Starting a
Yahoo!® Business
FOR
DUMMIES®

D1603179

Starting a Yahoo!® Business

FOR DUMMIES®

by Rob Snell

Wiley Publishing, Inc.

About the Author

Rob Snell loves e-commerce and all things Yahoo! Store. He is totally obsessed with search marketing and increasing his stores' conversion rates. He is a small-business owner, online retailer, search marketing/e-commerce consultant, Yahoo! Store developer, sometime bass player, and Steve Snell's brother and business partner. This is his first book!

Rob has been in retail literally longer than he can remember. Growing up in the family mail-order catalog and retail business meant summers and weekends of unloading truckloads of 50-lb. bags of dog food, waiting on customers, designing catalogs and magazine ads, and even programming the point-of-sale systems. He was shocked when his sister-in-law informed him that most other families didn't talk about search marketing or conversion rates over Thanksgiving dinner.

Rob has been into computers since 1981 when his mom bought him a Timex Sinclair ZX81. He's been online since 1990 and opened his first online store in 1997 when his brother stumbled across Viaweb (now Yahoo! Store). Since then, Rob has designed, developed, owned, and/or marketed hundreds and hundreds of Yahoo! Stores that have sold millions and millions of dollars worth of stuff. Rob has sold Superman comics, art supplies, Pokémon cards, refurbished Sun workstations, pewter dragons, dog supplies, car-top carriers, softball equipment, and even janitorial supplies.

Rob has a lot of experience as a small-business owner in many different fields. He started freelancing as a graphic design student and was booking and playing bass in several bands in college when he and his brother started a small chain of five comic book stores (which they sold in 2001). Rob spends his workdays helping his clients sell more stuff on the Internet and working with his family.

Rob now consults with retailers on improving their e-commerce sites and maximizing their search-marketing campaigns and is a guest speaker and lecturer on search marketing and e-commerce for small businesses. He posts somewhat regularly in his Yahoo! Store blog at www.ystore.blogs.com and can be contacted via e-mail at book@ystore.com. For more information, visit www.Ystore.com or www.robsnell.com.

Dedication

This book is dedicated to the memory of my father, W.C. Snell, who always believed in me even though he almost never agreed with me.

Author's Acknowledgments

Thanks to all the people who kept things going so I could write this book. Thanks to my family for your endless support, especially Mom and Steve. To Kathy for taking care of all her boys (and stocking the fridge). To my six nephews: Drew, Corey, Sam, Luke, Austin, and Cooper who always make me smile! Always do your best! Thanks to Uncle Paul for the good MSU tickets (and that 1979 boat ride). Thanks to Aunt Margaret and Uncle Mick for 1999 and for still holding my reservations.

To Rachel and Katie for your patience and understanding. To Nikki "I really think you need some more coffee" Ballard for all your help with the book and for keeping me sane. To Deb "WTFB" Wells. To Alesha "You really should write that book now" Calvert. (Hey, Innes!)

Thanks to all my friends for getting me out of the office, especially Devon, John and Kay, Todd and Melissa, Brian, Andy, and Victor. To Copy Cow and Gun Dog staff, especially Allen Giglio, Mike Yeager, and Selena for typing all my notes. Special thanks to Annie Dancer. Meals provided by Jay & Co. at the Veranda and Shipley Do-Nuts. Special thanks to all my wonderful clients who kept paying me and who put up with me being out of pocket for almost a year, especially Roy, Scott, Greg, John and Joe, Kevin, Leigh, John, Bobby, Larry and Jerry, Joey T., Mark, and Doug. Thanks to Craig Paddock, Joe Morin, Troy Matthews, and Mr. David Burke for keeping me in the loop and out of trouble. Or is it out of the loop and in trouble? See y'all this search conference season!

A very special thanks to Michael Whitaker, my good friend and this book's technical reviewer, for taking it easy on my redneck prose and making me look good by catching my mistakes. Thanks to Yahoo!'s Paul Boisvert for reviewing chapters and providing valuable input. This book is much better thanks to their comments, criticisms, and suggestions. I take complete responsibility for any and all errors and omissions. See Ystorebooks.com for errata. Thanks to the folks at Yahoo! Small Business who keep things running smoothly and make it almost too easy to sell stuff online (especially Jimmy

D, Rich, Mike, Maria, Vince, and Randy). Thanks to Paul Graham and the Viaweb folks for creating Yahoo! Store, but especially for getting me into this way back in 1997.

"How y'all doing?" to all my search conference folks, especially fellow author Andrew Goodman, Jill Whelan, Scottie Claiborn, Debra Mastaler, Bruce Clay, Mike Grehan, Tor Crockatt, Christine Churchill, Dan Boberg, Misty Locke, John Marshall, Tim Mayer, David (baaa!) Warmuz, Leslie Drechsler, Mike Reedy, and Danny Sullivan. Thanks to Brett Tabke and all of WebmasterWorld. Howdy to Champagne Jimmy, Shak, Oilman, Stuntdubl, DigitalGhost, WebGuerrilla, Mr. Bindl, Neuron, Calum, BakedJake, and SEOMike. Howdy to Istvan "RTML 101" Siposs, HarvestSEO, Chris Sims, David "FindStuff.com" Karandish, Steph and Ryan, and the MonsterCommerce volleyball team, Matt "Inigo Montoya" Cutts, Dr. Ralph Wilson, Sara Hicks, Roebuck, Carl, Kelly, Leigh Ann, Megan, and Jennifer Knight. Thanks to Lamkin, Mrs. Edon, Mrs. Werkheiser, David Allen, Harry Friedman, Jakob Nielsen, Seth Godin, Joe Field, Roy Wilson, and all the other folks who have taught me along the way! Apologies to the other 17 people I know I've forgotten.

Tonight's show is brought to you by the fine folks at Wiley Press. Extra special thanks to my infinitely patient project editor, Kelly Ewing. To acquisitions editor (and fellow bassist) Steve Hayes: Thanks for the gig! (to the Waffle House . . .)

Publisher's Acknowledgments

We're proud of this book; please send us your comments through our online registration form located at www.dummies.com/register/.

Some of the people who helped bring this book to market include the following:

Acquisitions, Editorial, and Media Development

Project Editor: Kelly Ewing

Acquisitions Editor: Steve Hayes

Technical Editor: Michael Whitaker (www.monitus.com)

Editorial Manager: Jodi Jensen

Media Development Specialists: Angela Denny, Kate Jenkins, Steven Kudirka, Kit Malone, Travis Silvers

Media Development Coordinator: Laura Atkinson

Media Project Supervisor: Laura Moss

Media Development Manager: Laura VanWinkle

Media Development Associate Producer: Richard Graves

Editorial Assistant: Amanda Foxworth

Cartoons: Rich Tennant (www.the5thwave.com)

Composition Services

Project Coordinator: Jennifer Theriot

Layout and Graphics: Carl Byers, Joyce Haughey, Lynsey Osborn, Erin Zeltner

Proofreaders: Laura Albert, John Edwards, Jessica Kramer

Indexer: TECHBOOKS Production Services

Special Help: Paul Boisvert

Publishing and Editorial for Technology Dummies

Richard Swadley, Vice President and Executive Group Publisher

Andy Cummings, Vice President and Publisher

Mary Bednarek, Executive Acquisitions Director

Mary C. Corder, Editorial Director

Publishing for Consumer Dummies

Diane Graves Steele, Vice President and Publisher

Joyce Pepple, Acquisitions Director

Composition Services

Gerry Fahey, Vice President of Production Services

Debbie Stailey, Director of Composition Services

Contents at a Glance

Table of Contents

Introduction

*T*hanks for taking a look at *Starting a Yahoo! Business For Dummies.* When the folks from Wiley Press approached me about writing this book, I think I may have come off as more than just a little cocky. I boldly asserted, "I am *the guy* to write this book." Why? I've lived Yahoo! Store since April 1997. I'm not saying I know more about Yahoo! Store than anyone else, but I do have as broad an experience with the platform as anyone I've ever met.

Around these parts, our Yahoo! Stores make the mortgage payments and then some, so we pay pretty close attention to what increases sales. Working with 300-plus retailers has opened my eyes to the myriad ways we all sell online using the same exact platform. I learn something new from every retailer I work with.

Also, I think I've worn almost every hat you can wear in the Yahoo! Store universe as both a retailer and an online store developer and marketer. I've been a new store owner, neophyte online store builder, entry-level HTML coder, graphic designer, product photographer, box packer, telephone order taker, shipping manager, e-mail marketer, customer service phone rep, RTML hacker, search engine optimizer, and sales copywriter.

I've also tried tons of different ways to sell online. Some have worked. Others haven't. Look, I'm not embarrassed to say I've made lots and lots of mistakes trying to stay on top of Internet marketing. Learn from them! If I'm still doing something today, it's because it works! I've had some home runs with sites that have made some of my clients rich (and me fat and happy), generating millions and millions of dollars in sales.

After nine years, I've found that it just takes a good idea, a little bit of luck, and lots and lots of good ol' hard work to be successful online. The better your idea and the better your luck, the more successful you'll be, but it really just comes down to who wants it bad enough. Opportunity shows up in work clothes. In this book, I give you the tools and show you the path that worked for me, but you have to do the heavy lifting.

About This Book

This book is filled with more than nine years of proven Internet marketing strategies and tactics sprinkled with online success stories and hard-learned lessons from Yahoo! Store owners who have successfully competed with the big online players. This book is paying a debt to all the retailers and other folks who shared information that helped me stay alive long enough to figure out what I was doing. I expect you to pass this knowledge on to future retailers. This book is what I wish I knew in April 1997. Anybody got a time machine?

In this book, you find answers to questions about:

- ✔ Creating an online store that sells
- ✔ Driving more traffic that converts into sales
- ✔ Profiting from keywords
- ✔ Processing credit cards online and offline
- ✔ Finding out what's really selling online
- ✔ Maximizing sales on an existing store

What You're Not to Read

This book is about store building with the Yahoo! Store Editor, which has been around in some form or another for more than ten years. I don't tell you how to build stores with Store Tags, the other way to build Yahoo! Stores, which I loathe. If you must build a store with Store Tags because your product catalog never changes, or if you want to use SiteBuilder, take this book back to the store and get your money back because about half of this book doesn't apply to you. On second thought, I get paid in royalties based upon sales, so, uh, keep this book and profit from all the marketing stuff in here. Store Tags users probably need *Site Builder For Dummies* (Wiley Publishing, Inc.) by Richard Wagner (or the specific *For Dummies* book for whatever software title you're using for store building). Every store owner can benefit from Yahoo!'s free Merchant Solutions Getting Started Guide, which is available on the Web at `http://help.yahoo.com/help/us/store/guides/index.html` for you to download and print.

This book is also not revealing any of my trade secrets or those of my clients. I'm not giving away the store here (pun intended). All the examples and screen shots have had specific store information removed, or I've been vague enough to protect client info. This book is also not about how to get rich quick; it's about how to get rich slowly. It's also not how to game the search engines for free traffic (which would make you a spammer).

Foolish Assumptions

When writing this book, I've made a few assumptions about you:

- ✔ You have a computer (a Mac or PC) and have basic computer skills.
- ✔ You're connected to the Internet with a high-speed connection.
- ✔ You either are a retailer or want to be a retailer.
- ✔ You want to know how to sell (more) stuff online.
- ✔ You're tired of working for The Man.
- ✔ You're not a communist, and you want to make some money.

This book is written for the independent business owner who feels pretty comfortable with computers. You can handle sending and receiving e-mail with attachments and are comfortable with software like Microsoft Excel, Microsoft Word, and QuickBooks. Some knowledge of graphics software (like Adobe Photoshop or Paint Shop Pro) is extremely helpful for editing product photos and creating store graphics, but it's not required.

How This Book Is Organized

This book is organized into six parts. I describe these parts in the following sections.

Part I: Finding Out about Yahoo! Store

Discover the basic geography of Yahoo! Store: the Store Editor, the Store Manager, and the published site. Find out about the different ways folks make money online. You also see how to find out what products are really selling and how you can save some time with a few simple tweaks to your Editor. Finally, it's almost like an episode of CSI where I dissect a real Yahoo! Store order from start to finish, examining every gory detail to determine the real cause of conversion.

Part II: Planning What's in Store

Preparing to build and design your online store is almost half the battle. In this part, you find out about doing the work yourself or outsourcing it to designers. I explore assembling the different elements before you start to build your store, designing your store to turn shoppers into buyers, creating effective internal store navigation, and using images to sell more product.

Part III: Building and Managing Your Store

This part tells you how the Editor works and shows you how to format your store with navigation buttons. You also discover how to create different types of pages: sections, items, the home page, search pages, and shipping info and contact information pages. You can read about how to sell more of the products you have by merchandising your store more effectively. I also check out the Shopping Cart and the new Checkout Manager. Finally, I cover the Store Manager, where you set all your tax and shipping calculations and process orders.

Part IV: Profiting from Internet Marketing

This part is my favorite. You need to be found when folks are looking to buy what you are selling. I cover keywords and introduce the basics of Internet marketing. You also find out about the specifics of paid search (Google AdWords and Yahoo! Search Marketing) as well as how to drive free traffic from search engines by optimizing your Yahoo! Store for Google, Yahoo! and MSN.

Part V: Making More Money with Your Yahoo! Store

This is my other favorite part of the book. After you have a store up and running, you've done the hard part: getting started. Improving an existing store is so much easier than launching a new store. In this part, you discover how to improve your store (based upon your stats), convert more of your existing traffic into buyers, e-mail your customer list to sell more stuff, and save time and energy by uploading products by the dozens.

Part VI: The Part of Tens

I love The Part of Tens. These chapters cover Yahoo! Store tools, add-ons, and upgrades. You also find out a little about RTML, the proprietary custom scripting language of Yahoo! Store.

Icons Used in This book

Look for these helpful icons to highlight specific points I think you should know about:

I'm all about giving folks action items or takeaways. When you see the Tip icon, you know that I'm sharing with you a way to improve your store or save time.

When you see the Remember icon, I'm reminding you that you need to know this bit of Yahoo! Store trivia for something to work.

I'm pretty careful to not be an alarmist, so when you see the Warning icon, don't think CNN scroll hype, think, "Danger, Will Robinson" because you're very close to something that could do you real harm — like a man-eating carrot (remember that episode?).

This icon highlights all the technical details that you don't really have to know to operate a Yahoo! Store, but you may want to know if you're a guru. If you're not interested, skip the text marked with this icon.

Where to Go from Here

Unlike a novel, you can read this book in any order. You can even skip parts, chapters, or entire sections within chapters, and you'll be okay. Skip to the end of the book and read about conversion rate, and then back to the part where I introduce the Store Editor, and then over to the design chapter, and you'll be fine. You don't even have to read the whole book. Use the Index and the Table of Contents to find what you want to read about and read only that information.

Running a Yahoo! Store isn't that difficult, but there are so many things you need to always be working on. The good news is that you don't have to memorize all of this stuff. Refer back to this book as often as you like.

"Talk to Me, Johnny . . ."

I need your feedback. Please e-mail me at book@ystore.com. It's really helpful for me to know what works and what doesn't. If you catch a mistake, let
me know, and I'll correct it. Visit www.YstoreBooks.com, which will have
additional information I wanted to include in the book, but couldn't because
Editor Kelly wouldn't let me have 600+ pages.

I also have a book-based newsletter, which you can subscribe to by e-mailing
newsletter@ystore.com. I don't promise a weekly newsletter, but I'll e-mail
you as often as I have something worth writing about. Visit my company's
Yahoo! Store Marketing and Development Web site at www.ystore.com. I also
have 100-plus posts about Yahoo! Store and search marketing at my blog at
www.ystore.blogs.com.

Part I
Finding Out about Yahoo! Store

"This is a 'dot-com' company, Stacey. Risk taking is a given. If you're not comfortable running with scissors, cleaning your ears with knitting needles, or swimming right after a big meal, this might not be the place for you."

In this part . . .

Yahoo! Small Business, Yahoo! Merchant Solutions, Yahoo! Search Marketing, Yahoo! Web Hosting, and Yahoo! Store. Wow! Sometimes starting a business on Yahoo! can be confusing, but don't panic. I do this for a living!

This part of the book gets you started building your online business with Yahoo! and fast! (I have a short attention span.) First, I explain all things Yahoo!, like how all these different parts work together. I also fess up and finally come clean about why I still use Yahoo! Store after all these years. (Because it works!) I also get you to plan your online business and examine different business models for selling stuff online. If you don't already sell something, I help you figure out what products to sell and then make sure that you can make a living doing so.

I like to get things moving, too. Chapter 3 is where the real action kicks in because I show you how to jump-start your store. You quickly dive into the Store Editor, create some sample sections and products, upload some images, and publish. You also publish your order settings and place a test order. Finally, I wrap this part of the book up and examine a real live Yahoo! Store order from beginning to end.

Yahoo! Small Business gives you the tools to build a successful online business, but you have to take the initiative and do the work. If you plan ahead, work hard, and take care of your customers, with a little bit of luck, you can build your online business and accomplish your goals and dreams.

Chapter 1

The Nickel Tour of Yahoo! Store

"Hey, Momma? Know what? If I take all my old toys that I don't play with anymore and sell them, I can take all that money and buy some new toys!"

— Sam Snell (my nephew), sometime around age 3

I've always wondered whether independent retailers are born or made. Is self-employment nature or nurture? Maybe self-employment isn't in the blood as much as it is in the air. I grew up in my parents' retailing business, so I can see where I caught the bug, but not my parents. Their parents taught school and sold insurance. I guess my folks saw opening their own store as the easiest way to be their own boss, own their own business, and get their piece of the American Dream.

This chapter is your introduction to all things Yahoo! Store. Thanks to its suite of online store-building and -management tools, Yahoo! makes it easy to start and run your own business. The Yahoo! Merchant Solutions service includes domains, Web hosting, e-mail, and Yahoo! Store. This chapter also provides you with an overview of the different parts of the Yahoo! universe, showing the different pieces and parts of Yahoo! I also discuss what Yahoo! Stores are, why I think Yahoo! Stores are swell, and the types of retailers who sell on Yahoo!

Exploring Small Business

Small business is really big business. It's an old story by now. The media have been all over it for ten years or more. "Small" business owners (and we don't like the word *small*) are the dynamo that powers the American economy, creating 70 percent of all new jobs. More folks are starting up new businesses than ever before, and the Internet makes becoming an entrepreneur easier than ever.

Retailing is also big business in this country. It's a very big percentage of our GDP. Americans really like to buy stuff, but how we buy is changing all the time. *We're buying more and more online every year.* Brick-and-mortar retailing is pretty saturated, getting overcrowded with big-box category killers selling everything from warehouse locations. Mom and Pop stores can't compete with the Wal-Marts on price or selection, so service is all you have when you're a little guy.

Retail customer service is pretty much dead. I'm really impressed if I get a cashier who smiles and thanks me for my business. Finding someone with real product knowledge who can answer my questions is whole 'nother trick. I've just accepted the fact that I have to become an "expert" about whatever I'm buying by doing my homework. There's this wide range of service in retail these days from virtually none (the big-box boys) to great service (high-end boutiques and better independent retailers).

All this change and the vacuum of decent customer service and product knowledge create a huge opportunity. If you have product expertise, are a subject matter expert in your niche of the woods, and enjoy dealing with folks like yourself, online retailing may be for you.

Get real for a minute. You're probably not going to get rich selling online with a Yahoo! Store. You certainly won't make a killing overnight, but it's a great way to make a comfortable living. You get to be your own boss and have a certain flexibility of schedule. Being able to work from anywhere (even at home in your PJs) is a big, big plus. Small-business retailing is more of a lifestyle business than a ticket for the IPO lottery. Retailing is an easy way to start a business, and selling on the Internet is a perfect way to start. You don't need mountains of capital, just a strong desire and a little bit of sweat equity, and you're in business.

Introducing Yahoo! Small Business

When you open a Merchant Solutions account at Yahoo! Small Business, you have a Yahoo! Store (which is what I call it, no matter what anyone else says).

Simply put, a Yahoo! Store is an online store hosted at Yahoo! — a Web store with your own domain name. Your Web site comes with a Shopping Cart and a secure checkout with a payment gateway. Plug in your *merchant account* (a special bank account for processing credit cards), and you can accept credit-card payments (and now PayPal payments). You also get tools to build and manage your store. These tools include the Shipping Manager tool to config-ure your store's shipping methods and rates, a product database, online sales and traffic reports, stats, and graphs to see how you're doing. You also get the Store Editor — a Web-design tool for store building. Yahoo! Store also has really good customer support (both toll-free by phone and e-mail) and excel-lent online help files.

Yahoo! Store is a great choice for building your online store. The platform has more than 35,000 stores and has been around since 1996, before Yahoo! paid $49 million for Viaweb in July 1998. There's a success track to follow. Other retailers have done well on Yahoo! Store, and maybe you can, too. Yahoo! Store is also a recognized name brand for shoppers, so potential customers feel more comfortable shopping with you.

Using Yahoo! Store also has secondary benefits: There's a big enough Yahoo! Store user base for a community to develop (www.ystoreforums.com). There's also a growing developer network of around 100-plus RTML guys and gals who specialize in designing and marketing Yahoo! Stores (http://smallbusiness.yahoo.com/merchant/designdir.php). Lots of business and design challenges have been met and overcome. There's a clear path to follow when building a Yahoo! Store, and many friendly folks are on the road and don't mind sharing tips and tricks with fellow Web retailers.

Okay. I'll admit it. Yahoo! is a bit expensive compared to bargain-basement Web-hosting and Shopping Cart software. Honestly, you'll pay more for Web hosting when you have a Yahoo! Merchant Solutions account, but I believe this expense is actually a good thing because you really do get what you pay for. Table 1-1 lists the different monthly hosting packages, where you either pay $40, $100, or $300 a month plus a percentage of your sales. This revenue share fee is 1.5 percent (ouch!), 1 percent, or 0.75 percent (depending on the type of account you get), but because Yahoo! has resources other smaller companies don't, you shouldn't mind sharing a little bit for what you get in return.

Table 1-1	Yahoo! Merchant Solutions Packages		
	Starter	*Standard*	*Professional*
Monthly hosting fee	$39.95	$99.95	$299.95
One-time setup fee	$50	$50	$50
Transaction fee	1.50%	1%	0.75%
Store volume	< $12K	$12K+	$80K+

Source: Compare Merchant Solutions Packages: http://smallbusiness.yahoo.com/merchant/compare.php

For example, huge surges in traffic aren't a problem when you have a Yahoo! Store. Yahoo! has an incredible load-balancing infrastructure so that you don't have to worry, for example, if your store gets mentioned on Oprah and 10,000 people suddenly swarm your store. I really don't understand all of this propeller-head stuff, but I've seen stores handle tons of traffic (10,000 people a day) and not crash. Yahoo! Stores can also handle the huge spikes in traffic, for example, like the Christmas rush, where the entire Internet is swamped with millions more shoppers than usual. If you have a very seasonal business where you go from a 100 people a day in the off season to 4,000 people a day in the peak season and 150 to 200 orders a day, Yahoo! Store may be for you.

Yahoo! is pretty serious about its Web-hosting business. It's not a sideline or an afterthought. Nowadays, anyone with a T1 line and a server can set up a box and be a "Web-hosting company," but sometimes it takes a $45 billion market-cap company to do things right.

Yahoo! Stores have a great uptime record, too. One of the reasons I don't mind paying a little bit more for Yahoo! Store than generic Shopping Cart Web-development packages or Web-hosting packages is that I've had a Yahoo! Store or Viaweb since 1997. I know of only two times that our store was either down or really, really slow. I can't say that about any other product or service that I've ever had, whether on the Web or not, including cell phones, air conditioners, 1-800 numbers, bank accounts, Lexus convertibles, iBooks, and so on. I'm not saying that Yahoo! Stores are bulletproof, but if someone is shooting at my online store, I would rather it be a Yahoo! Store than anything else.

Figuring Out Who Uses Yahoo! Store

Lots of different types of people use Yahoo! Store to sell all kinds of different things online:

- ✔ **Brick-and-mortar stores:** These stores include anyone from Mom and Pop retailers to large corporate clients who don't want to spend $250,000 for a custom e-commerce solution. These retailers supplement their brick-and-mortar store's income by double-dipping, with their inventory selling online and offline. Sometimes the tail wags the dog and the real "store" is simply a warehouse for the online store's products.

- ✔ **Stay-at-home moms (or dads):** These *mompreneurs* build their business by taking phone orders and packing boxes between changing diapers and making trips to soccer practice. This new demographic is exploding and, man, are these folks competitive! I had a huge base of mom-clients until a crop of stay-at-home mom store developers popped up. These Y!Moms had no overhead and rock-bottom store development prices and grabbed all the business! I love it when the "breadwinning" spouse has to quit his or her job to come home and help fill all these Yahoo! Store orders.

- ✔ **Nonprofits:** I've seen everyone from church groups to museums to social activists sell online to raise money or accept contributions. Even the American Red Cross had a Yahoo! Store to take donations!

- ✔ **Drop-shipping Web marketers:** These retailers only *drop-ship,* which means that they forward orders to a wholesale distributor who packs and ships the order for the retailer. Drop-shipping means no inventory, no warehouse, no killer overhead, and (sometimes) no employees. Drop-shipping retailers probably pay more for their products than retailers who stock and ship all their products, but drop-shippers have much less risk than traditional retailers. If you can find a great wholesaler who is also a drop-shipper, you can focus on customer service and Internet marketing (see Chapter 2). I have some great examples, but my retail clients would shoot me if I slipped and gave up their killer sources!

- ✔ **Mail-order catalogers:** These old-school, direct-mail retailers are embracing Internet marketing, and many catalog companies sell more through their online catalog than through mailed, paper catalogs. Catalogs are tremendously expensive to print and mail, especially compared to the relative bargains of paid-search advertising (see Chapter 18) and free traffic from search engines (see Chapter 19).

- ✔ **Inventors, authors, and musicians:** When you write a book or invent a product, no matter how cool it is, you can't sell it if shoppers can't buy it! Sometimes the Big Boys either won't carry a product or want big bucks for catalog placement or space on store shelves. If you can create a virtual product where folks can download a file like a program (www.rtmltemplates.com), an e-book (www.ytimes.info), or an MP3 file (www.laugh.com), you don't even have to ship anything!

Selling your own creation is probably the hardest road to Internet marketing success, but if you hit a home run, you're rich! When you sell the products that you make, you usually have a killer margin because you keep the manufacturer's, distributor's, and retailer's share of the pie.

- ✔ **Manufacturers:** I'm a retailer who firmly believes that most manufacturers shouldn't retail! I believe it's bad manners to compete with your retailers for the very same customers, but some manufacturers want to sell direct. It's a free country! The best compromise I've seen is when the manufacturer sells at full retail using its own *manufacturer's suggested retail price* (MSRP) and provides links to other approved online merchants who are free to sell at market price. See www.mailcarts.com for a manufacturer's site I did awhile back.

Deciphering All the Parts

Your credit-card statement lists Yahoo! Small Business (YSB) as your online landlord. Y!SB is the division at Yahoo! that you deal with the most.

Here are the other parts of Yahoo! you need to know about:

- **Yahoo! Search** (www.yahoo.com) **is a separate part of Yahoo!.** Just because you have a Yahoo! Store doesn't mean that your store will automatically rank in the top ten results at Yahoo.com when folks search for keywords related to what you sell. Yahoo! doesn't play favorites with stores or hosted sites, which is confusing to some new accounts. See Chapter 19 for tips on optimizing your store for all the search engines, especially the top three that drive 95 percent of Internet search engine traffic: Google, Yahoo!, and MSN Search.

- **Yahoo! Shopping is Yahoo!'s shopping portal and the public face of Yahoo! Search.** To be listed in Y!Shopping, you have to organize and submit your products to Yahoo! Product Submit. If accepted, your products get sucked into the Yahoo! Product Search database, showing up when customers search on http://shopping.yahoo.com. You pay for each click from Y!Shopping to your store based upon your industry (anywhere from 15 cents to $1). Yahoo! Merchant Solutions accounts do get 20 percent off list prices, though. See http://productsubmit. adcentral.yahoo.com/sspi/us/pricing to read about Yahoo! Shopping and other ways to market your store in Chapter 17.

- **Yahoo! Search Marketing (YSM) is the paid-search advertising part of Yahoo!.** You know what I'm talking about — those sponsored ads that appear at the top and to the right on Yahoo! and lots of other sites. See Chapter 18 on buying your way to the top with paid-search ads on Yahoo! (and its competitor, Google AdWords).

Examining Merchant Solutions

Yahoo! Merchant Solutions is the catchall marketing name for Yahoo! Small Business division's services package, which includes domains, business e-mail, Web hosting, and Store. Domains lets you register and reserve your domain name and control where it points on the Web. Yahoo! Business E-mail gives you 100 mailboxes with spam control and 17 other things e-mail does. Yahoo! Web hosting gives you traditional Web-hosting space where you can upload your files via FTP or the File Manager with 20GB of disk space. You also get 500GB data transfer, PHP support, log files, and more.

The "Store" part of Merchant Solutions is what used to be called Yahoo! Store and consists of the Store Manager and Store Editor. You can also use two completely different ways — Store Editor or Store Tags — to build and maintain your store. The store-building part of this book is about Store Editor. See Chapter 5 for more on why I use the Store Editor, and why I think you should, too.

The Store Manager is your virtual back office. You can process orders (review, edit, and export store orders), view Statistics (all the cool reports, graphs, and statistics to help you manage your business), configure Order Settings (Shipping Manager, tax settings, payment methods), maintain Site Settings, and promote your online store. You can read more about the Store Manager in Chapter 15.

The Store Editor is both an online store builder and a product database manager. You can create, edit, and organize your products on the Web by browsing a copy of your online store. Here you can also design, tweak, and update your store's look and feel and see your design changes behind the scenes. When everything's perfect in the Editor version of your store, click the Publish button to update the public version of your store. Use the built-in product and section page templates and customize your store by editing the look and feel settings on the global Variables page. Advanced users (or professional store developers, if you have the budget) can create a unique look by editing copies of RTML templates or by creating custom RTML templates from scratch. See Chapter 26 for more on RTML, the proprietary templating language and foundation of Yahoo! Store.

I still use Yahoo! Store and Store Editor today because they work

The reason I chose Viaweb (now Yahoo! Store Editor) to build my first online store back in early 1997 was because I wanted to sell stuff on the Internet, not code HTML or learn how to program CGI-BIN shopping cart scripts. I'm a retailer and a marketer, not a computer scientist! I had many reasons for choosing Viaweb:

✔ **Viaweb worked for me because I could do it myself.** Back in 1997, I literally had no Web store development budget, so I couldn't pay a Web developer what, at the time, was the outrageous price of $75 an hour to set up an online shopping cart. I was also highly motivated with the desperation that only comes from your momma saying, "Son, get my business online, and do it fast, or there won't *be* any business pretty soon. PetSmart is coming. . . ." One thing I did have was oodles of free time, thanks to my

business partner (and baby brother), Steve, who runs our day-to-day operations so well that I can disappear into a project (like this book!) for six months to a year when an opportunity presents itself!

✔ **Viaweb/Yahoo! Store was perfect for me because I also had no Web skills and virtually no online experience.** I had never "developed" a Web site. I was a newbie to the WWW in every sense of the word, playing on CompuServe since 1990 and posting in a few online comic book retailer forums swapping marketing tips. I did have a background in retailing and had owned my stores since I was in college. I also had my degree in graphic design from Mississippi State, but that was with tools from the Stone Age designing things on paper.

(continued)

(continued)

> ✓ **Viaweb also didn't require me to have any special software (that I really couldn't afford, anyway).** I could build my store online in the Store Editor (over a 28.8 modem dialup connection). All I had to do was copy and paste some product information, upload some pictures, tweak a few Variables, and I was online selling stuff, even though I had to learn store design and Internet marketing fast and in public in front of our customers!

The reason I still use Yahoo! Store today is because it works. I have yet to find a better way to sell online, and believe me when I say I'm always looking! To me, Yahoo! Store is the world's best online store-building platform. It's perfect for little guys who want to become big guys. You don't have to be a Web developer or even have an IT guy on staff. You build your store and then concentrate on building your business by taking care of your customers and selling stuff. Yahoo! takes care of all the propeller-head stuff behind the scenes.

Yahoo! Store can also scale with you as you grow. Power users can always tap into the awesome power of customizing store pages through RTML templates (see Chapter 26), as well as automating some order-processing functionality (see Chapter 15). Honestly, the only reason I ever learned custom programming with RTML was to be able to make search-engine-friendly changes to the templates (to get more traffic) and to make design changes to the store to improve sales (for example, moving my Add To Cart button higher on the page).

Paul Graham and Robert T. Morris (the RTM of RTML) did it right the first time with the Viaweb Store Builder software. The Store Editor has stood the test of time. The Editor I used in 1997 to build my first Viaweb store is remarkably similar to the Yahoo! Store Editor we use today. You get to see how your store looks in real time as you add products or make changes to the global Variables.

Back then, there weren't any *WYSIWYG* (what you see is what you get) HTML editors like today's Dreamweaver or FrontPage. Back then, you wrote your HTML code and then had to look in your browser to see what a page really looked like. I've been using the Editor for over eight years, which is an eternity on the Internet. Maybe this old dinosaur is stuck in his ways, but I love Store Editor and all things Yahoo! Store.

Chapter 2

Planning Your Online Small Business

In This Chapter
▶ Emulating successful online merchants
▶ Picking products that sell and generate repeat customers
▶ Looking at the different kinds of issues facing all kinds of retailers

*T*here are riches in niches, whether with popular products, products with limited distribution, or items that tend to generate repeat orders. In this chapter, I show you how to pick an online business model and how to do product research to discover which products sell on the Web. I also take a look at the different types of retailers starting a Yahoo! Store and cover brand-new retail startups, folks taking an existing business online, retailers migrating to Yahoo! Store from another platform, and existing Yahoo! Store owners opening multiple stores.

Choosing a Business Model That Works on the Web

Retailers on the Web have to have a different business model than traditional, real-world merchants. A *business model* is just a fancy name for the way a company actually makes money. What strategy works offline is probably not going to work online, which can make things complicated for folks who do business in both worlds. Locally, you may have no real competition within your trading area, but online you'll have a ton of competition. Your competitors are only a mouse click away, so you must be different. Differentiate your store's products from every other store selling the same things. I tell you how to do that in this chapter.

Selling online gives the little guy a fighting chance against the big category killers because smaller retailers are more nimble. When you're small, you don't need approval from marketing, legal, and IT to make a change on the

Web store; you just do it. The little guys can leverage their expertise, product knowledge, and enthusiasm, and provide a better shopping experience in many retail categories. On the Internet, you're not limited by your how many stores you have, your store's physical location, normal business hours, the size of your showroom, how much inventory you have, or the size of your staff. You're limited only by your creativity, your vision, your passion, and your work ethic.

Effective online retail business models remind me of cool retail shops I see in large metropolitan areas. These retailers tend to focus on these tight little niches that are big enough to make a comfortable living from but small enough to avoid the large discounters. For example, last year I was playing hooky wandering around in New York City. Instead of going to seminar presentations, I went shopping and found several cool, geeky stores that I loved. These retailers could only make it in the big, big city and/or by selling online or by mail order: Toy Tokyo (selling the coolest imported Japanese toys! See ToyToyko.com), St. Mark's Comics (selling every new comic book title published every week), and Forbidden Planet (selling tons of books, graphic novels, Japanese toys, and science fiction I couldn't find anywhere else).

In a large market, you have the advantage of being able to focus on one micro niche and be the expert in your subject area. The Internet is the largest market there is. Your Yahoo! Store gives you a shot at the millions of people shopping online every day, but only if you do something more than republish a copy of your suppliers' wholesale catalog. You have to do something to stand out from hundreds or thousands of potential competitors.

Here's a simple way to pick a business model: "Price, service, selection. Pick any two out of three." Another good one is "Do you want it good or fast or cheap? You can have it good and cheap, but it'll take forever. You can have it good and fast, but you'll pay a lot more. And you can have it fast and cheap, but it's not gonna be any good."

Your business model can be to lose money on the first sale just to acquire a customer and then make a profit on subsequent sales. Another model is to sell expensive items as cheap as you can and then make all your profit selling accessories, supplies, or extended warranties.

Another online business model is to use your industry contacts to bird-dog good deals. Some retailers have sweetheart deals with manufacturers and buy unsold inventory at rock-bottom prices, which allows them to have seemingly unbeatable prices. I know several apparel retailers who buy unsold stock from other boutiques for pennies on the dollar and then resell it online.

For example, my mom's brick-and-mortar store, The Dog Store, had a pretty simple business model based on service and selection. She sold a wide variety of premium pet food at competitive prices, gave great customer service, and had a very knowledgeable sales staff who could answer pet-care and -training questions. She built up a large base of repeat customers and sold them other products for training and taking care of their pets. When she opened her

Yahoo! Store in 1997, her business model radically changed. Mom couldn't offer pet food as a draw because (as dot-bomb poster child Pets.com discovered) you can't ship 40-pound bags of premium dog food and make any money, so she spent a lot more time on educating potential customers about pet-training supplies and equipment. Instead of doing this education in person, she made informative Web pages, personally replied to thousands of e-mail questions, and gave great customer service over the telephone.

You want to be *the place* to buy what you sell online, so focus on a niche. Be a cool, online boutique with a full selection and more product information than anywhere else. Don't sell 50,000 products. Don't be a general store. The old chestnut "You can't be everything to everyone" is not just a cliché.

Copy what works. Believe me. Someone has already figured out how to sell products online and make a buck. These retailers are the guys who understood that you have to make a profit and are still in business after the dot-com bubble burst. These successful retailers have already done the work. Copy what they're doing right, add your own personal spin on retailing, and you have a much greater chance of online success.

Picking Products That Sell on the Web

Picking what products to sell is tough. Most everyone I know started out selling one thing and ended up selling something else because they discovered a better opportunity. Your customers will tell you what to sell by what they buy or what they ask for that you don't carry. If someone can sell it through a catalog, you can sell it with a Yahoo! Store. Most people in America live in or near cities with pretty good access to shopping. If you sell the same stuff people can get down the street, you're simply offering convenience. You don't want to sell things that people can buy just anywhere unless you can beat everyone on price.

Finding popular and profitable niches

You need to sell a product that's popular enough so that you can make a living, and that's a lot easier to do when you make a decent profit on each sale. I would bet that every type of product that can possibly be sold on the Internet is being sold at this very moment.

Here's how to see what's selling on the Internet:

  ✔ **Look at the most successful retailers in your niche.** Check up on your future competitors. Usually stores will publicize their bestsellers in their Web store.

- ✔ **Visit the shopping search engines.** Look at Froogle.com, Bizrate.com, Yahoo! Shopping, and Shopping.com for their top sellers.

- ✔ **Look at Yahoo! Shopping Searches.** In your Yahoo! Store Manager, click the Shopping Searches link to see the past week's top 100 searches in Yahoo! Shopping. (Merchant Starter accounts don't get Shopping Searches, so you should upgrade.) Shopping Searches is a great way to see what folks are looking to buy. What's most popular on Yahoo! Shopping changes with the seasons. By the time a seasonal product is hot on Yahoo! Shopping, it's probably too late to cash in, but there's always next year.

- ✔ **Read the Shopping.com Consumer Demand Index at** www.shopping. com/cdi. This weekly report is also available in an e-mail newsletter. The folks at Shopping.com want you to know what retail lines are hot, and they want you to advertise your products with them.

- ✔ **See what's selling now at Yahoo! Shopping.** Visit http://search. store.yahoo.com/OT, and you see a sample of ten actual items that sold in the last hour at Yahoo! Shopping.

- ✔ **Look at completed auctions on eBay to see what's really selling.** Go to www.ebay.com and click the Advanced Search link, which takes you to the Search: Find Items page. Select the Completed Listings Only check box and then search for a product. The search results list only completed items.

- ✔ **Check out Terapeak.com.** This site offers even more information, with marketplace research on what products and categories are selling on eBay. Even though selling with auctions and selling through an online storefront are different, you can see some very interesting trends. For $16.95 a month, you can see what categories are hot, what specific types of products are having successful auctions, and what categories have unmet demand.

- ✔ **Research the highly popular keywords on eBay.** Go to http://buy. ebay.com, and you see hundreds of popular e-commerce keywords — from Acura Integra to Zippo lighters and everything in between.

- ✔ **Explore keyword tools like the Yahoo! Search Marketing (formerly Overture) Search Suggestion Tool, Wordtracker, and the Google Keyword Sandbox.** See Chapter 16 for lots more information about keywords. See which keywords are more popular (volume of searches) and which products are possibly more profitable based upon what advertisers are bidding because retailers don't bid for long on unprofitable keywords.

- ✔ **Look at Wordtracker.com's two Top 1,000 Keyword lists.** The long-term list reveals the most popular searches in the past eight weeks, and the short-term list shows the top 1,000 keywords in the past 36 hours. While most of these searches aren't exactly related to e-commerce, you can get some good ideas. Wordtracker is a paid service (around $200 a year), but you can sign up at www.wordtracker.com/topkeywords.html for free weekly e-mails with the Top 500 most popular keywords.

✔ **Ask your government what's selling.** Get the latest updates from the U.S. Census Department at www.census.gov/eos/www/ebusiness614. htm and see your tax dollars at work. Table 2-1 shows what's selling by line of merchandise in the e-commerce economy, according to the U.S. Census Department. You can easily find a ton of free information on e-commerce all over the Web by doing a search for site:gov e-commerce on Google or Yahoo!.

Table 2-1	What's Selling Online, According to the U.S. Census Department
Merchandise Line	*Percentage of Sales*
Computer hardware	16.70
Clothing, clothing accessories, and footwear	13.70
Other merchandise	12.30
Office equipment and supplies	8.60
Furniture and home furnishings	8.50
Electronics and appliances	7.20
Nonmerchandise receipts	6.50
Books and magazines	5.30
Drugs, health aids, and beauty aids	4.90
Music and videos	4.30
Toys, hobby goods, and games	4.10
Computer software	2.90
Sporting goods	2.90
Food, beer, and wine	2.20

From U.S. Electronic Shopping and Mail-Order Houses (NAICS 454110) - Total and E-commerce Sales by Merchandise Lines 2003

Look: You don't need to be the only store online selling what you sell. Selling on the Internet is like fishing in the ocean. There are enough fish out there for a lot of folks. You don't have to catch all the fish; you just need enough to feed you and yours.

I encourage clients who have been selling for awhile to "cream their line" or to focus on an existing niche within their product category that either does well or has potential. For example, I had a jeweler client who originally wanted to be a big online jewelry store and sell everything he sold in his real store in his Yahoo! Store. I looked at his product line and did a little keyword research.

We found a great little niche (and no, I'm not telling). This particular niche was a popular subcategory in the jewelry keyword universe. When we did our key-word research for these specific types of products, we found that there were enough keyword searches on a daily basis that if he got only 1 percent of the Internet business for this particular niche, he would do extremely well.

My jeweler client did very well because he focused on his bestselling prod-ucts. They were in the right price range of things that sell online, which in my experience has been anything priced up to $250. He also had great margins on these products. Also, he was somewhat protected from future competitors because the manufacturer wasn't looking for any new dealers. To sell its product line, you had to be a real jewelry store, but the manufacturer didn't care if you also sold online. Because the jeweler already had a relationship with the vendor, he was easily able to get databases and product photos. (See Chapter 8 for more info on perfecting product pictures.) He is selling lots of jewelry online and loves being a niche retailer. I told him it would work!

Promoting products with limited distribution

The last thing that you want to do is sell something that anyone else can sell online because too many retailers selling the same thing can totally saturate the market, drive down selling prices, and exponentially increase the cost of paid-search advertising. Sell products with lots of *barriers to entry,* or factors that make it difficult or expensive for new competitors to sell what you sell.

Barriers to entry can include exclusive marketing relationships, high initial orders, high minimum purchases, requirement of a physical store, geographic distribution restrictions, and minimum advertised pricing.

Barriers to entry are a double-edged sword. When you're a new retailer, you want to be able to open an account with a wholesaler, but after you're in, you don't want your suppliers to sell to your future competitors.

Here are a few points to keep in mind when promoting products with limited distribution:

✔ **Certain suppliers will only sell to "legitimate" retailers with proof of a physical location to protect their dealers from Internet-only competi-tion.** Selling out of a dorm room or basement is much cheaper than paying the overhead of a real store, and these dealers can undercut retailers who are paying for premium retail locations. Traditional stores have big bucks tied up in inventory and usually have high overhead with expensive employee payrolls, as well as infrastructure and administrative expenses. The manufacturers try to protect the companies who butter their bread because these dealers tend to carry the full line of products, order in larger quantities, and are usually more stable than dot-com startups. When you present yourself to these suppliers, you need to look as legitimate as you can.

- ✔ **Make sure that you have permission to sell online.** Some manufacturers and distributors don't allow their dealers to sell online, or they have Internet retailer restrictions. If retailers with a brick-and-mortar store get caught selling products online, they get cut off. Sometimes this rule creates a gray market because retailers can set up another company or sell through another retailer online, but folks going this route usually get caught.

- ✔ **Be certain that you can meet the minimum order or monthly volume.** Some distributors or wholesalers use sales volume to determine what discount retailers get. They don't want a lot of small dealers, but instead prefer fewer accounts who are really serious about selling their products. Look for wholesalers who offer a stair-step discount structure that seems to reward and protect their bigger retailers, because that's where you want to be one day.

- ✔ *Minimum advertising pricing* **(MAP) is a way manufacturers protect their offline retailers from heavy Internet competition.** With MAP, you can sell products for any price you want (because it would be price fixing if the manufacturer dictated the retail price), but you just can't advertise a price lower than the MAP, or you can lose your dealer status.

Competition is usually a good thing. Just because other online stores are selling what you want to sell doesn't mean that you shouldn't jump in and compete with them. When a lot of retailers are selling something online, that's usually a good indicator of a hot product line. If you can get the product, sell it at a competitive price, and make a profit, then do it. If you have product knowledge to give you an edge, get in there and compete with them!

It may not be too late

When we started selling Pokémon cards back in 1999, only three companies in the Yahoo! directory even had the word *Pokémon* in their Yahoo! directory listing. Now that the Pokémon phenomenon is over, you can still go to `http://dir.yahoo.com` and search for Pokémon. You find 24 categories for Pokémon with hundreds of sites listed. Even though we got in on the late beginning of the Pokémon boom almost by accident, by the end, hundreds, if not thousands, of people were selling the exact same products we were selling. Lots of competition didn't stop us from selling hundreds of thousands of dollars in Pokémon and related products, but by the time Wal-Mart had what we had, I knew the fun was over.

Retailing quality products and adding value

Sell quality products. You need to be able to stand behind what you carry. Make sure that what you sell is something that you would want to buy yourself. Sometimes it's hard to tell the quality of a product from a photograph and description. In the short term, you can make some money ripping people off by selling junk, but when you sell quality merchandise, everyone wins. Your customers are going to be happy when they get their order, you're not going to have a lot of returns, you spend less time on customer service issues, and you have happy customers who come back and shop again!

Your *returns policy* says a lot about how you feel about your products. Merchants with a 100 percent satisfaction guarantee or money-back policy have much higher *conversion rates* (percentage of browsers who actually buy something) than retailers with limited or no returns policies or high restocking fees. If you can reduce a customer's risk, he or she is more likely to buy from you.

Add value to what you're selling to distinguish your store from all the others selling the exact same products. Use your industry and product knowledge to help your customer solve her problem. Make sure that your customer gets all the accessories, equipment, supplies, or additional services that go with her purchase. I hate it when I buy something that needs a funky little battery or weird light bulbs, and I have to go back and buy something else. Sell me everything I need the first time.

For example, my good friend (and marketing guru) Brian Evans ordered a digital camera online. Immediately after receiving his order, the retailer called to thank Brian for his order and to point out that he didn't order several accessories he really needed, such as a protective carrying case, extra lenses, extra batteries, and so on. The retailer provided great customer service by making sure that Brian had everything he needed for taking pictures of his family for the holidays and ended up adding a couple hundred dollars in high-profit items to the sale.

When you're the expert, you can charge more. If you have tons of online content like buyer's guides or other helpful information, you don't necessarily have to always be the low-price guy to get the sale. People feel much more comfortable buying from the experts!

Selling products that encourage repeat orders

Sell products that encourage repeat orders. You want to sell products that people buy over and over again. Sell consumables: food that people eat, supplies that people use up, batteries that run out, items that people consume (such as vitamins or supplements), or clothes that wear out, go out of style, or get outgrown.

Sell products that have lots of new releases. Books, magazines, DVDs, video games, and lots of other entertainment properties always have new products coming out. We were in the comic book industry for more than 12 years, and every month we always had a new issue of the Superman comic book to sell.

In addition, you want to maintain a relationship with your customers and educate them about new products or other items you have that they may not know about so that you can sell them products again and again. Selling something to a previous customer is much easier than creating a new customer. Build up your customer list and market to them through e-mail. (For more on e-mail marketing, see Chapter 22.)

Maximizing your margins and price points

Every time I would brag about triple-digit sales increases to my father, he would invariably reply, "It's not what you gross, son. It's what you net." It took me a while to get that through my somewhat thick skull. Sometimes you can actually make more money (profit in your pocket at the end of the day) by selling fewer items when you concentrate on higher-ticket items with better profit margins. Here's how it works:

- ✔ **Sell things that have a decent *gross profit margin* (a percentage determined by the retail price minus the wholesale cost divided by the retail price).** Most of the retailers I see selling online have about a 30 percent margin. The most successful retailers who buy smart or create their own products have gross margins as high as 80 or 90 percent.

- ✔ **Sell products with an average order size of $50 to $250.** Anything much more expensive, and some folks have a hard time buying it online because they're afraid of getting ripped off or want to see it and hold it before they buy it. With some items, you can use the Yahoo! Store as a lead generator to get folks to call your 800 number. Anything less expensive, and you run the risk of doing a whole lot of work for little reward. Filling a $200 order takes about the same amount of effort as filling a $20 order. That's why I got out of selling comic books and baseball cards.

My general rule is to make at least $20 a box in *gross profit* (your retail sale minus your wholesale cost). Otherwise, it's not worth having me pack a box. Sell something that has a high enough price where you can actually make enough money filling the order to justify opening a new customer record, running the credit card, doing the customer service, and shipping the box.

✔ **Sell higher end products.** Customers shopping for budget or entry-level products seem to be much more price sensitive. Folks who buy the best products with all the latest features and gizmos generally have more expendable income, and they're much more likely to buy other things, too.

✔ **Don't try to be the lowest price guy on the Web.** There's always someone who will sell something lower than you, sometimes even losing money on every sale, whether they know it or not. When price is the only thing that matters to a customer, the sale tends to cause more headaches. I'd rather not make the sale.

I've been inside enough Yahoo! Stores in the past eight years to see that the retailers who are making all the money are the ones who buy low doing whatever they can to get the cheapest price from suppliers and then sell high by discounting as little as they have to. Lots of our suppliers give a 2 percent early pay discount if we pay an invoice within 10 days. Also, if we buy in bulk, by the pallet or case load, we get a better price. The bigger you get, the more volume you do, and the more negotiating power you have. From time to time, ask your suppliers how you can get a better discount.

When you sell the exact same thing as another retailer, and that seller discounts more than you, it can be difficult not to try to meet or beat his price. Try to get in there and compete with these folks. If they're discounting off retail price, I'll discount off retail a bit, but I'm not going to be the guy selling at cost plus $1.

✔ **Mix it up a little — discount some things and make full margin on others.** Even Wal-Mart uses *loss leaders,* where it sells items for little or no profit to get you in the store, where it hopes you'll buy something else. Wal-Mart tempts you with impulse items, which usually are the highest margin and most profitable items. You end up walking out with six or seven products that you didn't plan to buy. Do the same thing in your Yahoo! Store. Learn from the big boys.

Leveraging your knowledge and passion

If you're really into a subject, you can focus your product knowledge and passion into your Yahoo! Store. Turn your store into an industry resource about your subject matter area and make money by selling products.

Find a product niche you know something about. It may be your hobby or it could be job-related. Sometimes you find out things as an employee or know a lot about a particular industry. For example, if you work for a large manufacturer or distributor, you can see what types of products are selling, or you may hear of a business opportunity, or you might find a distributor who will drop-ship for you. It's important that you find what you sell interesting because you'll spend a lot of time writing and talking about your product lines.

Use your knowledge and passion to sell something that you're excited about. Folks can tell! You don't want to sell products you don't know about or care about. You'll be much more successful if you're excited about what you sell.

Building a New Business from Scratch

Building a new company from scratch is tough work. In e-commerce, the "commerce" part is harder than the "e" part. Putting together product photos and descriptions, designing a good Web store, and even getting ranked in the search engines are pretty easy. Selling something is a good bit harder. Turning that Web site into a viable business is a whole 'nother thing. Retailing is tough work, but if you like people and are into what you sell, it can be a rewarding way to make a living.

I probably take a lot of what I know about the "commerce" part of e-commerce for granted because I grew up surrounded by retail. My parents had a mail-order dog-supply business they started when I was 5. We were always going to the post office to check for orders, or collating and folding catalogs, or shipping boxes, or counting inventory. My folks opened their retail store when I was 11 or 12, and every summer after that, I worked the counter and unloaded truck after truck of dog food in the sweltering Mississippi heat. I guess most folks aren't as lucky.

Planning your business model on a napkin

The first thing I do when I am trying to figure out whether a new business model is going to work is to sit down at lunch with a napkin and look at the broad brushstrokes of a business. If you can make something work on a napkin and explain it to someone else, then odds are you'll be able to come up with a business model that can work.

I ask these kinds of questions: What is the gross profit margin in this industry. What is the average sale? How many visitors am I going to have to get to the Web site to make a sale? What percentage of the folks will return and buy stuff? What is the lifetime value of a customer? What other noninventory costs am I going to have? Is this something that I can do with low overhead, or am I going to need a 5,000-sq. ft. warehouse with 20 employees, a phone system, a network administrator, a bank of computers, and tons of overhead before I sell my first order?

Limit your overhead, and you limit your exposure. Dip your little toe in the retailing waters and see whether your new business is going to work before you quit your day job or blow your nest egg. The last thing you want to do as a retailer is buy yourself a job where you're making less money than you would make with a "real" job.

Using drop-shippers for fun, profit, and market research

Drop-shipping, where you take orders without ever touching the merchandise and your suppliers ship it directly to your customers, is a very effective way to sell online.

Launching a new online business

One of the things that I like to do when I'm launching a new retail business is determine the viability of the business from keyword searches to make sure that enough people are looking online for what I am going to sell. (I cover keywords in great detail in Chapter 16.) I also try to find out how many competitors I have and then pinpoint the most profitable products, which are usually the most popular products or those that have the best margin.

I quickly build a prototype store focused around a really small group of related products. I can build out a Yahoo! Store in a day or so with 10 to 15 products with a minimal amount of graphic design on the site. With paid-search ads (see Chapter 18), you can buy traffic almost immediately and get a pretty good idea of how your site will work. You can see initial conversion rates on the site, what products people buy, what pages people look at, and which keywords convert.

For example, I did an affiliate project with a friend of mine who sold hammocks. We were

selling the exact same hammocks that everyone else was selling online. We had the exact same product photos and descriptions, and our pricing was very similar because we had to be competitive. We were selling hammocks pretty much the same way everybody else online was selling hammocks. Big mistake.

Well-established retailers had much better margins because they were moving large volumes of hammocks. They had sweetheart deals with the manufacturers, and we had the worst possible discount with the distributor. We built the store and spent about $2,000 in paid-search ads on Google AdWords over a weekend or so to drive a ton of really qualified traffic across the site. We were able to see what products sold, what keywords converted, what ads converted for folks, and where folks went in the Web store. We ultimately realized that we were not going to make any money selling the same exact hammocks everyone else was, so we scaled down the project.

Here's how drop-shipping works: You establish an account with a drop-shipper who is usually a wholesaler, distributor, or sometimes another retailer with buying power and a large order fulfillment operation. The drop-shipper usually provides you with product pictures and descriptions for your Yahoo! Store. You market the drop-shipper's products online. When the orders come rolling in, you process the credit cards and then fax or e-mail the drop-shipping company the customer's shipping information. The drop-shipper then ships your orders and charges you wholesale cost and sometimes a drop-ship fee per box. Hopefully, your customer gets his order and you make a profit. It sounds almost too easy.

Drop-shipping has huge advantages. It lets you experiment in marketing a merchandise line without making a huge financial commitment for inventory that may or may not sell. Drop-shipping also allows you to avoid the tremendous overhead involved in storing and shipping merchandise. By leveraging someone else's inventory and personnel, you can put your little toe in a new merchandise line to see how it will sell in your Yahoo! Store. I know of many, many Yahoo! Store retailers drop-shipping their products all over the country, selling millions of dollars through their Yahoo! Stores.

Unfortunately, multiple problems can also occur with drop-shipping. If you're selling a very popular product, then odds are many other retailers will be using the exact same drop-shipper that you're using, so you may have lots of competition. While most drop-shippers are pretty good, you have little or no control over when your orders ship, so your customer service may suffer. You also pay drop-shippers more than your competitors who buy the same products direct from the manufacturer and warehouse and ship products themselves. Sometimes drop-shipping suppliers sell retail themselves, or hide the fact that they do by operating a separate company that does retail. Inventory can also be a problem. There's nothing more frustrating than having to refund a paying customer because your supplier can't fulfill the order. And, of course, some drop-shippers are better than others. If you find a good one, don't tell a soul (except me!).

Keep in mind that drop-shipping isn't for everyone. I like to have the product in my hands, which allows me to give better customer service because I know when I'm almost out of stock, and I know when a customer's order shipped. Drop-shipping works great when everything goes right, but when something gets screwed up, it can be a nightmare. I also get a better discount from wholesalers because I buy in much larger quantities, so it costs my wholesaler less to process my orders. Because I do my own shipping, I also don't have to pay a drop-ship fee on every box. These factors let me sell for less or make more money than my drop-shipping competitors. Sometimes I get to do both, which may make the difference between me making it and my competition not making it.

If you decide that drop-shipping may be for you, then check out the list of reliable drop-shippers recommended by Chris Malta's Worldwide Brands at www.worldwidebrands.com. He sells the Drop Ship Directory, which has a list of tons of wholesalers, retailers, and distributors who can ship products for you directly to your customers.

Looking before you leap

One of my clients called me to help build out his Yahoo! Store. He already had $25,000 cost-worth inventory in his basement before he knew whether he'd succeed. Fortunately, the guy is doing very well online, but making an inventory commitment of that size before you even get the first order scares the heck out of me.

A buddy of mine wanted to jump online and start selling Leap Pads right after they first came out. He contacted the manufacturer who told him his minimum order for the best wholesale pricing was around $50,000 cost. Ouch! For my friend to get his little toe into the Leap Pad business before he even filled the first order, he would have had to mortgage his house and buy an entire container load of products he was "pretty sure" he'd sell online.

My advice to him was to do some quick market testing and build a store to see whether he could actually sell the things online before worrying where he was going to get them. I suggested even going so far as to buy them at retail through someone like Amazon (even though he'd lose money) to avoid taking a huge gamble. After you start selling some product, then you make a deal with the manufacturer and actually make an inventory decision and get serious about selling. Long story short, the barrier to entry was too high, and he never got into e-commerce.

Taking an Existing Business Online

We took our existing retail business online when we were selling comic books and Pokémon cards, where we had around 5,000 different products. In my point-of-sale system, I had 25,000 different SKUs (stock keeping units), and we had 2,000 to 3,000 possible new products that we could sell every single month. To figure out what we wanted to sell online, I looked at what products we had the best discount on (the best profit margin) as well as what products tended to create repeat business.

We sold a lot of war games in our real stores where we'd sell the introductory boxed set at a steep, steep discount to get new customers into the game. Research showed that for every dollar that customers spent on the basic set, they'd spend $6 more on accessories — and these were hobbies where folks would spend $1,000. My online version of this business model was to do almost anything to get the customer and then make money selling her other stuff later. If I could get her to order from me online for a ridiculously low price and have a good shopping experience, then hopefully she would continue to buy from us again and again. It worked great!

Planning is everything! You have a much better chance for success when you map out a strategy for selling online than when you just put up a Yahoo! Store and hope to sell something. There are major differences between selling in the real world and selling virtually.

Creaming your most profitable products

If you're an existing retailer and you have an existing brick-and-mortar business, use the Pareto Principle (the 80/20 rule) to see what to focus on online. Twenty percent of your products probably generate 80 percent of your sales. You want to look at those products first and spend the time and energy to put those dudes online, and then later, when you have more time, add the other 80 percent of stuff that you sell to your online store. But odds are that you can cream your product line, just sell your bestselling items online, and still do most of the business with only 20 percent of the work that you would do by putting your entire product catalog online.

Leveraging existing inventory to the Web

If you already have a store, then you probably have a lot of inventory. Take some pictures, write some descriptions, and upload your products to a Yahoo! Store. Now your inventory is available in your real store and online in your virtual shop. You get double the mileage out of the same inventory. Eventually, when you start moving a lot of products, you want to be careful not to run out of stock on the popular products that you sell online.

Maximizing supplier relationships

When you have an existing business, you have a leg up on people who are just starting out because you already have a relationship with your suppliers. Use these tips to maximize your supplier relationships:

- ✔ **Existing retailers can use their real-world status to get product databases and images from suppliers.** For some reason, vendors tend to be stingy with product data. Manufacturers and wholesalers can give you additional content for your store, too. Just ask for permission to reuse articles or sell sheets, PDFs, owner's manuals, buyer's guides, or anything else that makes your store better.

- ✔ **Pick your suppliers' brains from time to time to keep up on industry trends.** Suppliers have a much broader view of the market than any one retailer, and they can give information on what's selling elsewhere with new product ideas you might not notice in your local market.

- ✔ **Encourage your suppliers to protect their existing customers by increasing the barriers to entry for new competition.** Suggest that they have large initial orders or higher minimum orders or require a physical storefront as a condition for buying wholesale.

- ✔ **Ask your suppliers for a link from their Web site to your Yahoo! Store.** When you do hundreds of thousands or millions of dollars a year in business with a company, it's really easy to get a link from its site to yours. Don't be afraid to ask for a link and hound the company as much as you can until you get that link. Links from manufacturers and other suppliers really give you a leg up on the competition because they help your search engine rankings, which I discuss in much greater detail in Chapter 19. You'll also get traffic and sales from these links. When potential customers are on the manufacturer's Web site, they're looking to buy, and I want to be one of those 10 or 15 stores with a link. If you don't ask, you don't get (a link), so ask!

Selling locally while shipping globally

When you sell both online and offline, sometimes you need two different sets of prices. There's more online competition, so you have to be much more price conscious when you sell online. But because your costs are lower selling online, you can actually make more online than you do offline.

However, the last thing you want to do is alienate your local customers, so my strategy has always been to use a different business name online and not use my Yahoo! Store as my company site. I won't deny that I sell online, but I won't rub it in my local customers' faces, either.

My brother and I went from not selling online to the Pokémon explosion with 80 percent of our sales volume suddenly coming from our Yahoo! Stores. Our business model changed, and it happened almost overnight. With four times the sales coming over e-mail, fax, and phone, it was easy to get distracted and neglect our local customers.

We were making so much more money selling online than we were offline, so we eventually sold our brick-and-mortar comic stores to concentrate on marketing our Yahoo! Stores selling comics, games, and gift stuff. This shift in our business model was a way to maximize our business and reduce our overhead. We also moved from an expensive retail shopping center to a cheaper industrial park warehouse and made more money by reducing our overhead. My mom's company now has a big warehouse that also serves a retail location, too. Sometimes you can have your cake and eat it, too!

Finessing manufacturer's descriptions

I tend to rewrite our manufacturer's descriptions on our bestselling products for multiple reasons:

✔ **Unique product descriptions distinguish you from the competition.** Your customer is probably looking at several different Web sites selling the exact same product at almost the same price. When your Yahoo! Store has much more product detail than the generic manufacturer's description with a different caption or product description, odds are that you're going to get the sale.

✔ **You can do better search engine optimization when you're writing your own product**

descriptions. Manufacturers tend to write for themselves. They use industry buzzwords and often refer to a product without using the words that shoppers are searching for.

✔ **You can show off your industry and product expertise in your sales copy.** When I shop online, I prefer to buy from sites that take a position and recommend which products I should buy. I want to know which products are better than others for my particular application. I also want to know that the folks I'm giving my hard-earned money to actually know about the products they sell.

Migrating to Yahoo! Store from Another Storefront System

Moving from another shopping cart system to Yahoo! Store can be confusing, but if you do your homework, assemble the right elements, and have a positive attitude, you can actually improve your store. About a third of my development clients started their stores on another shopping cart and wanted to move to Yahoo! Store and Merchant Solutions.

Making the transition

Even if you're not a Web developer or a super-geek, Yahoo! Store is still extremely easy for you to use. Of course, if you can export a database that has your product information in it, you have the graphic files and the templates that folks use to build your Web site, and you can export your pictures, it is very easy to take a feed, a database, or an export of another shopping cart store and turn that into another Yahoo! Store. See Chapter 23 for getting down with product uploads and Chapter 12 for info on creating products.

Copying your old site's look and feel

Copying the design of your old site to a new Yahoo! Store is important to give continuity to existing customers. You can build your store in three different ways:

- ✔ **Use the Yahoo! Store Editor and standard templates.** Use *Variables,* the global controls that control store layout and appearance, in the Store Editor to create a look and feel that is very similar to your other Web site. You can make a very nice-looking, easy-to-use, fast-loading, search-engine-friendly online store.

- ✔ **Use RTML to duplicate the HTML template from your other Web site.** Wrap that template around normal Yahoo! Store functionality. Copy your images to your Web-hosting account and you're all set. See Chapter 27 for more on RTML.

- ✔ **Use the new Merchant Solutions Store Tags to plug in access to your Catalog Manager product database and Yahoo! Store functionality into copies of your old store's HTML pages.** Store Tags allow you to put a little snippet of code on each HTML product page that says, "Hey, this is the product information for item *1234.*" When you change the name, price, caption, or even the picture in the Catalog Manager and you're using Store Tags, the Yahoo! Server changes the information on your Merchant Solutions HTML pages automatically. I don't build Yahoo! Stores this way and prefer using the Store Editor over using Store Tags.

Chapter 3

Jump-Starting Your Store

- -

In This Chapter

▶ Creating a new Yahoo! ID and security key

▶ Opening a new Merchant Solutions account

▶ Building your first store in Store Editor

▶ Creating, editing, and manipulating items and section pages

▶ Publishing your store and placing a test order

- -

So you're about to open a Yahoo! Store. Congratulations! You're now ahead of about 95 percent of folks who dream of doing their own thing, but never do anything but talk about it.

The most important thing you can do is start. Don't overthink it. Don't worry about picking the best domain ever. Just grab a domain, create a Yahoo! ID, and open a Merchant Solutions account.

In this chapter, I show you how to jump-start your online store. You create a new Yahoo! ID, open a Merchant Solutions account, and jump right into store building with the Store Editor. In the Editor, you create sample sections and product pages, upload some pictures, and publish your store. Finally, you place a test order.

When you see how fast you can get a working e-commerce site up and running, the entrepreneurial juices start to flow!

Registering with Yahoo!

You're ready to start your store when you have a domain name registered. If you haven't picked out a domain yet, take a look at Chapter 24, where I dive into the details of dot-coms and DNSs and help you master your domain. Before you get started store building or open your account, you need to register with Yahoo! by creating a Yahoo! ID.

A Yahoo! ID is your passport to all things Yahoo! Your ID is proof that you are who you say you are. With your ID, you can log in and edit your store, make changes to your domain name and e-mail accounts, export orders, and even cancel your store. A Yahoo! ID identifies you as the owner of a specific account, which gives you access to the back door of your online store. Your Yahoo! ID also stores the credit-card data you use to pay for your Yahoo! Small Business products and services.

Only the person with the master Yahoo! ID (login and password and security key) can access all the features of a Merchant Solutions account, including configuring domains and playing with the Web-hosting File Manager, among other things.

Creating your Yahoo! ID

If you have ever had a Yahoo! e-mail account, you have a Yahoo! ID. The ID is part of the e-mail address before the @ sign: the `whatever@yahoo.com`. If you have Yahoo! e-mail, you probably already have a Yahoo! ID, but I recommend making a new one for this store.

Before you create your Yahoo! ID, make sure that you can get to your e-mail because Yahoo! sends a confirmation message with a link that you have to click to verify your e-mail address. Create your Yahoo! ID by following these steps:

1. **Go to** `http://edit.yahoo.com`.

    If you're logged in with another Yahoo! ID, you have to log out. In the lower right corner, you see the text "Don't have a Yahoo! ID? Signing up is easy."

2. **Click the Sign Up link.**

    The Yahoo! ID signup page appears. Because it's going to be your permanent Yahoo! ID for the store, try to make it the same as your domain name. With 60,000,000 plus Yahoo! ID's, odds are your name is taken, but your can always use something like `yourdomain.com`.

    For example, my example store is `http://ystorebooks.com`, and my Yahoo! ID is `ystorebooks`. If that ID was taken, I would have tried `ystorebooks.com`. I have too many logins and IDs and passwords to remember these days, so I try to make my life easier when I can!

3. **Type your first name, last name, gender, and a whole bunch of other information and click the I Agree button.**

    The Registration: Please Activate Your Account page appears to ask you to check your e-mail for a note from Yahoo! Member Services.

Note: Eventually, you'll forget your password. Everyone does, so don't feel too bad. Fortunately, you'll have a security question with an answer that you and only you should know. Your Yahoo! Security Question is something like what is your pet's name, the name of your first school, or your childhood hero. Not only are you going to have to remember what the question is, but you're going to have to remember exactly what the answer is. Make your answer really easy, because you have to type it exactly right.

4. **Print this page and stick it in a file folder.**

   This way, you don't have to remember your security question or answer. I make a file folder with all of my Yahoo! account information, including the Yahoo! ID, password, security question, security answer, birthday, zip code on the credit card, alternate e-mail address, and (at least) the last eight digits of the credit card.

   Keep this info handy (but safe). When you have technical support issues, the nice people at Yahoo! Store Technical Support are going to ask you for this information to make sure that some unauthorized person isn't trying to fix your Yahoo! Store. I also keep my Yahoo! Security Key and my Security Key questions and answers on the same sheet of paper, but they're written in my chicken-scratch handwriting, which gives me the highest level of encryption.

5. **Go to your e-mail account and look for an important message from Yahoo!.**

6. **Click the Important! Click Here To Activate Your New Account link.**

   You see a page that asks for your Yahoo! password.

7. **Enter your Yahoo! password into the form and click the Verify button.**

   You see a page that says Your Alternate Email Address Has Been Verified. Now you have a Yahoo! ID.

Make sure that your credit-card information is current. When your card expires or is declined, Yahoo! sends you several e-mails and puts a warning notice inside your Store Manager. Eventually, Yahoo! Billing gives up and deletes your account with very little warning. Getting a deleted Merchant Solutions account reinstated requires several miracles happening at the same time.

Creating a Yahoo! security key

For additional security, there is also a second-level password called a *security key.* You have to type your security key every time you do anything involving credit cards or other really sensitive information, including configuring domains and editing or deleting accounts. If you haven't set up your security key, here's how to do it:

1. **Click the Change My Security Key link.**

   A page appears that says, "Your account does not have a Security Key. Sign up for a Security Key or continue."

2. **Click the Sign Up For A Security Key link, which takes you to the Yahoo! Security Key Sign Up page.**

   Choose your security key, select your forgotten security key question, and answer the question. Write this information down and put it in your file folder.

3. **Give Yahoo! your e-mail address, zip code, and country, and finally confirm the credit card in your Yahoo! Wallet to prove that you are who you say you are.**

4. **Click the Submit This Form button.**

5. **Click the Finished button to save all your changes.**

Opening Your Yahoo! Merchant Solutions Account

You need two things when you open your Yahoo! Merchant Solutions account: a Yahoo! ID and a domain name. You need to either have a domain name already registered at Yahoo! (see Chapter 24) or another registrar or register a brand-spanking new domain when you create your Merchant Solutions account. You also need a new Yahoo! ID and a Security Key, which you can read about in the section "Registering with Yahoo!," earlier in this chapter.

A Yahoo! Merchant Solutions account isn't the same thing as a *merchant account.* A merchant account is a business bank account with a company that processes your credit-card transactions for a fee and then deposits the money into your business checking account anywhere from 12 hours to 2 weeks later, depending on your account. To process credit cards, you need either a merchant account or a PayPal account (which requires using the New Checkout Manager). If you don't have a merchant account, Yahoo! hooks you up with its partner bank, Paymentech.

Figure 3-1 shows the Yahoo! sales page for the three different Merchant Solutions packages: Starter, Standard, and Professional. Yahoo! Store has a monthly fee of $39.95 for Starter, $99.95 for Standard, or $299.95 for Professional. Start cheap and upgrade later. Begin with Starter or Standard. When you start doing any real volume of sales, then start paying the $300 a month for Professional. Go to http://smallbusiness.yahoo.com/merchant to read up on the accounts. For more on comparing plans, read Chapter 1, where I talk about the differences in the three plans.

Figure 3-1:
Yahoo!
Merchant
Solutions
offers you
three
different
levels of
accounts:
Starter,
Standard,
and Profes-
sional.

Want to save $50? Every time I've opened a Merchant Solutions account, I got the $50 signup fee waived by calling the Yahoo! Sales line at 1-866-781-9246. A salesperson babysat me while I walked through the various steps and gave me a coupon code at the end of the transaction. The Yahoo! folks are always nice and helpful. I guess they give you the $50 because they figure they lose fewer customers in the signup process if they can answer any questions and walk you through it. Who knows whether this waiver will last?

Go to `http://smallbusiness.yahoo.com/merchant` to open your Merchant Solutions account:

1. **Click Starter (or Standard if you prefer) and click the Sign Up button.**

   The Search For Your Domain Name/Have A Domain Name page appears.

2. **Type your domain name in the search box and click the Continue button.**

   Yahoo! checks the WHOIS database (the public database of all the domain names in the world) and knows that it's a real domain name. You see a confirmation page with your domain name, your Merchant Solutions plan, and a button where Yahoo! double-checks to make sure that it's your domain name.

3. **Click the Yes, This Is My Domain Name button.**

   Yahoo! tries to upsell you to Merchant Standard or Pro, but you don't want that yet.

4. **Click the Keep Current Plan And Continue button.**

   You're asked to log in with your Yahoo! ID and password (if you haven't already logged in).

5. **Enter your Yahoo! ID and password.**

   A secure page appears, and it looks like Yahoo! wants some money:

   - If you've already created your Yahoo! Wallet, you need to verify you are who you say you are by typing your Yahoo! security key or by entering your credit card on file.

   - If you haven't created your Yahoo! Wallet, you need your credit-card number, the expiration date, the CV2 number, and your billing address if you want to set up a Yahoo! Store. Type all your information and click the Continue button.

   Yahoo! actually verifies your credit-card number while you wait, so it make take up to 2 minutes to place your order and to log in to your site.

   Be patient. It takes a couple of days or so for your domain name to propagate across the entire Web and point to your Yahoo! Store (whether you have a newly registered Yahoo! domain or a domain with another registrar.) Until then, you're able to edit and publish your store, which shows up on a temporary Yahoo! URL.

   You're making no long-term commitment to Yahoo!. I just signed a five-year lease on my retail location, so a month-to-month lease sounds pretty good. Yahoo! also auto-renews your order and charges your credit card each month until you tell it otherwise. Make sure that you keep your credit-card information current with Yahoo! unless you want to run the risk of getting your store shut off!

   If your domain was registered elsewhere, you need to change the DNSs (domain name servers) to point to Yahoo!'s name servers: `yns1.yahoo.com` and `yns2.yahoo.com`. Changing DNSs sounds worse than it is. All you do is log in to your account at your registrar, change the DNS settings, update your account, and wait a couple of days. Most registrars have an 800 number if you need help.

   The Small Business Home: Welcome To Yahoo! Merchant Solutions page appears. This page explains what a Control Panel is. You even get a Welcome e-mail message with plenty of information on how to get started the Yahoo! way. You can also go to the Getting Started guide, which you can download.

After you purchase Merchant Solutions, you have access to the Manage My Services console.

Jumping into Store Building

I can spend a lot of time yapping about what I do when I build a store and my store design philosophy for converting more shoppers into buyers, but I know you're chomping at the bit to get going on your own store.

Unlike most of the rest of this book, you need to do the rest of this chapter in the same order that I do, or you may not get the same results I do. Here's what you do to dive right in to building your store with the Store Editor (see Chapter 9):

1. **Configure the Store Editor.**

   Make store building easier by switching to the more powerful Advanced mode and turn off things that can slow you down. You also play with the global variables, which control the look and feel of the store.

2. **Create and edit some real pages.**

   Build sample sections and products, upload pictures, move the items around, rearrange the store, and create sample info and privacy policy pages. Edit the home page.

3. **Publish your store.**

   Now anyone in the world can see your handiwork.

4. **Place a test order.**

   Now you can see how fast you can actually get a real store up and running and taking orders.

Adding some test products and making a functioning store should take less than an hour unless you're pokey or get stuck on some design decisions. Don't make it pretty, just make it work for now!

1. Sign in with your Yahoo! ID and log in to Store Editor

Every time you do something in the Store Editor, you have to sign in with your Yahoo! ID and log in to your Merchant Solutions account.

1. **Point your browser to** `http://smallbusiness.yahoo.com/ merchant`.

   Figure 3-2 shows what you see when you sign in: your Business Console with Manage My Services with all your Merchant Solutions accounts. Each account has links to your Store Manager, web hosting, domains, and e-mail.

Figure 3-2:
The
Manage My
Services
page links
to your
Merchant
Solutions
account(s)
with links to
your Store
Manager,
web
hosting,
domains,
and e-mail.

2. **Click the Store Manager link.**

   Figure 3-3 shows the Store Manager page. The Store Manager is your virtual back office. It's the center of your Yahoo! Merchant Solutions account, where you access orders, study statistics, and control the order settings, such as tax, payment methods, and shipping methods and rates. Notice the page views and revenue graphs, which show you traffic and sales every time you log in. I discuss the Store Manager in minute detail in Chapter 15.

3. **Click the Store Editor link.**

   Figure 3-4 shows the Store Editor. You're now on the home page (index.html) in Edit mode. If you change the default Editor Entry Page under Controls from home page (the default) to Contents, when you click the Store Editor link on the Store Manager page, the Contents page appears instead of the home page. The Contents page is a hierarchical site map that shows all the objects in your store and the products and sections within each object. If you do see the Contents page, click the Index link to move from the Contents page to the home page.

The Store Editor is a working copy of your store, where you can manage all your products as well as make store design and layout changes. You control who has access to the Editor on the Store Manager's Access page (see Chapter 15), and the Editor is available only to your Yahoo! ID and any other Yahoo! ID's you let in the back door. You can make layout and design changes to your store, as well as add, edit, and delete products. When you're ready to make the changes public, click the Publish button, which updates the public version of your store almost instantly.

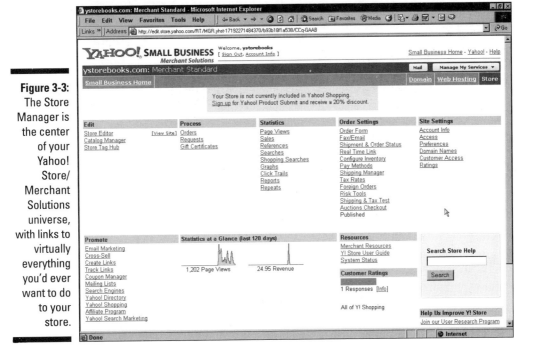

Figure 3-3:
The Store
Manager is
the center
of your
Yahoo!
Store/
Merchant
Solutions
universe,
with links to
virtually
everything
you'd ever
want to do
to your
store.

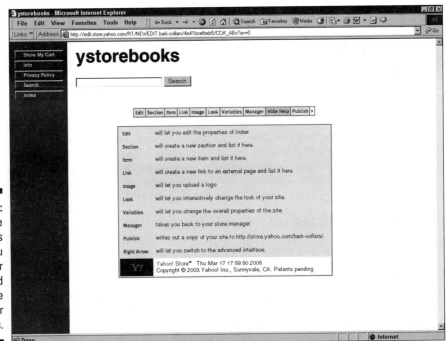

Figure 3-4:
The Store
Editor is
where you
build your
store and
manage
your
products.

Don't panic!

You can easily get confused when you have two versions of your store. Am I on the Editor? Or am I on the published store? Don't panic! It reminds me of that classic *Star Trek* episode where two parallel dimensions somehow collide, resulting in two Enterprises and two of every crew member running into each other. The only way you could tell the evil Captain Kirk and Mr. Spock from the good versions were their cheesy black goatees. Now that I think about it, one of those guys ordered from one of Mom's Yahoo! Stores.

If you're ever not sure which version of your store you're in — the Store Editor or the published site — look for the Edit Nav-bar; if you see it, you're in the Editor. You can also look at the URL in your browser's address bar. If you

see your domain name, then you're on the published site and need to log in to make changes to your site. If you see a URL that looks something like the following URL, you're in Store Editor:

```
http://edit.store.yahoo.com/RT/NEWEDIT.
        yhst-17192271484370/
        c7a5fd63345f/C5ccoAAH
```

The most common way to get booted out of the Store Editor and over to the published version of your site is by clicking links you made to the real version of your store. Notice that all the Editor-created links to your home page (home buttons, Name-image, Index, Button, and so on) point to index.html and not to www.*your domain*.com. These relative path links work in both the Editor and on the published site.

The Store Editor is already familiar to you because it's a copy of your site with an Edit Nav-bar stuck on top. Move around in your Store Editor the same way a customer navigates your published store. Click links, icons, and navigation buttons to get to the items or sections you want to edit. Each page has an Edit button (on the Edit Nav-bar), which you can click to edit the Name, Caption, Code, Price, Image, and other fields.

Figure 3-5 shows you the Edit buttons or Edit Nav-bar, which appears at the bottom (or top) of virtually every page of the Store Editor. The Edit buttons let you create, edit, and move pages around; make changes to your global *variables,* which determine the look and feel of your store; control and configure your Store Editor settings; and move around the Store Editor.

2. Configure the Store Editor for store building

You can configure the Store Editor for easier store building. Hide the useless stuff and crank up the Editor to Advanced mode. Following are my first round of tweaks:

✔ **Hide Help:** Click the Hide Help button to make all the definitions under each field go away. All you have to do is click the Help button, and they're back again. After about 5 minutes, the Help files just get in the way.

✔ **Turn on Advanced mode:** Click the little red arrow to the right of the Edit buttons to change the Store Editor from Basic mode to Advanced mode, which gives you access to all the fields, settings, and power tools the Store Editor possesses.

✔ **Move the Edit buttons to the top of your Editor:** Click the Config button. The Editor page appears to make your Store Editor behave.

3. Create sample pages

After you've poked around the Editor a bit, you can create some sample pages, edit them, upload pictures, make a product page, and make a special on the home page. Here's how to create a sample page:

1. **Navigate to the home page by clicking the Home button.**

   When you're on the home page, you can create a sample section.

2. **Click the Section button on the Edit Nav-bar.**

   Figure 3-6 displays a new section's Edit page, where you can enter page information like Name or Caption and upload images. For now, just give this section page a name.

Figure 3-5:
Your Edit
Nav-bar
tells you
where
you are,
helps you
navigate the
Store Editor,
and links to
everything
you need in
your Store
Editor
toolbox.

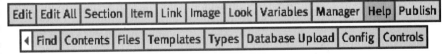

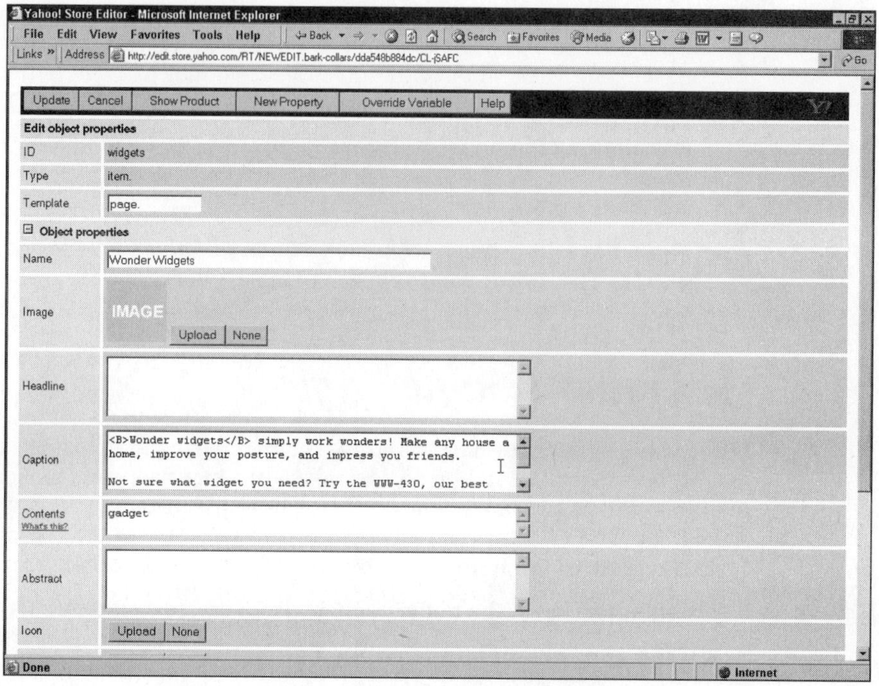

Figure 3-6:
The Edit
page for a
section or
item lets
you enter or
edit page
information
and upload
images.

3. Type the name in the Name field and click the Update button.

The page you created appears. Because you created a section on the home page, that section is part of the top-level navigation for the site. Any pages on the home page do double duty by also appearing in the navigation bar. Notice that the button text is from the text you typed into the Name field.

4. To add more information to the page, click the Edit button.

The Edit page for your section page appears. Notice that the ID is created from what you typed into the Name field, and the type is Item, even though it's a section page.

You can't edit Type or ID in Store Editor. After you create a page, ID and Type are permanent. I talk a lot more about IDs and Store Editor in Chapter 9.

Because this page was created with the Section button, the only Object Properties (the fields of an item, section, or other page) you see are Name, Image, Headline, Caption, Contents, Abstract, Icon, Inset, Label, Leaf, and Product-url.

5. Change the text in the Name field from whatever it is to something a little different so that you can see how edits change things.

6. **Add your text in the Caption field.**

For example, if I were creating a page on widgets, I might write the following in the Caption field:

```
<strong>Wonder widgets</strong> simply work wonders! Make any house a home,
        improve your posture, and impress your friends.
Not sure what widget you need? Try the WWW-430, our bestselling Wonder
        Widget! Order yours today and get free shipping.
```

7. **Click the Update button.**

The edited section page appears with the change to the Name appearing on the page itself in the Headline, as well as on the left on the button text in the navigation bar. Notice that the new Caption text appears.

Section pages need some text in the Caption, or they look kind of boring. I like to write a short paragraph or two to give customers a quick overview of the products in that section. Make the Caption text descriptive enough to show off your product knowledge, but keep it short enough to not push the products down the page and off the screen. Section pages with keyword-rich Caption fields are more search-engine friendly than pages with empty Captions. I talk a lot more about search engines in Chapter 19.

Captions are special fields. If you have two line breaks in your text, the Store Editor displays your text the same way. You can type limited amounts of HTML inside your Caption fields to format text, display images, and do almost anything else HTML can do. For example, I like to use strong tags around keywords to emphasize them. You can make important words or phrases appear bolder or darker by placing a `<strong>` tag before the text you want to emphasize and a `</strong>` tag after the text.

Upload an image to your section page

Section pages don't need huge images because they take up lots of room and push the products down the page, but they do need some kind of image to make a thumbnail if you show your contents or top-level navigation on the home page.

An image around 100 pixels tall by 100 pixels wide should match your text pretty well. You can use pretty much any JPEG or GIF files you have.

It's hard to sell anything without a picture, so you need to upload an image. Here's how to upload an item's image:

1. **Click the Edit button to edit your section page.**

You return to the Edit page, where you can upload an image.

2. **Scroll to the Image button and click the Upload button.**

The Image Upload page appears. You can upload images and other files from your computer to your Yahoo! Store.

3. Click the Browse button.

The File Upload window lets you browse your hard drive like you would in Windows Explorer when you're looking for files to open.

4. Browse to the image file you want to upload, select it, and click the Open button.

The path to the file on your computer is magically pasted into the field. It should look something like this:

```
C:\Documents and Settings\Administrator\Desktop\item.jpg
```

5. Click the Send button to upload your file to the Yahoo! image server.

When the file is finished uploading, the section page appears with the new image you uploaded.

Figure 3-7 shows my Wonder Widgets section page with an image uploaded.

Figure 3-7:
Section pages need love, too. Professional images and captions give customers confidence in your product knowledge and help sell more stuff!

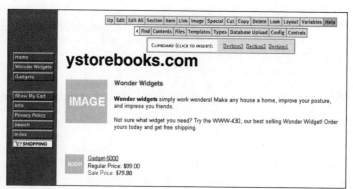

The Store Editor does all the heavy lifting on images so that you don't have to know HTML or know the URL or path to your image files. The Store Editor standard page template places your uploaded image where it's supposed to go. The Editor also automatically resizes your images to fit on the product page with the item-height and item-width settings under Variables.

Also, Store Editor makes thumbnails so that you don't have to! A smaller version of each page's image is created as a thumbnail for the home page or any section or product pages this item appears in. Pretty cool! I talk a lot more about images in Chapter 9.

You can also upload an image to a product or section page by clicking the Image button on the Edit Nav-bar. You can't delete an image from here, but you can upload a new one, bypassing the Edit page.

Create a sample item

An item (or product) page is just like a section page, but item pages display additional product fields, such as Code, Price, Sale-price, Orderable, Options, and so on, which are hidden on section pages.

Here's how to create an item:

1. **Navigate to your section page.**

2. **Click the Item button on the Edit Nav-bar to create a new item.**

   Now you're on the new item's Edit page, where you can type product information into the various fields. Notice how it looks almost like a section page, but with added product information fields.

3. **Type the name of your product into the Name field.**

4. **Type your code in the Code field.**

5. **Type your price in the Price field.**

6. **Click the Update button to create your first item.**

   The newly created item page appears with the name, the code, the price, and an Order button. The text on the Order button is set under Variables in the Order-text field. I always edit my Order-text and use Add To Cart or Add To My Order rather than Order or Buy.

When you create an item on a section page, that item appears on the section page as text and/or an image, which is linked to the item page. The item's link text on the section page comes from text in the item's Name field. The item's thumbnail image on the section page (if it has one) comes from the picture uploaded to the Image field unless the item has a separate image file uploaded to the Icon field, which replaces the Image as thumbnail. I talk a lot more about items and section pages in Chapter 11.

Edit the Sale-price and Option fields

Hey! You don't have to edit one field at a time and update. You can make all your edits at the same time, even when you create an item in the first place. I tend to edit, look at my changes, edit again, tweak something else, and edit yet it again. I love the fact that when you add product info or images to your Yahoo! Store, you get to see what your customers are gonna see as soon as you click the Update button. Those Viaweb folks did a great job creating the Store Editor!

I've broken editing these fields out as separate steps to minimize confusion. I'm throwing a lot at you in this chapter. Don't feel like you have to remember most of this material. I believe in open-book tests!

When you sell products online, you normally have to discount from a manufacturer's suggested retail price (MSRP) if you want to be price competitive. Here's how to show a discounted price using the Sale-price field:

1. **Navigate to your product page.**

2. **Click the Edit Item button to go to the item's Edit page.**

   The Price field appears on your page.

   Both Price and Sale-price fields take prices with or without dollar signs. Also, if an item only has one price, stick it in the Price field and leave Sale-price blank, or it will look funny. For example, if you leave the Price blank and type $79 in the Sale-price field, you'll wind up with text like "Regular Price $0.00, Sale Price $79.00."

3. **Type the discounted price in the Sale-price field.**

4. **Type the normal price (or manufacturer's suggested retail price) in the Price field.**

5. **Click the Update button to update the item.**

   The product appears with a Price and a Sale-price.

Many products you sell come in many different flavors of style, size, color, and other options. (See Chapter 12 for more options with option fields.)

Options are pretty easy to work with in a Yahoo! Store:

- The first word or phrase in the Options field is the option name.

- Each word or phrase after that is an option value.

- Surround phrases with quotes to keep phrases together as a single name or option.

- Multiple options are easy, too. Separate totally different options (such as color and size) with two line breaks by pressing the Enter key twice between separate options, which leaves a blank line between different options in the Options field.

Here's how to use the Options field:

1. **Go to your product page.**

2. **Click the Edit Item button to go to the Edit page.**

3. **Type your text in the Options field.**

   For example, I typed the following:

   ```
   Size Small Medium Large "Extra Large"

   "Gadget Color" Red White Blue
   ```

4. **Click the Update button to update the item.**

   Your item appears with drop-down menus for each option.

Add specials to your home page

Making a product a special simply places the item on your home page by putting the object ID in the Specials field of the home page. You can make items or sections appear as specials by editing the home page and just typing the object-IDs in the Specials field. For more than one product, type the IDs in the order that you want the specials to appear on the home page.

Here's how to feature a section or item as a special on the home page:

1. **Browse to the page you want to feature as a special.**

2. **Click the Special button in the Edit Nav-bar.**

   Figure 3-8 shows your home page with specials. Notice the thumbnail and link to the Gadget-5000 (or whatever else you made the special).

3. **Click the product's thumbnail or link.**

   The product page appears. Notice in the Edit Nav-bar that the Special button now says "Not Special." To remove the Special you created, all you have to do is click that button.

Figure 3-8:
Keep your home page fresh with specials. Feature bestselling items, which tends to make those products sell even more!

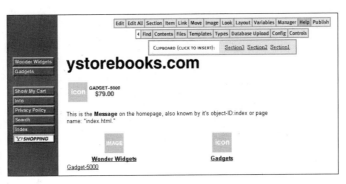

You can also make items or sections home-page specials simply by editing the home page and typing the IDs in the Specials field in the order that you want the specials to appear on the home page. The appearance of home-page specials is controlled by several settings on the home page itself and is covered in much detail in Chapter 12.

Introduce Variables by changing your button colors

Unlike each section or item page that has its own Edit page, only one Variables page exists. The settings on the Variables page determine the look and feel of your site. The Variables page is divided up into Colors and Typefaces, Image Dimensions, Page Layout, Button Properties, Page Properties, Store Properties, and Custom Variables. I cover all these variables in the book, but especially in Chapter 9.

Figure 3-9 shows the Variables page.

Here's how to change the color of the buttons across the entire site:

1. **Click the Variables button on your Edit Nav-bar.**

   The Variables Edit page appears.

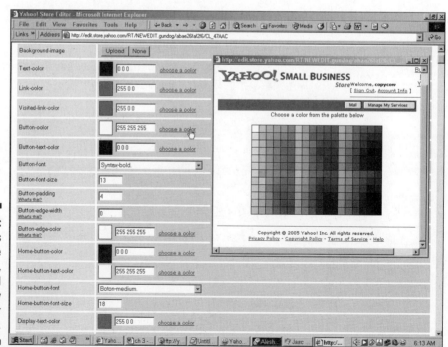

Figure 3-9: Variables determine the look, layout, and functionality of your store.

   2. **Scroll down to the Button-color variable.**

   Notice the color of the bar, three numbers in a field, and a link to Choose A Color. If you know the RGB number for a color, you can type it. *RGB* stands for *red green blue* and is how computer monitors display color. The number is the amount of each color, which is anywhere from 0 to 255.

   3. **Type 255 0 0 in the Button-color field and press Tab to move to another field.**

   Notice that the color of the bar changes from whatever it was before to a bright fire-engine red! Choosing 255 0 0 makes the color 100 percent red, plus 0 percent green, plus 0 percent blue, which is one of my favorite colors.

   4. **Scroll to top of the page and click the Update button.**

   Whatever page you were on before you clicked the Variable button appears. The buttons are red on every page on your site.

4. Publish your site, and you're live on the Web

You've made changes to your store, but only you can see what you've done. If you're ready to show your work to the world, you can publish to update the public version of your site by following these steps:

   1. **Browse to the home page by clicking the Home button.**

   2. **Click the Publish button.**

   The Publish Status page appears. If you want to keep editing, you can wait here until the Return To Editor link appears. If you want to see you changes (I do!), then go to your published site.

   3. **Click the Go To Manager link.**

   The Store Manager appears.

   4. **Click the View Your Site link to go to your Store Editor–built site.**

   The published version of your Store Editor–built store appears. It may be in one of several places, depending on how your domain's entry point is set up and whether you redirect all `store.yahoo.com` URLs to your domain:

```
http://store.YourDomain.com/index.html
www.YourDomain.com/index.html
http://store.yahoo.com/YourAccountName/index.html
http://store.yahoo.com/yhst-YourAccountNumber/
        index.html
```

5. Browse around the published version of your site and place a test order.

You're just getting started. As you build your store, you're really building your business. Don't worry too much about making money at first. Momentum is the main thing. Your store doesn't have to be the best site on the Web; it just needs to be *on* the Web. And soon!

I'm a big believer in implementing now and tweaking later. The faster you open your store, the faster you'll make the mistakes you need to make to discover the things you need to know to make your store a success.

Configuring Your Store Manager

Setting up your tax rates, shipping methods and rates, and payment methods is the second half of the equation when creating a store. By default, your Yahoo! Store doesn't collect sales tax, offers air and ground shipping with no shipping charge, and accepts only Visa as a payment method. To introduce you to the Store Manager's various features, you should set up sales tax rates, configure shipping methods and rates, create the order confirmation page and e-mail message, and activate your merchant order notification fax and e-mail.

After you make changes to the order settings, you see a red asterisk to the right of the Publish Order Settings link. Click the link to make your changes to the real store. After a moment, the changes have been made, the asterisk and link disappear, and they're replaced with the word *Published* so that you know that your settings match the real store settings.

Accessing the Store Manager

The Store Manager is like your back office in your Yahoo! account. When you log in to your Yahoo! ID, and then go to the Manage My Services page and `http://store.yahoo.com`, you must first go to the Store Manager before you can access the Store Editor.

When you're in the Store Editor, click the Home button to go to the home page. To return to the Store Manager, click the Manager button. Sometimes it's easier just to type `http://store.yahoo.com` and click the Store Manager link. You can also bookmark your Store Manager page for easy access.

Setting your sales tax rate

To set up sales tax, go to the Store Manager and follow these steps:

1. **Click the Tax Rates link under Order Settings.**

   The tax calculation page appears. You can change whether you collect sales tax, add or edit rows to your tax rules, or use the Auto Setup Wizard to set up your tax calculations. Use the wizard!

2. **Click the Auto Setup Wizard link.**

   The page that appears assumes that you're based in the United States.

3. **Click the Next button.**

   Now you're on the list of states that collect sales tax.

4. **Select the state(s) where you collect sales tax and click the Done button.**

   If you need to collect sales tax in multiple states, hold down Ctrl while you select the states.

5. **Change Tax Calculation for Customers to Calculate In Real-Time.**

6. **Click the Update button.**

   Notice that the Publish Order Settings link is back with a red asterisk.

7. **Click the Publish Order Settings link to publish the changes to your order settings.**

Configuring shipping methods and rates

Shipping Manager is located under Order Settings. In the Shipping Manager, you control your shipping methods, your shipping rates, and UPS settings. Shipping Manager also has links to register to use UPS Online tools (it's free!). Set up shipping methods before you set up your shipping rates. You can do so many things with the Shipping Manager; I recommend that you look at the full Yahoo! Resource and Help Files.

Setting up your shipping methods

In Yahoo! Store Manager, you can delete the default methods (Air and Ground) and set up your own shipping methods. Follow these steps:

1. **Click the Shipping Manager link under Order Settings.**

   The Shipping Manager page appears, where you can do all kinds of stuff. You want to set up Shipping Methods.

2. **Click the Shipping Methods link.**

   You see a page where you can edit shipping methods or change the display order.

3. **Click the Edit Methods button.**

   Now you're on the Edit Methods page of the Shipping Manager, where you have the following options:

   - You can select from General Methods, such as Downloadable, Two Day Delivery, Ground, Federal Express, First Class Mail, One Day Delivery, or Air.
   - You can add Custom Methods.
   - You can sign up for UPS Online Tools and use UPS's methods.

   I prefer to create my own methods and use a very simple shipping business model based upon getting new orders and eating some of my shipping costs as a marketing expense.

   I see increases in conversion rates and decreases in *dropped shopping carts* (folks bailing in the middle of an order) when I offer two ground methods: a free shipping promotional rate for orders over a certain amount and a flat rate amount for orders less than that. Here's how you can set up the same method:

   1. **Type** FREE UPS GROUND (on US48 orders over $99) **in the New Method Name field and click the Add button.**

   2. **Type** Standard Shipping (US48) $5.95 **in the New Method Name field and click the Add button.**

   3. **Deselect the Ground and Air defaults check boxes and click the Update button.**

      You return to the Ship Methods page.

   4. **Click the Change Display Order button.**

      The Change Display Order page appears.

   5. **Highlight the FREE UPS method, click the up or down arrows to make it first, and then click the Update button.**

      You have to Publish Order Settings, but after you do that, your new custom methods are live in the checkout.

Setting your shipping rates

You should be in the Yahoo! Store Manager. Here's how to delete the default methods (Air and Ground) and set up your own shipping rates:

1. **Click the Shipping Manager link under Order Settings.**

2. **Click the Shipping Rates link.**

   You see a page where you can edit shipping methods or change the display order.

3. **Click the Add Rule button to create a new shipping charge.**

   Now you're on the 5-Step Add Rule Wizard. Do the little ship-rate dance. The radio buttons are set to Specific Location, and Inside: US United States, which is fine.

4. **In Step 1 of the wizard, scroll down and click the Next button.**

   Note: UPS Ground to Hawaii and Alaska is available now, which I don't really understand.

   Step 2 of 5: Add Rule - Select Method(s) appears. The default And Ship Method Matches Any is fine.

5. **Click the Next button.**

   Now you're on Step 3 of 5: Choose a Rule Type page.

6. **Select Rate Table and click the Next button.**

   Now you're on Step 4 of 5: Rate Table Details page. The default is set to Based on: Taxable_Amount, which is fine. Because this rule is for folks who ordered more than $99, you really don't have to put anything here because this shipping method's rate is "free." However, you need to do something for the folks who order $10 and think they'll get shipping just because they select it. Nope!

7. **In the first field (From 0, Add $), type** 5.95.

8. **In the second field (From: ___), type** 99 **and click the Next button.**

   Now the checkout charges orders less than $99 the standard shipping rate of $5.95, whether or not the buyer chooses it.

   You're now on the Step 5 of 5: Override Setting page.

9. **Click the Done button.**

Note: I don't like Exclude All Other shipping rules. I don't want to override anything because I like to use an additive method of ship rates. For example, if someone from Hawaii orders something under $99, I'll add a non-US48 upcharge to the $5.95 rate. If someone from Alaska orders something over $99, eventually I'll have a separate non-US48 upcharge for those orders.

Setting your payment methods

In the Yahoo! Store Manager, you can add MasterCard, Visa, and American Express to your Pay Methods. Follow these steps:

1. **Click the Pay Methods link under Order Settings.**

2. **Type your Yahoo! security key.**

   Anytime you access or make changes to sensitive information, such as domains, your account information, account access, and customer credit-card info, Yahoo! asks you for a second-level password called your *security key* to verify your identity. If you don't have a security key, follow the prompts to create one.

   If you have a security key, you see the Pay Methods page, where you can apply for a new merchant account, configure your store to work with your existing merchant account, and add or edit the Payment Methods that appear on your checkout.

   If you've already set up your online credit-card processing, adding a card to your Payment Methods that your merchant bank account doesn't accept doesn't work, so don't try it.

3. **Change the radio buttons for the Payment Methods you want to add from No to Yes.**

   I select American Express, MasterCard, and Discover. For more information on credit cards, see Chapter 15.

   This page is a cool place to snag credit-card icons. Simply right-click the ones you want and save them to your desktop.

4. **Click the Done button.**

Working with order confirmations and merchant notifications

When a customer clicks the Place Order button, the next page he sees is his Order Confirmation page, which shows a copy of his order with a unique order number and verifies that the order was actually placed. Next, the customer gets an order confirmation e-mail with the same information. You can add text to both of these customer *touch points* (fancy marketer lingo for customer contact).

The Order Confirmation page

I like to thank the customer for his order and provide useful customer service info. This info reduces their stress, as well as the number of WISMO (where is my order?) phone calls. Include answers to frequently asked customer service questions. Let your customer know how long it will take to get his order and how he can contact you.

Merchants need to know about new orders, too! Depending on your Merchant Solutions package, you can get notified by e-mail, in the Store Manager, and/or by fax (Merchant Starter doesn't include faxes). I prefer to get order e-mails and faxes, but I'll upgrade later for that.

To customize the Order Confirmation page, follow these steps:

1. **Click the Order Form link under Order Settings.**

   Scroll down to the Order Confirmation message. The default message is "Thank you for your order. Please print this page for your records."

2. **Add the text you want to the message.**

   For example, you can include "This is the Order Confirmation message in Store Manager: Order Settings: Order Form."

3. **Click the Done button.**

   You're back in the Store Manager. Later, I'll can change my message to something really good.

The Order Confirmation e-mail

The Shipment Status page is where you can turn on shipment tracking and customer Order Confirmation e-mails, set a separate address to receive bounced e-mail notifications, customize your Confirmation e-mail and Status Update e-mails, and use the XML Update feature. I talk about all of these topics a bit more in Chapter 15.

You should be on the Store Manager page. Here's how to start sending and customizing customer Order Confirmation e-mails:

1. **Click the Shipment & Order Status link under Order Settings.**

2. **Type your e-mail address in the Order Confirmation e-mail field.**

3. **Scroll down to the Confirmation E-mail message and add the text you'd like to appear.**

   The default message is "This email is to confirm the receipt of your recent order from Yhst-*YahooStoreAccount*."

4. **Click the Update button.**

   You return to the Store Manager.

Auto–Order Notification e-mails

Here's how to start receiving merchant automatic order notifications every time you get an order:

1. **Click the Order E-mails link under Order Settings.**

   The Order System Settings page appears.

2. **Type your e-mail address in the E-mail To field.**

3. **Click the Done button.**

Publishing store settings changes and placing a test order

You can publish Order Settings by clicking the link. Go to the published site by typing your domain name in your browser or by clicking the View Site link in the Store Manager. Click around your new store. Place items in your Shopping Cart and actually place a test order.

Note: Until you open for business (and complete said checklist — see the next section), Yahoo! allows you to test orders. Your checkout works, but says "*yourdomain*.com is not open for business. Ordering is allowed for testing purposes only."

Sometimes it takes a little while to publish a large site. Don't try to go back to the Store Editor while your store is publishing; your store is working. If you try to publish more than five times, your store locks up, and it may take an hour or more to unlock. You then see the error message "You have more than 5 pending requests."

Opening for Business

After you've published the Store Editor, edited your privacy policy and info pages, and published your store settings, you see two links in the Store Editor in a message that says, "In order to open for business, you will need to complete all of the items in the open for business checklist." Here's what you do:

1. **Click the Open For Business link.**

2. **Fill in your merchant account bank's name, phone number, and your account number in the merchant account provider, provider phone number, and account number fields.**

3. **Click the Submit button.**

   Next, you see the Congratulations Message.

4. Continue to Manager Console and publish your order settings.

Your site is now current and has met Y! requirements.

Any changes to the Order Settings require publishing. If you're changing 17 things, wait until after you change the last thing to click the Publish Order Settings link to make your changes live on the real store. When the live store matches the Order Settings, the link disappears and is replaced with the word *Published.*

Remember, you're just getting started. As you build your store, you're really building your business. Don't worry too much about making money at first. Momentum is the main thing. Your store doesn't have to be the best site on the Web, it just needs to be *on* the Web. And soon!

Chapter 4

Anatomy of a Yahoo! Store Order

. . . .

. . . .

A journey of a thousand miles starts with a single click: Add To Cart. Nothing happens in e-commerce until a customer buys something. After that happens, watch out! You've got orders to pick and pack, credit cards to run, boxes to ship, and e-mails to send. Get this economy moving!

In this chapter, you get to see a real Yahoo! Store order from start to finish. I show you everything that happens from the first click to the Web store all the way through to the UPS truck pulling up to the customer's house. Watch the customer search on MSN, find my store in the search results pages, click my search listing to jump to my Web store, browse various products, place an order online, and discover everything else that happens behind the scenes to get that box to the customer. You can find out a lot from watching how real customers — not just browsers or tire-kickers — interact with your store. The secret to getting more sales is to attract more visitors who act like customers.

As you follow this order, watch as I point out the major attractions. (On your left, you notice the Shopping Cart. On your right, a secure checkout page.) The story ends happily with a satisfied customer who got what he wanted and a retailer who got an order and a brand new customer.

Examining the Timeline of a Real Yahoo! Store Order

This section gives you a timeline of an actual order placed in a real Yahoo! Store. I changed the customer's name and other personal info, but you can still see where he went and what he bought. As I walk you down the virtual shopping aisle, I point out features of the various elements of Yahoo! Store.

This overview includes the published pages of your Yahoo! Store; the Shopping Cart; the secure checkout collecting shipping and billing information; the order confirmation page and e-mail; and the tracking information and stats you get when someone browses and buys.

Finding the store in a search engine

Figure 4-1 shows a search on `http://search.msn.com` for dog whistles. Notice that the first result in the free listings in the MSN Search results is Gun Dog Supply, one of my mom's site. Not only did that #1 listing get a searcher to click on the result, but that searcher also converted into a sale.

Search engine optimization is extremely important, and I talk a lot about that in Chapter 19. In the search engine results pages, the link to the Web page comes from the title tag of that page. On a Yahoo! Store, the *title tag* is usually the text in the Name field. After the link is a snippet of text (also called the *abstract,* but not to be confused with the Yahoo! Store Abstract field) that comes from actual text on the Web page or from your Meta Description.

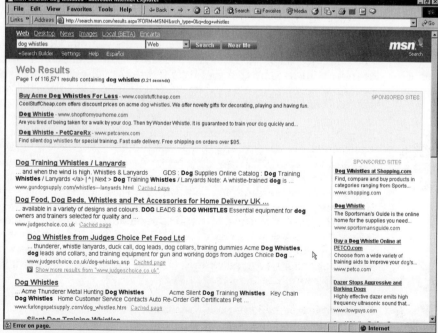

Figure 4-1: MSN's new search engine reveals that my page is #1 out of 116,571 results containing the phrase *dog whistles.* Guess it was a good day. . . .

The particular text in this example is from the *breadcrumbs,* the hierarchical text link navigation at the top of every page that shows the section, subsection, and product page. This text is very search engine friendly, but you have to customize your RTML templates to get these breadcrumbs to show up. I talk more about RTML and custom templates in Chapter 26.

Landing on a section page

Figure 4-2 shows my section page for dog whistles that was listed #1 for dog whistles in MSN. Notice that this section page contains both products and subsections, which have a thumbnail and a text link to the product or subsection. This particular page has two paragraphs of text in the Caption field, and the copy here is more for the customer than for search engines.

Note: This page uses custom RTML to display a tiny Order button on any orderable products. This experiment has resulted in additional sales, but having the Order button on section pages didn't really move the needle on increasing my conversion rate, so I dropped the little Order buttons for now.

Selling with a product page

Figure 4-3 shows a product page of the Acme Silent Dog Whistle. Product pages usually have a picture of the product (image), a headline, and a product description in the caption field, followed by the order functionality, which includes code, price, sale price, any options (like size and color), and an Add To Cart button.

Product pages are the most important type of page on your entire Web site. You sell more when people can see the Add To Cart button on product pages without having to scroll down. Bad product-page design kills more sales than anything I know other than super-slow-loading Web sites.

Notice that the Add To Cart button or Order button is *above the fold,* which means that you don't have to scroll to see it as long as your monitor resolution is set to 800 x 600, 1,024 x 768, or higher. The phrase comes from the newspaper industry, where *above the fold* means that the story or ad was important enough to appear in the top half of the page, literally above the fold in the middle of the paper.

Don't put too much information in your Caption field, especially if you use the factory preset templates. You need to have tons of online content (text and images) about the product because the more you tell, the more you sell, but long, long captions push the Order button way down the page.

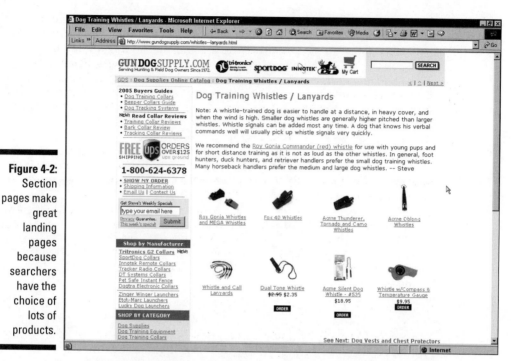

Figure 4-2:
Section pages make great landing pages because searchers have the choice of lots of products.

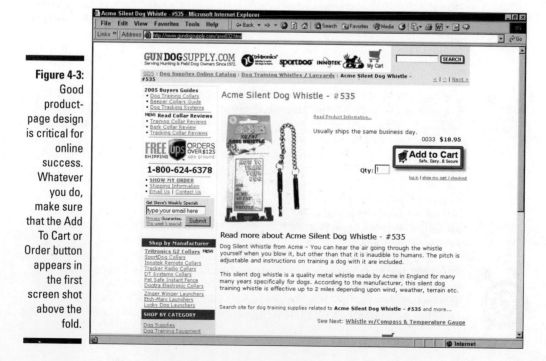

Figure 4-3:
Good product-page design is critical for online success. Whatever you do, make sure that the Add To Cart or Order button appears in the first screen shot above the fold.

With custom RTML templates, you can move the Order button above the Caption field so that it will always be above the fold. (Read more about RTML in Chapter 26.) With standard templates, I recommend this workaround: Create additional "More Info About The *Product Name*" pages. Place these reviews, additional photos, and customer comments pages either inside the product page itself (by putting the IDs in the *Contents* field like an accessory) or by simply linking to the pages from within the Caption field of the product. I talk a lot more about these topics in Chapters 11 and 12.

Use the following HTML code to link to additional information and content pages inside your Caption field (after replacing the page names and product names with real products). For more information on linking, check out the site navigation tips in Chapter 7.

```
More info: See <a href=more-info-id.html>product name</a> details,<a href=more-
            photos-id.html>product name photos</a>, and <a
            href=customer-reviews-id.html>product name customer reviews</a>.
```

Pushing the Shopping Cart

Figure 4-4 shows the Shopping Cart after the customer clicks the Add To Cart button on the Acme Silent Dog Whistle page. Anytime someone clicks the Show Order button, he's also sent to this page. The Shopping Cart shows a thumbnail of the product's image (linked to the page), the Name field (linked to the page), the unit price, the quantity, any options selected, and a subtotal for that line item.

Here's what customers can do inside the Shopping Cart:

- ✔ The Update Quantity button lets you change the number in the quantity field and update the Shopping Cart.
- ✔ Clicking the Keep Shopping button takes you back to the previous page.
- ✔ Clicking the Check Out button leads to the Shipping Info page in the Secure checkout.

The Shopping Cart always has the ID order, so it's easy to find in the Store Editor. (See Chapter 11 for more information.) You can link to your cart by going to `http://order.store.yahoo.com/cgi-bin/wg-order?`*your accountnamehere*

You want the look of your cart to match the look of your site as best you can so that the checkout process is seamless. I've seen solid increases in sales when clients changed their Shopping Cart page to match their site's look and feel. Read more about checking out the Shopping Cart in Chapter 14.

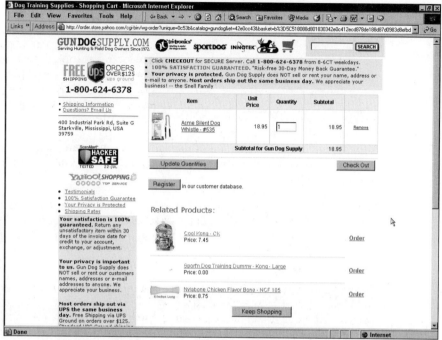

Figure 4-4:
When you
click the
Add To Cart
button, you
wind up
in the
Shopping
Cart.

I like to have as much control over the look and feel of my checkout as possible. By using custom RTML or the new Checkout Manager, my Shopping Cart can match the look and feel of the rest of my store. I also add text where I reassure the potential customer at the most critical time in the checkout process.

For example, I say "Order on a secure server or call 1-800-624-6378. Your privacy is protected. 100% satisfaction guaranteed. Risk-free 30-day money-back guarantee. Most orders ship out the same business day. We appreciate your business!" I show you everything I possibly can about how to make your site easier to use and how to sell more stuff in Chapter 21.

Regardless of the cart you use, when a customer is ready to pay and clicks the Check Out button, he's sent to the checkout pages on the Yahoo! secure servers. This is the first time in the order flow where the customer is on a secure server. The Shopping Cart isn't secure and doesn't need to be. You really only need a secure order form because that's where the real action is with personal information and credit cards.

You can always tell when you're on a secure server because the URL starts with `https` and a little lock icon appears in the lower right corner of your browser.

Checking out the Secure Order form

On the secure Shipping Info page, the customer enters her name and shipping address (including the country) and selects a shipping method. The shipping rate is calculated based upon how you set up the shipping tables; it's usually based upon a combination of shipping method and shipping address. Sales tax, if you collect it, is usually calculated based upon the location of the shopper using the zip code or state.

After typing the shipping information, the customer can click the Continue button to move on to the Billing Info page or click the Cancel button to return to the Shopping Cart.

Place a text message at the top of both the Shipping Info and Billing Info pages. You don't want to include a lot of text here because it will push the required fields down the page. For more information on this topic, see Chapter 15.

Shipping Info page

Figure 4-5 shows the Shipping Info page, where the customer inputs address and shipping method in the first page of the secure checkout. Notice the `https` in the URL in the address bar of the browser, which tells you that you're on a secure server. This page shows a summary of the customer's order, displaying the item name and subtotal of the order before shipping and tax are calculated. When customers click the Continue button, shipping and tax are calculated, and the Billing Info page appears.

If the customer forgets to fill out a field or types invalid information, Yahoo! Store returns an error message in red with a red asterisk by the field to be corrected. The customer can correct his error and click the Continue button again.

Billing Info page

Figure 4-6 shows the Billing Info page, where the customer inputs payment method, account number, and expiration date. The customer can also input his billing address, unless it's the same as the shipping address. E-mail address, a ratings request checkbox, and the Comments field round out the list of information I get from a customer.

At this point, the customer can either click the Cancel button to return to the Shopping Cart or click the Place Order button to place the order and proceed to the Order Confirmation page.

If you do real-time credit-card authorization, at this point the Yahoo! Store secure server queries your Merchant Bank through the gateway and attempts to get authorization for this credit-card sale. To get paid, you approve the transaction and either force a batch or autobatch between 6 and 11 p.m. PST. For more information on credit cards, see Chapter 15.

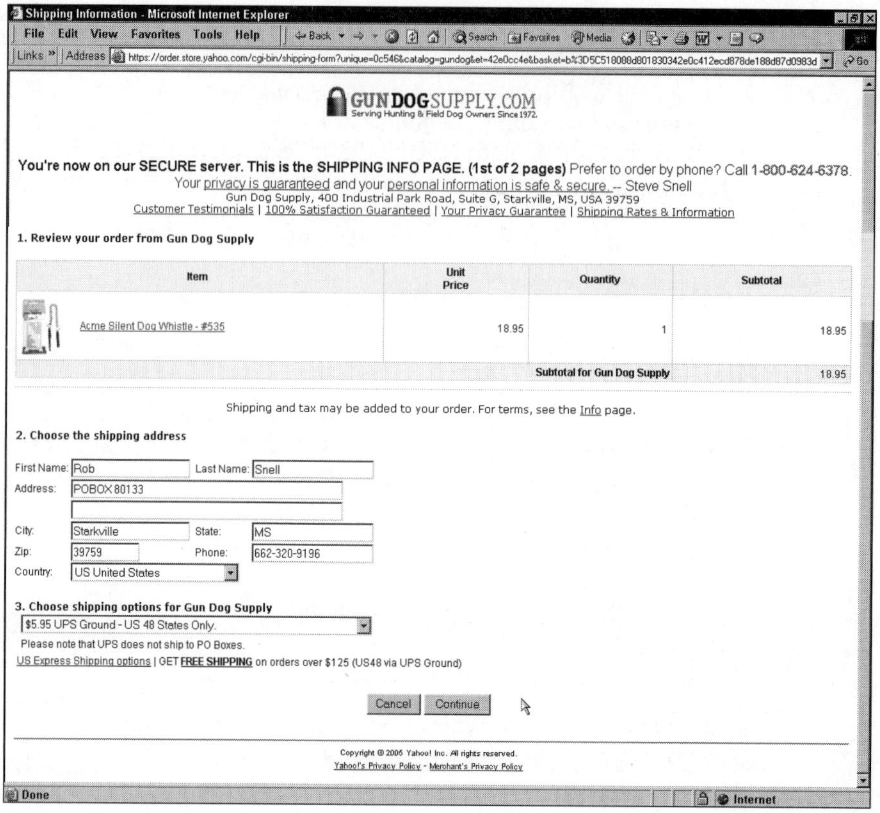

Figure 4-5:
The
Shipping
Info page is
the first
page of a
two-page
checkout.

If you process credit cards manually, then all the Yahoo! Store does here is collect credit-card information, which you can later verify, authorize, and charge.

Confirming orders and shipping 'em out

Figure 4-7 shows the Order Confirmation page, which is where you're sent when you click the Place Order button. This screen gives you the merchant's custom thanks message, your order number, and a link to your info page.

Almost instantly, a confirmation e-mail is sent to the customer's e-mail address that was entered on the Billing Info page. The retailer can also add some text to this information with contact information and answers to frequently asked questions.

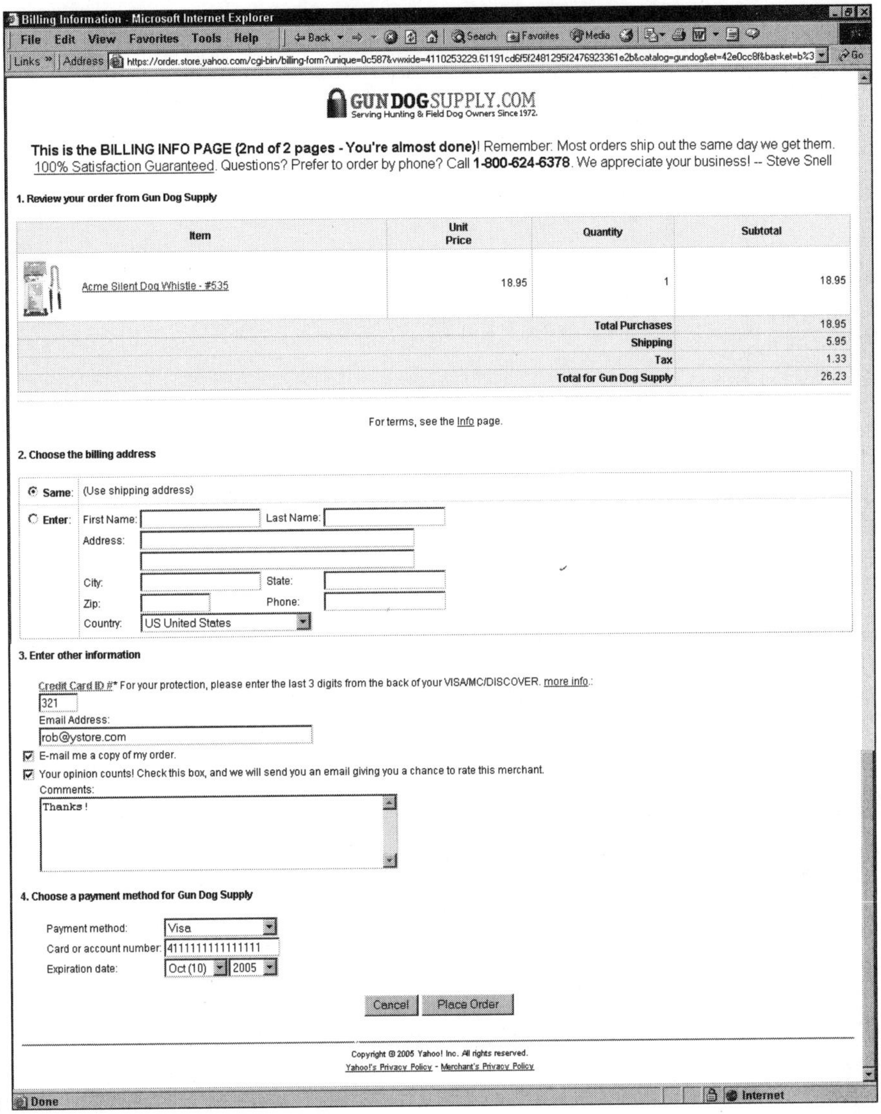

Figure 4-6:
The Billing Info page asks for billing information, the payment method and account number, and an e-mail address before the customer can complete the sale.

Receiving order notifications

After a customer places an order, Yahoo! sends merchants an order notification e-mail. To enable your merchant e-mail notifications, you must add your e-mail address to the Fax/E-mail page under the Store Manager. This order notification e-mail contains all the information the customer typed except credit-card information, unless you opt for encrypted e-mails. The merchant e-mail also shows the referrer, the entry page, and the converting keyword if the customer's order came from a search engine referral.

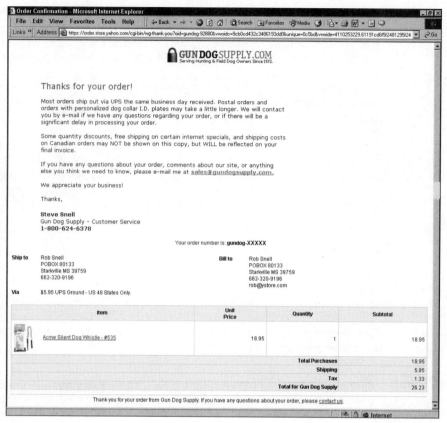

Figure 4-7:
The Order
Confirma-
tion page
tells the
customer
that his
order was
placed
correctly
and
contains the
same text
as the
Order Con-
firmation
e-mail.

If you have fax notification turned on, you also get a fax about the same time. In my warehouse, we use the faxes as pick tickets for the pickers and packers to pull the orders. An order is picked from the warehouse and placed in a box. The fax looks almost like the e-mail notification but does not have the credit-card information.

Merchant Solutions Starter-level accounts don't have the option to get faxes.

Processing orders

When you log in to the Store Manager, a red asterisk appears to the right of the Orders link so that you know that you have a new, unviewed order. After someone views that order, the red asterisk disappears.

Figure 4-8 shows the order as it appears in the Store Manager. You may have to scroll down to see all the information, but the order shows all the customer information, including shipping and billing information, what products the customer ordered, method of payment, shipping method and rate, tax rate, and more. The order also shows the referrer, the entry page, and the converting keyword if the customer's order came from a search engine referral.

Orders in the Store Manager keep credit-card data for only four weeks for security purposes. After that time, you can't access your customer's credit-card information, so print or export your orders ASAP!

At this point, an invoice is printed and the box is sealed with tape, marked with an order number, and placed in the shipping box line. Next, the day's data is exported from our POS software into the UPS WorldShip computer, where each box is weighed, the address is verified, and a label is printed and stuck on the box. UPS arrives about 4:30 p.m., and the box is on its way.

Taking care of details

Right before my UPS driver arrives to pick up my packages, I close out for the day. The UPS WorldShip computer dials up the big UPS computer and uploads the shipping data. Shortly thereafter, UPS sends e-mails from UPS to our customers that contain their orders' tracking number and anticipated arrival date of the package.

Figure 4-8:
Orders in the Store Manager show credit-card data for four weeks, and then the information is deleted to protect both you and your customer from fraud if your account gets hacked.

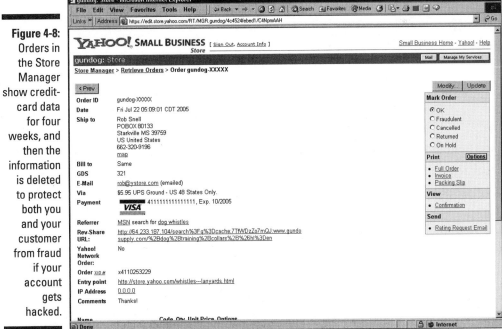

After an order has shipped, we send a personalized "Thanks For Your Order" e-mail to each customer. Customers receive their orders anywhere from the next day to a week later, depending on where they live and the shipping method they chose. When customers sign for their order, a copy of their signature and delivery information is uploaded to the UPS Web site in case we need to verify delivery.

A day or so after an order has been placed and all the stats in the Yahoo! Store have been updated, you can actually see the path a customer took as she placed an order by looking at the Click Trails (in the Store Manager under Statistics). I talk a lot about this feature in Chapter 20.

Order status e-mail

Yahoo! Store gives retailers the option of sending order status e-mails to let customers know that their orders are partially shipped, on back order, or shipped entirely. When you change a customer's order status, Yahoo! makes a note on the order and sends an e-mail to the customer. If you paste the tracking number into the order, this information is included in your order status e-mails.

I don't use order status e-mails because most of my orders ship the same business day. Before I have a chance to send an order status e-mail, I'm usually sending a tracking number e-mail.

Part II
Planning What's in Store

"Just how accurately should my Web site reflect my place of business?"

In this part . . .

I'm a big believer in planning your store before building your store. If I don't plan, I end up having to redo most of the work two or three times, searching for what I want. Even when I think I know exactly what I want in my head, I still sketch a quick design on paper before I start building anything!

In this part, I talk about getting everything ready before you begin store building. You can read about choosing a store-building tool (Pick the Editor! Pick the Editor!), explore whether you should build a store yourself or hire an expert to do it (Do both. Trust me, I explain!), and make a list of all the different design elements that make a store look like a store.

I also talk about what makes a good store design and why that subject is so very subjective. My definition of good store design is anything that increases store sales because that's extremely measurable and objective. Anything else is an opinion.

This part also covers store navigation. You can see how customers really shop online by searching your store, navigating with buttons and links, and clicking featured products and specials. I also address how you can design your store to make it easier for your customers to find exactly what they're looking for so that they will buy more stuff.

Chapter 5

Preparing to Build Your Yahoo! Store

. . . .

In This Chapter

▶ Choosing a store-building method: Store Editor or Web hosting with Store Tags

▶ Building what parts you can and outsourcing the rest

▶ Assembling all the elements you need before you get started

. . . .

*I*n this chapter, I tell you about two different ways to build your store: Store Editor and Web hosting with Store Tags. Choosing which way to build your Yahoo! Store determines how you maintain your store on a daily basis. You need to examine your options so that you can decide which way is best.

I also discuss the skills you need to build an online store. Take a good look at what you can do, what you can find out how to do, and what you need to hire someone else to do.

Finally, I lay out my list of the assets and elements you need to get together so that you have everything you need before you start store building.

Choosing a Store-Building Tool

You can build a Yahoo! Store in two very different ways: Store Editor and Store Tags. They are different faces for the same product database. With the default settings, Editor-built pages exist at `http://store.`*yourdomain*`.com`, while Store Tags are put inside HTML pages in your Web-hosting account at `www.`*yourdomain*`.com`. You get to choose where you point your www, and I prefer to have my Editor-built pages at the `www.`*mydomain*`.com` address. I show you how to point your domain and lots more in Chapter 24.

Store Editor

With Store Editor, you don't need any special software or Web-development skills. You simply build your store online using your Web browser and the Store Editor online software. Figure 5-1 shows the home page in edit mode.

As you add products, the Store Editor automatically creates Web pages for you. With Store Editor, your products are the pages. Editing the page for a product is the same as editing the product.

Store Editor requires no Web-development skills or special software. Nope. None. All you need is an Internet access and a Web browser. Store Editor may be for you if:

✔ You prefer to be able to work on your store from any computer, anywhere in the world with an Internet connection. All you have to do is log in and start working. All your work is stored on Yahoo!, not on your desktop computer.

✔ You have employees who maintain your online store.

✔ You have lots of products (more than 50), or products with lots of changes.

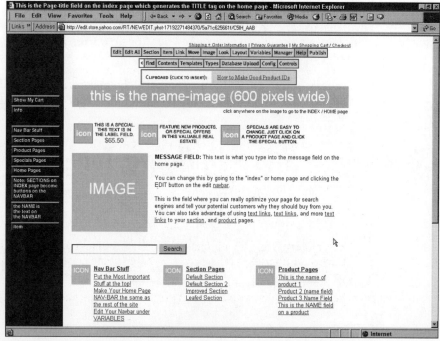

Figure 5-1:
Store
Editor is
essentially
the same
online store-
building tool
it was when
it was
created in
1996. This
figure is the
home page
or index of
the Store
Editor.

Why I prefer Store Editor

When it comes to deciding what's better for you, I'm biased. No bones about it. When it comes to store building and maintenance, I am completely biased toward Store Editor. Here's why: My mom can use the Yahoo! Store Editor, but she can't use Merchant Solutions Store Tags to save her life.

Most retailers are smart, independent, and overwhelmed with work. They have no desire to be a computer geek or Web developer. The whole point of Viaweb (now Yahoo! Store) was "no developer required."

This book is about store building with Store Editor. The Store Editor is easy to use, but it's also powerful.

Store Tags

Store Tags are a little different because you put Store Tags inside HTML pages you create with software such as SiteBuilder, Dreamweaver, or another HTML editor. Store Tags are magical bits of HTML code that you insert into your product pages hosted on your Web-hosting account. These snippets of code pull information from your product database so that changes to prices or descriptions in your product catalog are automatically updated in your Web pages. With Store Tags, you use Catalog Manager to create and maintain your product catalog, and you build and upload your Web pages using the HTML editor of your choice. With Store Tags pages, you have to manually update your category and section pages when you make additions or edits to your product catalog.

Store Tags require using additional software such as SiteBuilder (no HTML required) or professional HTML design software (like Dreamweaver), which makes my head hurt. Make anything other than a price change, and you, a skilled employee, or an outside firm has to edit and upload your edited HTML pages to your Web-hosting account.

Store building via Web hosting with Store Tags may be for you if:

- ✔ You already have a Web-hosting account and just want to add a Shopping Cart. Just upgrade your account, plug in some code, and you have an online store.

- ✔ You're a retailer who has few products, and they change rarely.

Choosing a store-building method: Another opinion

When it comes to picking a store-building tool and using it, my good friend (and technical reviewer of this book) Michael Whitaker of Monitus.com sums up his philosophy:

✔ Just because Web hosting with Store Tags is the new kid on block, don't assume that it is the better way to build your store. Many of the more successful and active Yahoo! Stores are built with the editor, but which store-building method you pick is dependent on your particular circumstances; carefully consider which features are important to you before you go charging off building your store. I personally still feel that building and maintaining your store with the Editor is easier for many merchants.

✔ After you have chosen your store-building tool, you should stick with it. If you use the Store Editor, create and manage products only in the Store Editor, and don't use the Catalog Manager. Conversely, if you use Web hosting with Store Tags, then only use the Catalog Manager to create and maintain your product catalog.

✔ You have larger corporate clients who need their pages to meet their marketing's branding design specifications.

✔ You have an ad agency or a Web-development firm developing your pages, and they're used to traditional Web-design methods or if your main Web designer is an HTML whiz.

Building a Store Yourself or Outsourcing It

You can build your store yourself, or you can hire someone to build it for you. You can even build it yourself and then just hire someone to clean it up. Sometimes, though, it's just better to break out the checkbook or the credit card and bite the bullet. It all depends on how much free time you have, how valuable your time is, and whether you want to spend your time learning store design and development if you're only developing one store. If you're starting out like I did with literally no budget, just dive in and fake it 'til you make it.

Doing it yourself

Building an online business requires ability in several completely different arenas: graphic design, programming, database development, Web design, copywriting, photography, and online marketing. You don't have to be an expert in all of them, but it helps to have a wide range of ability.

Make a list of your available skills as well as which skills you can learn. When you have a choice between learning a skill that will directly translate into making more money or learning a skill that will let you do cool stuff on the Web, make a careful choice. Decide how much time you really want to devote to learning and doing things that really don't help you sell more products. Do you want to be a retailer, or do you want to be a Web developer? The highest and best use of your time probably isn't learning the ins and outs of RTML, but taking care of customers, finding new products, and promoting your business.

Even if you do decide to hire someone to build your Yahoo! Store, I still recommend building a test store on your own just for the experience you'll gain. Because you'll probably maintain your own store and create and edit products in the Store Editor, you'll need to become familiar with using the Editor. When you get in there and poke around, you'll see that the Store Editor isn't so scary after all, even in Advanced mode. (I show you everything you need to know in Chapter 9.)

Outsourcing it

Anything you can do on or to a Yahoo! Store can be delegated or outsourced. You can hire folks to design your store from the ground up, create a custom logo, develop a corporate identity with unique colors and fonts, build your store product database, take product photos, write sales copy, perform search engine optimization on your site, custom-build RTML templates that do almost anything you want them to do, and even manage your orders and perform customer service. It all depends on your budget.

After you've decided that you need help, you have lots of choices to make. The first decision is the size of your budget, which determines who you can hire. I've seen prices for "building a Yahoo! Store" range anywhere from $300 to $20,000 and up. You can get a bargain using *offshore designers* (working anywhere from eastern Europe to India), college kids, or even professional designers moonlighting out of their basement. If you want a more "professional" experience, expect to pay up to $20,000 for a complete branding, marketing, and design package from top-drawer advertising agencies.

You get what you pay for. Most of the facelifts and site redesigns I see from the good design companies run between $2,000 to $3,000. When you get a facelift, sometimes the results are more than just superficial. Some designers improve the shopping experience, which can dramatically increase sales from your existing traffic by increasing your conversion rate (see Chapter 21). Also, many facelifts improve the way your site looks to search-engine spiders, too! For more on search engine optimization, see Chapter 19.

After you know what store building you can do and what you can't do or would rather not do, you're ready to look for some help with the heavy lifting. First, you have to decide what type of vendor you want to work with because there's a big difference between working with a freelancer or independent consultant and working with a large design company or ad agency:

✔ Advertising agencies and the bigger design firms have more resources, such as programmers, graphic designers, and Internet marketing consultants, all on staff. With a large design company, you never know exactly who's going to be working on your project. The designer you liked so much in the portfolio may no longer even work there. Depending on how much you pay, your project may be assigned to a junior-level designer or an intern. Unless you're a major project for the design firm, you probably won't be working with one of the principals of the company, but more likely an account rep, also known as a *project manager*.

Ask the right questions (such as who did the graphics on this site or the SEO on that site), and you'll get better access to the talent. Be a smart shopper for design services.

✔ You can find great smaller consultancies and freelancers if you can be flexible. When you hire an individual, you have a pretty good idea of the level of work that you'll get based on his portfolio. Remember that smaller firms and one-man-bands don't have the resources or organizational structure of a larger corporate firm, so you may have a more slightly relaxed working environment. Freelancers tend to come and go as they please, and working hours aren't usually 9 a.m. to 5 p.m.

Many independent consultants try to be all things to all people. No one can be great at everything. Make sure that whomever you hire specializes in exactly what you need.

Figure 5-2 shows the Yahoo! Store Developer Network. Yahoo! provides you with a list of designers, developers, programmers, and marketers who are (at worst) familiar with Yahoo! Store and Merchant Solutions and who have built at least three or more Yahoo! Stores. Yahoo! doesn't officially endorse the companies on the list, but (in my humble opinion) the directory is a very good representation of most of the world's top Yahoo! Store design talent. Designers are listed at no charge after they pass a review process. See the designers' contact information and links to portfolio pages at `http://smallbusiness.yahoo.com/merchant/designdir.php` for more info.

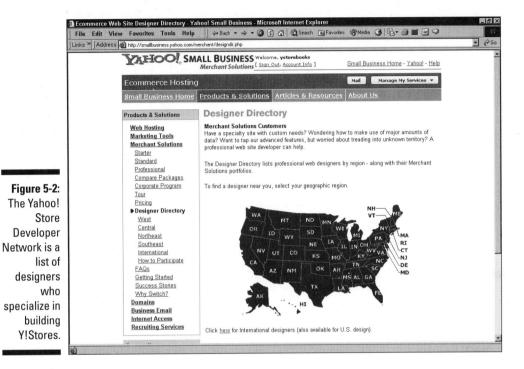

Figure 5-2:
The Yahoo!
Store
Developer
Network is a
list of
designers
who
specialize in
building
Y!Stores.

Gathering Elements and Assets

Whether you're building your store yourself or you're hiring a designer, you need more than just a logo and some product information to make a store. You need all the different design elements that make your store look like a store and not just another Web site. These elements include all your company's customer-service information and policies, HTML code for third-party software applications, a site map of what pages go where, and tons of little bitty things that no one ever thinks about until she starts to build a store. In this section, I give you a quick overview of the elements and assets you need to assemble before you start to build your Yahoo! Store.

Product data

Product information is what most people think about when they're getting ready to build a Yahoo! Store. Of course, you need a product database that includes the product name, code, price, sale price, and description. You also need individual product images. Don't forget such information as competing or more expensive or better suited products for up-selling, related products and accessories that you can use in the cross-sell database, and alternate sections and other ways of merchandising your products. (See Chapter 12 for more information on creating products.)

You also need to decide what products go where. Building a rough site map on paper can help you. I like to organize my stores into as many as seven major categories with no more than ten subcategories per section. If more than 20 products are in a subcategory, I break that subcategory into multiple subcategories. (See Chapter 7 for store navigation tips and tricks.)

Design elements

Often, it's the little things that make a store look like a store. Everything from credit-card icons to Add To Cart buttons shows your customer that your Web site is a Web store. Figure 5-3 shows a product page with several design elements.

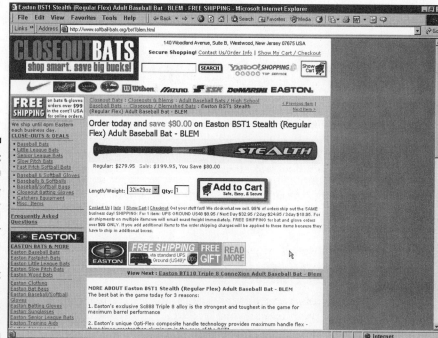

Figure 5-3:
Custom icons, buttons, logos, and other graphics are all the little things that make a store look like a store.

Here are the finishing touches to make your store look more real:

- ✔ **Logos and corporate identity:** You need multiple versions of your logo in Web-friendly file formats, preferably high-resolution .gif files. If you already have your corporate identity (colors and fonts) designed, your store designer needs to know your official colors and fonts. If you don't have a *corporate identity* (a fancy name for a logo and other branding elements), you can get one designed for you. Search on Yahoo! for logo design or corporate identity and be prepared to pay anything from $100 on up, depending on the quality of the designer.

- ✔ **Unique company graphics:** Usually, many other sites sell exactly the same thing that you sell. You have to do something to differentiate your store from all the copycat stores that are simply using the manufacturers' images and text. Collect any unique company graphics, images, or photos that help make your store look different from all the companies selling exactly the same thing.

- ✔ **Icons and buttons:** If you hire a store designer, she usually creates these elements, but it helps to know in advance that you'll need these buttons, bars, and icons. Poke around on the Web and find buttons and icons that you like. Find Search, Add To Cart, Show Cart, Info, E-Mail Us, and other cool icons that make a Web store look polished and professional.

- ✔ **Company logos and bugs:** Collect various logos and graphic *bugs* (tiny versions of logo graphics) from all the different suppliers, manufacturers, and industry trade associations you belong to, as well as of any consumer protection organizations that endorse your site. Trust symbols like Better Business Bureau seals and TrustE help make customers feel more comfortable shopping online. Contact your shipping company for official UPS, FedEx, and USPS logos. Your merchant account bank can provide you with credit-card logos such as Visa, MasterCard, Discover, and American Express. If you accept PayPal payments, grab that logo, too. Most companies can send you these graphics or offer them on their Web site for your convenience.

- ✔ **Yahoo! branding:** Having Yahoo! Store branding somewhere on your site is a good thing because you're using the Yahoo! Store secure checkout. See `http://help.yahoo.com/help/us/store/aboutms/aboutms-29.html` for cool new revised badges that say Hosted by Yahoo! and ecommerce by Yahoo! I also like to have a secure server icon showing on the product pages, and definitely in the Shopping Cart and on the checkout pages.

- ✔ **Manufacturer images:** Manufacturers are really good about letting you use their logo on your Web store. Nonetheless, make sure that you get permission before you use any photography or other promotional graphics off their Web sites because sometimes the manufacturers don't actually own these images.

✔ **Promotional images:** You need to create special promotional graphics if you have special offers like free shipping or 100 percent satisfaction guaranteed. You'll also want banners and micro-banners for the sites you sponsor or for folks who just want a link to you.

✔ **Candid photography:** Pictures of your store location or warehouse go a long way in establishing the fact that you're a credible business. If you work out of your house, use images of your work area with boxes and packing materials to show that you actually ship the things you sell. If you use a fulfillment center or a drop-shipper, see whether you can use photos of its location for added credibility. Pictures of you and your staff help humanize your company. Sometimes less-than-professional photography makes you look more real and less plastic.

It's okay to be a small company on the Web. Lots of folks like the fact that they get to deal with the owner of a company when shopping with a small business. Face it. Do you think Jeff Bezos packs every box at Amazon.com?

If you have photographs of people using the things you sell, use them on your Web site as long as you have permission. You don't have to have professional models to have good photographs.

Copywriting

Besides having great product descriptions in your Caption fields, you'll also need the normal pages every Web site has: your home page's intro copy, an About Us page, and good descriptions for your section pages.

Here is a good list of copywriting stuff you need to write for your site, including snippets, pages, policies, and other words:

✔ **Product availability:** You need a standard line about product availability on regular products. I like using "most orders shipped the same business day" when that is true. For out-of-stock, special order, or drop-ship items, it's also good to have a standard availability line such as "usually ships in four to five business days."

✔ **Contact us:** You need to collect your full contact information and your satisfaction guarantee, if you offer one — and you should!

✔ **Ordering information:** In your ordering info, include multiple ways to order: Internet, phone, fax, and mail; the credit cards you accept; and pricing information, including whether you wholesale or offer discounts on quantity pricing and the fact that prices may change without notice.

✔ **Shipping information:** In your shipping info, include which shipping carriers you use, the different shipping methods and rates, the cost and estimated delivery time of Express shipping, free shipping, and international shipping options, as well as what to do with returns and damaged packages.

✔ **Legal stuff:** I'm not a lawyer, but it would be smart to have your site's terms of use, trademark and copyright information, and privacy policy all over the site. Ask your favorite barrister.

✔ **About Us:** For the Company or About Us section, I like a Welcome To The Store letter, a page about your company's history, bios of the principals or owners, and customer testimonials.

✔ **Additional article:** For additional content, write articles about how to use the products you sell, create buyers' guides about all the different features and benefits of the different types of products you sell, and prepare a bestsellers list.

✔ **Search-engine copywriting:** For search engine optimization, the first thing you need is a keyword list of the top 200 keywords you want to rank well for. I talk a lot more about this topic in Chapter 16. For each section page and product page, you want to make sure that you have keywords in the name field (which creates the page title or title tag), a list of specific keywords around 18 to 36 words long, a 10- to 20-word keyword-loaded description of the page for the meta description, and great product and section descriptions in the Captions field.

✔ **HTML code:** If you use any third-party tracking solutions or e-mail services such as newsletters or E-Mail This Page To A Friend, you need the custom HTML code for those items as well. I also grab the HTML for Yahoo! Store functionality, including links to the cart, info page, privacy policy, and home page.

Chapter 6

Designing Your Store to Turn Shoppers into Buyers

· ·

In This Chapter

▶ Designing a store to meet your online retailing goals

▶ Exploring what is and isn't "good" design (Hint: "good" design sells more)

▶ Choosing colors, fonts, and page layouts for a better look and feel

· ·

Store design matters. Contrary to what your mother may have told you, people do judge by appearance. Your potential customers scrutinize your store design whether they're conscious of it or not. Every element of your Yahoo! Store from your company logo, colors and fonts, and quality of your product photography to the checkout flow tells potential customers about your company and influences their decision whether to buy something.

Just because a Web store looks professional doesn't mean that it *is* professional, but that doesn't stop your potential customers from making assumptions about you and your company based upon the quality of your store's design.

A well-designed store converts more shoppers into buyers with sales that result in happy repeat customers. That's it. I don't think there's really anything more important in e-commerce.

In this chapter, I explore the best practices of store design, push the design limits of standard Store Editor templates, examine various design elements, and help you create a professional-looking Yahoo! Store.

Designing Your Store to Sell

Your first design decision should be to determine what you want out of your Yahoo! Store. Are you looking to create a design masterpiece, an online retail money machine, or both? Here's my opinion about why you shouldn't have an opinion on store design until you see the sales numbers:

- **Good design sells.** A well-designed Web store communicates the value of the products you sell. Good design also underscores the professionalism of the company behind the products. Good design tends to give shoppers confidence in a retailer's ability to deliver and goes a long way toward increasing the likelihood that you'll convert a browser into a buyer.

- **A lack of design costs you customers, maybe forever!** It's too easy for shoppers to click the Back button and find 100 other retailers who sell exactly what you sell. It may be cliché, but my grandmother, Mimi, was right: You really *don't* get a second chance to make a first impression.

- **When potential customers look at your store, the emphasis should be on the products and the benefits of buying them, not on how cool your Shopping Cart or logo is.** The store is the frame, not the picture. I want customers to say, "Man! That product is exactly what I'm looking for. I'm ordering mine right now!" — not "What a cool-looking Web page. I love the site design. Who did that?"

- **When customers are less aware that they're being sold, the more they will buy.** By all means, romance and charm your customers as you educate them about what you sell, but the last thing I want you to do is say, "Now I'm about to romance and charm you." (That approach doesn't work so well when you're dating, either!) If you mislead customers, or exaggerate, or simply dump a bunch of hooey on them, you'll be out of business faster than Boo.com after the tech bubble burst.

- **People have strong opinions on what constitutes "good" design.** Rules abound regarding composition, use of color, contrast, balance, and harmony, but most opinions about design are just that: opinions. My opinions about effective store design are based upon how well the design helps me achieve the goals of my Web site (sell more stuff), not how much my girlfriend likes the pictures, logo, and navigation buttons.

Sometimes ugly Web sites have beautiful bottom lines

I've always heard and read that "ugly" Web design outsells "pretty" design. I was attending an affiliate marketing conference and was fortunate enough to eat lunch with one of the brilliant marketers who sold millions and millions of dollars of those X-10 spy cameras via pop-under banners. He told me that he thought the simple HTML Web pages sold better because they loaded faster than graphics-heavy pages. Basic HTML pages looked more like information pages from the early days of the Web and less like slick sales presentations. Regardless of why they converted better, simpler pages outperformed super-slick designs, so he stuck with what worked. This guy was always testing various design elements to maximize his results.

You can have an opinion on whether a store's design is good or professional, but there's no opinion on whether a change in design increased store sales. Numbers don't flatter or lie. Sales either go up or they don't. For the rest of this book, when I write *good design,* I mean anything that increases sales. Bad design is anything that doesn't increase sales or (gasp!) makes sales go down.

Looking through the Eyes of a Customer

Very simply, good design is about making conscious decisions about how the various elements of your store work together to create a positive online shopping experience by meeting the expectations of your target customers.

The design of your store is affected by many factors, but perhaps the most important factor is how customers view your store. Build your store with the average customer's experience in mind. It is so much easier to build a better store when you see exactly what your customers see.

Before you start building your store, know your typical customers' Internet access speed, operating system, browser software and version, and monitor *screen resolution* (the height and width settings in pixels). For example, if you sell reconditioned Sun servers and workstations to Fortune 500 IT department heads, your customers will have a different Web experience than customers of a NASCAR collectibles shop.

Here are three important design requirements:

- **Design pages to load quickly.** When pages download within 10 to 12 seconds per page for folks on dialup, the pages really fly on a broadband connection.

- **Make your store fit the two most common screen resolutions: 1,040 x 768 and 800 x 600 pixels.** You'll be safe if your store isn't more than 800 pixels wide.

- **Design your store using Microsoft Internet Explorer.** Most customers view my stores on the latest version of IE, but you still need to make sure that it looks good on AOL and the Firefox browser, too.

I talk a lot more about making your store easier to use in Chapter 21.

Choosing Logos, Colors, and Fonts

I don't think I can explain the intricacies of creating a viable corporate identity by branding through the use of logos, colors, fonts, and images in a single chapter, much less an entire book, but I am going to give you the keys to the kingdom for good store design.

Looking at logos

When you're in business, your logo represents your company more than any other single element. In the customer's mind, a professional logo equals a professional company. There's nothing that ruins a well-designed Web store faster than topping it with an illegible, unprofessional-looking logo.

You cannot afford to skimp on your logo. Hire a pro and spend what it takes to get a professional logo.

Your logo should be a distinctive color and font so that it stands out. Your logo also should match the look of your industry. It needs to look good and be legible in many different formats, locations, and sizes. Logos need to look good in color and in black-and-white. Logos need to be legible at any size: on your business card, plastered on the Goodyear blimp, or anywhere else your name could go.

Figure 6-1 shows a logo uploaded to the Name-image field (under Variables), which appears at the top of every page as a header graphic and also serves as a clickable link to the home page. I like to display my logo in the footer of every page, too, using the Final-text field (under Variables), where you can put HTML to call that image. See Chapter 8 for more info on images.

Mimic magazines

My good friend, Craig Paddock, Internet marketing consultant, gave me this design secret, which, by itself, is worth the price of this book: Design your store to match the look and feel of the magazines your customers read about the products you sell. What genius!

The best magazine designers have spent thousands of hours crafting a design that fits that specific industry and appeals to that specific demographic. Look at the magazine's colors, fonts, formatting of images, and even the tone of the writing to get ideas for your Web store. You don't have to literally copy a magazine's design, just emulate the flavor.

Look at the ads. Manufacturers spend hundreds of thousands of dollars hiring the best

photographers, graphic designers, and illustrators. Keep a file folder where you tear out various graphic elements you like.

For example, if you sell skincare products to women, your online store needs to have the production values of *Cosmopolitan* or *O, The Oprah Magazine*. When you sell home and garden products, your Yahoo! Store better look more like *Southern Living* or *Better Homes and Gardens*. If you sell contemporary designer furniture, take a look at *Metropolitan* magazine. Make sure that your stores look like the right magazine for its industry and not the latest cutting-edge skate punk 'zine.

How to get ideas for colors

If you don't have colors for your Web site, a great way to get ideas for your colors is to go to the supermarket and collect packaging of products you like, especially products that match your industry. Packaging designers are brilliant at capturing and communicating the essence of a product and motivating you to buy it.

Another way to gather ideas for colors is to collect photographs you like. When I find a great photograph, I scan a copy into my graphics program. I reduce the image dimensions to a micro-thumbnail about 10 pixels wide, which gives me a tiny palette of the most popular colors in that image.

Figure 6-1:
Upload a custom image to your Name-image field to go double duty with a single element: both branding and navigation.

Compelling use of color

Here are several concepts about color for your consideration:

- ✔ **Be consistent with the use of colors and fonts.** Use the same branding across your entire Web site and all other collateral materials, including your packaging, catalogs, brochures, business cards, letterhead, and anything else you send to vendors or customers.

- ✔ **Pick one dominant color and a secondary accent color.** These colors need to match your logo or complement your existing logo. Use these two colors across the store in your site navigation, links, site decoration, accents, icons, navigation buttons, headlines, and more.

> ✔ **Make sure that your corporate colors are high-contrast enough to look good in black-and-white.** Approximately 5 to 10 percent of males and 0.5% of females are somewhat color blind, so you're looking at a pretty decent-sized portion of shoppers. If your design looks good in black-and-white, most people who are color blind will be able to read it.

If you already have a logo or a corporate identity designed, you probably already know your site's colors in RGB. For example, one of my sites is red (255 0 0), white (255 255 255), black (0 0 0), and gray (102 102 102). *RGB* stands for red green blue. These numbers, which range from 0 to 255, tell your monitor how much to display of each of the three colors. For example, white (255 255 255) is made up of red, green, and blue at 100%. To display black (0 0 0), your monitor displays no red, green, or blue.

Picking colors on the Variables page

Changing colors on a Yahoo! Store is really easy. When you click the Variables button in the Store Editor, a page displays all the global variables of your entire Yahoo! Store. Many of these variables are colors. For example, the third variable is Background-color. Next to the name of the color is a color swatch showing you the color, a field with the RGB number of the color, and a Choose A Color link.

To change a color, type the RGB color code in the field or click the Choose A Color link, and a color pop-up window with Web-safe colors appears. When you click a color, the window closes, and the RGB number appears in the field next to a color swatch to show that you picked the right color.

Display text uses the vw-img text tag

Figure 6-2 shows how the Store Editor autogenerates good-looking text. It turns text into an image, drawing a picture of the text using the fonts you pick in Variables. Display text looks better than regular HTML text, but I'll give up pretty text for "ugly" HTML to make my site more search-engine-friendly.

Sizing up customers' monitors

Pixels are the dots that make up your screen and are the linear unit of measure for the Web. Each pixel can represent over 16 million colors (256 x 256 x 256 = 16,777,216) by turning up and down different combinations of red, blue, and green light.

The height and width of images are measured in pixels. Pixels display at different sizes on different monitors, depending on the size of the monitor as well as the screen resolution settings of the computer. Most folks have their monitors set at 600 x 800 or 1,024 x 768, which means your Yahoo! Store should be no wider than 800 pixels to look right on most monitors. I talk a lot more about screen resolution, load speed, usability issues, and other geeky things in Chapter 21.

Here's the code to make `vw-img` text:

```
<vw-img text="your text here" font=OCR-B. font-size=24
        text-color="#000000">
```

If you get any amount of search-engine traffic, look into getting around using the `vw-img` text tag and use CSS to format text. Your text looks pretty, but search engines can still read it.

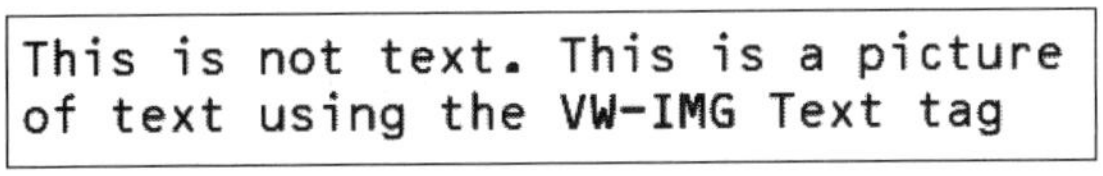

Figure 6-2:
Although it may look like text, the `vw-img` text tag really generates an image that looks like text. Try to highlight the text with your mouse.

```
This is not text. This is a picture
of text using the VW-IMG Text tag
```

Finding fantastic fonts

Here are several guidelines for using fonts:

- ✔ **Use a standard Web-friendly typeface.** Use the same font consistently across your Web site. Set the variable *Text-font* to Arial, Verdana, Times, or Georgia.

- ✔ **Pick a body copy font size that's easy to read.** I prefer to set the variable *Text-size* to 2 (the default) or 3. Be very aware of the age of your average customer. As we get older, smaller fonts are much, much harder to read. When your customers need larger fonts, they usually have larger wallets with more expendable income.

  I used to tease my mom about setting all her 21-inch monitors in a lower-resolution "Granny-mode" (800 x 600), which super-sized her screen fonts. It sure made her screen easier to read. After 15 years of staring at monitors all day long, I think she's about to get the last laugh, because I'll be wearing bifocals sooner than not!

Logos are more important than you realize

Manufacturers spend millions of dollars each year promoting their brand, which is associated with a logo. I found out last year exactly how much credibility logos give your site. To increase the load speed of one of my sites, I removed ten manufacturer logos from the header of the Yahoo! Store. Sales dropped by half, but it took me about 12 hours to notice it. When I did, I immediately put the logos back on the site, and sales jumped right back up.

You can upload manufacturer logos to individual product pages by using the *Inset* image field, but unfortunately, you have to upload these insets by hand. An alternative is to upload one manufacturer logo to your images folder and then use HTML to call that image with an image source tag in your *Caption*. Here are two different paths to an image:

```
<img src=/lib/youraccountname/
     logo.gif>
<img src=http://site.
     ystorebooks.com/images/
     logo.gif>
```

I also recommend putting micro-icons or very small manufacturer logos that link to the manufacturer's page in your stores header, Final-text, or sidebar navigation.

✔ **It's easier to read dark text on a very light background.** I prefer black text on a white background with absolutely no background image to obscure the text. The variable *Text-color* defaults to black (0 0 0), but please, please, please use a dark-color text on a white background! I talk a lot more about making your site easier to use in Chapter 21.

The Store Editor gives you 117 fonts to choose from, but only some fonts are good for navigation bars. Figure 6-3 shows the fonts I like. Pick a font that's easy to read at a small size. Narrower fonts work better because they don't take up as much room. For design consistency, pick a font in the same font family as the Display-text. I made a page that shows all 117 supported fonts in all their glory: See www.ystorebooks.com/all-fonts.html.

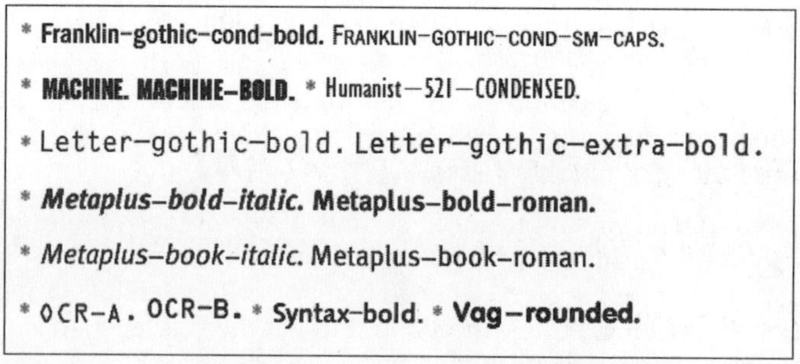

Figure 6-3:
The Store Editor supports 117 fonts.

* Franklin-gothic-cond-bold. Franklin-gothic-cond-sm-caps.

* MACHINE. MACHINE-BOLD. * Humanist—521—CONDENSED.

* Letter-gothic-bold. Letter-gothic-extra-bold.

* *Metaplus—bold—italic.* **Metaplus—bold—roman.**

* *Metaplus—book—italic.* Metaplus—book—roman.

* OCR-A. OCR-B. * Syntax-bold. * **Vag—rounded.**

Chapter 7

Exploring Store Navigation

. . . .

In This Chapter

▶ Figuring out how shoppers navigate

▶ Exploring the Editor's navigational elements

▶ Using Site Search for better navigation

▶ Optimizing your store with simple text links

▶ Introducing advanced navigation with RTML

. . . .

*W*ell-designed store navigation is crucial for the success of your online store. Most shoppers don't enter your store through the home page. They enter your store sideways and land on a product or section page. If you want a prospective customer to find what she is looking for, the navigation needs to show who you are, where she is in your store, and where she can go from this page.

Folks navigate stores by clicking featured products; by browsing your store's hierarchy of sections, subsections, and products; or by using your site's search engine to find information.

In this chapter, I cover the different ways shoppers navigate your store, introduce navigational elements, and explain how the Store Editor automatically creates most of these items for you. I also show you how to add text links and introduce some cool things you can do (or hire someone to do!) with advanced RTML templates to max out your store's navigation.

Introducing Store Navigation

Store navigation really comes down to communicating two things:

✔ This is where you are.

✔ Here's what you can do.

Make it really easy to get around on your site by showing shoppers where they are now and where they can go from here. Improve store navigation by removing anything that gets in the way of shopping.

Seeing how customers shop

Figure 7-1 shows a detail of a click trail. If you want to see how individual customers navigate your store, look at Click Trails under Statistics in the Store Manager, which shows you the path or click trail of specific customers. (Merchant Starter accounts don't get to see Click Trails, and if that's what you're using, you need to upgrade to use this feature.) Pay attention to users who place an order. You'll see how they page back and forth between similar products, read your Info page, add and remove items from their carts, and then finally place an order. You can discover a lot about how shoppers navigate your site by diving into the click trails.

Figure 7-1:
The details
of a Click
Trail show
you what
pages the
customer
looked at
before
placing an
order.

Time	Page
Sep 25 14:23:37	Pet Safe Dog Fences & Dog Training Collars
Sep 25 14:23:48	Petsafe Instant Fence - Wireless Dog Fence PIF-300
Sep 25 14:25:32	Wireless System with Single Transmitter
Sep 25 14:25:59	In Ground Pet Containment System Installation Guide and FAQ
Sep 25 14:33:39	Petsafe Instant Fence - Wireless Dog Fence PIF-300 into shopping basket
Sep 25 14:33:40	Show shopping basket
Sep 25 14:35:45	Gun Dog Supply SHIPPING & CONTACT INFO
Sep 25 14:37:11	Place order gundog-
Sep 25 14:37:42	Thanks!

Take a look at every page and ask yourself what you want customers to do on this page, and then make sure that they can easily do it! I talk about making your site easier to use in Chapter 21.

Use every navigational tool at your disposal to make it easy for your customers to shop:

✔ **Have a consistent navigation scheme across your entire store.** Stores built with the Editor using standard templates have navigation buttons across the top or down the side that link to the top-level sections and buttons that link to built-in store functions.

✔ **Display your company logo on every page and link it to the home page.** The Store Editor automatically displays your logo on every page when you upload your logo to the variable Home-image. You get two features for the price of one: branding and navigation. You can also use the variable Name-image. Upload an image (preferably a 100-pixel-tall x 650-pixel-wide graphic) as a header to brand pages. The Name-image also links to your home page.

✔ **Link to your Shopping Cart on every page with the Show-order button.** I prefer a link to the cart to be in the upper right corner, which can be by using RTML or by sticking some HTML code in the Head-tags field on the Variables page.

✔ **Link to your Info page on every page with the Info button.** Use the Info button as well as links to Info, Contact Us, Information, and any other utility pages in the footer of every page. Use the variable Final-text for these links.

✔ **Flatten your site.** The deeper your site is, the more levels you have, and the more clicks it takes for your customers to find what they want. Don't bury pages too deep in your site. I try to limit my sites to five levels of pages at the most.

✔ **Separate the shopping pages from the customer care and content pages.** Group related merchandise together. Focus on five to seven major product categories. Feature your most popular items on a bestsellers' category page. Make a separate content section. Include articles like Buyer's Guides, product Frequently Asked Questions (FAQs), and other product-related content. Create a Customer Care section with links to About Us, Contact Us, Shipping Information, Terms & Conditions, FAQs, Link/Resources, and any other customer service information that's important, but doesn't need to be mixed in with the items you sell.

✔ **Call navigational elements what they really are and be consistent!** For example, the default text for the button that add items to your Shopping Cart is Order and is determined by whatever text is inside the Order-text field under Variables. To see what's inside your cart, you click the Show-order button, and the text on this button comes from whatever text is inside the Show-order-text field under Variables.

Change the text to Add To My Cart or Show My Cart, which sounds like less of a commitment than Order or Buy. I also think the word *my* gives ownership to the cart. Before the potential customer got to the product page, she probably didn't even know she had a Shopping Cart on your site. Now she does!

You are here: Store Editor navigational elements

Navigational elements are the text and images that tell you where you are on a Web site and help you navigate from one page to another. Figure 7-2 shows you that the Store Editor is really just a collection of built-in navigational elements that you wrap around the products and sections of your store.

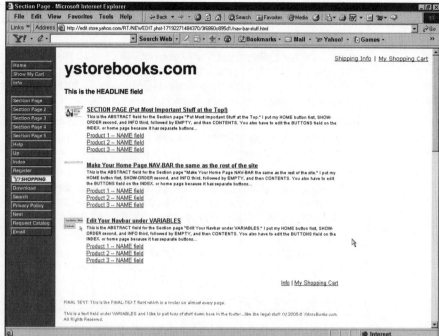

Figure 7-2:
Store
Editor—built
pages can
display
links to a
section's
subsections
and items,
as well as
links to the
contents
of those
subsections.

Here's what you see in the Store Editor:

- **Your domain name is branded across the top of every page in your store.** This Banner-Text displays the text from the variable Title and links to your home page.

- **The name of each page shows at the top of each page.** If you use the Headline field, it replaces the name. Display-font, Display-font-size, and Display-text-color variables control how the text looks. The name is also used as the `<Title>` tag, which appears in the left-uppermost corner of your browser's window.

- **Navigation buttons exist for all major built-in store functions.** These navigational helpers exist before you create the first product or section page and include my favorites like Home, Info, Show-Order, and Up/Next, and all the ones I don't use, like Privacypolicy, Register, Help, E-mail, Search, Mall, Catalog Request, and more.

- **Top-level navigation buttons are created automatically.** When you create a new section page on the home page, Store Editor automatically creates a button to that section on the navigation button bar on every page in the Store Editor.

- **Links, thumbnails, and Order buttons are also created automatically when new pages are created.** When you create a product, an Order button appears. A small thumbnail image and text link to that product automatically appear on its section page. If you feature that item on your home page as a special, a thumbnail appears on the home page with the price and a link to that product.

✔ **New pages are automatically searchable.** When you create a page, the Name, Code, and Caption fields of that page are automatically added to your store's internal site-search database. Even if you bury a page deep down in your store, search makes it easy to find!

✔ **Checkout navigation is already set up for you.** See Chapter 14 for more on how the new 2005 v3 Cart allows unbelievable control over cart and checkout navigation.

✔ **Add more navigational text links.** Store Editor stores can have HTML text links to sections, products, and utility pages across the entire site in the Final-text footer of each page. You can also add simple text links inside Caption fields cross-referencing different products and sections.

✔ **Maximize navigation by adding custom RTML.** RTML, Store Editor's proprietary template language, makes it possible to add navigational functionality to Store Editor–built stores, giving you advanced features like breadcrumbs, Previous/Up/Next buttons, and more, which I introduce in Chapter 26.

Navigation button bars

The Store Editor has built-in navigational button bars, which format the site and link to your top-level categories, as well as your home page, Info page, and Shopping Cart/Checkout. You have two options of page-format: Side-buttons, with buttons running down the left side of the page, or Top-buttons, with buttons appearing above the product or section page content.

You can find all these controls on the Store Editor's Variables page, and I talk a lot more about navigation buttons in Chapter 10.

Make clickable buttons look clickable. You can make your store's navigation buttons look raised by making the variable Button-style either Solid or Incised.

Product/section navigation

Imagine your store's navigation like blocks on a pyramid. The home page is the top block and the uppermost level. All the top-level navigation pages (sections within the home page) are on the second level of the pyramid. All the subsection pages and product pages within those sections are on the third level. Products within those pages are on the fourth level, and so on.

Figure 7-2 shows you an example of how every Store Editor page can show you navigation to at least three levels: links up to the home page, links down to the sections and products within the page you're on, and (if you turn Contents on under Contents-elements) links deeper in the site to the pages within those pages.

You control which elements appear on section pages with the variable Contents-elements, which lets you show an image, the page's name, or both. I also recommend displaying the Contents as links. *Contents* are the pages inside of a page, and when you display Contents on a section page, the products (or contents) of each subsection page appear as text links.. Shoppers can easily click a product link to totally bypass the subsection page and jump straight to the product page.

Because the average shopper views only five pages, the faster you get him to a product page, the greater the chance you have to sell him something.

When you're on a section page, you see thumbnails and links to all the pages (products and subsections) inside that section page. Thumbnails are automatically generated from the Image file for each product or section page. If you want, you can upload a separate image for the thumbnail by uploading an image to the Icon property. The size of the thumbnail image, shown in pixels, is determined by the variables Thumb-height and Thumb-width.

I like to make my thumbnails as small as I can, anywhere from 45 x 45 pixels to 65 x 65 pixels. The template automatically creates links to all the sections and products inside a page. The name of each page is used as the anchor text or link text (the text inside the link).

Here are some other navigation tips for product and section pages:

- **Maximize section pages by listing the contents of subsections on the section pages.**

- **Show as many thumbnails as you can above the fold.**

- **Write short section descriptions within the Abstract field.** Tell a little more about what's inside a section page. Feature more popular products and use links within those abstracts.

- **Focus attention on your bestselling or most profitable products.** My experience has been that a large percentage of your sales comes from a small handful of your products, so use links, navigation buttons, and home-page specials to lead your customers to these popular items.

- **Make browsing easier with Up and Next buttons to help your customers view more product pages.** When you bump up your page views, your sales usually follow because your customers spend their time shopping instead of figuring out how to navigate your site.

- **Cross-link related merchandise inside caption fields.** Feature related products and accessories on individual product pages.

- **Consolidate similar subsections into fewer sections.** If you have only one or two of an item, you really don't need a separate section for it.

✔ **Make links inside the cart and checkout pages open new windows.**
Use the target attribute `target=_blank or new` inside your anchor
tags to keep folks on task to complete their order. I talk a lot more about
the new checkout in Chapter 14 and discuss usability and conversion
rate improvements in Chapter 21.

Linking to optimize navigation

Text links are extremely important navigational tools for users and search
engines. Your site automatically creates text links to all the sections and
products within a given page, but I like to add a text-link site map with anywhere from 20 to 30 text links at the bottom of every page. Figure 7-3 shows
text links in the footer of a page featuring popular keywords linking to my
most popular pages.

Figure 7-3:
Text links in
the Final-
text appear
as a footer
on almost
every Store
Editor page.

Here are some guidelines for navigational links:

✔ **Underline your links to make the text look like links.** The Store Editor
underlines your links automatically, but some folks override this setting
with CSS because they think it looks better when folks have to mouse
over a link for it to show the underline. Please don't do this!

✔ **If words are not links, then don't underline them.** Why they ever
invented the underline tag, `<U>. . .</U>`, is anybody's guess!

✔ **Link to your most valuable pages with your most valuable keywords.**

✔ **Use relevant keywords in *anchor text* (the underlined words inside a
link).** Keyword-rich link text is good for users (so they'll know what the
linked page is really about) and for search engines (so they'll know what
the linked page is really about, too!). For example, if this paragraph was
text on a Web page, it would be better to say "Read about using relevant
keywords in anchor text." than to say "Click here to read about using relevant keywords in anchor text."

Links and the text within those links are extremely important to search engines. Search engines use a process called *reputation analysis,* which reads the anchor text to know what the pages linked to are about. For example, if you link to a page with the anchor text "cheap iPod accessories," then search engines figure out that that page is probably about cheap iPod accessories, especially if those exact words are also on the page. I talk a lot more about this in my search engine optimization chapter, Chapter 19.

Here is a simple text link:

```
<a href=cheap-ipod-accessories.html>Cheap iPod Accessories</a>
```

This simple HTML code creates a link to the cheap-ipod-accessories.html page on whatever domain you're already on. I put this code in the Final-text field under Variables.

Links with just href=*pagename*.html are called *relative URLs* because they don't move you to another domain, but assume that you just want to move to another page in the folder on the same domain where you already are. Because all Store Editor–created pages are in the same folder, relative URLs work both in the published store and within the Store Editor.

Make a list of 10 to 20 of your best pages and link to them with the most relevant keywords in the anchor text.

Here are links to three sections, centered, with keywords in the anchor text, which are separated by the pipe character:

```
<div align=center>
<a href=section1.html>Section1 Keyword Phrase</a>  |
<a href=section2.html>Section2 Keyword Phrase</a>  |
<a href=section3.html>Section3 Keyword Phrase</a>
</div>
```

Figure 7-4 shows an example of a page that links to other pages within the Caption field. Here's an example of good internal linking inside a Caption field. Notice the model number is inside the anchor text:

```
All of these WidgeCo-2000 Widgets work great indoors,
but if you're looking for a portable widget, try the
battery-powered <a href=widget430.html>Widget 430</a>
```

Figure 7-4:
Text links in
the caption
make it
easier for
customers
to browse
your store.

**Tom Dokken of Dokken's Dog Supply
has created the ultimate retriever
training dummy: The Deadfowl Trainer**

Dokken Dead Fowl Trainers encourage your retriever to make a proper pick
up and hold while discouraging your water dog from shaking ducks. Dokkens
Dead Fowl Trainers float in water even when punctured.

Retriever training scents may be injected directly into the duck's foam body for
added realism. Dead Fowl Trainer Internal Scent System To scent your DeadFowl Dummy: Inject
the duck scent into the foam duck body. The foam body is designed to hold the training scent in or out
of the water.

For water dog training, Dokkens Mallard Dead Fowl Trainer has no equal when it comes to life-like
appearance. You may choose the more visible (whiter) ducks: Pin Tail deadfowl, Blue Bill Deadfowl
trainer, or Red Head Dokken models for younger, less experienced dogs.

Shopping by Searching Your Store

Every Yahoo! Store has an internal search engine that lets a user search
pages from your online store and delivers high-quality search results. Your
store's search page is located at www.*yourdomain*.com/nsearch.html or
http://store.*yourdomain*.com/nsearch.html, depending on how you
set up your domain.

When you search for a keyword, your internal store search looks for that
word or phrase in the Name, Code, and Caption fields.

Figure 7-5 shows an example of a store's internal search-engine results page
with the first ten most-relevant pages. Search results are ranked in order from
most to least relevant. Orderable items with prices show a small thumbnail
image, the name of the page (which is also a link to that page), a small snippet of text, and the selling price from either the Price field or the Sale-price
field (if it has one). Sections or other nonorderable pages show up with the
page name as a link and display a snippet of text with the keyword.

Here are some things you need to know about your site search:

✓ **Modifying the look of your search page is easy.** The way your search
page looks is determined by settings in the global Variables when you
use standard templates.

✓ **Use the Code field for quick internal searches.** When someone performs
a store search, Yahoo! looks for that keyword phrase in the Name, Caption,
and Code fields. Each item has a Code as a unique product identifier. For
example, if you have a customer on the phone and want to show her a specific product — say, the Flextone Canada Goose Call page — instead of
telling her the full URL, tell her to do a store search for that product's
Code. Say "Do a store search for 1238."

Figure 7-5:
Internal store searches look for the keyword query in the Name, Caption, and Code fields of products and sections.

✔ **Name products what customers call things.** Add keywords to your Caption fields. Help pages rank better in your internal search engine by naming your products in English, not just using the brand or trade names.

For example, my distributor says a product is called "SCOTT JRT JR TISSUE, WHITE," but customers search for "Scott toilet paper." If the phrase "toilet paper" is not in the Name or Caption field, the page a customer is really searching for may be buried under less-relevant results, like under the Scott paper towels and Scott napkins pages.

✔ **Account for typos and misspellings.** If the same customer couldn't spell (or just made a typo) and searched for "scot toilet paper," the only word store search finds is *paper,* so *paper cups, paper vacuum bags, and paper baking cups* show up before any Scott toilet paper. To account for misspellings and alternate names of products, you can add text to the bottom of the caption field of the relevant section page. "Sometimes referred to as *misspelling, other misspelling,* or *yet another misspelling,* and so on." If you don't want to clutter your section pages, create special pages with keyword-loaded captions designed to get caught up in your internal store search results and then link to the relevant product or section pages from those misspellings pages.

✔ **Put a message with text or links on the search results page.** Add text or links to appear right above your search results pages by adding the text to the Caption field of your ID:nsearch page. Add links to your best-selling products, buyers' guides, and your FAQ or list your 800 number to help people who can't find what they're looking for by searching.

✔ **Put search all over your site.** Yahoo! gives you the option of adding a Search button to your navigation buttons. This button simply links to your `nsearch.html` page. It's really better to have a search box on every page. When I use standard templates, I add a bit of HTML code inside the Final-Text field under Variables for an easy search box. Replace *accountname* with your store's account name/number. Older stores have alphanumeric store account names, such as webstore-design or gundog-intl. Newer stores (September 2003 and later) have accounts like yhst-17192271484370. Here's the code:

```
<form name=vw-form method=post
action="http://search.store.yahoo.com/cgi-bin/nsearch">
<input type=hidden name=vwcatalog value=accountname>
<input name=query type=text size=30>
<input type=submit value=Search></form>
```

✔ **Try some cool linking tricks.** Linking to store search results pages allows you to do some really, really cool things, like create extremely relevant landing pages. What's a more relevant page for a searcher than a store search page showing the ten most relevant items and sections?

For example, we sell only a few types of Flextone duck calls. If I wanted to show a shopper all the Flextone duck calls, I could link to my Flextone duck calls section page, which may or may not have all the calls we sell depending on how vigilant I am at merchandising. A link to an internal store search for flextone+duck+calls would search all items and sections.

Link to store search results pages with URLs like this:

```
search.store.yahoo.com/cgi-bin/nsearch?catalog=accountname&query=
        keyword+phrase
```

Replace *accountname* with your store's account name/number. Replace *keyword+phrase* with your real search phrase. You can separate words with a + sign or with %20, which is just a fancy way to encode a space character.

✔ **See the search phrases used on your store.** Yahoo! shows you exactly what words folks use to search your store. You can see these keywords under the Store Manager's Store Searches. This information is extremely valuable to see what keyword phrases are most popular, as well as what products folks can't find easily with your internal navigation.

✔ **Hide pages with Nosearch tags.** Sometimes you don't want a particular page to show up in your internal store search results. All you have do is add a `Nosearch` tag to the Caption field, and the internal search engine ignores that page. I use the `Nosearch` tag to hide coupons, testimonials, and newsletter pages and to move pesky pages that seem to rank well for popular keywords for my own internal store search. Here's the tag that you paste inside the Name or Caption field:

```
<!--NOSEARCH-->
```

The NOSEARCH tag also excludes the product from being included in Yahoo! Shopping, so be mindful of that as you use it. See Chapter 17 for more on Yahoo! Shopping.

✔ **Make all pages searchable.** The prebuilt function pages, such as home page, privacypolicy, and the info page, have valuable information inside nonsearchable Intro-text, Message, and other text fields. If you use the standard templates (page.) in the Store Editor, a simple workaround makes this information searchable. All you do is create a New-Property Big-text field named Caption and copy the text from the unsearchable fields into the Caption field. The information doesn't actually display on the store, but it will be searchable.

To see this search hack in action, visit `www.ystorebooks.com` and search for *secret home page search test.* You can see the text in the results, but it exists nowhere on the visible home page. Pretty cool! You can use this trick for misspellings, too.

Chapter 8

Selling with Pictures

. . . .

In This Chapter

▶ Picturing possibilities with images

▶ Compressing photos and other files

▶ Uploading images to the Store Editor

▶ Collecting graphics and converting images to Web-friendly formats

▶ Selling with super product photography

. . . .

*P*icture this: Good photography sells your products by showing all the details. Imagine what someone needs to see before he buys. The more expensive an item, the more pictures you need to sell it. Professional pictures produce profits.

Manufacturers' product photos usually work okay, but often their photos are barely adequate. Fortunately, Photoshop fixes most faux pas. Great product photography takes your store to a whole 'nother level. A picture of a person actually using the product you want to sell thrusts the customer into an imaginary world, where she can visualize the benefits of buying.

Stand apart from all the other cookie-cutter retailers with your own unique and professional graphics. Custom graphics like logos, icons, navigational elements, and buttons turn your Web site into a store that sells stuff.

Yahoo! Store makes managing Web images easy because the Editor automatically creates thumbnails images for you and displays product images at a consistent size across the site. You don't have to be a graphic designer. You just upload your images and away you go. In this chapter, I show you how to upload photos to the Store Editor and balance good-looking graphics with super-fast downloads for dialups. I also point out the different types of images in a Yahoo! Store, show you how to compress files, and optimize your pages for speedy downloads!

Looking to Images to Sell More Stuff

Images are a lot like donuts. The more you have, the heavier you are, and the slower you move! I'll admit it, I can't seem to eat just one! (Ummm, Shipley's!) I tend to gorge on images, too. I'll upload a big, beautiful 75KB product photo, and then hope I can crunch the heck out of everything else to get a fast-loading product page.

In the good ol' days, some designers just made a picture of a Web site in Photoshop, chopped it into four or five pieces, and uploaded the graphics. The image-only Web-design method gives you a beautiful-looking Web store with absolute control over the appearance. There are only two downsides: You don't get any free search-engine traffic because the search engines have no idea what your site is about, and the half of the country on dialup or "slow" broadband will never be able to shop your site because it will take too long to load. Hopefully, you don't care about free traffic or losing half of your potential customers. (I'm teasing!)

Addicted to images

Some retailers are more interested in having a beautiful Yahoo! Store than having a profitable Yahoo! Store. I think you can have both, but if I really had to choose, I'd rather have a profitable, ugly store than a beautiful, unprofitable one.

A few years ago, I was doing some online marketing consulting for a retailer who owned one of the most beautiful Yahoo! Stores I have ever seen. His designer (who I won't name) was a master of Photoshop and had skillfully designed a beautiful storefront with huge sweeping splashes of color, mixed with brilliant photography, and custom section navigation buttons with literally every color of the rainbow. It was the crown jewel of this designer's portfolio, which admittedly kicks my butt up and down the street in the "make it pretty" department.

The reason this fellow called me was because he was working 60 to 80 hours a week between filling orders for his Yahoo! Store and still working

full-time at his "real" job because his online store was grossing maybe $10,000 a month in revenue. Ouch! Store sales were so low because it loaded so slowly. I think the average page size was around 200K, which is about four or five times as big as it should be. Holy cow!

A few days later, another client called. This retailer had just passed the million-dollars-a-year mark in sales, and he wanted to keep on trucking. While we were talking on the phone, my million-dollar-a-year client e-mailed me a link to my new marketing client's store. "That's the one! I want my store to be just like that one!" What a freaky coincidence!

I told him, "My friend, trust me, but you don't want a store like that one. I can't tell you why I know or what I know, but I'd bet dollars to donuts that guy would trade stores (and sales) with you in a heartbeat." Remember: You want a store that looks good *and* sells good!

Look: There is a very precarious balancing act between having nice images with plenty of detail and having Web pages load too slowly because of either large image files and/or too many image files. (For more on this topic, see the sidebar "Addicted to images.") Usability guru Jakob Nielsen says that you have about 10 seconds for a page to load before the average visitor gets impatient and clicks the Back button. Nowadays with broadband, folks are even more impatient than ever. I talk a lot more about usability and improving conversion rate and stalking Jakob Nielsen in Chapter 21.

There is a direct relationship between fast-loading Web pages and higher conversion rates. Remember that about half of Internet users in America are still on dialup. The faster your page loads, the more pages the average visitor will look at. The more pages they look at, the more they buy.

Deciphering Image Formats

I could talk for days about the gory details of image and file formats for Web graphics, but as a retailer, you need to know only a few things: There are two image file formats that matter, JPEG and GIF:

- ✔ **JPEGs are for photographs.** Shown in Figure 8-1, the JPEG file format gives you the option to compress your images by removing details that may not be visible in a Web browser. I compress my JPEGs about 15 percent in Paint Shop Pro. Be careful. When you overcompress your JPEGs, your image looks like a photograph that has gotten too close to a flame, and all the little bubbles pop up.

- ✔ **GIFS are for graphics with flat areas of color, such as logos (see Figure 8-2).** This file format gives you up to 256 different colors. GIFs are *bitmap* files. Zoom in on a GIF file, and you see a map of bits of color, which looks like a sheet of graph paper that's been colored in. Be careful here, too. Overcompress your GIF files, and they look crunchy and pixilated like a fifth- or sixth-generation photocopy.

Web graphics are low-resolution graphics usually designed at 72 dpi (dots per inch). Lower-resolution images have smaller file sizes, which translates into faster download speeds. When you print a GIF or JPEG file, it may look choppy, distorted, or pixilated because most black-and-white or color printers have a print resolution of anywhere from 300 dpi to 1200 dpi.

Figure 8-1:
Use the
JPEG file
format for
photo-
graphs. This
is my puppy,
Georgia.

Figure 8-2:
Use the GIF
file format
for graphics
with flat
areas of
color, like
logos or
product
packaging.

Image files have two different sizes:

- **Display size:** This is the height and width of an image measured in pixels.

- **File size (or weight):** This is how much space the image takes up on your hard drive, measured in bytes, kilobytes (KB), megabytes (MB), or even gigabytes (GB), depending on how large the file is.

File size is still important. Even though most people have broadband at work, and about half of the United States is on broadband at home, you need to compress your images and aim for a total file size (images and other files) of no more than 50K for a fast-loading Yahoo! Store.

Just for reference, a 3.5-inch high-density (HD) floppy disk could store 1.44MB or about 25 fast-loading Web pages including images. In contrast, a CD-ROM can hold 650MB of data, which is about 13,000 fast-loading Web pages including images.

Working with Product Images in the Store Editor

If you've used any other Web-hosting setup, you'll soon notice that Yahoo! Store Editor handles files a little differently. Product images are resized to fit product pages. *Thumbnail images* (smaller versions of the product images) are automatically created for these products to show on section pages. You can also override thumbnails and upload your own custom image to the Icon property of an item or section page to have a thumbnail that's not just a small version of the product page's image.

One cool Yahoo! Store feature is that the Editor automatically resizes your product images to display consistently across your store, almost no matter how big an image you upload, as shown in Figure 8-3. You can upload images up to 2MB file size (but don't — 100K max!) and still have consistent-looking product images.

Here are a few things you need to know about images uploaded to the Editor:

- If your uploaded image is the same size or smaller than your Item-height/Item-width variables, the product page displays the image at the original size.

- If your uploaded image is larger than the Item-height/Item-width, the Store Editor redraws that image as a GIF file. Clicking the image takes you to the full-size image.

- If your uploaded image is way too big or is an illegal file format, you see what I call the "Red Square of Death" instead of the image. Upload a Photoshop file to the Image property on an item to see what I mean. To fix this square, simply upload a GIF or JPEG, and if the file is too big, simply resize your file and upload it again.

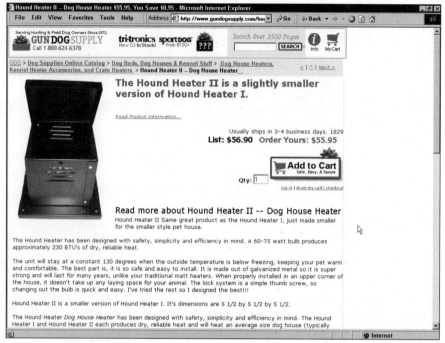

Figure 8-3:
Store
Editor auto-
matically
resizes
product
photos to fit
your page
layout.

For example, upload an 800-x-800-pixel JPEG as a product image. If your Item-height and Item-width settings are 300 x 300, the Yahoo! store is automatically going to redraw your big honking JPEG file the size that it's supposed to be. Sweet! (See the sidebar "My preferences for Store Editor image sizes," later in this chapter, for more on sizing your images.)

When you upload an image file larger than Item-height and Item-width, the resized product image becomes a clickable link to a page showing the full-size version of the image you uploaded. Uploading large product images may be very appropriate for certain types of products (jewelry, electronics, or furniture) that have details you may miss in smaller product images. For example, you can show a smaller product image on the item page at 300 x 300 pixels, and when a user clicks the picture, the original image is displayed full-sized.

Don't rely on Yahoo! to resize your product images. Compress your JPEGs and size them down to your preferred display size (I like 300 x 300 pixels) to maximize load speed.

My preferences for Store Editor images sizes

Because most folks surf the Web with monitors set to 800 x 600 or 1,024 x 768 screen resolutions, any images with a display size larger then these settings would be too big. I prefer my product photos to display at about 300 x 300 pixels. If I upload big, big images, I want them no larger than 800 x 600.

I like my thumbnails to be anywhere from 45 x 45 to 95 x 95 pixels, depending on how many items I have on a section page. Autogenerated thumbnails at this size tend to be anywhere from 4K to 8K. You can double your page's load speed by optimizing these images (in your graphics program) down to about 2K and uploading them to the Icon field.

If you want to see how big an image appears on the Web, simply right-click it and choose Properties from the shortcut menu that appears;

this shows the location, width, height, and size of the image file (see figure).

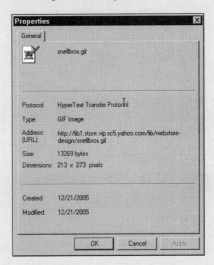

When an uploaded JPEG file is taller or wider than the Item-height or Item-width settings under Variables, the Store Editor redraws the file as a shorter and/or narrower GIF file but with a much larger file size than a JPEG of the same image. Bigger file size = slower download speed = less page views = fewer shoppers converted into buyers = less money in your pocket. Consider resizing all your product images to fit within whatever your Item-height or Item-width Variables settings are.

Uploading Images to the Store Editor

You can upload images to the Store Editor in several ways, but most folks upload images by hand, one page at a time. Here's how to upload images:

- ✔ You can browse to the page you want and click the Image button in the Edit Nav-bar and upload the GIF or JPEG from your hard drive to the Y! Image Server.

- ✔ You can browse to a page, click the Edit button on the Edit Nav-bar to go to the Edit page, and then click the Upload button to the right of the Image property.

✔ More advanced users can use the Bulk Image Upload feature under Controls. Create a *zip file* (a compressed archive created with WinZip software, available at `www.winzip.com`) where you name each image file with its ID so that the Store Editor "knows" which picture goes with which product. For example, if a product's ID was 12345, then the name of the graphics file would be `12345.gif` or `12345.jpg`. Zip all your image files into a single zip file and visit the Controls page in the Store Editor to upload the file, which magically hooks up all the images with the right products. For more information on this topic, see this book's companion Web site at `www.ystorebooks.com/bulkimageuploads.html`.

Nothing sells like more details, and nothing shows details like more product photos. If you want to upload a second picture, such as an alternate product shot, use the Inset field, as shown in Figure 8-4. For more than two product shots on an item page, upload the image to your Web-hosting account and use an HTML image source tag in your Caption field to show the image like this:

```
<img src=http://site.yourdomain.com/images/filename.gif>
```

Figure 8-4:
Use the Inset field to upload and display a second product photo.

It's impossible to keep people from downloading your images because they must download an image to even view it in their browser. You can take all kinds of steps to make it more difficult for unscrupulous people to steal your images, but it's almost impossible to stop someone, especially if he knows anything about computers. Personally, I'm more concerned about direct competition stealing my images than with someone in an unrelated field on a Web page I'll probably never see. Put your domain name on your best images!

Finding Product Images

Most of the time, the image files I use to create my Yahoo! Store product images come from manufacturers' Web sites. Make sure that you have permission before you do use someone else's images. If you're selling a company's products, it will most likely let you use its product photography on your Yahoo! Store. Images are often already formatted for the Web (JPEGs and GIF files) but usually need to be compressed or optimized. I also like to brand these images with my logo or domain names as a *watermark* (a subtle translucent mark, such as logo or text, used to brand images) to keep competitors from just copying my images and uploading them to their Web sites and benefiting from all my hard work.

Watermark your photos with your company name, domain name, and/or copyright information.

Fortunately, watermarking is relatively easy. Depending on the graphic software you use, make a new layer for the text, but reduce the opacity to about 15 or 20 percent so that the text is translucent.

Always get permission before using anyone else's images. Not only is it very bad manners to steal images from other Web sites, it's also probably a violation of copyright law.

The worst thing you can do is steal images from competitors who can use this mistake to get you kicked out of your Yahoo! Store, get your site removed from the search engines, and sue you for up to $100,000 per copyright violation. I'm not a lawyer, but you need to keep your nose clean. I have one competitor stealing lots of my images, and my lawyer wants this image-thief to pay for his summer home in Mantachie.

You can also find images through other means:

  ✔ **Request manufacturers' CD-ROMs.** Manufacturers who supply catalog retailers with product images can provide you with high-resolution TIFF files even if they don't have Web images for you. These super-huge image files (around 2,000KB) need to be resized and compressed in your graphics software to a more Web-friendly 72 dpi (around 40KB or smaller).

✔ **Scan catalogs, brochures, and sale sheets provided by distributors and wholesalers.** Turning these images into Web-ready product photos takes a little more work. You have to scan them with a flatbed scanner at about 300 dpi, remove any hickeys, dirt, or telltale signs of the printing process, and then shrink them to about 72 dpi. If you sell flat items smaller than 8½ x 11 inches (such as books or DVDs), flatbed scanners are better and quicker than digital cameras for creating quality product images.

✔ **Take your own product photos.** With the magic of today's digital cameras and the editing power of graphics programs, you don't have to be a professional photographer to get professional-looking results. Sometimes you have to fiddle with your setup a bit to get it right, but after you get going, you can knock out a ton of photos in a hurry. If you get half-decent photos, you can clean them up in your graphics program lickety-split! (For more on graphics programs, see the next section in this chapter.)

Tweaking Your Images

When you're working with images, you need several things: a better-than-average computer with a decent monitor, a large hard drive, and graphics software for creating and modifying images. You can also use a flatbed scanner, a mid-line digital camera and other camera equipment, a CD burner, and some other form of external storage, such as a removable hard drive or tape backup.

You also need special software to create or edit Web graphics. As shown in Figure 8-5, I use Paint Shop Pro. I've been using the same software ever since 1997, when I got a demo version. You can get your copy for around $129 (or maybe less). I also think Adobe Photoshop is cool, but it has way too many features that most folks never use and costs a lot (around $695). Photoshop is the industry standard for designers with tons and tons of tutorials and other resources on the Web. I'm old and cheap, and pretty much stuck in my ways by now. Both Photoshop and Paint Shop Pro have batch-processing features for automating repetitive tasks for editing images, which can save a lot of time if you work with lots of product images.

No matter which graphics software you choose, it needs to enable you to do certain basic things to your images:

✔ **Take screen shots:** Most graphics programs have a screen shot function. Turn it on, click a button, and then whatever image was on your screen is now captured and saved inside your graphics software, where you can manipulate it. Use screen shots as the foundation for a complete redesign or to quickly capture logos or other design elements from your site.

Yahoo! Store's very own Senior Technical Content Producer Paul Boisvert says, "There is a neat extension for Firefox out now called Screengrab (`http://andy.5263.org/screengrab`). It allows you to right-click to get the area inside the browser, and more importantly, it can scroll to get a full browser window. This feature will probably be standard in Firefox within a few versions, but this may be a good little tool for Firefox users."

✔ **Crop the excess space around an image:** Remove excess *negative space* (the white space around an image) to make images load faster and improve the look of product photos and autogenerated thumbnails.

✔ **Add a 1-pixel border to the outside of an image:** I prefer my product photos to have white backgrounds so that the objects appear to float on the page. Sometimes a light gray border really defines the image, but sometimes a dark border is just too much. Whether you should add borders to product images totally depends on your site design.

When you add borders to one product image, you really need to add a border to every product image, or your site looks inconsistent. Autogenerated thumbnails with 1-pixel borders tend to look a little sloppy, so you need to make custom icons for each one. I really like the look of a 1-pixel border around the edges of a 95-x-95-pixel thumbnail.

✔ **Adjust image parameters such as contrast, brightness, color balance, and so on:** You can radically improve the quality of a photo by making subtle changes to various settings in your graphics software, but be careful not to overtweak your images or fall into your work and lose all track of time.

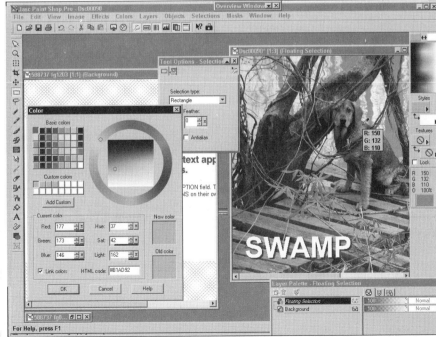

Figure 8-5:
Even though Photoshop is the industry standard for creating and editing images for the Web, I use Paint Shop Pro because I'm cheap and it works, and it has since 1997!

✔ **Export an image as a GIF or JPEG file:** There is always a trade-off between the quality of an image and how big the file size is. When you convert an image to either GIF or JPEG formats, the resulting image file size is much smaller, but this compression degrades the image quality. For this reason, I usually work with a copy of an image file rather than the original file so that when I need to start over, I can just go back to my original file. (For more on these formats, see the section "Deciphering Image Formats," earlier in this chapter.)

Working with Text Inside Graphics

Different graphics programs have different ways of adding text to images, but there are several universal truths:

✔ **It's better to work with a high-resolution image in your graphics software and then export the image as a lower-resolution file.** If your original image file is a GIF file with 256 colors (8-bit), increase the file bit-depth from 8-bit to 24-bit, which gives you up to 16 million colors, create your file, and then save it and compress it as a GIF.

✔ **Create your text graphics at their real size so that you can see how fonts display.** Sometimes when you resize images with text, the text becomes illegible.

✔ **Anti-alias your text.** Sometimes you'll see graphics or text on sites where folks didn't *anti-alias* the text, which is a feature on most graphics programs that smoothes the edges of fonts by blending the font color into the background color. If you don't anti-alias fonts in images, words look choppy or have the jaggies, as shown in Figure 8-6.

Figure 8-6:
Working with text and images can be a little tricky. Anti-alias your text and make sure that your image bit-depth is set to millions of colors.

anti-aliased text
jaggy text

Part III
Building and Managing Your Store

The 5th Wave   By Rich Tennant

"I see you're creating products on our Yahoo! Store site that don't actually exist yet. I didn't know Catalog Manager came with a delusional fantasy mode."

In this part . . .

This part contains everything I wanted to know back in 1997 when I started building stores. I'll be candid here. I love building stores with the Store Editor. The Editor is an extremely powerful and easy-to-use store-building tool, but I would hardly call some of the intermediate or advanced functions intuitive.

Hey! I've been working with the Store Editor since way back when, but sometimes I still need help figuring out where some feature is located. For example, I'm always looking for the switch that moves the Edit Nav-bar to the top or bottom of the page (Config) or the one where you make folks who are using the Editor sign in using their Security Key (Controls).

In this part, I dig into all the details of store building using the Store Editor and Store Manager. You can find out about designing your store's navigation buttons and creating product pages, section and subsection pages, info pages, and even the most important page on your site, your home page. I share all the good tips and tricks I've picked up in the past eight or nine years of store building.

After you build your store, I show you how to sell more products using Store Editor features, such as home page Specials and Shopping Cart Cross-sells. You also find out about the new Checkout Manager and Shopping Cart, which give you a previously unknown level of control over checkout design. Finally, I wrap up this part of the book with pretty much everything you need to know about mastering the Store Manager, which is a pretty big chapter with a lot of information on setting up your store with shipping methods and rates, setting tax rates, and most importantly, processing orders!

Chapter 9

Store Building with the Store Editor

*T*he Store Editor is a powerful online tool for building your Yahoo! Store and managing the products you sell. You can control the look and feel of your store from settings on the global Variables page. In addition, you can create, edit, and delete products in a hidden copy of your store so that you see exactly what customers will see.

The Store Editor is easy to use, too. New retailers and Webmasters can make good-looking stores in no time at all without additional software or programming skills. Power users can tweak templates to create customized stores designed to convert shoppers into buyers.

In this chapter, I introduce the Store Editor, explore Editor geography, discuss basic store-building concepts, show you how to tweak your settings for maximum power editing and how to navigate the Store Editor, get you started creating new products and sections, and give you an overview of the store Variables page. The Store Editor makes it easy to make more with a Yahoo! Store.

Getting Started in Store Editor

The Store Editor is the tool you use to build your online store and manage your products. Most successful store owners use the Editor almost every single business day. The Store Editor is also the tool you use to manage your virtual store and merchandise.

Settings on the global Variables page determine how the basic store templates display product information, including store layout, colors, fonts, text size, and more. Power users have even more control by modifying copies of existing templates or building new templates from scratch. I introduce RTML templates in Chapter 26.

Because the Editor is a copy of your store, you can see your site the same way your customers do as you manage your product pages. The Store Editor is really just a copy of your Yahoo! Store with the Edit Nav-bar stuck on top of it. Every product page, section page, and function page in your store has its counterpart inside the Store Editor.

The Store Editor comes with additional controls, such as the global Variables page where you edit settings to control the look and feel of the site. It also has tools for advanced users, such as Database Uploads for quick and easy product uploads; Types and Templates to help customize your products; and other advanced Editor settings, which I cover later in this chapter in the section "Meeting the Edit Nav-bar buttons."

Editing your store

Your store has two versions: the public (or published) version of your store and the hidden Store Editor version of your site:

- ✔ You can see the published version of your store at `http://store.yahoo.com/yhst-youraccountnumber` or at your domain name. I delve into the details of domains in Chapter 24.

- ✔ The Store Editor is where you make changes to your store's design and product info and is accessible to only Yahoo! IDs listed in the Store Manager's Access panel. You control who gets in the back room.

Edits you make in Store Editor are invisible to store visitors until you click the Publish button. Thanks to the Store Editor, you can make major changes to the navigation, design, layout, products, and pricing on your Yahoo! Store without everyone in the world seeing what you're doing. You can make wholesale changes to the design of your Web site and publish the changes only when you're ready for the site to launch.

To get started editing your store, follow these steps:

1. **Go to** `http://smallbusiness.yahoo.com/services` **and log in with your Yahoo! ID and your password.**

   The Manage My Services page appears.

2. **Click your store account link.**

   The Store Manager page appears.

3. **Click the Store Editor link.**

   A copy of your store's home page appears, and you're now inside the Store Editor, where you can make edits.

Notice the Edit Nav-bar floating above (or below) your store page. You know you're in the Editor when the URL in your browser starts with `http://edit.store.yahoo.com/RT/NEWEDIT/`*youraccountname*, or you see the Edit Nav-bar. Notice the Publish button in the upper right corner.

Multiple people can work inside the Store Editor at the same time, as long as they're not working on the same pages. When someone does try to edit a page that another person is already editing, a warning message pops up to the second person: "Locked. Sorry, this resource '{ID of page}' is currently locked by another user. Either click on Clear Lock to remove the lock, or click on Cancel to try again later." Don't select Clear Lock unless you want to screw up what the other person's doing.

Publishing your edits to the Store

The Publish button has two states: Publish and Published. When the button is cream-colored and says Publish, changes have been made inside the Store Editor, but the published version of the site has not yet been updated.

When you're ready to publish your changes to the Store Editor, follow these steps:

1. **Click the Variables button and then click the Update button right before you publish to force the Store Editor to generate and publish every single page.**

   The Store Editor is pretty smart and knows which pages you edited since you last published. To save time and resources, the new Store Editor generates and publishes only the pages it knows you edited. When products appear on multiple pages, sometimes the information on section pages or custom templates doesn't get updated, so always update your Variables before publishing.

2. **Click the Publish button.**

   The Publish Status page, shown in Figure 9-1, appears to monitor the published progress and refreshes every five seconds. The Store Editor generates the HTML pages reflecting your changes and then uploads those HTML pages to the Yahoo! servers. (This process takes anywhere from 30 seconds to 15 minutes.)

If you don't care to watch your progress, click the Store Manager link to exit. I usually go check my stats or something while impatiently waiting for the store to publish. You can tell when the Editor is finished publishing because a link back to the Store Editor appears.

Figure 9-1:
The Publish Status page tells you where you are in the publishing process.

After you publish changes, the Publish button turns gray and says Published. However, the moment you edit anything at all, for example, you access the Variables page or click Edit and change a single property on a product, the Published button changes back to a cream-colored button.

No one can see the changes you've made in the Store Editor until you click the Publish button.

By default, the Publish button appears only on the home page (next to the Manager button), but you can add these site buttons to every page by clicking the Controls button and changing the Site Buttons setting to Every Page, which puts a Publish and Manager button on every page. I get more into the Controls in just a little bit in the "Setting the Controls for the Editor" section.

Here are some things you need to know about publishing your store:

- ✔ **When the Store Editor is publishing, you can't work inside the Store Editor.** If another person's editing the store when someone clicks the Publish button, the other person's version of the Editor freezes. If he happens to be editing a particular page, those edits are lost.

- ✔ **Don't click any Store Editor links while the store is publishing.** Also, don't try to log back in to the Store Editor from inside the Store Manager. Five or more clicks on any Store Editor link locks up the Store Editor for a lot longer than it takes for the store to publish. Be patient!

- ✔ **Publishing the Store Editor publishes both the Store Editor and the Catalog Manager (if you even use it).** Publishing doesn't publish the Order

Settings, such as changes made in the Store Manager to Shipping, Taxes, or other back-end settings. I talk about the Store Manager in Chapter 15.

✔ **Sometimes it takes a while for the Store Editor software to publish your site.** The amount of time usually depends on how many products you have. Bigger stores take longer to publish. I usually use publishing as an excuse to step away from my computer and stretch my legs.

✔ **Sometimes old pages get stuck in your browser.** For example, if you just changed the price on a product and have published the store, but the product page you see is the old page with the old price, the problem may be that the old page is cached in your browser. Click the Refresh or Reload button in your browser when you view the published version of your store to make sure that you're seeing the most current version of the page.

Customizing Your Editor for Editing

The default settings for the Store Editor are pretty helpful to new retailers, but you'll find a bunch of stuff in the way after you know the basics. When I log in to Store Editor for the first time, I have to make my nest. Here's what I recommend, which I describe in the following sections:

✔ Switch to Advanced mode. (See the section "Switching to Advanced mode," later in this chapter.)

✔ Move the Edit Nav-bar to the top of your Editor pages. (See the section "Moving the Edit Nav-bar," later in this chapter.)

✔ Hide the Help button. (See the section "Meeting the Edit Nav-bar buttons," later in this chapter.)

✔ Add the Find and Publish/Manager buttons to every page. (See the section "Meeting the Edit Nav-bar buttons," later in this chapter.)

✔ Tweak a few other settings. (See the section "Meeting the Edit Nav-bar buttons," later in this chapter.)

Publishing protocols work

Because multiple people are always editing our stores, before we can publish, someone yells, "Can I publish the store?" and a chorus of "Fine by me!" echoes throughout the warehouse unless someone is in the middle of something, and then you can hear him holler, "No! No! Don't publish! Whatever you do, do *not* publish!"

Switching to Advanced mode

The Store Editor is in Regular mode by default, and you need to access some power tools provided by Advanced mode. It's easy to understand why retailers may be hesitant to jump off into Advanced mode with warnings like the following:

> "The Advanced Editor is designed for experienced programmers — all protections against damaging your store are turned off. In Advanced mode it is easy to damage your store or break pages beyond repair. For that reason, we recommend it only for experienced programmers."

Okay. No sweat! You bought the right book. Raise your right hand and repeat after me: "I am an experienced programmer." Then click the little red arrow to the right of the Edit Nav-bar to change the Store Editor from Regular mode to Advanced mode. The Editor shifts into Advanced mode. Notice that a second row of buttons appears on the Edit Nav-bar with functions that weren't available to the basic user in Regular mode.

Moving the Edit Nav-bar

The Edit Nav-bar, shown in Figure 9-2, is the Swiss army knife of the Store Editor. The Edit Nav-bar helps you navigate the store, lets you Edit pages, or changes settings in the Variables or Controls pages.

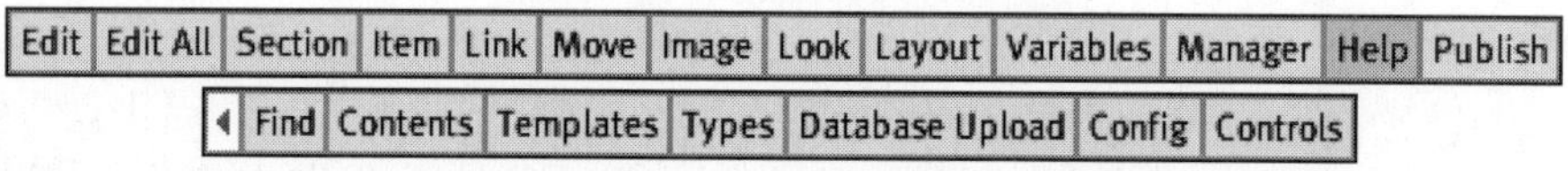

Figure 9-2:
The Edit Nav-bar is the Swiss army knife of Nav-bars.

| Edit | Edit All | Section | Item | Link | Move | Image | Look | Layout | Variables | Manager | Help | Publish |

| ◀ | Find | Contents | Templates | Types | Database Upload | Config | Controls |

One of the first things I do is move the Edit Nav-bar from the bottom of every page to the top of the Store Editor so that I don't have to scroll to the bottom of the Editor every time I want to make a change. Save your finger and the scroll wheel on your mouse and do the same:

1. **Click the Config button.**

   The Config page appears.

2. **Change the Edit-button-position from Bottom to Top.**

3. **Click the Update button.**

    The last page you were on in the Editor appears, but this time your Edit Nav-bar is at the top of the screen. It's magic!

Meeting the Edit Nav-bar buttons

The Edit Nav-bar is your friend. Here are some of the Edit Nav-bar buttons and what they do:

- ✔ **Edit:** Click the Edit button to open the Edit page of whatever page you're currently on. Using this button, you can add, edit, or delete text in the various fields or upload images.

- ✔ **Edit All:** Click this button to edit all the items inside a section at once. Edit All lets you edit the Name, Code, Options, Price, and Sale-Price fields. Edit All displays ten items at a time. You can save your work as you edit each group of ten items.

- ✔ **Section:** Click this button to create a new section page.

- ✔ **Item:** Click this button to create a new item page.

- ✔ **Link:** Click this button to create a Link-object, which is the Store Editor's way to create hypertext links to other Web sites without coding HTML. Who needs HTML anchor tags when all you have to do is know the URL? Simply name the Link and away you go. Link-objects have Name, URL, Image (for a thumbnail), Abstract, and Label fields. Most of the time, Link-objects are used for making objects for a links or a resources page. Sometimes I use Link-objects instead of a copy of the same ID.

- ✔ **Move:** Click the Move button for an easier way to reorder navigation buttons or products inside your section pages. Click the Move button, click the item you want to move, and then click where you want it to go.

- ✔ **Image:** Click this button to jump to a shortcut to upload a graphic to the Image field on a section or item without having to first click the Edit button. Unfortunately, you cannot delete an Image, only upload a new one, which overwrites a previously uploaded file.

- ✔ **Variables:** Click this button to open the global Variables page, which affects the look and feel of almost every page in your store. This page is where all the action is!

- ✔ **Manager:** Click this button to jump back to the Store Manager. The Manager button appears only on the home page unless you change the Site Buttons setting under Controls To Every Page, which puts a Publish and Manager button on every page; this change can save you a click or two. I put Site Buttons on every page on stores I work on by myself, but not on pages where multiple people work on the site at the same time because it's almost too easy for someone else to publish while you're in the middle of something!

✔ **Help/Hide Help:** Click this button to turn Store Editor Help on and off. If you don't need Help all the time, turn it off because the Help labels and definitions take up a lot of screen real estate.

✔ **Publish:** Click this button to publish your store. Publish makes the Store Editor generate a new copy of your site using the RTML templates you assign to each page to crank out an HTML page, generates any new images you need, and updates the published version of your store to match the changes you've made in the Store Editor. The Publish button appears only on the home page unless you change the Site Buttons setting under Controls to Every Page.

✔ **Find:** Click this button to open the Find By ID form, where you type or paste in the ID of a page you want to jump to. Remember, IDs must be lowercase, or the Store Editor gets confused. I highly recommend that you turn on the Find button on the Controls page (set the Show Find Button setting to Yes).

✔ **Contents:** Click this button to open the Contents or site map page, which displays a hierarchical site map of your Yahoo! Store.

✔ **Templates:** Click this button to go to the Templates page, which shows you a list of the 80 or so built-in RTML templates and any custom templates you've created. From this page, you can look at the built-in templates (but not edit them), copy existing RTML templates that you can modify, create new RTML templates, and delete old RTML templates. RTML is dangerous fun. Check out Chapter 26 for more on RTML.

✔ **{Page2}:** When you're on a page using a custom template, the name of that custom template appears on the Edit Nav-bar instead of the Templates button. Click that button to fire up the RTML edit page for that template. The regular Template button is a click away in the Edit Nav-bar.

Notice the period after the name of each of the types and templates. The period tells the Store Editor that the type is a prebuilt type and can't be edited. Also, when you're in the RTML Editor, the last button on the second row of the Edit Nav-bar displays the ID of the last page you were on, so you can easily make changes to your template and then click that button to see the changes on a page using that template.

✔ **Types:** Click this button to load the Types page. You create custom types in the Editor to use in conjunction only with custom RTML templates, so beginners need to steer clear. The Types page is where you can create custom types (with custom fields), add new fields to existing custom types, and delete unused custom types. See all the built-in types (such as empty., info., item., link., main., norder., privacypolicy., raw-html., and search.), any custom types you created, and custom tables you created in the Catalog Manager.

A type in the Store Editor is very similar to a table in Catalog Manager. *Types* and *tables* are lists of fields or properties that an object can have. For example, the built-in Type (item.) is the default and is used for sections and products. Every ID that's an (item.) type has Name, Code, and Price fields so that you can add this information every time you create a new page.

✔ **Database Uploads:** Click this button to go to the Database Uploads page, where you can upload CSV files to create and modify sections and items. I live for database uploads and gush in much detail in Chapter 23.

✔ **Config:** Click this button to jump to the page where you edit various Store Editor settings, such as the position of the Edit Nav-bar (top or bottom of the store), your leafed product page settings (see Chapter 11), and more.

✔ **Controls:** Click this button to explore the Store Editor Controls page, where you can upload images in bulk, change your Default Editor Mode, place Publish and Manager buttons on every page, and more.

✔ **Look:** Click this button to make site-wide changes to the design by choosing one of 14 color schemes. Ignore the Look button, or at least be cautious when using this tool, because it overrides any changes you've made on the Variables page. You can show/hide this button on the Controls page.

✔ **Layout:** Click this button to change the appearance on individual pages by modifying the number of columns and alignment. I'd avoid using the Layout button because of the potential for overriding any existing work. This button is hidden unless you turn it on from the Controls page.

✔ **Red Arrow (left side):** Click this arrow/button to return to the Regular interface of the Editor. The red arrow on the left side of the Edit Nav-bar indicates that you're in Advanced mode. When you click the arrow, you return to Regular mode, and all the Advanced mode Edit Nav-bar buttons disappear and the red arrow appears on the right side.

✔ **Red Arrow (right side):** Click this arrow/button to switch to the Advanced interface of Store Editor. The red arrow on the right side of the Edit Nav-bar means that you're still in Regular mode. Go ahead and click the Controls button and change the Default Editor Mode setting to Advanced so that you'll always be in Advanced mode. Then you can have access to the all the wonderful features of the Store Editor.

✔ **Up:** Click this button to go up to the section page (Parent object) of whatever page you're currently on. The Up button appears on the Edit Nav-bar only when you're on a page with a parent page.

Navigating the Store Editor

You can browse around the Store Editor by clicking Nav-buttons, thumbnail images, and text links just as you would on any other Web site:

- ✔ **Click navigation buttons or icons and text links to find the page you want to edit.** Clicking buttons or icons is the easiest way to get around inside the Store Editor and is very easy to do on a small site with a few sections. However, if your site has thousands of products and hundreds of section pages, navigating this way is more difficult.

- ✔ **Add Up and Next buttons to your Nav-buttons (under Variables: Nav-buttons) to make it easy to browse from one product to the next within the same section.** See Chapter 10 for more on buttoning down your store's navigation.

- ✔ **Browse around on the Contents (site map) page.** Contents displays the ID (linked to the page in Edit mode), Type, Template, and Contents of every page (object) of your store.

Figure 9-3 shows the Contents page, which displays the entire navigational structure of your store with an expandable site map. Your home page (ID:index) is at the very top of the hierarchy. All the top-level section pages (pages in the Contents field of your home page) appear directly below the home page. These top-level sections are arranged in the order that the pages appear on your site.

On the Contents page, when a section page (parent) contains other pages (children), the IDs of the these child-pages appear below the parent page as links to the pages in the Store Editor. It looks scarier than it is. After you get the hang of it, it's pretty easy to navigate.

You can expand and contract your store's site map by clicking the + or – sign to see the contents of each section. Click the + button to the left of the ID to expand the site map to see all the pages inside that parent page. Click the – button to hide the contents. A Show Parents button appears when an ID is in multiple sections. Click that button to see all the parent object-IDs with links to those pages.

At the bottom of the Contents page are the *orphaned pages,* which are pages not inside any other page. Because they aren't linked from another page, it seems almost impossible to find these orphaned pages by browsing about the site. Every so often, I scroll down to the bottom of the Contents page, click the first orphaned ID to see what the page is about, and figure out whether it needs be placed within a section page or simply deleted. You can always cut the orphaned page to the Clipboard and move it to a section page. See Chapter 12 for more info.

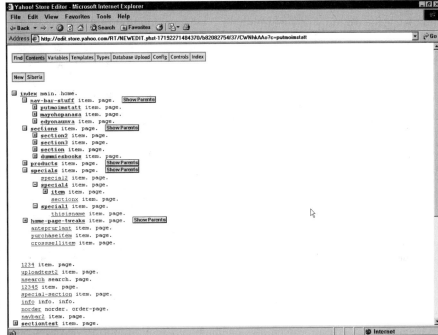

Figure 9-3:
The
Contents
page, or site
map, is
where you
can see
the entire
hierarchy of
your online
store.

Finding pages by knowing the ID

When you know the ID of a page, you can use the Find button to jump to that page instead of browsing around in the Store Editor to get to it. As long as you know the ID, you can even find IDs of objects that are cut to the Clipboard or orphaned. To use the Find button, first you need to turn it on under the Controls page in the Store Editor by setting Show Find Button to Yes. Click the Find button on the Edit Nav-bar, which zips you over to the Find By ID page. Type the ID of the page you want to find and click the Find button, and the page magically appears.

You must type the ID in lowercase letters and make sure that no space appears at the end.

Bookmarking Editor pages with consistent URLs

I got this tip from long-time Yahoo! Store developer Brian Bock (www.bock. com). You can bookmark pages in the Editor to save time and trouble. First, go to the Controls page and set your Editor Entry page to the home page, and then use these direct Editor URLs to jump straight to any ID in the Editor. These URLs work as long as you're logged in to your Yahoo! ID and that ID has permission (under the Store Manager's Access link) to access your Store Editor. Here's the format for direct URLs linking to specific IDs:

```
http://edit.store.yahoo.com/RT/NEWEDIT.yourstoreaccount/id.html
```

Setting properties on the Config page

The Config button takes you to a page where you change your Store Editor's settings and Leaf configurations and set the default types and templates. Set the Edit-button-position to Top. If you use custom Types and Templates, set the default items and sections to match those custom Types and Templates; otherwise, do not touch these settings. Config is also where you configure how your Leafed pages look. I cover this topic in Chapter 11, where I talk about the many different looks of section pages.

Setting the Controls for the Editor

Figure 9-4 displays the Controls page, which contains helpful tools and settings for the Editor. This page shows the last time you published the store with a time and date stamp and shows any error messages.

Tweak your Controls page to save time and energy, as well as eliminate needless clicks, so that your Store Editor is ready to rock from the moment you log in. Here are my favorite settings for Controls:

- Set the Default Editor Mode to Advanced to have access to every Editor feature.

- Set Site Buttons to Yes so that you see the Publish and Manager buttons on every page.

- Leave the Editor Entry Page set to the home page so that you can bookmark Editor URLs.

- Don't use the Look and Layout buttons because they can mess up your store.

- Set Show Find Button to Yes because Find is the easiest way to jump to a page when you know the ID.

- Set Color Code Input to your preference. To me, the color white is 255 255 255 (not #ffffff), so I use Decimal color.

- Set Index Page Size to 50 or 100, which is better for search engines. I talk a lot more about search engines in Chapter 19.

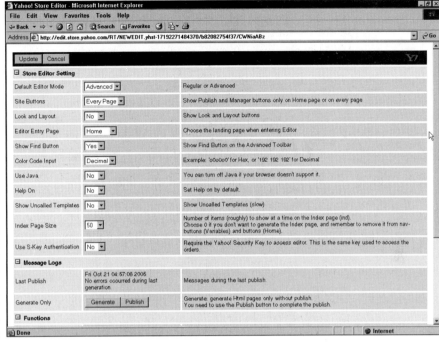

Figure 9-4:
The Controls page has all kinds of nifty features for customizing your Store Editor.

✔ Keep Use S-Key Authentication set to No unless you want to type your Security Key about once an hour. It's good security for the Editor if you need it.

✔ Search Objects By Some Property is a really cool feature. You can search the various fields (Name, Code, Caption, Abstract, Contents, Headline, Ship-weight) of every ID to see which IDs either contain something, equal something, are empty, or are nonempty. It's really great when you know you have a page named something-something-8675309 and just can't find it!

✔ Multiple Image Upload is where you upload your .zip files full of images named the same as the ID you want them to upload to. I cover image uploads in Chapter 8.

✔ Edit by ID is pretty handy when you've done something (with a broken table or JavaScript) that makes the page not load and not show the Edit Nav-bar.

Controlling Look and Feel with Variables

Setting global Variables isn't something you do every day, but you'll live on this page the first time you set up your store's look and feel. I cover the various Variables in great detail throughout the book, but here's an overview of all the Variables with references to the chapters that contain the nitty-gritty information.

Click the Variables button to go to the Variables page (see Figure 9-5) where you can change all kinds of parameters to control the look and feel of your Yahoo! Store.

Clicking the Help button causes a helpful definition for each setting to appear. Also, see the Help page at `http://help.yahoo.com/us/store/edit/variables/variables-01.html` for more info.

- ✔ **Title:** Change the Title to the name of your company and/or your domain. The default is your domain name or your account name. The Title appears in the banner text on the top of every page until you upload a Name-image graphic. This text also appears in multiple places across the site, especially in the old Shopping Cart and Checkout, so be careful what you type here!

- ✔ **Email:** This e-mail address is the official site's e-mail address and appears on the info.html page.

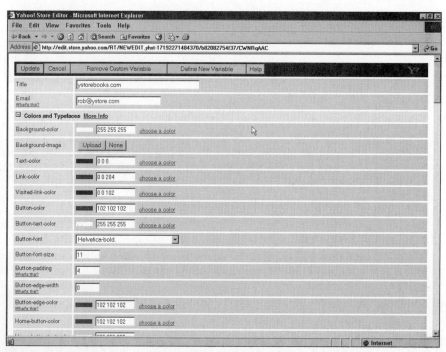

Figure 9-5:
The Variables page is where you adjust the global settings that control the look and feel of your Yahoo! Store.

Colors and typefaces

Believe it or not, variables in the Colors and Typefaces section control the appearance of various hues and fonts across the site. It's electric!

- **Background-color:** Use white (255 255 255) or a very light gray.

- **Background-image:** Don't use a background image. It makes the text hard to read.

- **Text-color:** Use black or a very dark color.

- **Link-color:** Use blue or a color that matches your logo.

- **Visited-link-color:** Use a color that's darker than your link color.

- **Display-text-color:** Pick the color of your headlines.

- **Display-font:** Choose a font from the drop-down menu from the many, many fonts. I prefer Syntax-bold.

- **Display-font-size:** Measured in points. Choose anywhere from 16- to 36-point type.

- **Text-font:** Choose an HTML font face for Captions and link text. I like Verdana or Arial. Times, Helvetica, and Georgia work, too.

- **Text-size:** Choose an HTML font size. The default is 2, and I also like 3.

- **Label-color, Label-font, and Label-font-size variables:** Control the look of the Specials on the front page if you choose As-Thumbnails for the Specials-format. For more on these Variables and Specials, read Chapter 13.

- **Banner-font-size:** Overrides the banner font size, which is based on the length of your domain name. Instead of using this field, upload a name-image header graphic (about 650 x 75 pixels). To me, banner fonts look really unprofessional. The color of the banner is the same color as the home-button-text-color.

- **Emphasis-color:** Determines the -color for the Price if your Price-style isn't set to Quiet.

Buttons get their own chapter! Chapter 10 covers Button-color, Button-text-color, Button-font, Button-font-size, Button-padding, Button-edge-width, Button-edge-color, Home-button-color, Home-button-text-color, Home-button-font, and Home-button-font-size.

Image dimensions

I fully cover images and Image Dimensions Variables in Chapter 8, including Thumb-height and Thumb-width, Inset-height and Inset-width, and Item-height and Item-width.

Page layout

Page Layout variables determine how your pages look, how thumbnails and product links display, and which elements show on the various pages. If a page has Leaf set to Yes, then these settings are overridden by the settings on the Config page, covered earlier in this chapter in the section "Setting properties on the Config page."

- ✔ **Page-format:** Determines whether your buttons go on the top or along the side.

- ✔ **Page-width:** Set in pixels. I keep my pages less than 800 pixels wide.

- ✔ **Name-image:** Clicking the Name-image graphic takes you to the home page. The Name-image appears as the header on every page and serves as both branding and functionality, which makes it your most important graphic. Upload a 750-x-75-pixel Name-image for Top-button stores, or a 600-x-75-pixel Name-image for Side-button stores).

- ✔ **Head-elements:** Controls whether Image and/or Display-text-title (the Name/Headline) appear on nonleafed pages. Sometimes I don't display Image to free up screen real estate on section pages.

- ✔ **Head-style:** Determines the alignment of the Head-elements, the Image, and the Headline. I prefer left-aligned pages, but right-aligned works, too. Using Centered eats up a lot of space on product pages, so I don't use it.

- ✔ **Columns:** Controls how many products are in each row. I prefer three or five. More items per column displays more products per screen shot.

- ✔ **Column-width:** Determines how tight your columns look. Fixed makes all your columns the same width. Variable makes columns with items with more text wider, so the pages breathe a little more.

- ✔ **Row-pad:** This is the space (in pixels) between rows. The default is 15 pixels.

- ✔ **Contents-elements:** Determines which elements show on nonleafed section pages, which I talk about a lot more in Chapter 11. I select Image, Screen-text-title, and Price for nonleafed section pages. Select or deselect multiple options in the list box by holding the Ctrl key (Mac: the ⌘ key) and clicking elements on or off with your mouse.

- ✔ **Contents-format:** Use Vertical for nonleafed section pages because sections display vertically centered thumbnail image, text link, and price (if it's an item) in minimal space. Vertical allows you to get more products in the first screen shot, above the fold. Ell displays the text link to the right of the thumbnail in a separate column. Wrap is just like Ell, but information wraps around the thumbnail in the same column, and Pack displays the image full-size, with no border or space between elements.

✔ **Bullet-image:** Use the image field to upload a custom image to replace the bullet.

Button properties

For more on navigation buttons and related Variables, check out Chapter 10, which is dedicated to navigating button Variables.

Some properties are only used for some settings. For example, if you use Button-style:Icon with custom images for buttons, you can upload GIF files to these image Variables: Up-image, Next-image, Show-order-image, Home-image, Info-image, Privacypolicy-image, Help-image, Search-image, Index-image, Download-image, Register-image, Request-image, Email-image, and Mall-image.

Here are the Button properties you need to know about and what they do:

✔ **Button-style:** Select Text, Solid, Incised, or Icon (Custom images).

✔ **Nav-buttons:** Determines what buttons show up on your Nav-bar. I like to use Home, Show-order, Info, Empty, Contents, and sometimes Up and Next. I don't really use Help, Index, Register, Mall, Download, Search, Privacypolicy, Request, or Email.

✔ **Mall-url:** If you use the Mall button (which links to Yahoo! Shopping by default), you can change the URL here. I don't use this field unless I need the Mall-button to link to another related site.

✔ **Info-text:** This is the text on your Info button. For Top-buttons, I use "Info" because it's short. For Side-buttons, I use "Shipping Info" or "Shipping Information."

✔ **Request-text:** This is the text on your Catalog Request button. Don't use this button because the Catalog Request form is very clunky.

✔ **Privacypolicy-text:** This is the text on your Privacy Policy button. Don't use this button because Nav-bar real estate is so valuable. Instead, link to your privacypolicy.html page in your Final-text field with something like this:

```
<a href=privacypolicy.html>Privacy Guarantee</a>
```

Page properties

Variables under Page properties control the text in four fields. Really take advantage of your Final-text field and carefully choose how you present your contact information and links to shipping and ordering info.

- ✔ **Keywords:** Whatever words you put in here go in your Keywords meta-tags on your home page.

- ✔ **Head-tags:** Lets you put HTML code inside your Head-tags field. Use for CSS, for JavaScript, or to call external files, such as third-party tracking scripts. Please don't override this variable if you can help it because one day you'll have to undo all that hard work. Trust me. The Head-tags variable is only visible in the Advanced mode of Store Editor.

- ✔ **Final-text:** This text-field is at the bottom of every page. On standard template stores, I load this field with contact information, text links, a search box, trust symbols, and anything else I think customers need to see before they buy from me.

- ✔ **Address-phone:** A text field used on the home page if selected in the Page-elements field. See Chapter 11 for more on the home page.

Store properties

Variables in Store properties control the appearance of order functionality, such as the way prices look, the way options appear, and what text appears on your Order buttons. If you change only one thing on the Variables page, please change the Order-text from Order to Add To Cart. One guy who read my blog fixed his Order button and tripled his sales with no increase in traffic. Of course, your mileage may vary. . . .

- ✔ **Price-style:** Determines the formatting of prices. I prefer Normal or Big. Quiet does not show the price on section pages. Normal uses emphasis color for the color of price. Big uses Display-text for prices, which may be too much for some stores.

- ✔ **Regular-price-text:** Text that appears before the Price only when there's a Sale-price. I prefer Retail, MSRP, List, Catalog, or similar language.

- ✔ **Sale-price-text:** Text that appears before the Sale-price when there's a Sale-price. I prefer a call to action (a phrase telling someone to do something) or words that add value, such as "Order yours for," "Only," or "You pay," "Ships Free for only," "Save at," and so on.

- ✔ **Order-style:** Determines how options appear. Normal just lets the options fall where they may, depending on the length of the text. Two-line kicks all the options down to the second row. Multiline kicks each option down to a separate line, which looks better for stores with products that have a lots of options.

- ✔ **Secure-basket:** Determines whether the old cart is on a secure server. The default is No. If you select Yes, you move your Shopping Cart to a secure server. At first, this sounds like a pretty good idea, but it's not because you really need a secure server for Checkout pages, where customers enter personal information and credit-card info. Shopping Cart pages contain only product information. Secure servers are much, much slower than regular servers because they have to verify and encrypt every little thing, which only slows down the shopping process and cuts into your sales.

- ✔ **Compound-name:** Selecting Yes adds the section name to the product name in the Cart and Checkout.

- ✔ **Order-text:** Text that appears on the Order button on Product pages. Please, please, please change this text to Add To My Cart or Add To My Shopping Cart because it converts at a much higher rate than Buy or Order.

- ✔ **Show-order-text:** Text that appears on the Show-order button. I prefer Show Cart or Show My Cart. Make this wording match what you call the Cart (basket, order, whatever) in Order-text.

- ✔ **Families:** A field for legacy stores for cross-selling.

- ✔ **Cross-sell-text:** Text that appears in the cart above your cross-sell items. I prefer "Related items:" or "Customer also bought these products:".

- ✔ **Currency:** A currency symbol. Put the almighty $ here.

- ✔ **Thousands-mark:** Use a comma unless you're in Europe.

- ✔ **Decimal-mark:** Use the period unless you're in Europe.

- ✔ **Quantity-text:** Change to " for " (without the quotes, but with a space before and after). Text appears on quantity pricing. It looks better to me than a slash.

- ✔ **Minimum-order:** Set a dollar amount for your minimum order. I prefer to let my shipping cost fix piddly orders. If someone wants to order a $1.25 nameplate and pay $5.95 for shipping, so be it.

- ✔ **Minimum-quantity:** Set a minimum quantity for orders.

- ✔ **Availability:** Choose a global standard delivery time. You can override this variable on custom or drop-ship items.

✔ **Need-ship:** Set to No if you don't ship products (e-books, newsletter sub-scriptions, donations, and so on).

✔ **Need-bill:** Override to No on free items.

✔ **Need-payment:** Override to No for free items.

✔ **Personalization-charge:** Lets you charge for monograms.

✔ **Ypath:** Sets the category for Yahoo! Shopping.

✔ **Shopping-url:** Ancient field that's no longer used.

Custom variables

If you have custom RTML templates using custom fields, you can create new properties on the Variables page. Click the Define New Variable button, name your field, and select the field type, and your custom fields appear at the bottom of the Variables page. See Chapter 26 for more on RTML.

Chapter 10

Pushing All the Right Buttons

. . . .

In This Chapter

▶ Choosing where your navigation buttons go

▶ Discovering Function and Contents buttons

▶ Making your site look good and easy to use with navigation buttons

▶ Maximizing your site's most valuable real estate with navigation buttons

▶ Customizing your site with Icon buttons and custom graphics

. . . .

Navigation bars give form and function to your online store. These buttons provide navigation and define the look and layout of your Yahoo! Store. The buttons allow shoppers to navigate your Web store and buy things.

The Store Editor has built-in navigation button bars that link to your top-level categories (sections) and to major store functions, including your home page, info page, Shopping Cart/Checkout, and more.

Navigation buttons are easy to edit, configure, and customize to match the look and feel of your site. You can make a good-looking online store that's easy to navigate with just a few tweaks to the Variables page.

In this chapter, I'm really going to press your buttons. I explain the differences between top and side buttons, compare Contents and Function buttons, show you how to control which buttons appear and in what order, look at the various Variables that control the look and feel of standard buttons, and show you a few tricks to customize your store. Max out your Yahoo! Store with standard Store Editor templates without ever touching or customizing RTML (or even knowing what that means).

Navigating Yahoo! Store Buttons

Store navigation is extremely important because the easier you make it to navigate your store, the more products people look at. The more products people look at, the more stuff you sell. Standard Yahoo! Store navigation buttons are easy to create and edit. You use them to create a professional-looking, easy-to-navigate storefront. You control where the buttons appear on the page, which buttons appear, and in what order. You choose the button colors, the font and size of the button text, and even the words that appear on the buttons. You can even create a custom look by uploading graphic buttons.

Call them navigation bars, navigation buttons, Nav-bars, or button bars, but whatever the name, navigation buttons do many things:

- ✔ Navigation buttons are the most important design element on a standard Yahoo! Store. They determine the look of the store with button colors and fonts.

- ✔ Buttons frame your store, too. They determine the width of the store by the number of buttons in your navigation bar, text on the buttons, button-font-size, and spacing between buttons.

- ✔ Buttons brand the store on every page with your logo and company colors and fonts.

- ✔ Navigation buttons link to your major product categories — the top-level products and sections on your home page.

- ✔ Buttons link to Yahoo! Store's prebuilt function pages (info, show-order, search, and so on).

- ✔ Navigation buttons let your customers navigate your online store, but they also work in the Store Editor.

Figure 10-1 shows an example of Yahoo! Store with the Page-format set to Side-buttons side-by-side with the same store with the Page-format set to Top-buttons. Notice that the Side-buttons store has room for five or six section buttons, but the Top-buttons store has fewer section buttons with much less screen real estate eaten up by navigation. Everything's a trade-off!

Figure 10-1:
Compare
the same
store with
side buttons
and top
buttons.
The size of
your store
determines
whether
you choose
Side-buttons
or Top-
buttons for
your Page-
format.

Exploring the Different Types of Buttons

Yahoo! Store gives you two types of buttons:

- ✔ **Function buttons** link to the various prebuilt Yahoo! Store function pages, such as your Shopping Cart, your store's search page, its alphabetical index, and so on. Every Yahoo! Store has these function pages, whether you use them or not.

- ✔ **Contents buttons** are the buttons that link to your top-level navigation and mirror whatever sections or products you put on your home page.

Function buttons

Your Yahoo! Store's 15 Function buttons are the most important navigational elements of your store. Every single page of any online store needs a link to the home page, a link to customer service information, and access to the Shopping Cart. Store Editor's navigation buttons make this easy.

A Home button gets folks to the home page, which they can use as a starting point for navigating your store. An Info button links to your store's `info.html` page and lets customers read your terms and conditions, shipping methods, and payment methods and provides full contact information to give even the most skeptical customer a reason to trust and buy from you. A very prominent Show Order button links to your store's Shopping Cart and secure checkout, which makes shopping easy and reminds customers to buy what they stuck in their cart.

Paul Graham (the creator of Viaweb, now called Yahoo! Store) and his team did a really good job of building these store functions into the Editor software. The Store Editor makes it easy to add the functionality you want and remove the functionality you don't want because buttons are easy to turn on and off in the Variables page.

Variables are global settings that affect the entire site. For example, when you click the Variables button in the Edit Nav-bar, make the Button-color property 0 0 0 (black), and click the Update button, suddenly every single one of your pages has black buttons. Change your mind, click the Variables button, change it to 0 0 255 (blue), and click the Update button, and now, every single one of your pages has blue buttons. I talk about Variables ad nauseum in Chapter 9.

I'm very picky about what Function buttons I stick on my navigation bar. The screen real estate taken up by your navigation buttons is extremely valuable because every page of your store shows these buttons. The more clutter you have in your navigation bar, the harder it is for your customers to find what they want.

Of the 15 Function buttons, the only Function buttons I must use are Home, Show-Order, and Info. Sometimes I use the Empty button as a spacer between my Function buttons and my Contents buttons. Sometimes I use the Up and Next buttons for easier browsing if my store has Top-buttons.

Usually, I prefer to have my Page-format variable set to Side-buttons. Under Variables, I set my Nav-bar to show Home (1), Show-Order (2), Info (3), Empty (4), and Contents (5). I don't use the rest of the Yahoo! Store Function buttons, but I do link to some of the function pages at the bottom of every page in my footer (found in the Final-text field on the Variables page).

Figure 10-2 shows all 15 Store Editor Function buttons on a Top-buttons store in an alphabetical list as follows. Notice that just a space appears in the Empty button spot.

Figure 10-2:
There are 15
Function
buttons:
Download,
Email,
Empty,
Help, Home,
Index, Info,
Mall, Next,
Privacy-
policy,
Register,
Request,
Search,
Show-order,
and Up.

Download Email Help   {Title}   Index {Info-text} 🐾 Next {Privacypolicy-text} Register {Request-text} Search {Show-order-text} Up

✔ **Download:** This button is for stores who sell downloadable products, such as PDF files, MP3 files, and so on. The Download button links to the Order Confirmation page, which displays a link to download the file after someone has made a purchase.

✔ **Email:** This button creates a `mailto:` link to the e-mail address entered under the Email field under Variables.

Clicking a `mailto:` link automatically opens the default e-mail software on a PC. I prefer to have the e-mail address at the bottom of every page by sticking a text link in the Final-text field under Variables like this:

```
<a href=mailto:email@yourdomain.com>email@yourdomain.com</a>
```

✔ **Empty:** This creates an empty space on the navigation bar, which works as a divider between your Function buttons and Contents buttons.

On Top-buttons stores, I use it as the second-to-last button to separate the Up and Next buttons from the other Function buttons for easier browsing.

✔ **Help:** This button links to the Yahoo! Store Help For Buyers Ordering page, which tells shoppers how to find something, how to buy something, what to do when problems occur, and more.

✔ **Home:** This button is a link to your home page or `index.html`. When you have Side-buttons, the word Home appears on the button. When you have Top-buttons, the text in your Variables: Title field appears on the button. You can also upload a custom image (such as a logo) to the Home-image field under Variables. If you don't upload a custom image, you control the look of the home-button with the fields home-button-color, home-button-font, home-button-text-color, and home-button-text-size.

✔ **Index:** This button links to the alphabetical index, or `ind.html`, page. Every Yahoo! Store has one whether or not it has the button.

✔ **Info:** This button links to your `info.html` page, where you put your contact info, shipping information, and terms and conditions. The text on this button comes from the Info-text variable, and the default text is Info.

✔ **Mall:** This button links to the URL in your Mall-URL field under variables. By default, that URL points to Yahoo! Shopping and displays a Yahoo! Shopping logo. Replace this logo by uploading a new image to the Mall-image field under Variables.

✔ **Next:** This button links to the next object in the Contents field of this object's parent section. For example, if you were on the first product inside a section of 20 products, clicking the Next button takes you to the second product. The Next button is a great way to make your products and sections easier to browse.

✔ **Privacypolicy:** This button links to your `privacypolicy.html` page. The text on this button comes from the Privacypolicy-text setting on the Variables page, and the default text is Privacy Policy.

Yahoo! requires you to have a page that explains how you collect, use, and distribute private customer information. I prefer to not use this button and have a text link in the footer of every page by using the Final-text field under Variables. Protecting your customers' privacy is extremely important, but a link to your privacy policy page belongs at the bottom of the page, not in your navigation bar. To link to your `privacypolicy.html` page, copy this code:

```
<a href=privacypolicy.html>Privacy</a>
```

✔ **Register:** This button links to the register login screen, which is still used by some ancient Yahoo! Store owners (like me). The new Checkout Manager is not compatible with the old Register function, so don't use it.

✔ **Request:** This button links to your Catalog-Request form. Because you can't do a lot of customization with your catalog request form, I seldom use this button or the form. The text on this button comes from the Request-text setting under Variables, and the default text is Request Catalog.

✔ **Search:** This button links to `nsearch.html`, which is the default search page on every Yahoo! Store. I never use this button because I prefer to have search functionality on every store page. I stick a snippet of code in the Final-text field under Variables by placing this little bit of HTML code, which calls a search box:

```
<form name=vw-form method=post
action="http://search.store.yahoo.com/cgi-bin/nsearch">
<input type=hidden name=vwcatalog value=storeaccountnamehere>
<input name=query type=text size=30><input type=submit value=Search>
</form>
```

✔ **Show-order:** This button links to your Shopping Cart at `http://order.store.yahoo.com/cgi-bin/wg-order?youraccountnamehere` or the new checkout Shopping Cart. The text on this button comes from the Variable Show-order-text, and the default text is Show Order. I like to make my Show-order-text say Show My Cart.

✔ **Up:** This button links to the parent page of the current page you're on. For example, on a product page, this button links up to the section page. On a top-level section page, the Up button links to the home page. If the current page has no parent page, this button does nothing. I like to use Up and Next buttons on Top-Buttons stores.

Contents buttons

Figure 10-3 shows the home page of a store with six objects (sections and products) on the home page and on the navigation buttons. When you create a product or a section on your home page, Yahoo! Store automatically creates a button that links to that page in your navigation bar. The text on the button comes from the Name field of the item or section. Notice that the navigation buttons are in the same order as IDs in the Contents field.

These navigation buttons are called Contents buttons because the object-IDs of these sections or products are inside the Contents field of your home page. You can see the Contents field of your `index.html` page by browsing to your home page and clicking the Edit button.

For example, when you're on the home page and click the Section button in the Edit Nav-bar to create a new section, Store Editor automatically adds that top-level section to the navigation bar. If you create a product on the home page by clicking the Item button, that action also creates a button linking to that product on the navigation bar.

Figure 10-3:
Six Contents
buttons
appear on
the home
page. Any
pages you
create or
move to
your home
page
become
top-level
navigation
Contents
buttons.

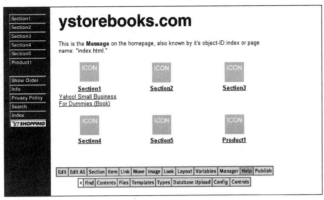

Evaluate which section pages are your most valuable real estate. Your top-level sections are usually the pages that get the most page views. I talk a lot more about deciding which five to seven sections to feature in your navigation in Chapter 13.

You have to click the Publish button on the home page in Edit mode after making any changes in the Store Editor to make the published site show the results of all your labor. If you don't, you'll be the only one who can see you new, improved navigation!

Choosing Page-Format: Top Buttons or Side Buttons

Yahoo! Store lets you put your navigation buttons either on top of the store, or on the left side of the store. You control this placement with the property Page-format, which is found on the Variables page. Side buttons and Top buttons are very different looks for your store, and each has pluses and minuses:

- ✔ Side buttons visually anchor the page to the left and give you plenty of room to list your major categories down the left-hand side (up to 30 buttons, in total).
- ✔ Top buttons center the page and take up much less real estate, but give you virtually no room to promote categories.

In this section, I talk about what I like and don't like about both settings.

Side buttons

When you open your Yahoo! Store account, your Store Editor's Page-format is set to Side-buttons by default. Side buttons are pretty hard to screw up, which is probably why it's the default setting. (I've seen some people do some pretty horrible things to Yahoo! Store navigation bars!)

Here are several solutions for Side-buttons stores:

- ✔ **Show how many types of cool things you sell.** Maximize your Side-buttons real estate with this Side-buttons recipe: I prefer to have the Nav-buttons field show Home (1), Info (2), Show-order (3), Empty (4), and Contents (5). Sometimes I stick the Next (5) button right after all the Contents buttons for easier browsing.

- ✔ **Use short names for top-level products and sections.** Really long section names make your navigation bar too wide. Because the text in the Name field of each top-level section or item is also used for the text on Contents buttons, you need to use relatively short names for these sections or products.

- ✔ **Show your logo at the top of your navigation.** Create a custom graphic with your logo, 1-800 number, and the word (Home) about 175 pixels wide. Upload this image as the Home-image under Variables. This Home-image automatically appears instead of the Home buttons whether or not you use the Icon setting under Button-Type on the Variables page. Make sure that the names of your sections aren't longer than your logo is wide.

- ✔ **Make sure that your store is visually balanced.** When you use Side-Buttons, your site can look lopsided. This unbalanced appearance is especially true if you use a very dark color for your Button-Color or Button-Edge-Color. Experiment with lighter versions of the color to see what looks best.

Top buttons

With top buttons, the width of the navigation buttons determines the width of the site. I like my top buttons to be no wider than 770 pixels and to match the width of my Name-image. The width of Top-buttons navigation is determined by many factors, including how many function or Contents buttons you show, which buttons you show, the text on the buttons, the font size of the text of the buttons, the Button-padding, and the Button-edge-width.

Keep these tidbits in mind for tip-top Top-buttons:

✔ To keep your site less than 800 pixels wide, you have to make some pretty hard choices about which buttons get that very valuable real estate. I prefer to show Info (1), Contents (2) with two or three categories at most, Show-order (3), Empty (4), Up (5), and Next (6).

For example, if you have 17 sections on your home page and you use every single Function button, you can wind up with a six-foot-wide Yahoo! Store.

✔ Figure 10-4 shows that Top buttons don't need a Home button if you upload an image to the Name-image under Variables. This graphic appears above your navigation bar, links to your home page, and is perfect for branding your site with a logo as well as using for navigation. Simply add the word *Home* to your graphic, and you have an instant Home button! For example, type **Home** in 8-point Helvetica type right below your logo in the `Name-image.gif` file to make it pull double-duty as a branding and navigational element. Not using the Home button frees up extra real estate on a Top-buttons navigation bar for an additional Contents button, or maybe for a slightly larger font for button text to make the buttons easier to read.

✔ Top-buttons make it easy to use Up and Next Function buttons because you can stick that Next button as the last button in the upper-right corner. It's so much easier to browse from product to product, almost like a slide show. You just keep clicking that Next button. The easier it is to navigate your store, the more products people look at. The more products people look at, the more stuff you sell. It's that easy!

Figure 10-4:
Top buttons take up less screen real estate and are better for stores with fewer products and sections.

Editing Your Navigation Buttons

Deciding which buttons are on your navigation bar is actually harder than editing the buttons. You actually control the order of navigation buttons and which buttons appear on almost every page from three different settings in two different places in the Store Editor: the Nav-bar property under Variables and the Contents field and Button property on the Edit page of the home page:

- ✔ The Nav-bar property on the Variables page lists all the Function buttons available (Info, Show-cart, Index, and so on), enables you to control which Function buttons appear, and lets you determine button order for every page but the home page. To the right of the property is a Change button. Clicking the Change button pulls up an edit list, which is an alphabetical list of all the buttons. (A little field appears off to the right of each button name.) Number the buttons you want to appear in the order you want them to appear. Any button without a number doesn't show up.

- ✔ The home page's Buttons property acts just like a home-page-only Nav-bar to let you have different Function buttons on the home page. For example, you probably don't want a Home button on your home page.

- ✔ You also control where the block of Contents buttons appears by where you sequence the Contents in the Nav-bar edit list, but the order of those buttons is determined on the home page by the order of the IDs in your Contents field.

Working with Function buttons

To add, remove, or change the order of Function buttons (for every page but the home page), follow these steps:

1. **Click the Variables button in the Edit Nav-bar.**

   The global Variables page appears.

2. **Scroll down to the Button Properties section to the Nav-Bar setting.**

   You see a list of which buttons are showing (separated by commas).

3. **Click the Change button.**

   The Nav-bar's edit list, an alphabetical list of all the buttons you can have in a Nav-bar, appears.

   Each button has a position field to the right of it that is either empty or has a number in it. When the position field is empty, the button doesn't show up. When the position field has a number in it, that's the position of the button. When the Contents property has a number by it, all the Contents buttons are in that position. With an edit list, you control which elements appear and the order in which they appear. You can use some, all, or none of the buttons.

4. **Type the following numbers into the fields to the right of the following button names and delete any numbers next to any of the other buttons: Home (1), Show-order (2), Contents (3), and Info (4); then click the Update button.**

   The Variables page reappears, and if you scroll down, you can see that the Nav-buttons property shows the names of the buttons you selected, in the order you selected. At this point, you can either change the Nav-buttons settings again, click the Cancel button at the top of the page to abort the whole thing, or click the Update button to update your buttons.

5. **Scroll to the top of the Variables page and click the Update button to accept the changes.**

   Your page appears, and the Nav-bar displays the Home button; the Show-order button; the Contents buttons: (whatever pages have IDs in the Contents field of the home page); and the Info button.

Fiddling with Contents buttons

Contents buttons display on the Nav-bar in the same order that the sections or products appear on the home page, which is determined by the order of the IDs inside the Contents field of home page. Change the order of these object-IDs, and you change the order of the Contents buttons in the navigation bar.

Note: You need to be in the Store Editor's Advanced mode to see the Contents field. You can tell that you're in Advanced mode because you have a two-row Edit Nav-bar. If not, click the little red arrow to the right of the Edit Nav-bar.

To change the order of your Contents buttons, all you have to do is change the order of the object-IDs inside the Contents field of the home page: Edit the page, type the IDs in the Contents field in the order you want them to appear, and click the Update button. For example, say that you have five sections on your home page and in your Nav-bar, and you want to do two things: remove section 4 and make the fifth section the first button.

Right now, the Contents field of your home page shows the following:

```
section1 section2 section3 section4 section5
```

All you have to do is change the text inside the Contents field to this and click the Update button:

```
section5 section1 section2 section3
```

Remember that you have to click the Publish button on the home page in Edit mode to make the published site reflect any changes you make in Store Editor.

Like many things in Store Editor, the home page is a little weird. and I talk about its various quirks and peculiarities a lot more in Chapter 11. The home page uses a different template (Home.), which makes the page display differently. The home page also generates completely different navigation buttons than the rest of your store using the Buttons property. Buttons control which Function buttons appear on the home page and the order of those buttons on the home page's navigation bar and acts just like its cousin, the Nav-buttons property (from the Variables page).

Access the Buttons property by clicking the Edit button on the home page. Click the Change button for an edit list of the available buttons and their position. Number the buttons that you want to appear in the order you want and update them. It's pretty straightforward.

If you've made any changes to the Button settings on your home page, editing your home-page buttons can be very confusing, especially if your home-page Button property doesn't show the contents anymore. I prefer that the navigation on my home page looks like every other page, so I make sure that my Button settings on the home page match my Nav-bar settings under Variables.

Overriding Variables is fine for a few notable exceptions, but please, please, please, do not override variables as a design strategy. A few years ago, I spent about half of my time on a Yahoo! Store facelift project removing overwritten variables.

Editing the text on the buttons

Editing the text on Contents buttons is really easy because the text on the button is the text in the Name field of the section (or item or link) on the home page.

Editing the text on function buttons is almost as easy because you just go to Variables and change some text. You can change text on the Info-text, Privacypolicy-text, Request-text, or Show-order-text. The text on the Home button is "Home" when Page-format is set to Side-buttons. The text on the Home button is determined by the Title field under Variables when Page-format is set to Top-buttons. The rest of the Function buttons cannot be changed, but you don't need to use most of them anyway!

Figure 10-5 shows the section page's Top-buttons with the renamed function pages.

Figure 10-5:
Edited text on navigation button bar.

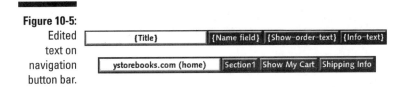

Editing the Appearance of Navigation Buttons

You control the appearance of your store's navigation buttons on the global Variables page with several different parameters. You determine which Function buttons appear and their order with the Nav-buttons fields. Total customized looks are possible by uploading custom graphics to the Icon fields for each button.

In print production, 72 points equal an inch. Size your text anywhere from 8 points to 25 points, depending on what looks good for the font you choose. Make sure that the font size is large enough to read but not so large as to screw up your site by making the Nav-bar wider than about 250 pixels for Side-buttons stores or 770 pixels for Top-buttons stores.

Button-Styles

Here are the basics about selecting Button-styles:

✔ Choose the Button-style you want: Text, Solid, Incised, or Icon. Figure 10-6 shows top buttons with three different Button-styles: Text, Solid, and Incised.

 • Text buttons are flat with no definition.

 • Solid buttons have raised buttons with drop shadows, but the button-text is flat.

 • Incised buttons are raised like Solid buttons, but the text is incised or cut into the buttons to look more three-dimensional.

If you want people to use your navigation buttons, make the buttons look clickable. That's pretty easy! I prefer Solid or Incised buttons because clickable-looking 3-D buttons tend to get clicked.

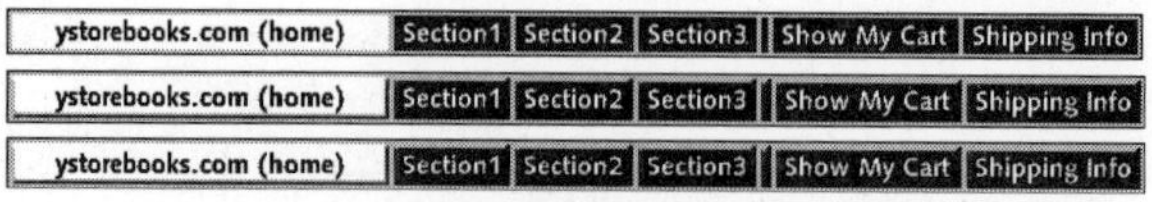

Figure 10-6:
The three
standard
navigation
Button-
styles are
Text, Solid,
and Incised.

ystorebooks.com (home)	Section1	Section2	Section3	Show My Cart	Shipping Info
ystorebooks.com (home)	Section1	Section2	Section3	Show My Cart	Shipping Info
ystorebooks.com (home)	Section1	Section2	Section3	Show My Cart	Shipping Info

✔ Text, Solid, and Incised styles are controlled by several Variables settings and show the text from the Name field of the sections on your home page.

✔ The Icon Button-style lets you upload your own graphics for much more control over your store's look. The Icon or thumbnail image of a section becomes the graphic for each Contents button. Upload custom images to the Variables page for every single Function button, (Home-image, Show-order-image, Info-image, and so on).

Home button variables

Home button variables work the same way that other button variables work. If you don't upload a logo to your Home-image, you can make your Home button have a slightly different Home-button-color, Home-button-text-color, Home-button-font, and Home-button-font-size.

I recommend uploading a logo to your Home-image, but if you really want to use these four variables, make your Home button stand out! Make your Home button the exact opposite of your other button colors or make the home-button-font the bold version of the font. Another option is to make the home-button-font-color a slightly darker or brighter color than your regular buttons.

Button spacing variables

You can build better buttons with these variables:

✔ **Button-padding:** The space in pixels inside the buttons between the button text and the edge of the button.

✔ **Button-edge-width:** The space (in pixels) between the buttons on all four sides. The default is 0.

✔ **Button-edge-color:** With Top-buttons, if there's no Button-edge-width, the Button-edge-color doesn't show. With Side-buttons, the Button-edge-color determines the color of the left stripe behind the navigation buttons. Make your Button-edge-color slightly lighter than the Button-color to get the buttons to pop off the page.

Creating a Custom Look with Icon Buttons

Yahoo! Store gives you some very cool options using Icon buttons to get a custom look for your store without ever touching RTML (see Chapter 26). First, you build your store with standard navigation buttons and then use that layout as the foundation for a design using custom Icon buttons. It doesn't matter whether you use top or side buttons.

Take a screen shot of an existing Yahoo! Store and build a custom façade right on top of the foundation with your graphics software. After the design is complete in your graphics software, all you do is save it as a GIF file, reopen it, and chop up the buttons for each Contents and Function button. Then upload the images to the Icon fields for each section and Function button and switch the Variable Button-style to Icon, and you're all done.

Figure 10-7 shows you the same navigation bar in four different phases. First you see the standard navigation bar, where the Page-format is set to Top-buttons. The Nav-bar is set to Home, Contents (with three section pages), Info, Show-order, Up, and Next. Button-style is set to Incised. These settings create a pretty standard navigation bar.

The second image shows the same navigation bar as seen in a graphics program with a 50-x-750-pixel rectangle drawn around it and with vertical lines showing the different buttons.

The third image is the same navigation bar with the vertical button dividers shifted around a little to give less space to the Home button and spread the real estate around a little. The fourth image shows the final design in the graphics program, and the white space makes it easy to see the different buttons.

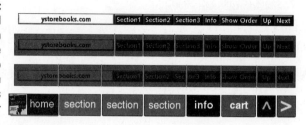

Custom Function buttons

You can create and upload a custom graphic to each Function button on the Variables page, including Up-image, Next-image, Show-order-image, Home-image, Info-image, Privacypolicy-image, Help-image, Search-image, Index-image, Download-image, Register-image, Request-image, Email-image, and Mall-image.

Custom Contents buttons

You can also create and upload custom graphics for each Contents button for your custom Icon navigation bar. Simply upload the custom Icon button to the Icon field on each top-level section on your home page. I think you should know the following before creating a custom look with eye-popping Icons:

- ✔ When you select Icon as the Button-style, Yahoo! Store automatically puts the Icon for that section where the button goes. If you don't upload an image to the Icon field on a section, the Store Editor places the thumbnail of the image for that section, which can look really strange.

- ✔ If the section has no image uploaded to the Image or Icon field, then the Store Editor centers the text in the name field just like a flat-looking text button.

When you use Icon buttons, you really need to create custom graphics that fit the navigation bar and upload them to the Icon field for each section, or your store will look really weird.

Making custom icons

Creating custom icons can be kind of complicated. Here are a few more concepts to consider:

✔ All your buttons have to line up just right. Before you start designing buttons, figure out exactly how much screen real estate you're willing to give up for your navigation. Your navigation needs to be large enough to be easy to use, but no larger. Make your Icon buttons around 50 to 75 pixels tall, and make sure that the total width of the Nav-bar is somewhere between 750 and 780 pixels. Sometimes overly ambitious custom navigation pushes the Order button below the first screen shot on product pages, which is bad!

✔ I like to take a screen shot of my site with simple text buttons and design custom Icon buttons on top of those text buttons. I use Paintshop Pro, which is a poor man's version of Adobe Photoshop. I create a single GIF image, compress the heck out of it, chop it up into the various Contents and Function buttons, and then upload it.

Most shoppers really need to be able to do only three things: browse back to the home page, read up on your shipping information page, and then finally, get back to their Shopping Cart so that they can check out. The Store Editor makes it easy to add the buttons you want and make them look they way you want without knowing a lick of HTML.

Navigation Bar Resources

Building better buttons can be an ambitious undertaking, so take a look at these resources for more info:

✔ Yahoo! Store Help page on navigation button bars:

```
http://help.yahoo.com/help/us/store/edit/edit-24.html
```

✔ Yahoo! Merchant Solutions "Getting Started Guide," Chapter 6.

✔ *Don't Make Me Think,* Second Edition, by Steve Krug (New Riders Press, 2005). This is one of my favorite books on usability, and Steve's thoughts on navigation and buttons are second only to those from Jakob Nielsen.

Chapter 11

Designing All Kinds of Pages

. . . .

In This Chapter

▶ Producing other pages that sell

▶ Homing in on the perfect front page

▶ Selling with section pages

▶ Informing customers with friendly FAQ pages

. . . .

*W*hen most folks think of designing an online store, they think of producing product pages. While products get all the attention (and sales), shoppers would never make it to the product pages or be able to buy without the other types of pages that organize these products and make shopping possible: the home page, section pages, shipping info page, Shopping Cart, internal store search results page, and several other built-in function pages.

Your home page is the most important page on your site. Designing a home page is hard enough, but wrestling with a totally different template only compounds the confusion. Your info page is second only to the home page for giving customers the confidence to buy. You can display products on section pages in so many different ways that it sometimes makes my head hurt.

In this chapter, I share with you what I've learned in eight-plus years of using the Yahoo! Store Editor to create a professional-looking, easy-to-use, customer-friendly merchandising machine of a home page that search engines love. I show you how to set up sections that sell, give you the inside scoop on info pages, and help you format your Function pages: Shopping Cart, search results page, privacy policy, and the alphabetical index.

Introducing the Home Page

Your home page is the most important page on your Yahoo! Store. It needs to load fast, look good, and tell prospective customers who you are, what you do, and how they can find what they're looking for within seconds. If your home page doesn't communicate effectively, you'll lose valuable traffic and sales as browsers bail from your store.

Figure 11-1 shows you how a home page serves three completely different functions: branding, merchandising, and customer service.

- ✔ **Branding:** Your home page must present your company as a credible, professional store to give shoppers the confidence to buy something.

- ✔ **Merchandising:** Your home page organizes and displays products three different ways for three different types of shoppers: featured specials on the front page for frustrated shoppers who need some guidance, a store search for someone who knows exactly what she's looking for, and navigation links and buttons for category clickers and browsers.

- ✔ **Customer service:** Your home page should offer fast and friendly customer service with text links to help pages, shipping information, and FAQ pages. It should also give good contact info so that customers with problems can get a real person on the phone ASAP!

Figure 11-1: Your home page is the most important page on your Yahoo! Store.

Optimizing begins at home

Your home page is also your most powerful weapon in search engine optimization (SEO). (I dive into SEO in Chapter 19.) If you haven't already done the following, these next three points will pay for the price of this book a hundred times over:

- ✔ **Tweak your title tag for top rankings.** Most of the links pointing to your store point to your home page, which means that your home page has the highest link popularity (search-engine power) of any of your pages. Because the title tag is widely accepted as the most important on-page element for SEO, it's super-important that the title tag of your home page contain your most valuable keywords to improve your rankings in the search engines.

Using your company name or domain name as the only text in your home page's title tag is bad, second only to not even having a title tag at all. A good title tag needs four or five of your top keyword phrases arranged in a compelling sentence. Your home page's title tag comes from the text inside your Page-title field on the home page. For example, my page's title tag on `www.YstoreBooks.com` is *Yahoo! Stores For Dummies: Yahoo! Merchant Solutions and Store Editor tips. No RTML required at YstoreBooks.com.*

✔ **Use your best keywords in text on your home page.** Use the Message field and Intro-text fields to write an overview paragraph of your business, but don't just spew out a list of keywords. Establish your expertise. Write about what you sell, why you sell it, and why folks should buy from you. Compose two- to three-sentence paragraphs summarizing your section pages, paste the text in the Abstract field on each section, and then display these Abstracts on the home page.

✔ **Link to your most popular product and section pages on the home page with descriptive anchor text.** Use converting keywords as the *anchor text* or *link text* (words inside the links). These linked words tell search engines what these pages are about and get your pages higher rankings in Google, MSN, and Yahoo! search engines. Having popular keywords link to popular sections on your home page helps customers get to what they're searching for even faster.

Designing your home page

You want your home page to match the look of the rest of your site, but don't use the exact same layout because you don't want it mistaken for just another page. The Store Editor's home page template (home.) is structurally different from other Store Editor pages and gives you a lot more flexibility than the regular (page.) template. I wish Yahoo! would give the regular section and product pages the versatility of the home page template (hint, hint!). The key to the layout and design of the home page is found in using the various Page-elements: Address, Buttons, Contents, Final-text, Image, Intro-text, Message, Name, Search, and Specials.

Figure 11-2 shows the Edit page for the home page. You can see most of the home page's fields, including the Page-elements setting, which is an edit list just like the Nav-bar setting (see Chapter 10). Click the Change button to the far right of the Page-elements label on the home page to see (or change) this list of elements and their position. Place a number in an element's position field to make the element show on the home page in the order of the position number.

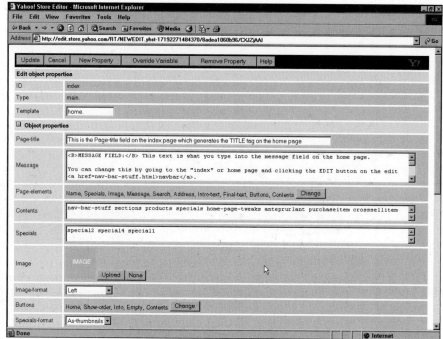

Figure 11-2:
The Edit
page for
the home
page is
different
from every
other Edit
page.

Keep in mind that elements with empty position fields don't appear. Elements with the same number display in alphabetical order. These on/off switches on elements give you an incredible amount of control of the appearance of your home page.

Think of Page-elements as rearrangeable chunks of content:

- **Text chunks:** Intro-text, Message, Address/Phone, and Final-text fields where you can insert limited bits of HTML.

- **Image chunks:** Image and Name (which either calls the Name-image graphic or the big ol' ugly Banner-text) where you can upload images.

- **Contents chunks:** Thumbnails and links to pages with IDs in the Specials and Contents fields. Specials can either match the appearance of the Contents set on the home page's very own Columns/Contents-elements/ Contents-format or have their own formatting as images with the setting As-thumbnails. Read extra-special details in Chapter 13.

✔ **Other chunks:** Search and Buttons (if you have a Page-format:Top-buttons store).

The settings on your global Variables page still determine most of the look and feel of the store, even on the home page. Page-format controls whether you have navigation buttons on the top or side of your store. The text in Final-text and Address/Phone fields come from the Variables page.

What's different about the home page is that some settings are independent of the Variables settings of the same name (or similar names) so that the home page can have a unique look:

✔ **Buttons:** Instead of using the navigation button bar from the Variable setting Nav-bar, the home page uses the Buttons setting on the home page. Buttons works the same way as Nav-bar with an Edit position list to determine which buttons show up and how they are ordered. Chapter 10 is all about the buttons.

Different buttons on the home page make sense for several reasons. Home-page visitors need different navigation than shoppers deep within your site. Most folks visit your home page as an entry point to your site or use your home page to start a new task. Also, you really don't need a link to your home page on your home page.

✔ **Contents (and Specials):** The home page has its own Contents-format, Contents-elements, and Columns settings. These settings control how the contents appear (and sometimes the Specials), and they work the same way their counterparts on the Variables page do. Remember, top-level sections appear on the home page because their ID is in the Contents field of the home page.

Maximizing home-page Page-elements

Prioritize the various elements on your home page. Figure 11-3 shows an example of how you can present your most important information in the first 500 pixels, the first screen shot of the page (also called *above the fold*). Any content for search engines or just less important information goes down lower on the page.

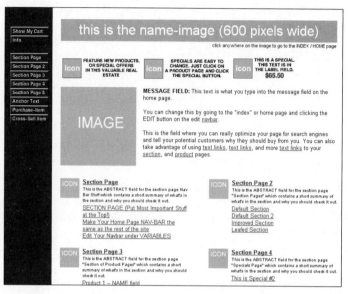

Figure 11-3:
This top
page of the
Ystorebooks
sample
home page
shows the
Name,
Specials,
Image, and
Message
elements in
the first
screen shot.

Here's how I make a homerun-hitting home page:

- ✔ **Buttons:** When I have a store with Top-buttons navigation, I place my buttons at the very top of my home page for a slightly different look than my interior pages.

  Make sure that you don't have Home or Up/Next buttons because they don't work on the home page.

- ✔ **Logo/Branding:** At the top of the page, I like to have my Name-image graphic, which is usually 600 x 100 pixels, with logo and tagline, 1-800 number, accepted methods of payment, physical address, and any other trust symbols I can stick in there without crowding it up too much. See Chapter 21 for more on creating trust to convert more shoppers into buyers.

- ✔ **Specials:** After the logo, I like to have a single row of product specials featuring something new, something at a crazy clearance price, and my bestsellers, which I try to rotate on a regular basis. Use Specials-format:As-thumbnails.

- ✔ **Image and Text:** Next, I use my Image (Image-format:Left) and Intro-text for some customer-friendly text with HTML links to both products and customer service sections of the site. This text is both customer-friendly and search-engine friendly. This text and image block is usually about 200 pixels tall. Upload a 200-pixel-tall JPEG for your Image graphic to make sure that it fits the page and loads faster than a larger-sized image.

✔ **Search:** I like to show the Search box after the Image and Text (see the preceding entry). You can do this by calling Search in the Page-elements field of your home page, but that puts the search box aligned to the left, which looks a little cockeyed.

A better way to put a search box on your home page without custom programming is to paste this code into the Message field:

```
<div align=center><form method=get
          action=http://search.store.yahoo.com/cgi-bin/nsearch>
<input type=hidden name=catalog value=youraccount>
<input name=query type=text size=30><input type=submit value="Search">
</form></div>
```

Replace *your account* with your Yahoo! Merchant Solutions account name or number. For example, my www.ystorebooks.com account is *yhst-17192271484370,* but my legacy account for www.robsnell.com is webstore-design.

✔ **More Text:** After the search box, I have a small bit of text in my Message field and then show my Contents.

✔ **Contents:** The home-page template is really cool because it lets you display your contents differently than on section pages or leafed pages by using its very own Contents-format/Contents-elements/Columns settings.

I usually choose a "show-'em-what-you-got layout," where I set Columns to 1, Contents-format to Ell or Wrap, and Contents-elements to show Screen-text-title (which is the Name), Image (the thumbnail), Abstract (if there is one), and Contents (which lists all the subcategories and products within each section). Make sure that each top-level navigation section page has a couple of descriptive paragraphs in the Abstract field on each of those sections.

In addition, here is some other home-page stuff I forgot to squeeze in here:

✔ Scratch a long-winded welcome message. No one is going to read it. Think short and sweet, peppered with text links to products and info pages.

✔ Use a professional photograph featuring a person using what you sell. Advanced users shouldn't use the Image field because it's not a clickable link to whatever you're selling. Instead, upload a smallish JPEG image (200 x 200 pixels or so) to your hosting account and use the Intro-text field for the HTML. Make it a clickable link going to the product shown in the photo.

✔ The Specials field shows all the IDs for items that you've selected to be featured on the front page with the Special/Not Special button. You can also type or cut and paste IDs into this field for faster editing.

Selling with Super Section Pages

A *section page* is really any regular page that doesn't have an Order button. Sections usually have items (or other sections) inside them. I have several kinds of section pages: top-level navigation/master section pages, subsection pages, and "empty" section pages for additional content pages, such as articles, buyers' guides, and reviews.

Top-level section pages usually contain subsection pages

I like having two different looks for section pages: leafed and not leafed. Figure 11-4 shows how I don't mind my *leafed* section pages resembling my product pages. A page is leafed when the Leaf setting on the Edit page is set to Yes, which changes the way the page looks and how the products display. Instead of using the product display settings under Variables, the template uses the leafed-product display settings under the Config page. Leafed pages just give you another way to show products on pages.

Figure 11-4:
This leafed section page shows how you can have two different looks to section pages when you set Leaf=Yes and adjust the leafed settings under Config.

A good example of a leafed section page is www.ystorebooks.com/nav-bar-stuff.html, which shows a section page of sections. Notice how showing the Abstract gives you more information about what a section is about.

Here's how I like to design my section pages:

- ✔ **I like these master section pages to have nice Caption fields.** These paragraphs of text illustrate my product knowledge and expertise, pointing out the key features that solve customer problems.

- ✔ **I feature my bestselling products with text links inside the Caption field.** This text is search-engine friendly, as well as user friendly, to drive traffic to my better-selling items.

- ✔ **Sometimes I use the Abstract field on subsections contained in these pages.** This text points out the differences between the subsections, as well as adds search-engine-friendly text to my master section pages.

- ✔ **I also don't like to use the Image field on a section page.** Images tend to push the products down lower on the page. If I don't want an image, but I still want that section to have a thumbnail image, I usually upload an image to the Icon field.

- ✔ **Another way to have image-free sections is to upload an image, but not show it on the section page.** Override the Head-elements variable and set it to show Display-text-title (only) by deselecting the Image.

- ✔ **To get a different look for my master section pages, I change the Leaf setting from No to Yes.** Under Config, I set Leaf-contents-elements to Image, Screen-title-text, Abstract, Contents, and Price. I set Leaf-contents-format to Ell, and I set Leaf-Columns to 1.

The Leaf setting is also a bit confusing for some folks, but leaf it up to me to explain it: You can tell whether a page is leafed by how product thumbnails look on that page. For example, on my mom's site, I can tell that a page is set to Leaf=No when I see five product thumbnails per row with the links underneath. I know a page is leafed (Leaf=Yes) when I see one product thumbnail per row with the link to the right of the thumbnail, a brief text description of the item, and text links of the contents underneath that.

Items created with the Item button are leafed by default (the Leaf setting is set to Yes). Items created both on the Contents page via create New Object and items created with database uploads are also automatically leafed. Here's where I get a little crazy: I like to leaf some section pages, too, especially when they contain subsections and not just products.

Because I also have the element Contents selected in the Contents-elements variable, section pages show thumbnails and links to the products, as well as links to all the pages inside those pages. For example, if you were on the Pets section page containing links to the Dogs, Cats, Rabbits, Lizards, and Snakes subsections, links to all the subsection pages appear so that you can jump straight to pages about Great Danes, German Shepherds, or Yorkshire Terriers.

In theory, the average visitor is going to look at four or five pages on your Web site. The reality is that certain customers look at 15 or 20 pages, while other visitors bail out after the first page view. You want to do everything you can to minimize the number of clicks it takes for a visitor to reach your product pages.

Subsections contain products

I want my section pages to show the wide variety of products that I carry, and Figure 11-5 shows how subsection pages that display tons of products allow me to show the depth of my inventory in the first screen shot.

Figure 11-5: This subsection page shows how I like to display more products in the average screen shot.

Here are a few tips for working with section pages:

✔ **I really like to show the price on section pages.** Displaying the price on section pages keeps folks from having to drill down to the product level to see the price and then come back up to keep browsing.

✔ **Sometimes I place my products in descending order by price.** Because higher-priced items appear before lower-priced items, more expensive items have a better shot at getting seen.

✔ **I like to feature my bestselling product in the upper-right corner of my section page.** For example, if I have a five-column layout, the fifth product is usually my bestseller because that's the position that gets all the clicks. Your eye goes straight to it.

Here's what I do on the Variables page to format section pages with items:

- ✔ I set Contents-elements to show Image, Screen-title-text, and Price.

- ✔ I set Columns to 5 to show five thumbnails on a row.

- ✔ I set Contents-format to Vertical, which centers the Name under the thumbnail and centers the Price and/or Sale-price under that. This way, I can display the largest number of products in the first screen shot. A good example is at `www.ystorebooks.com/products.html`, where I can see 20 products above the fold on my monitor. The more products shoppers can see on the first screen shot, the more likely they are to drill down to the actual product level.

Use empty section pages for content

You can also use empty section pages for content pages, buyers' guides, comparison charts, and reviews. All you have to do is type your text into the Caption field and upload a picture to the Image field. These content pages don't have to contain any products or subsections.

If you need to have super-long descriptions about your product, sometimes it's better to actually create separate content pages, such as review pages and buyers' guides, than it is to muck up the caption. For example, I like to have these additional content pages inside the products they talk about, which means the ID of the "More Info About Product *X*" page is inside the Contents field of the Product *X* item page.

Contents, Contents, Contents, and Contents

The word *contents* means several things in the Yahoo! Store Editor, which can be very confusing! Remember this tip, and you'll be fine: Contents really means only one thing: the stuff inside other stuff.

- ✔ ***Contents* usually refers to the field on almost every page (the home page and every section and item page) that contains the IDs of pages inside it.** Pages with IDs in the Contents field are called *parent pages,* and the pages contained within them are referred to as *child pages.* For example, a section page called Super-Heroes (the parent) can have the IDs Superman, Batman, Wonder Woman, and Flash (the children) inside the Super-Heroes' Contents field.

✔ *Contents* **is also a button on the Edit Nav-bar.** This links to the Contents (site-map) page that displays your entire store's hierarchy as a list of IDs, where you can expand and contract IDs to see pages within other pages.

✔ *Contents* **is also an element inside the navigation buttons.** The Viaweb guys really should have called it Homepage-Contents because it really refers only to the home page's Contents field. When Contents is selected in Variable setting: Nav-bar (and its very similar cousin on the home page: Buttons), the Store Editor makes a navigation button for every single page on the home page.

For example, if you have 25 sections on the home page, every single section gets its own button. You can always see which IDs are inside the home page by looking on the Contents (site-map) page or by editing the home page and scrolling down to see the list of IDs in the Contents field of the home page.

Now you see why folks easily get confused about the settings that control how Contents display on various pages. The three settings that control how sections display items contained within them are Contents-elements, Contents-format, and Columns:

✔ **The Contents-elements setting literally controls which elements (or fields) from items in the Contents field show on section pages.** The elements you can choose from are Image (thumbnail), Bullet, Screen-text-title (text links), Display-text-title (text as an image or display-text), Abstract, Caption, Price, Order, and Contents.

✔ **The Contents-format setting controls how the elements chosen in Contents-elements are formatted on the page.** Choose Vertical, Ell, Wrap, or Pack.

✔ **The Columns setting controls how many items appear in the same row.** Set your Columns to an odd number because odd numbers look more balanced than even numbers. I like three or five items per row.

What is really confusing is that these three settings (Contents-elements, Contents-format, and Columns) exist in three different places: on the home page, on the Variables page, and on the Config page under the leaf settings.

The following adds to the confusion about the different types of contents:

✔ **Home page Contents:** Pages with IDs inside the Contents field of the home page appear on the navigation button bars as Contents buttons (see Chapter 10). If you also want to show thumbnails and text links of those pages *on the home page,* such as a regular section page, you have to turn on Contents under Page-elements. These thumbnails and links are formatted according to the home page's own Contents-elements, Contents-format, and Columns settings.

✔ **Section Contents:** The Variables settings Contents-elements, Contents-format, and Columns are easy to see in action because Variables control the appearance of pages created with the Section button (and here's the important part) because the Leaf setting is set to No.

✔ **Item Contents:** Item pages (sometimes called *product pages*) display IDs inside the contents field differently because the Leaf setting is set to Yes.

✔ **When you create a new page on the Contents page, the Store Editor doesn't know whether you're creating a section page or an item page.** The Store Editor sets the all the item fields to Yes (Orderable, Taxable, and Leaf), which also happens when you upload "sections," which the Yahoo! Help files swear up and down you can't do. (You can upload section info using load files, but it's confusing and my tech reviewer says it's a workaround.) See Chapter 23 for more on database uploads.

✔ **Heaven forbid that you override the Contents-elements, Contents-format, and/or Columns Variables on a page.** When you do, your over-ridden Variables override the real Variables setting and control how Contents display, even if the page is leafed.

When you click the Section button to create a new section page, the Store Editor creates a page where Leaf=No so that the Contents-elements, Contents-format, and Columns are controlled by those settings on the Variables page.

The defaults are Contents-elements=Screen-text-title, Image, and Price; Columns=2; and Contents-format=Ell, which means that on any section page, pages in the Contents field display two columns per row. If an image exists on a page contained in Contents, an autogenerated thumbnail appears with the size determined by the Variables Thumb-height and Thumb-width, and the text link appears to the right of thumbnail image.

Exploring Other Function Pages

Your Store Editor comes with several prebuilt pages. Here they are with their ID (and what they are): index (the home page), info (information and policies), privacypolicy (your privacy policy page), norder (the Shopping Cart page unless you use the new Checkout Manager), nsearch (the Search page), and ind (the alphabetical index). I cover the home page in the section "Introducing the Home Page," earlier in this chapter. The new Checkout Manager (see Chapter 14) lets you customize your Shopping Cart and Checkout in the Store Manager. The following sections contain info on customizing the rest of these pages.

Editing your info page

A complete and professional-looking info page is extremely important. Most of the folks who are adding items to their carts look over your info page before placing an order. Figure 11-6 shows a sample of text from an info page that has stood the test of time since April 1997.

Figure 11-6:
Often the information and the quality of the presentation on the info page are the difference between a completed Shopping Cart and a dropped Shopping Cart.

Your info page is linked to from the Shopping Cart and Order Form. This page is the second-most checked page by shoppers looking to give you money, so do your info page up right!

Click the Find button on the Edit Nav-bar to go to the Find By ID search form. Type **info** in the ID field and click the Find button on the form, which takes you to the Info page. The Info page's template (info.) is similar to the regular (page.) template, but instead of having a Caption field, three text fields are available: Greeting, Address-phone, and Info. Your e-mail address (from Variables:Email) also appears on this page before the Info field.

Here's what I like to do with each field on my Info page:

✔ **Image:** Upload your picture or a picture of your warehouse or office. Anything you can do to look more "real" makes Internet shoppers feel more comfortable about placing an order with you.

✔ **Greeting:** Write what I call a "Howdy!" message. I like to offer a 100 per-cent satisfaction guarantee, as well as point out what someone needs to do if he has a problem. You should also talk about how fast orders ship and discuss product availability.

- ✔ **Address-phone:** List a physical address, all your phone and fax numbers, hours of operation, and a contact name.

- ✔ **Info:** Type all your shipping information, policies, terms and conditions, international shipping info, and answers to frequently asked questions. The Info field is a *smart field,* which means that it recognizes the line breaks you created when you press Enter.

Steal ideas from other good info pages. Ask your lawyer before you post anything that may be a binding contract, or you can get in trouble with the *The Man.*

Creating your privacy policy page

Yahoo! requires you to post your privacy policy on a page that tells customers what information you collect from site visitors, what you plan to do with this information, and who you share personal information with. Again, talk to your lawyer, but I think the simpler the policy, the better. Check the Yahoo! Store Help file at `http://help.yahoo.com/help/us/store/ edit/edit-20.html` for more info on online privacy or search on your favorite search engine for *writing a privacy policy.*

Use language to reassure shoppers that you won't spam them or sell their personal information to spammers (if that's your policy). For example, my privacy policy is "Your personal information is protected. We do not sell or rent our customers' names, addresses, or e-mail addresses to anyone."

To edit your privacy policy page, click the Find button on the Edit Nav-bar, which takes you to the Find by ID page. Type **privacypolicy** in the ID field and click the Find button to go to the privacy policy page. Click the Edit button, type your privacy policy into the Info field, and click the Update button.

Editing your Shopping Cart

You don't really want to mess with your Shopping Cart or norder page, because what you see in Editor isn't really what you get on a published site. If you make any changes to the `norder` object, publish your site and immediately place a test order to see what the cart looks like on a real order.

Trying to customize the Shopping Cart is difficult without using custom RTML templates (see Chapter 26) because there's no Final-text field or way to put custom text in the cart. Fortunately, the new Checkout Manager and Shopping Cart fix a lot of limitations of the old cart. (Read more in Chapter 14.)

Also, see Chapter 21 for more info on improving your conversion rate. For example, you can override your Name-image in the Shopping Cart and upload a more specific graphic designed to complete more carts, something pushing a special offer or 100 percent satisfaction guarantee.

Editing your store's Search page

Yahoo! Store has an excellent internal search engine. Store Search looks for your keyword phrase in the Name, Code, and Caption fields in every page on the site. Every Yahoo! Store has the same page (nsearch.html) for basic search. I talk a lot more about how internal store search works in Chapter 7.

Looking at your alphabetical index or site map

Every store built with Store Editor has a built-in sitemap/alphabetical index. The ind.html page lists the name of every page in your store in alphabetical order and provides links to it.

You can't directly edit the ind.html page by browsing to it, but you can always use the Controls: Edit by ID tool. You control how many links appear on the ind.html page with the Index Page Size setting under Controls in the Store Editor. Because some search engines (in theory) count up to 100 links on a page, you're better off having 50 or 100 links per ind.html page. See www.yourdomain.com/ind.html for the published version of your index.

Chapter 12

Creating Product Pages with the Store Editor

*P*erfecting your product pages is a never-ending project. Converting browsers into buyers with pages that perform is a priority. Creating a great item page is a pretty precarious balancing act. Have too little product info, and prospects don't purchase. But have big, bloated pages that bury buyers in BS and you end up with bupkus. In this chapter, I explore object IDs, which are the building blocks of the pages in the Store Editor. You discover how to organize and optimize your objects, as well as how to create, delete, move, and improve your items. Finally, you find out how to get the 411 on fields.

The look of your product pages depends on two things: the information inside fields on the page and the settings of the Variables, which control the formatting. In this chapter, I look at all the product page fields and the kind of data they hold and explore what you can do with them. I also dissect a product page, pointing out the properties, and verify the Variable settings that control the layout and appearance of the page.

Exploring Store Editor Concepts

My goodness, some of this Store Editor stuff seems complicated! I just want to sell stuff. Feel free to skip ahead to the next section on creating, editing, moving, and deleting pages if you don't feel like thinking right now.

Sometimes you need to work with the Store Editor for a while to get the hang of these ideas. You really don't have to understand all these concepts to sell stuff online using the Store Editor, but finding out about objects and their IDs, the parent and child relationships between sections and items, and page organization with Paths and Contents makes using the Store Editor much, much easier.

Let me see some ID

Every Store Editor page has its very own *alphanumeric ID,* which is the unique identifier for that page and is used in the Store Editor for many things:

- The ID is how the Store Editor identifies which page you're working on or referring to with links and all other Editor functions.

- The ID determines the Store Editor URL of a page. For example, `http://edit.store.yahoo.com/RT/NEWEDIT.`*`youraccount`*`/`*`id`*`.html`.

- The IDs inside the Contents field of a page determine what pages are inside that section or product page.

- The IDs in the Specials field of the home page determine which pages are featured as specials.

- The ID of a page serves as the page's HTML filename on the published version of the site. For example, the published page for the ID widget-2000 is found online at `www.`*`yourdomain`*`.com/widget-2000.html`.

- The ID of a page must be unique and can contain only letters, numbers, and/or dashes. IDs are not case sensitive. For example, the IDs *widget* and *WIDGET* actually refer to the same page. Links to pages need to have the ID in lowercase letters, too. For example, a `WIDGETS.html` link may work in the Editor but doesn't on the published site. Link to `widgets.html` instead.

- The Find button requires IDs to be typed in lowercase letters.

- Page IDs are permanent, so after an ID is created, you can't change it. If you try to create a new page on the Contents page and use an ID that already exists, the Store Editor is pretty smart and makes the new ID the old ID plus a 1 or other character.

- If you upload new product information using an existing ID and click the Add button, the newly uploaded information updates the old product. If you click the Rebuild button, your store is rebuilt from scratch.

Getting positive ID on products and sections

Be consistent when you create the IDs of products and sections. Some retailers use the Code field for the product page IDs, which makes a lot of sense because Merchant Solutions stores must have unique codes as well.

Here are more tips on how to create good IDs:

✔ **You have little or no control over the page's ID when you use the Section or Item buttons to create pages.** The Store Editor generates an ID based upon the first couple of letters of each word you type into the Name field.

For example, when I manually create a page with the name "Make Good Product IDs," the Editor creates a mysterious and unique random ID: *magoprids*. A better ID is something like *how-to-make-good-product-ids*.

✔ **You can trick the Editor.** Getting your clients or employees who create new pages in the Editor to quit using the Item or Section buttons is almost impossible. I found that you can type up to 14 characters with no spaces or dashes in the Name field and click the Update button to force the Editor to use that as the ID.

✔ **You determine a page's ID when you create pages through database uploads with the ID field.** If no ID field is in the CSV upload, the Editor uses the Code field as the ID. If no Code field exists, the Editor creates an ID named *gen-sym* plus a number.

✔ **You have absolute control over a page's ID by using the New button on the Contents page to make a new page.** When you create a page from the Contents page, whatever text you type into the ID field becomes the object's ID. The only time this trick doesn't work is if a page already exists with the same ID.

Doing a little extra work to write good IDs while you create products and sections will make your day-to-day management of your store easier. When you know the ID of a page, you can move products and sections around a lot easier because you have a pretty good idea what a section contains. For example, IDs like *louisville-baseball-bats* are easier to decipher than the mystery of what's inside the *lobabat* section. Read `http://help.yahoo.com/help/us/store/edit/regular/regular-62.html` for more information on IDs and codes.

Exploring Parent-Child Relationships

The Contents page is a site map and shows the unique relationship between section pages and item pages, called the *parent-child relationship*. This metaphor is used to explain how section pages contain subsection and item pages.

The following bullet list is rated PG. Parental guidance is suggested:

- **Item pages exist inside section pages.** This is because the IDs of the items (children) are inside the Contents field of the section page (parent).

- **Parent pages usually show child pages with thumbnail images and text links to those pages.** This is an overcomplicated way of saying that section pages have links and pictures of items inside them.

- **Pages can be the child of one page and the parent of another, just like people.** For example, if you have a Books section on your home page containing ten books, the section page is the child of the index.html or home page, but is the parent page of the ten item pages. One exception is that the home page or index page should never be a child page.

- **Pages can have an almost unlimited number of parent pages.** For example, imagine that you sell flashlights and have a hundred different flashlights that all use the same type of D-cell batteries. Instead of creating a different battery for each flashlight, you can create one item page with the object ID: d-battery and place this accessory in the Contents field of each flashlight.

- **Some pages don't have parents and are called *orphan pages*.** Don't be sad. They don't live in orphanages like Little Orphan Annie did, and they probably get enough porridge to eat. They're Web pages, not people. You can find these pages at the bottom of your Contents (site map) page.

- **When you move pages, you change the parent-child relationship.** For example, if you accidentally create the Pets section inside the Dogs section, you can move the Pets section to the home page and then place the Dogs section inside the Pets section.

- **When you delete a parent page, you also delete all the children pages inside that page, even if they exist somewhere else.** Be careful!

- **When you create a section on the home page, you make that section the child of the home page.** When you create a item in a section page, the item is the child of the parent section page. Pages can be both parent and child.

- **Objects/pages created on the Contents page (the site map) are orphans the second you create them.** You need to place the IDs inside the Contents field of the parent sections you want them to go in. I cover this topic in more detail in Chapter 11.

✔ **Creating products in the Store Editor and Catalog Manager is almost exactly same thing.** Catalog Manager products have no path information (where they sit in your Store Manager's hierarchy), because Catalog Manager products have no Contents or Path field, but listen to my technical reviewer, Mike Whitaker, when he says use one way or the other.

✔ **Some pages don't have children.** Some item pages have children, but the child pages are *NIL templates,* which are objects that only show their properties on a parent's page. For example, when you click the Accessory button on the Edit Nav-bar of an item page, you create an object that doesn't have its own page, but the Accessory can have a Name, Code, and Price. An Accessory displays product info and (usually) an Order button on the item page it was created on.

Producing Profits with Product Pages

The appearance of product pages is important. Not only is the information in the Name, Caption, and Price field important, but the variables that control how that information is displayed are also sometimes as important.

If you want to see the various fields available on any product page, browse to your favorite product page and click the Edit button. Click the Types button on the Edit Nav-bar and click the link for (Item.) type to see all the fields on a product page:

ID: This field displays the ID for the page and can't be edited.

Type: This field displays the page's type, which just means what type of page it is. The type determines which fields a page has.

Template: You can edit this field if you want to use custom templates. Templates determine what information from a page actually shows up on a page and how it looks. RTML templates are programs that crank out HTML pages when you click the Publish button. See Chapter 26 for more on RTML.

Name: The name of a page is one of the most important fields because so many other functions use the text in the Name field as the default. The text in the Name field does the following things:

✔ Text from the Name field appears at the top of the product page as a display-text headline unless you specify different text inside the Headline field

✔ Text from the Name field is used for the Title tag, unless the field Page-title exists

✔ Text from the Name field is used as the anchor text or *link text* (words in a link) on its parent section pages where this page appears

✔ Text from the Name field is also the text in the label by the thumbnail image when you feature a page on the home page as a Special (unless you specify different text in the Label field)

✔ Text from the Name field is used as the text on the Navigation button bar when a page is a top-level section page (exists on the home page with its ID in the Contents field of the index.html)

All these reasons are why you should be very descriptive when you enter the Name field. For example, naming a product "Hulk T-Shirt" is okay, but "Incredible Hulk T-Shirt from 1973 Marvel Comics Hulk #108 cover — Green 100% cotton Beefy Tee" is better because it has more keywords that potential shoppers can type into search engines.

You can't rank well in the search engines for words that don't exist on your store's pages. Well-written Name fields (think lots of keywords) give you a better chance to rank well in search engines, as well as Yahoo! Shopping. I unlock the secrets of keywords in Chapter 16. For Yahoo! Shopping info, jump to Chapter 17.

Image: You can upload an image file in a GIF or JPEG format of the item here. Click the Upload File button. Click the Browse button to find the image on your hard drive. Click the Upload button to send the image file to this item. A thumbnail image appears so that you can see that you uploaded the right graphic. (See Chapter 8.)

Code: The code of an item is usually the item's product ID number or UPC code or some unique number so that you know exactly what the customer is ordering. You can search by code. Code is also used in the Cross-sell database.

Price: Not simply a number field, this field can also contain quantity discounts that are automatically calculated by the Shopping Cart. The format is kind of strange: first the price, then the first quantity break, then the total price at that quantity, then the next quantity break, and then the total price at that quantity. For example, to show that T-shirts are $20 each, three or more are $15 each, and ten or more are $10 each, you type the following in the Price field:

```
20 3 45 10 100
```

Sale-price: If you put the item on sale, list the sale price here. Lots of people put the list price, or the manufacturer's suggested retail price (MSRP), in the Price field to show the discount that the shopper gets from your Yahoo! Store.

Orderable: This field determines whether an item has an Order button. Set Orderable to No when you're temporarily out of stock on an item.

Options: Use this field to specify product options, such as size or color. The Options field is really cool! The first word on a line is the name of the option. The second word is the first option in the pull-down menu. For example:

```
Color RED WHITE BLUE
```

You need to be aware of the following while exploring your options:

- ✔ **Option phrases:** Put straight quotes (" ") not curly quotes (" ") around multiple words or phrases for the Options field to treat the phrases as a single concept. For example:

```
"Color of Flag" "REDCOAT BLOOD RED"
"ROYAL BLUE" "WHITES OF THEIR EYES WHITE"
```

- ✔ **Multiple options:** Separate multiple options with two hard returns (press Enter twice). For example:

```
Color RED WHITE BLUE

Size SMALL MEDIUM LARGE X-LARGE
```

- ✔ **Option upcharge:** You can also add an upcharge by putting a plus sign and the upcharge in parentheses inside an option. For example:

```
Size SMALL MEDIUM LARGE X-LARGE "XX-LARGE(+$5.00)"
```

- ✔ **Inscription:** Figure 12-1 shows an example of an Inscription, which is a specialty Option function, replacing the drop-down menu with an input field where customers can type information for monogramming or other personalization. The format for Inscriptions is Option-name *Inscription* number, which is the number of characters in the field. For example, here's an Inscription for a 20-character dog tag:

```
"Dog's Name" Inscription 20
```

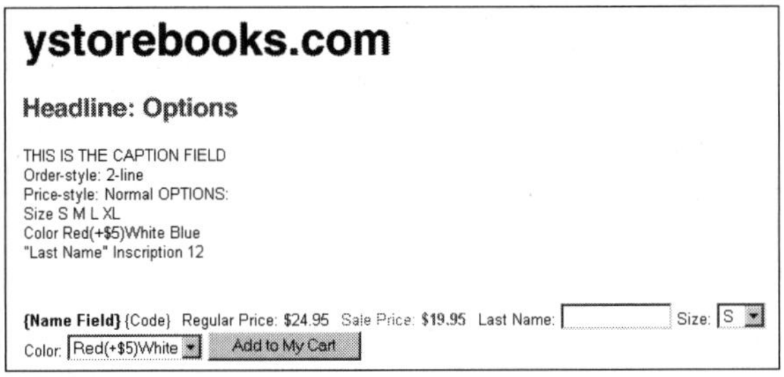

Figure 12-1:
This product page has three options: Last Name (which is an Inscription field), Size, and Color, which shows an upcharge.

ystorebooks.com

Headline: Options

THIS IS THE CAPTION FIELD
Order-style: 2-line
Price-style: Normal OPTIONS:
Size S M L XL
Color Red(+$5)White Blue
"Last Name" Inscription 12

{Name Field} (Code) Regular Price: $24.95 Sale Price: $19.95 Last Name: [   ] Size: [S ▾]
Color: [Red(+$5)White ▾] [Add to My Cart]

> ✔ **Personalization charge:** If you want to charge for this added service, use the Personalization-charge setting under Variables. If different items have different costs to personalize, just override the Personalization-charge variable on each product.
>
> *Note:* In this chapter, I use ALL CAPS to differentiate between the options and the name of options. You have the option of not doing that on your store.

Formatting options can be a little hairy. If you don't format your options exactly right, and you have your Store Manager set to validate options (the default), customers will not be able to check out when they try to order items with incorrectly formatted option fields.

For this reason, I go into the Store Manager to the Order Settings page and set the Item Options Validation field to Allow Items With Unrecognized Options. This setting can be potentially dangerous and allows malicious hackers to change prices when adding items to the cart, but you shouldn't have a problem if you see and/or touch every order. (See Chapter 15 for more about the Store Manager's Order Form settings for validating options and formatting. Also check out `http://help.yahoo.com/help/us/store/store-44.html` for more info on validating options.)

Headline: Anything you type in this field overrides the Name field and appears as display-text to the right of (or below) the item's image and above the caption. I always use the Headline field because of a quirk in the item template. If you don't have any text inside the Headline field, the name displays here. If you do, the template also shows the name to the left of the Order button. This little trick helps you with search engines. When I do a database upload, I usually use both Headline and Name fields to take advantage of this "feature." Eventually, I try to write a compelling headline for each product that touts the benefits of buying the product.

The headline is a *smart field* that recognizes line breaks in text created by pressing the Enter key within a field. The only other fields that recognize line breaks in fields and show them on the page are the Label and the Info field on the Info page.

Figure 12-2 displays a product page. Notice how line breaks in the text help you tighten up pages with long names or headlines. If a headline is wider than the space between the right side of the image graphic, then the headline is kicked down beneath the image. This results in wasted space to the right of the photograph. I manually insert a couple of hard returns, and I break up unusually long headlines into phrases of two or three words per line that make sense.

Figure 12-2:
Line breaks
in the text
help you
tighten up
pages.

Caption: This is the description of the item that appears below the Image and Headline fields. You need to use lots of keywords in several sentences to help you with the search engines. You also need compelling reasons for your shoppers to buy this product, so list the benefits of the product.

Abstract: This little-used text field can appear on section pages or on the home page if you select Abstract in the Contents-elements field. I use the Abstract to put teaser copy or a synopsis of the caption to pull customers into a product page. Abstracts look better when the Column variable is set to 1 and the Contents-format variable is set to Ell or Wrap. I sometimes use <small> tags in my Abstracts to make the text a bit smaller.

Icon: You can control what thumbnails appear on section pages with the Icon field. The Store Editor automatically generates a thumbnail image for every product or section with an image. The Icon property allows you to customize your thumbnail by uploading another image. Just like the other thumbnails, the size of the icon is determined by the Thumb-height and Thumb-width settings under Variables.

Sometimes the autogenerated thumbnails look a little funky. Focus on a particular product detail or use a logo for an icon to make a better thumbnail. Icons take more work, and they take a lot of time to upload by hand, but you can get faster loading and better looking pages.

Inset: The Store Editor lets you upload a secondary image to a product or section. Most folks who use this feature upload a small manufacturer's logo, about the size of a thumbnail, which appears to the right of the image. You can also put a detail photo here. Inset-height and Inset-width are set under Variables.

Label: If you use this field, this text appears on your home page Special when you select the home page setting Specials-format: As-thumbnails. If you don't, the Name field appears on the home page. The Label field is like the Headline field, which remembers hard returns or line breaks. Break up long lines of text by pressing Enter every two or three words to kick text down to the next line. If you don't, long text labels display on one line, which looks weird and pushes the next Special off the page.

Ship-weight: This field allows you to use the weight-based tables to determine shipping cost in the Store Manager's Shipping Manager.

Taxable: If you have set up the tax calculation, you can use this field to exempt nontaxable items from sales tax.

Download: You can use this field to sell soft goods. Upload a PDF, MP3, or other file to be downloaded from the Checkout Confirmation page.

Family: This is the old way to *cross-sell,* or group related products together. When a customer adds an item with a family to the Shopping Cart, he's offered three related items from the same family. See Chapter 13 for more on the new, much improved cross-sell feature.

Product URL: This field is the URL of the published product page used by Yahoo! Product Submit for inclusion into Yahoo! Shopping. I talk a lot more about Yahoo! Shopping in Chapter 17.

Looking at Product Elements

Almost every page on your Store Editor–built store has the same template showing Nav-buttons, the Name-image header, and the Final-text footer. What's unique on a page, or what's inside the boilerplate template, is what some folks call the *pagelet.* With basic templates, items and sections are built pretty much the same way. I discuss what the properties (fields) are and what settings control them in the following paragraphs. Here are the elements in the order that they appear.

Title tag: The Title tag of the page comes from the Name field (unless you have created a new property named: Page-title, type: text).

Head tags: The Variable: Head-tags allows you to stick code inside your head tags field. Use it for calling CSS or JavaScripts. Although you can't see the code on the page, every HTML page should have a head tags section, which shows browsers (and search engines) meta or hidden information about the page's structure, content, and appearance. It's not wise to override the Head-tags variable, even though you need to do so to have unique meta descriptions or meta keywords. If you want to do this kind of SEO, look to RTML for relatively simple SEO custom programming in Chapter 26.

The variable Keywords creates a keywords meta-tag on the home page. If you don't use custom RTML, feel free to override the Keywords variable on every page to create a custom keywords meta-tag for each page.

The variable Head-elements determines whether pages show the image and/or the Display-text-title or neither. The variable Head-style determines the alignment of the Head-elements. I prefer left-aligned pages, but aligning your image and text to the right works, too. A center-aligned image eats up a lot of real estate on product pages, because it kicks the headline down under the Image, so I don't use it. For leafed pages, the -Config's Leafed-head-elements and Leafed-head-style setting do the same thing.

Product photo: The image comes from the page's Image variable, and the maximum height and width (in pixels) is controlled by the Variables: Item-height and Item-width. If your image file is taller or wider than these constraints, the template generates a smaller version of the image, which you can click to go to an empty page to see the larger original image.

Unfortunately, this resized image file is reformatted as a GIF file, which is a pretty heavy file format for photographs. Either upload big images (up to 600-x-800-pixel JPEGs) with lots of details or right-size all your images to fit within the Item-height and Item-width settings for faster loading images.

Product headline: The text from the Display-text-title is from the page's Name field unless there's a Headline. The look of the display-text is controlled by the following variables: Display-text-color, Display-font, and Display-font-size.

Additional photo: If you upload a second image to the Inset image field on a product, it shows up right under the headline as a thumbnail with the maximum size set in pixels by the variables Inset-height and Inset-width. Click the inset image to see the larger uploaded file. I like to upload manufacturer logos or secondary product photos to the Inset field.

Product description: The Caption field appears next. The font is controlled by the variables Text-font, Text-size, and Text-color. Captions are HTML text, which is very search-engine friendly. The caption is a versatile field because you can insert HTML tags like `<strong>` tags around keywords to format your text to look better. You can also add links like `<a href=moreinfo. html>More info</a>` into the Caption field.

Order functionality: Next is my favorite part: how folks order. Here you show the product's price, product options (such as sizes and colors), quantity discounts, product availability, and an Order button. Sometimes on product pages with multiple options and quantity pricing, this order functionality can get kind of hairy-looking.

Product availability: The Availability variable is a global setting, which is turned off by default. It's really good manners and good business to tell customers the standard delivery time for a product. Customers hate ordering something and finding out that you can't ship it.

Unfortunately, you have to choose an average standard delivery time for all your products. When you have custom or drop-ship items that may take longer to ship, you can then override the Availability variable on a product-by-product basis.

When you select an Availability from the Variables page (or override the Availability variable), the Store Editor forces you to choose from several different availability messages. There's gotta be an availability that suits your business, but if not, database uploads may be for you because they give you total control over the Availability field. You can upload whatever text you want. Chapter 23 fully explores database uploads.

Product name: If you have any text in your Headline field, the text inside the Name field appears here as bold text.

Product code/SKU: The Code field needs to be unique for each item. Codes appear on the product, Shopping Cart, and Checkout pages, and even in the order confirmation e-mails. Most people don't know this, but your store's internal search functionality searches the Name, Caption, *and* Code fields. Cool! Use the manufacturer's product number, SKU, or UPC code as an item's Code because some folks search for products by the numbers.

Product price: The price is formatted differently based upon several factors, including the presence of a sale price or quantity pricing. If you have a regular price and a sale price, text labels appear before each number. Edit the Regular-price-text and Sale-price-text on the Variables page.

Price-styles: This variable controls the look of prices on product and section pages and the home page when you use specials. Figure 12-3 displays Normal (the default), Quiet, and Big Price-styles. Keep the following in mind when working with Price-styles:

- If Price-style is set to Quiet, prices are formatted the same as the Normal setting with bold formatting.

- If Price-style is set to Normal, the price appears without bold. If there's a Sale-price, the Sale-price is displayed in bold as well, and the color of the Sale-price comes from the variable Emphasis-color.

- If you have Price-style set to Big, the sale price appears bigger in Display-text-title, which matches the headline font, but the color is controlled by Emphasis-color.

Product options: Product options (like color or size) appear as drop-down menus. The variable Order-style determines how options are formatted:

- ✔ Normal lets the options fall where they may, depending on length of the text.

- ✔ Two-line inserts a line break after the name, which kicks the code and all the options down to the next line.

- ✔ Multi-line kicks each option down to a separate line, which looks a lot better for stores that offer a lot of product options, such as apparel retailers.

Figure 12-4 shows how Quantity pricing displays a little differently. For example, if the regular price is $12, your Sale-price is $10, and you have a buy-12-or-more price of $5, the Store Editor displays your price like this:

```
Regular Price: $12.00    Sale Price $10.00, 12/$60.00
```

Figure 12-4:
Quantity
pricing
displays on
the bottom
of the
product
page.

This is the Headline

This is the Name Field

QTY-PRICE Regular Price: $24.95 Sale Price: $20.00, 2/$30.00, 5/$50.00   Add to My Cart

The text in the Quantity-text variable separates the quantity and the price when you discount an item with quantity pricing. I think 12 *for* $60.00 reads better than 12/$60.00. Change the / (slash) to the word *for*, and your price looks like this:

```
Regular Price: $12.00    Sale Price $10.00, 12 for $60.00
```

Order button: The text on the Order button comes from the text in the variable Order-text. Make that text Add To Cart or Add To My Cart for a higher-converting product page.

After all the order and price stuff, any IDs inside the Contents field display according to how you have your Leaf settings on the Config page, with thumbnails, links, text, price, and sometimes an Order button.

Maintaining Your Pages in the Store Editor

In this section, I cover the basics of creating and maintaining a new store in the Store Editor, including new ways to create pages, effective editing, how to move pages, and painless page removal with a primer in deleting pages. If your inventory changes pretty often or you have new products coming in, you'll spend a lot of time creating and editing pages. More time on the site means more money in the bank!

Creating new pages inside the Store Editor

Creating a new page in the Store Editor is easy. All you do is click the appropriate button, type the page's name, and click the Update button:

✔ To create a section page, click the Section button. The Store Editor creates a new section and takes you to that new section's Edit page, where you can type info or upload images.

✔ As shown in Figure 12-5, an Edit page is simply a Web form with all the different fields for an item or section. Type some text in the Name field, type a brief description in the Caption field, and click the Update button. Your changes appear on the page. If you're happy with your work, keep on trucking. If not, simply click the Edit button, which takes you back to the Edit page, and make any desired changes. Pages created with the Section button are not leafed, and the Orderable, Taxable, and Leaf fields are automatically set to No.

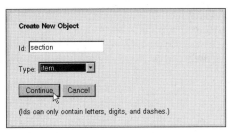

Figure 12-5:
The Edit
page for a
section
page.

✔ To create an item page, click the Item button. A new page is created inside the page you were just on. The Store Editor is pretty smart and anticipates that this new item page is going to be a product. The Edit page, where you can input the Name, Code, and Price fields, appears for this item. The Orderable, Taxable, and Leaf fields are automatically set to Yes. Pages created with the Item button are also leafed so that when you add accessories to an item page, they'll have an Order button.

✔ To create an Accessory, you need to be on an item. If you are on an Item page, the Item button on the Edit Nav-bar is replaced by the Accessory button. Click the Accessory button to add a product to the Item page. Accessory items are NIL templates, which means that they don't have their own page, but exist only on this item page.

Store Editor pages can change back and forth from section to item to accessory and back. All you have to do is change a few settings on the Edit page and add (or remove) some missing information. The Show Product/Hide Product button makes the hidden product fields appear or disappear. These product fields are Code, Price, Sale-price, Orderable, Options, Ship-weight, Taxable, Download, Family, and Gift-certificate. These fields exist on the section pages, but you just can't see them until you click the Product button. I use the words *item* and *product* interchangeably because a product is something you sell, but an item can really be anything.

Here's how to switch pages from sections to items to Accessories and back:

✔ To make a section an orderable item, set Orderable and Taxable to Yes, input a Code and a Price, and change Leaf to Yes. Click the Update button, and you now have an orderable product.

✔ To change an item to an Accessory, first you must be in the Advanced mode of Store Editor. Edit an item and change the template field to NIL, which makes it a NULL page.

✔ To make an Accessory into an item (with its own page), you must be in the Advanced Store Editor. Edit the item and change the Template field from NIL to "Page." (without the quotes but with the period) and click the Update button.

Advanced users can create new pages in other places, too: on the Contents page and by performing database uploads. These other ways of adding pages give you more control over the pages and allow you to do things you just can't do by clicking the Item, Section, or Accessory buttons. Here's how I like to add pages to my sites:

- ✓ **Create items or sections on the Contents page.** Click the Contents button on the Edit Nav-bar, which takes you to the Contents (site map) page. Figure 12-6 displays what you see when you click the New button. Type the ID and select a type to create a new page. Creating products in Store Editor from the Contents page gives you total control of the ID, but the page isn't inside a section page anywhere and is considered an orphaned item. The page has the same settings as an item page (the Orderable, Taxable, and Leaf fields are automatically set to Yes).

- ✓ **Add thousands of products and sections with the click of a mouse.** Click the Database Upload button on the Edit Nav-bar, upload a CSV with your new or updated product information, and click either the Add or Rebuild button to update your store. Be careful. Creating products with a database upload lets you control the ID, determine the Path (where pages exist in your store's navigational hierarchy), and control the contents inside each page, among other things. Read the full details in Chapter 23 before you start shaving with a chain saw.

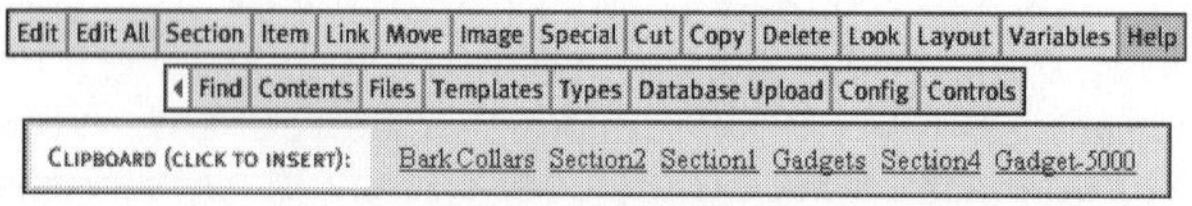

Figure 12-6:
Creating
pages on
the Contents
page gives
you the
most control.

| Edit | Edit All | Section | Item | Link | Move | Image | Special | Cut | Copy | Delete | Look | Layout | Variables | Help |

◀ Find | Contents | Files | Templates | Types | Database Upload | Config | Controls

CLIPBOARD (CLICK TO INSERT): Bark Collars Section2 Section1 Gadgets Section4 Gadget-5000

When you create multiple items that are almost the same, it would be nice if you could use a Clone button to create a new item with copies of all the same settings. Unfortunately, this Clone button doesn't exist for the Store Editor. The best way to create many similar, yet slightly different, products or pages is to use the Database Upload feature. Create a CSV file using Microsoft Excel, create a record with the original info, and then copy the record, changing the ID field for each variation of the product you have. Save the CSV and do a database upload. I cover product uploads in loving detail in Chapter 23.

Editing product and section pages

Editing product and section pages is easy with the Store Editor. To edit a page, browse to that page in the Editor and click the Edit button. Add or edit text, upload images, or change prices. Click the Update button to save your changes and then preview that page in the Store Editor. If you like what you see, click the Publish button to make your edits to the live site. In a few moments, the real version of the store is updated with your changes. You don't have to publish after every page you change, but I do like to publish every hour or so as I'm working in the store to keep the published store updated.

When you click the Edit button, the Edit page for that object appears, and you can see the properties of the specific page in an HTML Web form that lets you add, edit, or delete information in various fields (Name, Image, Code, Price, or Caption). After you make your changes, you can accept your edits by clicking the Update button or opt not to save them by clicking the Cancel button.

When you click the Edit button on a page, you're only editing that one page. When you click the Variables button and change settings, you're making changes to the global Variables settings that affect virtually every page on your store. There is only one Variables button, not a Variables button for each page. This point confuses some folks.

Also, when you click the Edit All button on a section page, you can edit the Name, Code, Price, Sale-price, and Options for all the items in that section in one spot.

Moving pages by cutting to the Clipboard

The Clipboard and Cut function make it easy to move pages around in the Store Editor. Here's how it works: Browse to the page you want to move and click the Cut button on the Edit Nav-bar to cut the page from whatever page it was inside (removing the ID from the Contents field) and place it on the Clipboard. The page appears just under the Edit Nav-bar as the name of the product as a text link. Just browse to the wherever you want to move the page and click the name of the page on the Clipboard to insert the cut page as the last object on that page.

Using the Cut function removes the page from every other section or product page it appears in. This deletion may be a problem if the page appears inside many products and sections. Okay! Here's some Clipboard content for your consideration:

- **Editing pages on the Clipboard is tricky.** One way to edit them is to temporarily paste the page on another page, edit that page, and then cut it to the Clipboard again after editing it. A better way to edit pages cut to the Clipboard is to use the Find button. Type the page's ID to jump straight to the page and click the Edit button to go to town.

- **Cutting a page to the Clipboard makes the cut page an exiled item so that it doesn't appear on the published site.** These pages look okay in the Editor but are invisible on the published site as long as the page is marked by a button at the top of the Unexile page.

- **You can place exiled pages into section pages by typing or pasting the ID into the Contents field, but the pages are still exiled.** Exiled pages may work in the Editor and look like good links, but the links aren't clickable on the published site, and visitors trying to get to the page from search engines or by typing the URL straight in their browser either get an error page or are dumped to your home page.

- **If a page was on the Clipboard and then got knocked off (for whatever reason), it may still be marked exiled.** Exiled pages are bad news because the pages don't work on the published version of the site, but they look okay in the Store Editor. You don't really know you have a problem until you publish and poke around on the published version of the site. When customers complain about links not working or pages disappearing, it's usually a case of an exiled page.

- **The only way to fix an exiled page is to click the Unexile button.** Unexiling a page and clicking the Publish button makes the page available on the published site.

- **To see all the exiled pages in your store, go to the Contents (site map) page and click the Siberia button.** A page appears displaying all the IDs of the exiled pages, whether or not they appear on the Clipboard.

When you do a database upload (see Chapter 23), pages on the Clipboard get dumped back into the site because, for some bizarre reason, all exiled items get unexiled. These dumped items from the Clipboard become *orphaned pages* (pages without parent pages linking to them), and you can find them at the bottom of the Contents page (site map). These pages appear in your internal store site search results. Search engines can find them, which means that customers can find them and order items you thought you took off the site.

Copying pages into more than one section

Sometimes you want a product to appear in more than one section. For example, say that you sell a hundred different flashlights, and they all use the same size batteries. Instead of making 100 different accessories with the exact same information, just copy the batteries onto every flashlight page.

A faster way to put the same product into multiple section pages is to insert the ID of the page into the Contents field of every page where you want that page/object to appear. Browse to the section page, click the Edit button, type the ID, and click the Update button. Repeat for each additional section page.

Deleting pages

Deleting pages can be scary! When you delete a page, you delete all the pages inside that page, and the pages inside *that* page, and so on, and so on, and so on, as well as every single reference to all those deleted IDs in any other page on your site. When you click the Delete button on a section or item page, you get a list of all the IDs you're about to delete accompanied by a very scary warning message:

> *"Warning: You are about to delete: {name of ID}. Deleting will remove all instances of the above-listed item(s) and or section(s) throughout your store - not just the items on this page. Deletions are not recoverable. Are you sure you want to delete?"*

This message is your only chance to reconsider. Carefully read through the list of IDs and click the Yes button if you're certain you never want to see those pages again. After you click the Yes button, your deleted page(s) are gone forever. This point is super-important: All the pages inside that page (pages with IDs in the Contents field) get deleted, too, even if the pages exist elsewhere. So if you delete a section containing section pages with tons of subsections with potentially hundreds of products, who knows how many pages you're deleting. Talk about collateral damage!

To remove IDs from any particular page without deleting anything, simply edit the section page, scroll down to the Contents field, highlight the object ID with your mouse, and press the spacebar. If the page is the child of many other pages, you aren't really orphaning that product. If the object doesn't exist inside any other pages, it will be orphaned, and you can find it on the Contents page or by using the Find button.

When I delete pages, I usually create a new temporary page with the ID delete-me-please. Then I paste all the IDs of all the pages I want to delete in the Contents field of the new delete-me-please page and click the Update button. If I'm really sure, I click the Delete button on the Edit Nav-bar and then click the Yes button, and all those pages are gone forever.

Chapter 13

Merchandising to Sell More

· ·

In This Chapter

▶ Picking the products you prefer to push

▶ Merchandising products across the entire site

▶ Cross-selling in the cart

▶ Navigating the virtual aisles

· ·

Merchandising your online store is one of the keys to online retail success. How you display your products on your Web site determines which products get exposure. The products that people see are the products that get sold.

Remember that the average visitor to your Web site will only see four or five pages. You have a lot of control over which pages the average customer sees by which products you feature on your home page and how you design your store's navigation. (For more on home-page design, see Chapter 11.)

In this chapter, I show you how to pick which products you should push, how to organize your section and category navigation to get the most bang for your buck, and how to maximize your most valuable real estate.

Specializing in Bestsellers

I could make this chapter extremely short if my editor, Kelly, would let me get away with it. Here goes: 99 percent of Yahoo! Store merchandising is taking your bestselling products and slapping them up on your front page where everyone can see 'em. That's it. Trust me. It's better than free money.

Half of the people who hit your site visit your home page. Put your specials near the top of your home page (within the first screen shot), and maybe you'll see 150 percent increases in sales per product like I do. You can cross-sell from the Shopping Cart all you want, but 90 percent of the people who visit your site will never add an item to their cart. Cross-link, accessorize, upsell, and add on like crazy, but effective home-page specials kick your "You want fries with that?" up and down the block.

It's the little things that getcha!

Uh-oh! I may have just done you wrong in trying to drive home a very important point. The reality is that most small-business retailers don't maximize the effectiveness of their home page specials, but that's where most people get the biggest bang for their buck. If I can't get retailers to do the big, easy things, how can I ever get them to accessorize, cross-link, upsell, and add on to every single customer?

As a retailer and a consultant, I tend to try to be a home-run hitter. I like to swing for the fences and knock it out of the park. I like to run the bases and do the little dance. Home runs are fun, but the reality is that bunts and singles and sacrifice flies win baseball games. I recommend that you do both. When you have a new breakout product that looks like it could be a home run, then swing for the fence. But with your average, ordinary, everyday sale, just try to get the guy to buy some batteries, too. Think of it as a sacrifice fly to bring in that guy on third base. No matter what you do, brilliant merchandising is not going to double or triple the sales of the majority of your products.

Featuring specials

The Store Editor gives you an easy way to feature items, sections, or other pages on your home page with the Specials feature. *Specials* are thumbnail images and text that link to a featured product or section. Figure 13-1 shows you an example of a home page that makes good use of specials.

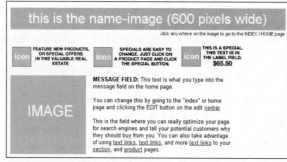

Figure 13-1:
A home page with three specials on it.

Keep your site looking fresh by rotating new items and bestsellers as home-page specials. Show as many specials as you want on your home page, but I think anything more than two rows is wasted space. I prefer five-column rows showing the thumbnail, a text link, and the price.

Making something special

To make an item a special, browse to that item in the Store Editor and click the Special button, located in the middle of the Edit Nav-bar. The Editor creates a special link to that item on the home page and takes you there to see it.

To remove a special, you need to browse to the item or section page that is the special, and the fastest way to do that from the home page is to click the special's thumbnail. When the product page loads, look at the Edit Nav-bar. Notice that the Special button now says Not Special, which reminds you that this page is a featured item on the home page. To remove this item from the specials, click the Not Special button, which removes the link from the home page. The Editor whisks you back to the home page to show you it's gone.

The Special/Not Special feature works in both Regular and Advanced mode. If you see one row of buttons, you're in the Regular mode of Store Editor. Click the little red arrow that appears on the far right side of the Edit Nav-bar to switch to the Advanced mode. When you see two rows of buttons on the Edit Nav-bar, you're in the Advanced mode of Store Editor, which gives you access to all kinds of powerful store-building and -editing features. Click the button on the far left side of the Edit Nav-bar to return to Regular mode.

There's a quicker and better way to add or edit specials when you're in Advanced mode. Browse to the home page and click the Edit button to edit the home page. When you have specials on your home page, the object-IDs of the products or sections appear in the Specials field in the order that they appear on the page. This field acts just like another Contents field, where you control the specials by adding, shuffling, or removing object-IDs from the Specials field.

Victoria's other secret

If you don't believe me, I'll let you in on Victoria's Other Secret. There I was in sunny California at Search Engine Strategies, and I happened to be eating lunch with the former marketing something-something of Victoria's Secret. Guess who got to go to merchandising school and find out about maximizing the most valuable real estate on your home page by rotating and testing product specials?

Now I don't kiss and tell, but I discovered that some companies live and die by home-page specials. Some companies like to put three specials on the home page because that real estate is more valuable than any runway model. Within an hour, one special gets pulled because it's not, uh, fully supporting someone's well-developed marketing goals. I guess even supermodels live and die by that conversion rate. Work it, baby!

Here's how to manage specials a little bit faster by editing the home page:

- ✔ **Make an item a special.** Type the object-ID of any product or section in the Specials field and click the Update button.

- ✔ **Remove a special from the home page.** Delete the object-ID from the Specials field and click the Update button.

- ✔ **Change the order of the specials on the home page.** Change the order of the object-IDs inside the Specials field and click the Update button.

Editing the look and feel of specials

To change the appearance of home-page specials, click the Edit button on the home page. When the Edit page appears, scroll down until you see the Specials-format setting, which controls the two different ways specials appear: As-thumbnails or As-contents. Figure 13-1 shows a page with the Specials-format set to As-thumbnails, which is the default setting and renders specials links as images with a thumbnail and label. As-contents displays specials just like the Contents look on your home page.

Showing specials As-thumbnails is really good for new stores that haven't figured out how to maximize the use of the Contents formatting settings, which are kind of convoluted.

These different elements control the appearance of specials:

- ✔ **Thumbnail:** The thumbnail image is automatically generated from the item's Image field unless you uploaded a separate image to the Icon field. The thumbnail image's size is controlled on the Variables page by Thumb-height and Thumb-width settings, which are set to 45 pixels by default.

- ✔ **Label text:** The label text (which really isn't text, but a GIF file image of text) comes from an item's Label field, unless it's empty and uses the item's Name field instead.

- ✔ **Label settings:** The appearance of the label text is controlled by three settings on the Variables page: Label-font, Label-font-size, and Label-color. The default settings are Helvetica-Bold, 10, Black (0 0 0), which makes the label text read okay, but the letters are always all caps, which is harder to read.

Match your Label-font to the other fonts you use on the site, but don't make your Label-font-size too big. I see a lot of new Yahoo! Stores with huge labels! Keep your Label-font-size smaller than your Button-font-size or Display-font-size.

- ✔ **Price:** The price comes from the real selling price, whether that's the Price or the Sale-price (if there is one). If the Variables setting Price-style is set to Quiet, then price shows only on the item page, not the section or the home page. The color of the price is controlled by the Variables setting Emphasis-color.

Specials As-thumbnails show up only in one row, so the number of specials you can have is limited to the page width. Also, unlike specials As-contents, the Name field doesn't automatically kick down to the next line. If the name of a product is too long, it looks funky! Fortunately, the Label field comes to the rescue. You can either type a short, snappy label or, because the Label field is a "smart" field that remembers line breaks, type a few words, press Enter, type a few more words, press Enter, and type the rest of your label on the third line.

Specials shown As-thumbnails are images (even the text is a picture of text), not a graphic, so you don't get the benefit of anchor text for search engine optimization. I cover SEO in Chapter 19.

Figure 13-2 shows Specials As-contents, which look just like your Contents. The Contents of the home page are your top-level categories, which are determined by which Object-IDs are inside the Contents field of the home page.

Figure 13-2:
Specials-
format:
As-contents
formats
specials and
sections on
the home
page the
same way.

When you use the Specials:As-contents setting, the look of both your Contents and specials is controlled by the home page settings Contents-elements, Contents-format, and Columns. On almost any other page, the look of Contents is controlled by the Variables with the same names.

Figure 13-3 shows the Edit page of your home page, which has separate Contents-elements, Contents-format, and Columns settings than the rest of your site, so you can go for a slightly different look here. I talk about formatting your section pages with these variables and the Leaf setting in Chapter 11.

Figure 13-3:
Contents-
elements,
Contents-
format, and
Columns
control the
appearance
of Contents
and specials
when the
Specials-
format is set
to As-
contents.

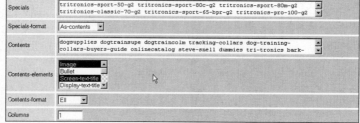

Troubleshooting specials

Don't panic if specials don't show up on your home page when you think they should. Specials are turned on by default, but you (or your designer) may have changed your Page-elements settings. To make sure that the specials element is turned on in your home page's Page-elements setting, browse to the home page, click the Edit button, and take a look. A list of all the elements shows up in the order that they appear.

For example, I'm showing all my Page-elements on http://Ystorebooks.com: Name, Specials, Image, Message, Contents, Address, Intro-text, Final-text, Buttons, and Search. Click the Change button, and the Edit List Position (Page-elements) form pops up, where you can change the numbers to the right of the elements' names to alter the order the elements appear on the home page. If you don't want certain elements to appear, remove the number from the Order field. I talk a lot more about Page-elements and other settings unique to the home page and other pages in Chapter 11.

Make sure there's at least one real Object-ID in the Specials field, too. It's easy to make a typo if you're just typing in the object-IDs. If you're using Specials-format:As-contents, make sure that some elements (Image, Screen-title-text, Price, and so on) are selected in Contents-elements. Also, take a look at your Variables page and make sure that Label-color and Link-color aren't the same color as your background.

Picking What Products to Push

Knowing how to promote products and merchandise your Yahoo! Store is important, but knowing which products to promote can be the difference between making it and not making it. When selecting products to feature or to make a special on the home page, I look at overall sales volume, how much profit I make per sale, and which products generate repeat business and appeal to customers who are more likely to buy again and again.

Use the Store Manager's Sales report to determine your products for merchandising. I take my bestselling products and look at several different factors: revenue (sales), page views (popularity), number of orders, and number of items sold. Product sales history is more about merchandising than it is about statistics. In Chapter 20, I show you how to use your Sales report to find which products to push and which sections and categories deserve the largest portion of navigational real estate based upon what's really selling.

Here's how I decide what products to promote:

- **Most of the time, a little sells a lot.** For most retailers, 20 percent of their products drive 80 percent of their sales. Looking at a real Yahoo! Store's sales for April 2005, 700 different products sold that month:

    - The top ten products accounted for 35 percent of the revenue.

    - The top 40 products accounted for 60 percent of the revenue.

    - The top 120 products accounted for 80 percent of the revenue.

    Make more by prominently displaying these top items. Highlight or feature these bestsellers within their various categories to maximize sales.

- **Nothing succeeds like success.** Pushing what items are already selling can give you a lot more sales with just a little more effort. It's far easier to take a solid seller and turn it into a star than it is to get a slow-moving item moving at all. Push the fact that your bestsellers are the bestsellers. Most people feel more comfortable buying what other people bought. If it's popular, it may not be the best, but it's probably not the worst! I can increase a bestseller's sales by 10 to 15 percent just by adding "bestseller" to the name. Sounds sort of obvious, but it works!

- **Promote products that encourage repeat orders.** I also like to push the pages that sell products to folks who tend to become repeat customers. I am much more interested in getting a customer for life than I am in simply making a single sale. I push anything that needs refills, or wears out, or gets used up, or gets read or watched and has new releases coming out.

✓ **It's not what you gross, it's what you net.** If my dad said that once, he said it a thousand times. It's taken me awhile, but I finally get it. I promote the stuffing out of products where I have a higher profit margin. All things being equal, if a customer is trying to decide between two products that cost about the same and solve the same problem, I'm going to push the product (or the distributor or manufacturer) that gives me the better discount and the fattest margin. Sometimes that extra 5 or 10 percent profit is the difference between making it and not making it.

Making small improvements to your top-selling product pages can result in huge increases in sales, but the opposite is also true. You can screw up a perfectly good product page by trying to "fix" it. Be careful. Make small changes and track your results. If something doesn't work — or shoots your sales in the foot — it's easy to undo that last change and try something else.

Merchandising Top Sellers with Navigation

Generally, a typical Yahoo! Store's top-level navigation is divided evenly between the seven or eight major categories reflecting the breadth of the store's product mix. My experience is that more than half of a store's sales comes from its top two or three product categories. What's funny is that the subsections of these super-categories often outsell the nonperforming top-level categories, even though the nonperformers get all that valuable navigation button bar real estate. Pretend you're looking at licensing revenues for all the starters on a pro sports team —say, Michael Jordan, Scottie Pippen, some guy who looks kinda familiar, some other guy, and that guy no one ever remembers. I bet Michael Jordan's Pez dispenser revenues alone outsell the rest of the team's total licensing revenues combined.

Your business probably isn't exactly what you envisioned when you started it, but hey, you're selling something. Here's an idea: Let your customers tell you what's important on your Web site by where they go and what they buy.

For example, when Steve and I started selling comics and popular culture collectibles way back in 1988, we let customers' buying habits determine how the stores were merchandised. We actually allocated physical retail floor space and merchandising in our stores based upon what product categories generated the sales and profits.

Do the same thing with your store's site-wide navigation. Take your best-selling category and pull the top three subcategories up into the top navigation. Add these subcategories to your home page, add these pages to your navigation button bar, and give them the space they deserve.

My best experience with allocating site-wide navigational real estate by sales volume has been to take the best "shop by manufacturer" pages and include them in the global site navigation and top-level category pages. For example, if you sell MP3 players, chances are that Apple's iPod is your #1 seller. Instead of making a customer drill down into the MP3 Players section and then into the iPod section, move the Apple iPod section to the top of the heap. The iPod accessories are popular, too, so that category may warrant a top-seven spot for this hypothetical electronics retailer.

Figuring out what to feature when you have no track record

If you're a new retailer, it's hard to figure out what products to merchandise because you have no idea what's going to sell. You have no sales history to fall back on, no data to mine. You can be patient and wait for six months and let your customers tell you what to promote, but if you're as aggressive as I think you are, you want to take action now. Here are ways to find out what products to promote:

✔ **Ask your suppliers what's hot.** Your wholesalers, dealers, distributors, and manufacturers sell the same products you buy from them to many, many other retailers. Hopefully, your supplier won't tell you exactly what items your direct competition is selling, but many times you can get companywide bestsellers, top-100 product listings, and other aggregate industry information. If lots of other folks are selling it, consider moving it to the top of your promotions list.

✔ **Check out the competition.** Lots of times, your best competitors will tip their hands and give you valuable information about what's selling for them. Poke around their Web sites to see what products they promote as popular or bestsellers.

✔ **Go shopping at Shopping.com.** Shopping.com releases a weekly list of bestselling products. Figure 13-4 shows the Shopping.com Consumer Demand Index, which offers lists like Top 20 Shopping Searches and What's Hot, as well as a graph of what's jumping this week online. See www.shopping.com/cdi for what's moving and shaking in e-commerce.

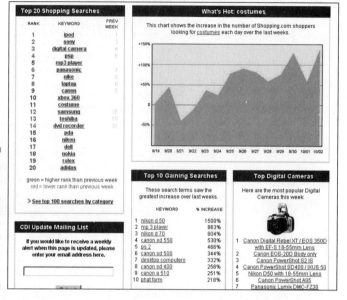

Figure 13-4:
Shopping.
com
releases
a weekly
list of
bestselling
products.

✔ **Watch the big boys, too.** When Amazon.com or other category killers are promoting specific products on their home pages or section pages, you can be absolutely certain that this real estate is generating revenue, whether through direct online sales or kickbacks for product placement by the manufacturer. Hide and watch!

✔ **Pay to play.** Buy yourself some test traffic. Spend the big bucks on a Pay-Per-Click advertising blitz (which I talk about in Chapter 18) and watch where all the traffic goes.

Featuring products across the site

You have many opportunities across your store to feature products. You can promote new items, special offers, and featured products on the home page. On section pages, you can add links to recommended products inside the caption, as well as feature bestsellers. On product pages, you can feature similar and even competing products with Compare To links. You can also upsell by linking to higher end, best-in-class products. You can also display supplies, accessories, and related items on every product page. When someone adds something to the Shopping Cart, you can use the cross-sell feature to show three related products or accessories.

Speeding up the clock with paid search

Several years ago, I spent around $2,000 buying paid-search keywords and sold around $5,000 worth of hammocks in an affiliate pilot project. In the end, I lost only a little bit of money after paying for the hammocks ($3,500 wholesale cost) and some overhead (around $500), but I discovered which pages and products generated sales a lot faster than I would have otherwise.

Paid-search advertising allowed us to buy the most valuable keywords and turn several thousand shoppers loose in our store. We saw where they went and what they bought. We found out that our most popular products were buried way too deep in the Web site.

This research convinced us to move these products to the top of the home page and feature them as home-page specials. We also discovered that even though our site was organized into seven major sections, the majority of our sales came from two sections and all their subsections. The first thing I did after that campaign was to upgrade the subsections from those two super-selling sections to top-level section navigation.

Here's how I recommend featuring products across your site:

✔ **Maximize your home-page real estate.** Make one row of five specials across the top of your home page. Rotate these on a weekly basis. Include a loss leader, a new product, and three of your bestsellers from different sections. Do anything you can to make the offer more exciting. If you can, do a limited-time offer. Push new products in their own section.

✔ **Push bestselling products on section pages.** Sprinkle hypertext links to specific products within the captions of other products. For example, on Mom's duck calls section page, I link to a related waterfowl identification book. This link is not only helpful to customers, but it's also very good for search engine optimization as well.

Figure 13-5 shows how I push to the top three products that I would really prefer to sell. I have a higher profit margin on these products, the product pages convert extremely well, or these products are my best-selling products in this section. Emphasizing your bestsellers on your section pages helps customers like me who may not want to evaluate every possible product you sell, but just want to find something that'll do the job and buy it.

Also, often times the last icon on the right of the first row gets all the clicks. Put your bestselling or most profitable product here. Whatever link gets the clicks gets the chance to convert a browser into a buyer.

Figure 13-5:
Feature your
bestselling
products on
your section
pages by
linking to
them directly
from the
Captions
field and
featuring
them in your
first row of
products.

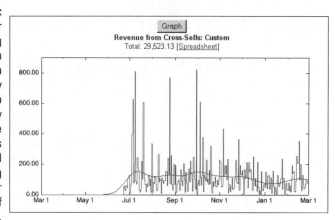

▶ **Upsell on the product pages.** Product pages are the perfect place to upsell better merchandise. Make sure that your customers explore all their options before deciding what to buy. As a shopper, I hate nothing more than buying the wrong version of what I really need. You're actually doing me a favor by trying to sell me the best product for my needs.

A real-world example of upselling is when retail salespeople start showing you the top-of-the-line models and then work their way down the product line until they find a product that has both the features you need and a price you can afford. Unfortunately, you can't control what products customers look at first, but you can gently push people to the products you think they should consider.

On mid-line or bargain-level products, link to more expensive products with text like "Need more features? Consider the S-class Widget 600." Link to best-in-class or feature-rich, top-of-the-line products.

▶ **Accessorize the product pages.** Product pages are the perfect place to sell shoppers everything they possibly need to get the most out of their merchandise. If a product needs batteries, sell batteries on the product page. Push extended warranties, refills, and any accessories that make sense.

If a particular product has multiple accessories, take three to five accessories and bundle them with the original product to make a kit, gift basket, or ultimate version of the product. Throw in a little something extra for free for a very inexpensive promotion and an easy upsell.

Finding $30,000 in Sales by Using Cross-Sell

Cross-sell is a relatively new feature for Yahoo! Merchant Solutions, which is available for all accounts except those using the Starter package. The Cross-sell feature uses item codes to connect items placed in the cart with corresponding cross-sell items. Not only can you use cross-sell to suggest other related items when someone adds a specific product to her cart, but when someone buys one item, you can also give her a discount (as a percentage or a dollar amount off) on other specific items. You can also set start and end dates for promotions and special offers.

I used to believe that the Cross-sell feature was more clutter than it was worth because when a shopper gets something into the cart, I like to get out of her way and let her check out. When someone is in the mood to buy, I try to do two things: make sure that she has everything she needs and then get out of her way. I am obsessed with removing clutter from the shopping process. Remove all impediments to buying. Anything that gets in the way of closing the sale is gone.

I'll admit it. I was wrong! Here's a cool story that illustrates the point that you don't need to close the sale until you make sure that the customer has everything he needs.

Figure 13-6 shows how a new client's site generates around $100 a day in additional sales from cross-sells. That's $36,000 a year. You can also see what products are being cross-sold because items bought from cross-selling have little + signs next to them on the individual Order page.

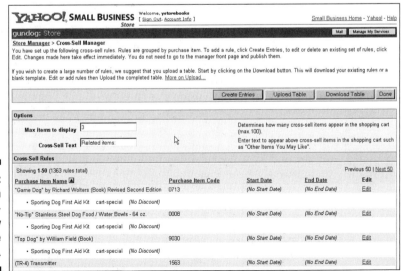

Figure 13-6: Sales from cross-selling show up on the graph.

The best part about cross-selling products is that these sales are most likely ones you wouldn't have gotten otherwise, so all the gross profit really goes to the bottom line. Usually, there's no additional cost on the sales, because you can just throw something extra in the box. Sweet!

As long as you know a little bit about cross-selling, you're ready to try it out. Go to the Store Manager under Promote and click the Cross-Sell link. If you haven't already turned on Cross-Sells, click the Get Started Now link. Figure 13-7 shows you the page where you can either create your cross-sell items by hand, or you can create a table or CSV file with a list of product codes and the corresponding codes of items you want to cross-sell with those products.

Figure 13-7:
Create
cross-sell
items in
the Store
Manager
under
Cross-Sell.

Retailers with large stores will probably never get around to listing three to five items for every item in their store. I recommend starting with the top 100, and doing ten products a day until you start seeing some results. When I don't have a specific cross-sell item for a product, I like to have what I call a global cross-sell item. A global cross-sell works great until you take the time to hand-pick three or more cross-sell items for every single product in your Yahoo! Store.

Stop and look at each product and figure out three to five things that someone buying this product also needs. Take a look at the orders for this product. Look at the other products people bought when they purchased this product. Consider those products as well when you create your cross-sell database. The more time and thought you put into a product's cross-sell items, the better your cross-sells will do for you.

Here's something easy to do that starts getting results immediately: Pick a popular product that appeals to the broadest range of customers and offer it as a default cross-sell on every product.

Do these two things: (a) Change the Code on that product to Cart-Special and (b) create and upload a cross-sell table with a row for each product with each product's code in the purchase-item-code field and the code Cart-Special in the every cross-sell-item-code field.

Here's the cool part: Anytime you want, you can change what product is the cart-special by changing which product has the code Cart-Special. This rocks!

Before you can create a Cross-Sell table to upload, you need a list of all your product codes. You can get this list of codes by exporting your products under Catalog Manager, under the product summary of the Controls in the Store Editor, from the XML feed, or by using a third-party export tool like David Burke's Ystore Export tool at `http://ydev.visualfuture.com` (see Chapter 23).

Cross-sells let you give free gifts with the purchase of selected items! I got a 20 percent increase in conversion rate by offering a free gift with a purchase on one of our Yahoo! Stores. These free gifts cost us about a dollar, but the perceived value to our customers is much, much higher. Our inventory of free gifts changes quite frequently, and I can tell when we have a lame free gift because sales tend to drop!

Make the discount on a cross-sell item 100 percent, which makes that item free. Pretty cool! People can drive you crazy with free gifts, though, so be careful. Some folks try to get something for nothing and will do things like try to edit the quantity on their free gift. Make sure that you include proper disclaimers and terms and conditions on your free gifts just in case.

Merchandising Products in Other Ways

After you've figured out your most profitable categories and which items to cross-sell, look at other ways to shop. You never stop coming up with new ways to organize your products. See how your customers shop your store to determine how you merchandise your Yahoo! Store. Perhaps they do one (or more) of the following:

✔ **Shop by product type:** I prefer to group my merchandise in categories by product type. It's pretty easy to figure out category names, too. Category names should be the generic keywords that most shoppers use when searching for what you sell. By researching basic keywords (which I talk about in Chapter 16), brainstorming, looking at the competition, and asking some real customers how they shop, you can figure out exactly what your main category navigation should be.

✔ **Shop by manufacturer or brand name:** I also like to group products by manufacturer or brand name. Brand-name pages are also keyword loaded. Sometimes your manufacturer pages will be your most popular pages. Brand names are a very safe way for consumers to shop. For example, I don't know a lot about patio doors and windows, but if I buy a top brand like Pella, I think I should be okay.

✔ **Shop by problem (or solution):** Lots of customers search for solutions to their problems rather than by the specific name of a product or prod- uct type. For example, if you sell dental hygiene supplies, create a Shop By page called Ten Best Products To Cure Bad Breath, where you put the alcohol-free mouthwash, the tongue scrapers, the dental floss, and related products. I generated a lot of free search-engine traffic to one of my dog sites when I created content pages about solving dog-training problems: how to stop dogs from unwanted digging, how to stop dogs from chewing, how to crate-train dogs (potty training), and how to stop dogs from barking. Most of this content was free training information, but I also linked to various products from these pages.

✔ **Shop by customer type:** You can classify your customers into several different categories: beginner, intermediate, and advanced users; ama- teurs, semi-pros, or professionals; personal, small business, or corporate/ government customers; and so on.

✔ **Shop by name (author, artist, and musician):** When I sell books, I also like to create a Shop By Author or Shop By Artist category, where I can feature all the creator's work and include a short biography. These author pages are also great for linking to other resource pages.

✔ **Shop by bestselling products:** You can feature your top ten bestselling products across the whole store, as well as bestsellers by section and by product type. For example, on a strollers section page, you could high- light your top three bestselling baby jogging strollers.

✔ **Shop new arrivals:** Create a new arrivals section, where you can feature the latest products to arrive in your online store. Feature this section on the home page, too.

✔ **Shop by occasion:** Make special sections for each gift-giving holiday that applies to your business — Mother's Day, Father's Day, birthdays, Valentine's Day, and especially Christmas.

✔ **Shop by price:** Price is a great way to merchandise products, especially higher-end retail. Lots of people have a dollar amount in mind when they're shopping and either can't or won't spend any more or less.

For example, a few years back, I was looking to buy a bass amplifier, and I made up my mind that it was going to cost around $1,000 to get what I needed. The sales guy kept showing me $400 and $500 amps. They were nice, but didn't have enough thump. Argh! I kept saying, "I want something bigger. I want something louder. I have to compete with the world's loudest drummer." Finally he got it, and I got the amp I wanted. Mo' bass!

Would you like fries with that?

Retailing super-consultant Harry Friedman likes to tell this story at his retailing seminars. Harry tests his client stores to see how many times their salespeople will add on to an existing sale after someone has decided to buy something. He sends mystery shoppers into his clients' retail stores with a no-limit American Express card, with instructions to say yes every single time the salesperson adds on items to an existing sale. For example, someone selling a suit may suggest a belt, or socks, or a tie, or a sport coat, and the mystery shopper says yes every time. It's pretty funny (but probably not to the retailer) to see how few add-ons salespeople will attempt before they decide that you've bought enough and decide to cut you off.

Recently, I had a chance to try out this approach when I bought an Oreck vacuum cleaner. I wanted to see how many times the phone rep would add on. First, I bought the vacuum cleaner. Next I bought a year's worth of bags. Then I bought a multipurpose pocketknife. Next I bought an air filter, and at that point, I was getting a little nervous. I bought another multipurpose pocketknife, but then he stopped. Whew! I'm glad I did my add-on experiment, but if anyone wants a deal on some pocketknives, give me a holler. . . .

Chapter 14

Checking Out the New Shopping Cart

. . . .

In This Chapter

▶ Exploring the new Checkout Manager's many features

▶ Designing your cart to match the look and feel of your store

▶ Selling more by streamlining checkout pages

. . . .

A well-designed Shopping Cart and secure checkout are extremely crucial elements of any successful e-commerce business. Your checkout needs to be easy to use as well as inspire trust and confidence in your company as shoppers consider giving you their money and personal information.

In the past, Yahoo!'s checkout lacked customization options and was one of the biggest liabilities of the Yahoo! Store platform. I have never liked the checkout, but I just got over it instead of worrying about something I couldn't change. Well, suffer no more, Y!folks. Not only are the new Shopping Cart and Checkout Manager real, they're spectacular!

The new Checkout Manager is extremely well organized and well thought-out. You now have control over the cart's and checkout's flow, appearance, navigation, branding, fields, checkout buttons, and functionality.

In this chapter, I discuss all the cool, new changes in the brand-new Checkout Manager. I really love the new cart and Checkout Manager. They're screaming! When this cart becomes the real checkout procedure (probably by the time you read this book), it's gonna rock! Bear in mind that the new Checkout Manager was in beta at the time of this writing. By the time this book is published, there may very well be some feature changes, so check out the Yahoo! Help files for the most current info.

Introducing the New Checkout Manager

I'm happy to introduce the new V3 (Version 3) checkout. The more I dig into it, the more impressed I am with all those smart folks in Sunnyvale in the Store division at Yahoo! Retailers have been waiting for these changes for a long, long time, but it looks like it was worth it! The checkout is a control freak's dream! Now you can customize everything.

Eventually, the new Checkout Manager will become the default checkout for new Merchant Solutions accounts, so a lot of the things mentioned in this chapter won't show up on the Store Manager for new accounts.

Whew! The new Checkout Manager has more than 100 pages of documentation in the Yahoo! Store Help files, so this chapter is really more of an overview of what you can do than how to do everything you can possibly do. For all the details, download Yahoo!'s excellent "Getting Started Guide for Checkout Manager" at `http://help.yahoo.com/help/us/store/manage/checkout` and read over the Help files there, too.

To start playing around with the new cart, you must turn on the Beta test by clicking the Store Manager link to the Checkout Manager (Beta) and accept the Beta agreement. Click the Test Your Checkout Manager Settings link, which takes you to a page where you can set the test cookie on your machine so that you can place test orders in the New Checkout without mucking about with your real store.

Exploring the Checkout Manager

The new Checkout Manager is accessible from a link in the Store Manager under Order Settings. Checkout Manager is divided into four separate modules:

- **Global Settings,** which controls checkout flow and the checkout wrapper (HTML for navigation and branding) and is covered in the section "Controlling Checkout Flow with Global Settings," later in this chapter.

- **Page Configuration,** which defines page titles, whether top and/or side navigation appears, and head tags and gives you total control of standard and custom fields and their labels, and is covered in the section "Configuring Elements with Page Configuration," later in this chapter.

- **Visual Customization,** which determines the look and feel through Global styles (either default Visual Styles, a custom-configured Visual Style, or totally customized CSS); with Font, Text Links, Sections and Sub-Sections, and Checkout Buttons; Progress Indicator, and Checkout Buttons with Button Labels (text); and Button Style (CSS Button, HTML

Button, Text Link, or Image Button). See the section "Customizing Your Visual Design," later in this chapter, for more info.

✔ **Advanced Settings,** which controls Order Button Behavior, Special Handling (Downloadable Goods, Gift Certificates, and No Cost Goods), Item Option Validation, and the Revert panel, where you can revert back to the published settings or the default settings for the Checkout Manager. For more info, read the section "Tinkering with Advanced Settings," later in this chapter.

Poke around the Checkout Manager's four modules. Make a few small changes and save them. Publish your Order Settings. Place a test order (see the next section) and see how what you did looks in your cart. Make notes about what you want to change.

Testing your settings

Figure 14-1 displays where you preview changes to checkout settings in an enhanced preview function of Checkout Manager. This preview is so much better than the old preview of the cart and order form.

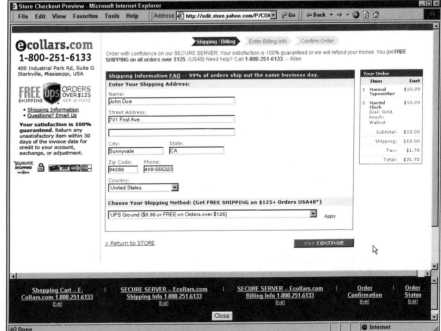

Figure 14-1: See how your changes look in the enhanced preview of Checkout Manager.

You can also place real test orders on your store through the new cart without enabling the Checkout Manager for your customers. When you first activate New Checkout Manager, the special Yahoo! *cookie* (tracking file) redirects you from the old cart and checkout to the `store.yahoo.net` checkout on the published site so that you can see exactly what your customers will see with the new checkout. If you hate your changes, you can also revert to the system defaults or revert to the current published version of the checkout.

Be careful when you revert! If you've published your checkout settings, then you can revert to them, but if you revert to system defaults, all your changes are undone and all your hard work is gone forever!

Publishing your new cart

You have to publish Order Settings to update saved changes to the Checkout Manager (whether you're just testing or have enabled the real deal). If you're testing the Checkout Manager, after you publish Order Settings, you'll be the only one who can place test orders and see the new checkout. If you've enabled the new Checkout Manager (which I don't recommend yet), your published changes are live for everyone to see.

Anytime you make a change, you need to save it. You can save by choosing Save, which just saves your changes, or Save & Preview, which takes you to a Preview window, where you can see what your changes look like on a sample order. If you're at a stopping place and like what you see, go back to the Store Manager and Publish Order Settings to make the saved changes live on your published store.

The easiest way to kill your sales is to screw up something in the checkout, so I always place a test order on another computer after making any changes to any part of checkout, Shopping Cart, or Shipping or Tax settings to make sure that I haven't blown up something. If I'm making major changes, I ask an opinionated third party, like my brother or my assistant, Nikki, because I know that they'll really tell me what they think!

Controlling Checkout Flow with Global Settings

Flow, the number of pages for each step in the checkout process, includes the Shopping Cart, Shipping Information, Billing Information, optional Order

Review, and Order Confirmation stages. You can place each checkout stage on a separate page or design a true one-page checkout that merges the cart with shipping and billing info. You can also have a regular cart with a merged shipping and billing page for a faster checkout.

Click the Checkout Manager link in the Store Manager and then click the Global Settings link. The Global Settings' Flow Settings page appears with clickable tabs that link to the Checkout Wrapper and Checkout Settings pages.

Flow settings

You now have total control over the Order Flow from Cart to the Confirmation Page with the new Flow settings.

On the Flow settings page, Checkout Options lets you choose either single page or multipage checkout. Single page lets you to have a true one-page checkout with shipping and billing on the Shopping Cart page, if you want, which is good for single-item stores. (Make sure that you set your cart to secure under the Variables page.)

The Shipping and Billing information page can be on the same page or separate pages. As Figure 14-2 shows, when you collect shipping and billing information on the same page, the checkout feels a little crowded, so I recommend a multipage checkout here. The shipping charges, based on dollar amount and default shipping method, show in the Shopping Cart (which is really cool), but watch out!

If you have same-page shipping and billing and remove the Order Review like I do and if you have additional shipping rates (based on other shipping methods, zip code, country, or state) or charge sales tax (unless the customer selects the shipping method and clicks the Apply button), the customer sometimes doesn't get to see the real total until after he places an order. Some folks are going to be royally ticked off when you charge them more than you said you would.

Here's a quick fix: You can always add text to the message in the shipping methods section that says "Make sure you click the Apply button to see the cost of your chosen shipping method."

The Shopping Cart section can be top- or right-aligned. This section isn't really the Shopping Cart, but the Order Summary on your checkout page, which shows what someone bought with the code and options. Pick Align Right to move the cart to the right, which pulls all the checkout functionality closer to the top of the page.

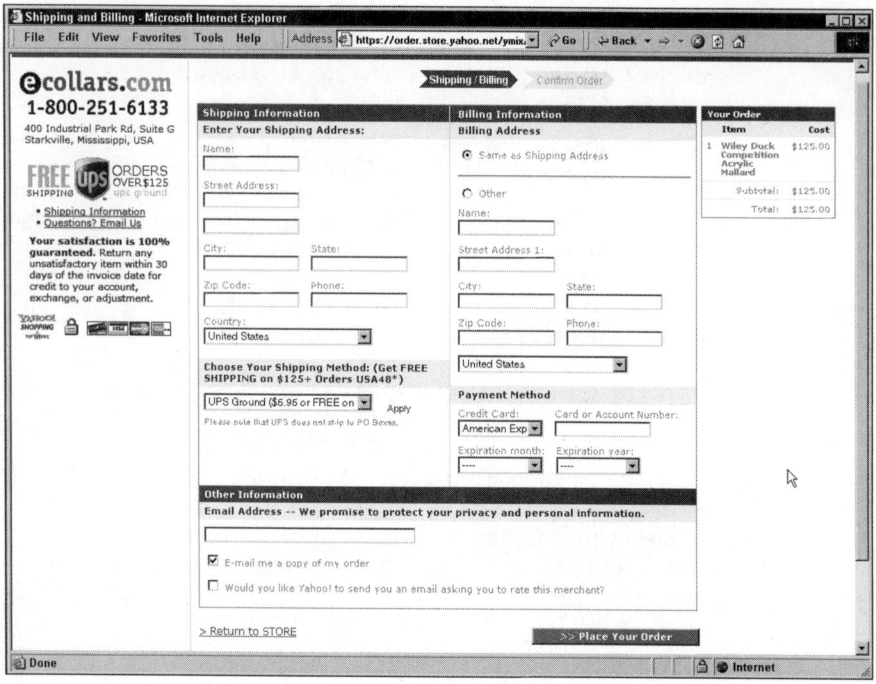

Figure 14-2:
A combined Shipping and Billing page may look a little crowded.

You can set the Order Review Page to Show (the default) or Hide. I call this page the "Are you really, really sure you want to give me money? You can still back out" page. I recommend turning off Order Review if you have separate Shipping and Billing pages because you'll get more orders. However, if you merge these pages, keep the Order Review page to stay out of trouble.

Checkout Wrapper

Checkout Wrapper is Yahoo!'s branding/navigation fix, which is the key to the look and feel and consistency of experience during checkout.

The Checkout Wrapper has two parts:

- **Company branding:** You can upload a logo to Checkout Wrapper's Company Image field, but don't, because you're limited to a 250 x 50 GIF file. Instead, choose Display Text and delete all the text in the field. Save your changes. Use the HTML fields for branding with your logo.

- **Checkout regions:** Keeping a consistent look and feel across the site through the checkout is much easier with Top Navigation, Side Navigation, and Footer text fields for HTML.

I recommend matching the branding and navigation of your regular Yahoo! Store pages with these text fields, but don't use the Top Navigation field (header for HTML) unless you absolutely have to. Top Navigation pushes all the checkout functionality down lower on the page, and folks have to scroll to see the Continue or Place Order buttons.

Instead, use the Side Navigation field and put your branding, trust symbols (such as the Yahoo! Shopping 5-Star rating, HackerSafe logo, TrustE logo, and so on), and reassuring links to privacy policies in the Sidebar text field.

After you put the HTML code in the Side Navigation field and save, you still have go to the Checkout Manager's Page Configuration module, enable Display In Checkout Page, and click the Save button for each stage of the checkout where you want the Side Navigation field to appear (Cart, Shipping Info, Billing Info, Order Review, or Order Confirmation).

Checkout settings

You can use checkout settings to enable Customer Ratings and Gift Options, switch to alternate URLs for utility pages, and enable Yahoo!'s third-party (read: paid) services.

Configuring Elements with Page Configuration

Page Configuration is where you can configure the various checkout page elements: customize Page Titles, display custom HTML, add HTML and JavaScript to the head tags field, add custom fields, and have total control of standard fields and their appearance with labels. Also noteworthy is the fact that Page Configuration changes according to the Flow Settings in Global Settings. It's magic! Page Configuration shows you only the number of pages in your checkout flow, whether you use a single-page or multipage layout, or choose to show a review page.

Page Settings

You can control each page in your checkout flow with Page Settings fields, including the text fields Title and Page Message, as well as the Top Navigation Bar (display or hide), Side Navigation Bar (display or hide), and Pay Using PayPal.

Max out your checkout by making the most of these important text fields:

✔ **Page titles:** Title tags appear in the upper left corner of your browser window. You can improve your checkout's Page Titles for branding and giving shoppers confidence. Instead of a lame Page Title like "Shipping Information," try something like "SECURE SERVER: My Shipping Info: *YourDomain*.com (1-800-555-1212)."

✔ **Message fields:** A simple text box allows you to put text or simple HMTL on each Checkout page right above the checkout functionality. Add order information and trust-building messages to woo customers at the most important stage in the buying process. Keep text in the message field as short as possible so as to not push the big green button down any lower on the page than you have to.

Page Sections

Page Sections displays all the sections and fields for each of the different checkout stages and is where you can add, edit, or hide standard fields and add, edit, hide, or delete custom fields. You can turn sections on or off, too, if you don't use them or want to streamline the checkout process.

Embedding marketing and trust messages within the structure of the new Checkout Manager is an efficient way to get your message across using what used to be wasted space. For example, I edit and rename Section Names to add useful shipping information or marketing messages. For example, I change "Shipping Address" to "Shipping Address: Most orders ship out the same business day." Also, I like to expand "E-mail Address" to "E-mail Address: We promise to protect your privacy and personal information."

Fields

Figure 14-3 shows how you control section labels and formatting. You can edit, hide, or delete standard fields; edit the text on field labels; or hide individual field labels completely. You also can add, edit, and delete custom fields and control the type of field, length, acceptable data input, and so on.

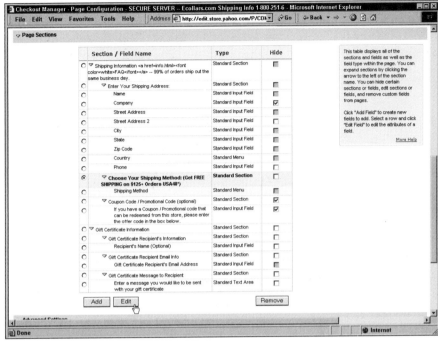

Figure 14-3:
The Page
Configura-
tion screen
is where
you edit
fields
for each
Checkout
page.

Here's what you can do to fields:

- **Hide redundant or unnecessary fields and field labels.** You can turn on or off individual fields. Use Do Not Display Field Name In Checkout to keep the field, but not show the label.

- **Change the type of buttons** from radio buttons to drop-down, and so on.

- **Edit field names.** You can now rename the field labels for every field within checkout. For example, change Coupon to Source Code (Optional) to reduce the "I'm getting screwed because everyone has a coupon but me!" factor, which can kill your conversion rate.

- **Add custom fields.** Collect additional information or enhance checkout with text. Also, enhance your design by placing these custom fields at the top or bottom of any section.

Advanced Settings

Here's what's you can do inside Advanced Settings:

- ✔ **HTML Head Section:** Put JavaScript or HTML code inside the head tags field for each page in the checkout. For example, you can stick in tracking code from Yahoo! Search Marketing (formerly Overture) or Google AdWords to help you see which paid-search ads converted into sales. See Chapter 21 for more info. Merchants familiar with CSS can also use embedded styles to override their global CSS styles set by Checkout Manager.

- ✔ **Cookie Check Alert:** The Yahoo! Shopping Cart requires cookies for customers buying multiple items. *Cookies* are very small files that Web servers place on computers to identify and track users. On the Shopping Cart page, you can turn the Cookie Check Alert on or off and edit the text in the Cookie Alert Message. This text appears to shoppers who don't have cookies enabled in their browser settings. The Yahoo! Store cookie can also store limited amounts of information and remembers customer info (except any credit-card data) typed into Checkout pages for two weeks. This cookie saves repeat visitors from having to retype all their info and helps convert more return visitors when they see that they don't have to retype all their personal data.

Customizing Your Visual Design

You have almost total control over the visual design of the Shopping Cart and checkout. Visual customization lets you use the default settings and edit those with a Variables-like interface controlling the fonts and colors. Advanced users can have almost total control using CSS (cascading style sheets) to format text. CSS is a relatively new way Web designers use global style codes to format HTML pages.

Technical reviewer Michael Whitaker says that you should not use a custom CSS unless you're, in fact, proficient with CSS and have the ability to test the way the checkout looks on different browsers and platforms.

Global styles

Global styles control the appearance of fonts, text links, colors of sections and subsections, and appearance of Checkout buttons. Choose Default Visual Styles, Configure Visual Styles, or Custom Uploaded CSS. Go with the default look or control the look of the cart with Editor-style fields where you choose colors and fonts or control the look with custom CSS. Simply download the CSS file, modify it at your leisure, re-upload it, and you're done.

Progress indicator

A progress indicator is a way to show shoppers where they are in the checkout process and how far they have to go. Choose custom graphics or CSS (which I like better). Here are few things you may want to try:

✔ **Change page titles in the progress indicator.** Add calls to action in the Checkout page names in the progress indicator to tell folks what to do. For example, instead of simply saying "Shipping Information," I prefer to use "Enter Shipping Info." You have only 25 characters, so you can't go too crazy.

✔ **Choose progress indicator colors and fonts to match your style.** I prefer grayed-out text for visited and not-visited checkout stages.

✔ **Upload custom images for progress indicators.** When you upload your own custom images for progress indicators, you have to upload three separate versions of each step of the checkout process: visited, not visited, and current. Also, Step 1 is not the Shopping Cart like you'd think, but Shipping Info (or Shipping and Billing if combined). Limit your images to 170 x 25 pixels.

Checkout buttons

This trick is one of my favorite things about the new cart! Now you can replace all the Checkout buttons with custom image buttons or standard HTML buttons, or you can just customize the default CSS buttons, which I prefer. You can control the text with Button Label text and the look with Button Style.

Edit text on Checkout buttons to improve conversions. Use a call to action and capitalization for emphasis. For example, I change the Cross-sell button's text from Order to Add To Cart. In the Shopping Cart, I change the Checkout button to Proceed To Checkout. On the Billing Info page, I change Place Order to Place Your Order.

You can edit a Checkout button's type, too. I change the pesky little Apply button that appears on the Shipping Info page to the right of Shipping Methods from a CSS button to a text link to deemphasize it. The Apply button is too close to the Continue button at the bottom of the page for my taste!

Tinkering with Advanced Settings

Advanced Settings is where they stuck everything else. I recommend not worrying about Item Option Validation and setting it to No. For more information on Item Option Validation, go to Chapter 15.

Also, the Revert panel lets you jump backward in time to the published settings or all the way back to the default settings for the Checkout Manager. Take good notes because you lose everything if you totally reboot!

Jumping to the New Cart

Hey! The new cart has bugs. The beta secure servers are a bit slower. Don't click the Enable Checkout Manager link unless you're sure. I have a real store that I play with, and it probably costs me eight to ten orders every time I enable the new cart, but I'm finding out enough monkeying around with it to make it worthwhile by the time they roll out the new cart.

If you do decide to enable the cart, you can jump back to the old V1 or V2 checkout by clicking the Disable Checkout Manager link in the Checkout Manager.

Chapter 15

Mastering the Store Manager

*T*he Store Manager is order-processing central, your virtual customer service headquarters and online control panel to configure and manage the backend of your Yahoo! Store. The Store Manager is where they show you the money! You can review, manage, and process your orders, submit credit-card statements, and view statistics and reports of how well you're doing.

New store owners use the Store Manager to set up their stores by customizing secure Checkout pages; setting up tax rates, shipping methods, and rates; defining international order rules; writing customer notification e-mails; configuring and uploading inventory; controlling which user IDs have access to the store; managing mailing lists; and lots, lots more.

This chapter is an overview of the Store Manager's many features with some cool Store Manager tips and tricks thrown in. In my world, I focus on building and marketing stores. When someone clicks the Place Order button, that's when the customer service folks usually step in. You need to know all about the Store Manager, so I'm breaking out the good stuff for you. I've discovered a lot watching my brother and regular clients manage their stores for almost ten years, and now I get to pass it on.

Getting (Store) Help When You Need It

Everything changes. Staying on top of all the new features of Yahoo! Store is tough! Seems like almost every time I look up, the fine folks in Sunnyvale at the store division at Yahoo! keep adding useful features to the Store Manager. Lately, most of the improvements are backend features like the Shipping Manager (integrated with UPS Online), the new Checkout Manager (Chapter 14), Risk Tools (customized credit-card approval rules), and most recently PayPal as a payment method or alternative to a Merchant Account.

When you find that you need help with all these new features, the Help files are just a step away. Fortunately, Yahoo!'s online Store Help files have kept pace with all the updates. Although it doesn't seem that long ago when the online Store Help files for Store Manager were a little skimpy (and almost nonexistent for store building), they now rock! Yahoo!'s own king of content, Paul Boisvert, and the Yahoo! Store folks do an outstanding job writing helpful, retailer-friendly online documentation.

Needless to say, it's hard to stay on top of all the new information coming out. To keep this book from turning into a four-volume set, I'm going to cop out more than once and point to the helpful Store Help files. Here are my favorite ways to get information and stay current on all things Yahoo! Store:

- ✔ **Get some help (online).** More than a thousand pages of searchable online Help files detail exactly how features of the Store Manager and other Yahoo! Store elements work. Start at `http://help.yahoo.com/help/us/store` and browse around or use the search box in your Store Manager.

- ✔ **Download the Getting Started Guide.** Yahoo! now also offers a free online e-book, *Getting Started with Yahoo! Merchant Solutions.* This 384-page guide covers everything you need to know about opening your store, with specific details on how to do the nuts-and-bolts stuff. You can download this PDF file by right-clicking the link at `http://help.yahoo.com/help/us/store/guides` and choosing Save Target As.

- ✔ **Download other guides.** Yahoo! also offers these helpful downloadable guides in a PDF format: *Open for Business Checklist, Checkout Manager Guide, Order Processing Guide,* and the *Store Editor Variables Guide.* Download them all.

- ✔ **Check the System Status page.** While not exactly a Help file, this link goes to an extremely helpful System Status page, which displays any technical difficulties going on with the Editor. Hmmm. A little bird tells me that this page may switch to a blog pretty soon. Cool! That means retailers can subscribe to the RSS feed and get system status updates via their news reader, `my.yahoo.com` pages, e-mail, Yahoo! Messenger, wireless phones, or all of the preceding.

Getting Anywhere from Here

The Store Manager (see Figure 15-1) is the navigational hub for all things Merchant Solutions. With the click of your mouse, you can jump to all the different Merchant Solutions tools: Domain, Web Hosting, E-mail, and the store-building and product-management tools. Update your Yahoo! info under the Manage My Services button, which links to your billing info (`http://billing.yahoo.com`) and contact information as well as the Manage My Services page (`http://smallbusiness.yahoo.com/services`), with links to all the Yahoo! products and services assigned to your Billing ID.

Click the Store Editor link, and you're magically transported to my favorite store-building and product-management tool, the Store Editor. (See Chapter 9 for lots of information about the Store Editor.) Adjacent to that link is the View Site link, which whisks you to the published version of your store.

If you use the Yahoo! Web-hosting method for store building, the Store Manager has links to Catalog Manager and Store Tags Hub. The Catalog Manager is where you manage products and tables, track inventory, upload and download items, and publish changes when you've finished updating information.

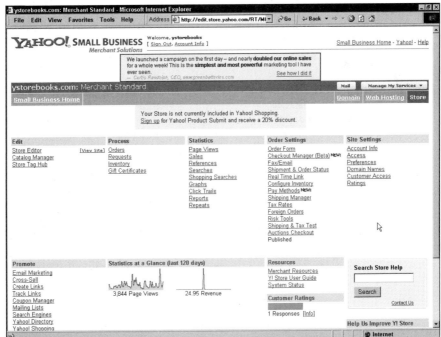

Figure 15-1:
The Store Manager is the hub of your e-commerce universe.

Inside the Catalog Manager, you can add, edit, and delete items; add custom fields to product pages; view and update inventory; and publish changes in your product database. You can also adjust products and inventory information by hand or by uploading a CSV (comma separated value) file. The Store Tag Hub organizes all the tools you need to use Store Tags, including a wizard for generating store tags for specific products, prebuilt modules of Store Tags code, and various Store Tags documentation. (For more information on choosing a store-building method, read Chapter 3 and `http://ystorebooks.com/storetags.html` for more information about the Store Editor and Store Tags.

Shipping and Managing Orders

Every Yahoo! Store owner I know uses the Store Manager somewhat differently. Usually this system depends on how each merchant processes orders and the volume of sales he does. I often get excited about the different technical ways we can solve a problem, but sometimes the simplest system is the best. Low-tech is sometimes the best answer, especially when the folks using the system are technically challenged. (I'm *not* picking on you, Mom!)

Low-tech order-management solutions

Some folks barely use the Store Manager at all. After their shipping methods and rates and taxes are set up, they're done with the Store Manager unless something changes. These retailers use order-notification faxes as pick tickets and invoices, process credit cards offline outside of Yahoo!, and use paper-based methods to manage customers, orders, and inventory. These folks send shipping confirmation e-mails by hand by responding to the order-notification e-mails. For these retailers, their Yahoo! Store is a marketing tool, and the Store Manager has a lot of untapped potential.

I know of stores tracking more than 50 orders a day that are still using a paper-based system — a 3-ring binder with a list of order numbers, customer names, and a status code sits beside the phone. This method works even when the power is out and there are no real tech-support issues, but this solution won't scale if a company's sales double year after year.

Other folks simply use Yahoo! Store as a store-building and order-collection tool and export customer and order data to use in third-party programs. There are all kinds of cool features in the Store Manager that the majority of my clients never use because by the time you need them, you're probably ready for more powerful third-party inventory, customer service, and order-management tools.

Go with the (order) flow

The folks at my mom's warehouse use merchant-order faxes for pick tickets and place picked orders at the beginning of the processing line. At the beginning of each shift, Allen exports customer and order data from the Yahoo! Store Manager and imports that data into Microbiz, a somewhat generic general retailing inventory program (inherited from Mom's retail store that she's almost outgrown). This cycle happens a couple or three times a day.

David opens up Microbiz, pulls up the customer's record, double-checks the pick ticket, and creates an invoice, ringing up all the items in the box. David then runs the credit card. When he gets an authorization code, he rings out a Microbiz invoice, which removes the products from inventory and adds the order to the customer's history. He prints two copies of the invoice: He places one inside the box for the customer and tapes one to the outside of the box for our records. The box is then packed and sealed and placed next to the digital scale by the UPS Shipping workstation.

Next, Jonathan imports customer shipping data to the UPS computer's free UPS shipping software called UPS WorldShip. He pulls up the customer record, creates a shipping record based on ship method and weight of the box, and prints a label. Jonathan sticks the label on the box and puts the box by the loading dock, where it waits until the UPS guy shows up. UPS WorldShip also assigns tracking numbers, organizes and summarizes the daily pickup data at the end of the day, and finally e-mails customers with their shipping notification, estimated delivery date, and a tracking number.

High-tech order-management solutions

Some merchants use the Store Manager every single day. These merchants live inside the Store Manager, processing credit cards online by first getting authorization when a transaction is made and then completing the sales by clicking the Sale button as they ship orders. These retailers use the Store Manager as an order-management tool, too, updating order status settings and sending tracking information from one central location.

Sometimes the Store Manager runs painfully slowly, especially during peak usage times when other retailers are using the Manager. The Store Manager is slow to begin with because you're on a secure server, but there are other reasons, too. Some Store Manager functions require a lot of heavy lifting (creating order summaries and large export files). Stores with thousands of products take longer to do product- and order-related functions (order-related reports and stats, database inventory, and so on). Finally, you're sharing resources with 35,000-plus other Yahoo! Store owners on a limited number of servers. There's a reason I code RTML and play with the Store Manager at 4 in the morning. It's so much faster!

I completely avoid using the Store Manager when I can during regular business hours around the Christmas shopping season. On Mondays, the Manager seems particularly slow because retailers are processing orders from over the weekend. The best way to not bog down the Store Manager is to avoid performing multiple Manager tasks at the same time and always wait for one process to finish before firing something else up in the Manager. Check out `http://help. yahoo.com/help/us/store/troubleshooting/troubleshooting-09. html` for more methods to make your Manager move.

However, just because the Store Manager is slow, it doesn't mean that the published version of your store is slow. Unlike the extremely powerful multi-million dollar load-balancing system that handles the millions upon millions of Yahoo! Store shoppers every single day, you share a Store Manager with multiple merchants.

Power-user solutions

Power users export order info out of their Store Manager, import that info into third-party tools to process and ship orders, and then export and upload the updated info back to the Store Manager. Doing all the data crunching and order processing offline gives you the best of both worlds: You get to use all the power of the Store Manager with almost none of the drawbacks. You don't have to deal with limited Internet bandwidth or server-sharing issues, but you also can automate everything and not have to touch each order by hand.

Super-advanced users who can program or have access to programmers can actually have Yahoo! post the order info right into their own secure server at the same time Store Manager gets the order. These guys can process orders and generate an order status update file, which they e-mail to Yahoo! Changing the order status to "shipped" automatically triggers a customer-shipping notification e-mail. See `http://help.yahoo.com/help/us/store/order/ retrieve` for more info. Merchants with a Starter account need to upgrade to get access to these features.

Third-party order-management software

Maybe I'm just grumpy, but I prefer to use anything but the Store Manager for managing inventory, my customer database, sales reporting, e-mail, and so on. You can visit `http://help.yahoo.com/help/us/store/guides` and download useful application notes about some of these Yahoo! Store–friendly third-party services and tools including, UPS Online Tools, Paymentech, QuickBooks, Stone Edge Order Manager, and OrderMotion. I have clients using one or more of these software packages. Here are some popular order-management solution options for you to consider, with my commentary:

- ✔ **Mail Order Manager (M.O.M.), from Dydacomp:** I have Yahoo! Store clients who swear by Mail Order Manager. One of my long-time clients actually gushes when he talks about M.O.M.'s drop-shipping capabilities. M.O.M. is available in several different versions, which allow you to buy what you need and trade up later. Dydacomp offers modules for customer management, order entry, order processing, inventory, purchasing/receiving, accounting, point of sale, list management/mailing, and so on. For a $25 refundable deposit, you can get a fully-working trial version that comes with a coupon good for $100 off the purchase of a system if you decide to buy. M.O.M. (www.dydacomp.com) is priced from $995 for the SOHO version.

- ✔ **StoneEdge Order Management Software:** Designed for stores doing anywhere from 10 to 2,000 orders per day, StoneEdge (www.stoneedge.com) lets you manage customers, inventory, and orders from your desktop. StoneEdge folks support Yahoo! Stores and several other shopping carts, such as MonsterCommerce (Hey, Steph!), Miva, eBay, and ShopSite. Multiple Yahoo! Stores aren't a problem as long as Codes are the same on each store. This software is priced from $995, depending on the features and support needed.

- ✔ **QuickBooks:** Lots of Yahoo! Store owners must use QuickBooks based upon the number of questions I see posted online. My brother, Steve, uses the online version of QuickBooks (http://quickbooks.intuit.com) for bookkeeping, but I don't really see QuickBooks as an inventory or customer-tracking tool unless you have a really small number of products, customers, and orders.

- ✔ **OrderMotion:** Imagine being able to afford a site license to a million dollar enterprise-level order-management software. If you were processing tens of thousands of orders a day, it would run you less than a buck an order! OrderMotion has a progressive pricing model that assesses you a minimum monthly charge, but what you pay is based upon how many orders you process.

  OrderMotion is an online multichannel Yahoo! Store–compatible order-management and inventory control platform with a killer feature-set. Because it's an online application and you pay a per-order fee, you can have as many of your employees use it as you have PCs with Web access at no additional cost. While it's a little more expensive than some other software, I believe you get what you pay for. I have several clients using the software, and they say the additional cost is worth all the extra time you get. Just FYI: I'm making the jump to OrderMotion as soon as I finish this book, so watch my blog at http://ystore.blogs.com for tales from the migration.

Processing Orders — Show Me the Money!

The Store Manager is where you process orders, catalog requests, and gift certificates. You can view orders one at a time, view a range of orders, view or download a summary of orders, print anywhere from one order to hundreds, and export your orders in a variety of formats.

When you get a new order, a red asterisk (or star) appears by the Store Manager's Process Orders link to let you know you have work to do. This red star displays only for unviewed orders (or catalog requests) and disappears after the first person looks at all the new orders, which can be confusing when multiple people use the Editor. Don't assume that you have no new orders just because you can't see the red star. Personally, I keep a watch on incoming orders by always keeping an eye on my merchant-order notification e-mails.

Taking orders all the way to the bank

I want to see some orders! Here's how you get to the orders so that you can ship some stuff and get some money. To view any or all of your orders, click the Orders link, which takes you to the Order Manager page (see Figure 15-2). This screen summarizes customer order data since your store first opened, with links to new orders, canceled orders, returns, and orders on hold.

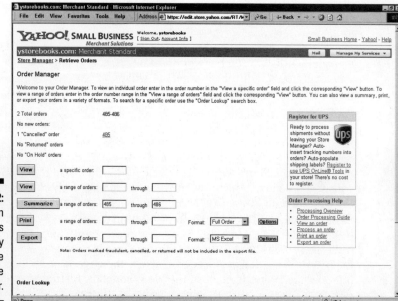

Figure 15-2: You can access orders only through the secure server.

You can use the Order Manager to access individual orders by order number, view a range of orders (which is slower to load), print orders (up to 1,000 at a time), view a summary of orders, or export orders (up to 3,000 at a time) in a variety of standard formats.

You can view specific orders in many ways, but the easiest way is to type an order number inside the View A Specific Order field and click the View button. The order appears with all the information collected in the checkout process, including Shipped To info, Bill To info, e-mail address, payment information, IP address (from the buyer's ISP), merchant-rating information, repeat customer information with links to previous orders (if any), and store merchant notes. Here are things you can do in the Order Manager and what you need to know about managing orders:

- ✔ **Modifying orders is relatively easy.** Click the Modify button, and you can change the shipping or billing information, edit what the customer ordered, add items, or recalculate shipping and tax. When you modify an order, you're reminded to verify prices and item codes. Click the Done button to save your edits. Here are some things to think about when you modify orders:

  - • **Use Merchant Notes.** When you change the status of an order, your Yahoo ID, the date, and what you changed shows up under Merchant Notes. You can also type notes to yourself. Just remember to click the Update button to save your changes.

  - • **Delete bad orders.** Mark bad orders as fraudulent, canceled, or returned so that you don't have to pay Yahoo!'s revenue share percentage on sales where you never got paid. You have 90 days to mark an order as a return to get your revenue share fee returned. When you mark an order as canceled, an e-mail is sent to the customer to notify her.

    Cancel bad orders before fraudulent customers have a chance to rate you. Merchant ratings e-mails usually go out two weeks from the day the customers placed their orders.

  - • **Don't scheme.** You can't cancel all your orders (or just the really big ones) and not have to pay the *revenue share fee,* which is a percentage of your sales that Yahoo! collects as an additional cost of doing business on its platform and pays for things like the multi-million dollar load-balancing infrastructure and Jerry Yang's PB&J sandwiches. When a certain percentage of your orders gets canceled, Yahoo! starts looking. Y! reserves the right to contact your customers and see what's up.

- ✔ **Summarizing a range of orders** shows you the order ID (linked to the individual order), customer name, address, number of items, subtotal, order date, marked (for deleted orders), and % Completed. Click the Export To Excel link at the bottom left of the page to download the data in a CSV file. Sometimes I use the View Summary feature a little after midnight to get a current daily sales figure. (I guess I'm a little obsessed, especially toward the end of the month when I'm really close to breaking a sales record.)

✔ **Printing orders lets you choose to print the full order, an invoice, or a packing slip.** When you print a range of orders, each order is printed on a new page. Click the Options button to change the file format from PDF to PostScript or HTML (but why would you?).

✔ **Exporting orders is an easy way to get customer and order data out of the Yahoo! Store and into another order-management system.** Exports are available in the following formats: Microsoft Excel, Microsoft Access, Generic CSV, Mail Order Manager (M.O.M.), QuickBooks, PC Charge, XML, and Plain Text. Click the Option button to set specific M.O.M. parameters. You can export up to 3,000 orders at a time, and bad orders (marked fraud, canceled, or returned) aren't included in the export file.

Exporting orders in Microsoft Excel gives you the option of downloading individual data files or all the tables zipped up in a *tar file,* a zipped or compressed file that can be opened with any standard compression utility, such as WinZip. (See www.winzip.com for a free trial download.) For more information on exporting orders and file types, see the Yahoo! Store Help pages or the documentation.

Searching for that one special order

Sometimes you need to find an order very quickly with very little information. The Store Manager's Order Lookup feature (hidden at the bottom of the Order Manager page) is pretty helpful, even if it's limited to orders from the past year. Search results supposedly show only the first 50 matching orders, too. Now you can search orders by name, phone number, e-mail, address, city, zip code, last four digits of a credit-card number, or order date.

Zip code is probably the best way to search using Order Lookup because zip codes are short and easy for customers to give over the phone, most folks know all their possible shipping zip codes, and you probably don't have that many orders from the same zip code in the course of the year.

Handling catalog requests

I used to use the Catalog Request form on my Yahoo! Stores to collect e-mail addresses. Click the Catalog Requests link to go to a page that should be called the Catalog Request Manager (but it's not). Here, you can view specific catalog requests, view a range, summarize, print, and/or export catalog requests. You control the fields on the Catalog Request form with the Order Settings' Order Form page.

Changing order numbers

By default, every Yahoo! Store starts out on order number 485. I highly recommend asking Y! to change your order number so that sneaky competitors can't figure out exactly how many sales you've had since you opened for business simply by placing an order and doing a little math.

Call Yahoo! Technical Support at 1-866-800-8092 (press 2, 2, and then 2 for Merchant Solutions) and ask the rep to change your order number. If the first guy to answer the phone says he doesn't know what you're talking about or can't do it, just ask for a supervisor. Remember that you can only increase the order number, and after the Store Support folks change it, they can't change it back. Be sneaky yourself!

Working with Credit Cards

Real-time online credit-card processing is pretty cool. Your customer places an order; types in his card number, and billing info; and clicks the Send Order button. The credit-card number, expiration date, billing address info, and *CVN* (credit-card verification number — sometimes called the CVC, CVC2, CVV, or CVV2, which is the 3-digit verification code found on the back of a Visa or MasterCard) get sent through the gateway to the Merchant Bank. Then your customers' credit-card company (the issuing bank) compares the data on file with the information your customer just submitted through the order form.

This point is where the Risk Tools kick in. Depending on how you configure Risk Tools, for example, if the billing zip code and/or phone number on the order doesn't match the same info in the credit-card file, the transaction is flagged for review. After the transaction is authorized, that money is held in your customer's account, but it's reserved for you after your merchant bank verifies the card info and gives you an authorization code. When you ship the order, you click a button to charge the customer's card. Later that night, a batch with all your orders is sent through the credit-card gateway, and the money is swept from your customers' credit-card bank to your merchant bank. Depending on the specific terms you have with your merchant bank regarding how long it can play with your money, that money (less your merchant bank's percentage fee) is transferred to your bank account within a few days or more. E-commerce is pretty cool!

For security purposes, Yahoo! deletes credit-card numbers after 30 days. Also, credit-card authorizations are good only for seven days, so make sure that you reauthorize any orders shipping more than seven days after an order was authorized.

Setting up credit-card processing

To set up online credit-card processing for an existing account, you need to contact your Merchant Account bank and make sure that it's compatible with FDMS Nashville. To get your Merchant Account bank to set up things on its end, it needs to know the following:

- **Product Name:** Yahoo! Store FDMS gateway
- **Product ID:** 819000
- **Vendor Name:** Yahoo!
- **Vendor ID:** 190

Then you need to have your Merchant Account number, the bank's name, and your MID and TID numbers. Open the Store Manager and click the Order Settings link under Pay Method. Now click the Payment Processing Setup and Management link. Because you already have a merchant account, click the Set Up Existing Merchant Account link, and paste the information into the corresponding fields. Go back to the Store Manager and publish order settings, and then place a test order with a real credit card.

If you have questions, Yahoo! Store tech support is very helpful in setting up credit-card processing. Sometimes your merchant bank will give you a test Discover card number to use to verify that your transactions are coming down the gateway to your merchant bank for approval.

Check out `http://help.yahoo.com/help/us/store/order/order-23.html` to download Yahoo's very helpful document "Merchant Solutions Payment Processing Guide" (1.4MB, Acrobat PDF).

Processing online orders

Here are some things you need to know about online order processing:

- **When you use real-time online credit-card processing, you have to click the Sale button on each individual Yahoo! Store order to charge the customer's credit card.** Clicking the Sale button (see Figure 15-3) puts the transaction into your daily batch and charges the customer's credit card after you close when the batch is submitted to your Merchant Account bank. The card's issuing bank sends the money to your Merchant bank, and you eventually get paid.

- **If you made a mistake on an order before a batch was submitted, you can void the sale and charge the correct amount.** Voided charges don't appear on the customer statement; only the corrected charge appears.

✔ **If you catch a mistake after the batch has been submitted, you have to issue a credit and then run a second corrected charge.** The credit appears on the customer's statement.

✔ **If you forget to click the Sale button, you don't get the money!** Don Cole of YstoreTools.com has a cool tool to make sure that you have charged every single customer that you're supposed to charge. If you process credit cards online, then you must get Don Cole's YstoreTools Yahoo! Store Order Checker (`www.rtmltemplates.com/order-checker.html`). Don's nifty utility double-checks orders to make sure that they're either canceled or they were shipped and charged. This relatively simple piece of software doesn't do any other charging or processing, but for $99.95 for the first year, it's worth every penny! Additional subscriptions are $30 a year.

Figure 15-3:
You process credit cards by clicking the Sale button on each individual order as you're ready to ship.

Process through authorize.net

Amount: 72.22   Sale | Void Sale | Credit

[Submit batch] [Review batches]

Handling manual transactions

When you have phone orders or additional charges for online orders, you have a couple of choices. You can place the orders online yourself or process the order as a manual transaction. Placing an order through the store creates a record of the order with an order number and gives you access to all the features of the Store Manager, but you pay the revenue share fee.

You also can click the Manual Transactions link under Process. This link appears only when you have activated online credit-card processing. Here, you can process nonstore orders received offline by phone, fax, or mail. You process offline orders just as you process online store orders. You can obtain an authorization, process the sale, or apply credit. You can also void sales or credits, but only before the batch has been submitted. In addition, you can charge customers for sales of additional items. Manual transactions aren't subject to the Yahoo! revenue share fee, but like Momma always says, "You get what you pay for. . . ."

Processing cards offline

Many of my clients don't process their orders online because they get a very low credit-card processing (%) rate from their local bank. Sometimes a local bank can be more competitive than an online processor because of the volume of business the retailer does locally. For example, I know of one multimillion dollar Yahoo! Store that still hand-keys orders through a terminal (just like in a retail store) and saves up to $40,000 a year because of a preferred local rate. Call your banker and ask what she can do for you.

Configuring Order Settings

My guess is that eventually the Store Manager's Order Settings fields (shown in Figure 15-4) will be moved to the Checkout Manager when it comes out of beta testing to become the official checkout method.

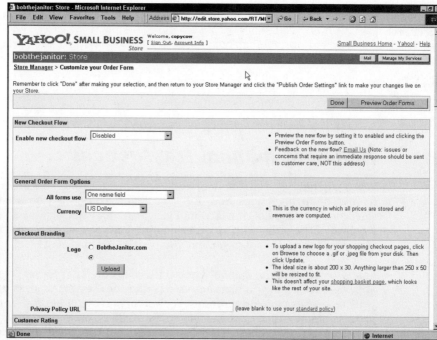

Figure 15-4:
Order Settings allow you to customize the order form and more.

Customize Order Form (Checkout)

The Order Form link is located in the Store Manager under the Order Settings heading. Clicking the Order Form link takes you to a page where you can update the following fields and settings:

- ✔ **New Checkout Flow:** This setting allows you to use the second version of the Shopping Cart (on all orders or just Yahoo! Shopping orders), which arguably looks better than the old Viaweb checkout. I still recommend using the old version of the Shopping Cart checkout. In 2006, Yahoo! plans to offer a more customizable checkout called the new Checkout Manager, but until then, use the old Shopping Cart. See Chapter 14.

- ✔ **Checkout Branding:** Upload a 250-x-50-pixel logo to appear at the top of the Checkout pages; otherwise, text from the Title variable (usually your store's name or domain name) appears.

- ✔ **Gift Options:** Offer Gift Wrap (on the Shipping Info page), set a Price (either per order or per item), and turn on the Gift Message, which is a comments field to let customers specify a message to be included with the order.

- ✔ **Shipping Info Message:** Add text and simple HTML here to appear at the top of your Shipping Info page. The Shipping Info page is the first page in the checkout that is hosted on the secure server. To increase customer confidence, I link to my Customer Testimonials, 100% Satisfaction Guaranteed, Your Privacy Guarantee, and Shipping Rates & Information pages. To keep the customer on task, these links open new browser windows with code like so:

  ```
  <a href=http://www.yourdomain.com/info.html target=_blank>Shipping Info</a>
  ```

  Most of the customers who start to order drop their Shopping Carts right here before completing all those pesky fields, so anything you can do to assure customers helps increase the number of folks who order. I add a message like this:

  "You're now on our SECURE server. This is the SHIPPING INFO PAGE (1st of 2 pages). Prefer to order by phone? Call 1-800-555-1212. Your privacy is guaranteed and your personal information is safe & secure. — Your Name"

- ✔ **Billing Info Message:** When customers make it to this point, they really want to buy. Of the folks who make it this far, 95 percent place an order. I like to put a message like this on the Billing Info page to close the sale:

  "You're almost done! Enter your billing info and payment method. Your 100% satisfaction is guaranteed. Order online with confidence, or if you

prefer, call us at 1-800-555-1212. 99% of orders ship out the same business day. — Your Name"

Both the Shipping Info and Billing Info pages let you edit the existing fields and add custom fields:

- **Edit Standard Fields:** Use the Yes/No drop-down list to control which fields appear on the page.

- **Edit Extra Fields:** Add, edit, and delete custom fields that appear on the Shipping Info and Billing Info pages. These custom fields appear below Shipping Options on the Shipping Info page and after the Billing Address block on the Billing Info page. Unfortunately, you can't change the order of custom fields, so you have to create them in the order you want them to appear.

  When you click the Add New Field link, you choose the page where the field appears (Billing, Shipping, or Catalog Request). You can edit extra fields to move fields from the Shipping Info page to the Billing Info page if a custom field makes more sense there. You also choose the type of field (Text, Hidden, Text Area, Info, or Check Box), the length of the field, the field name, and a description. You then choose whether the field is optional or mandatory.

✓ **Order Confirmation Message:** This is the text that appears on your Thanks For Your Order page, which is what the customer sees directly after clicking the Place Order button. This field is also where you place the tracking code from Google and/or Yahoo! for conversion rate tracking, which I discuss in greater detail in Chapter 20.

I like to reassure the customer on the Order Confirmation page that she will actually get what she ordered, and if something goes wrong, I'll be here to back up the sale. Be friendly and reduce buyers' remorse as well as reduce *WISMO* (Where Is My Order?) phone calls and e-mails to your customer service staff. Thank the customer for her order, include any information about delivery time and product availability, and even link to your FAQ pages.

I use the same information here that I do in my Thanks For Your Order page:

Thanks for your order! Most orders ship out via UPS the same business day received. Postal orders and orders with personalized products may take a little longer. We will contact you by e-mail if we have any questions regarding your order, or if there will be a significant delay in processing your order.

Some quantity discounts, free shipping on certain Internet specials, and shipping costs on Canadian orders may NOT be shown on this copy, but WILL be reflected on your final invoice. If you have any questions about your order, comments about our site, or anything else you think we need to know, please e-mail me or call 1-800-555-1212. We appreciate your business! — Your Name

✔ **Order Status Message:** I don't really use the Order Status page for customers, but if you do, the Order Status Message field is the place where you can place a text message.

✔ **Catalog Request:** Edit the Catalog Request Form Title, add a test message, and add or edit extra fields.

✔ **Advanced Features:** Be careful in making customers jump through too many hoops, such as forcing them to format addresses a certain way or limiting the lengths of fields. Use Field Length Limits to set the length of fields to match databases. Choose whether the Order Button increments quantity or simply takes the customer to the cart page when that item is already inside his Shopping Cart. Here is where you turn on the Got Email collection setting, which adds customer e-mail addresses to your database. You can also activate Webloyalty's Reward Banner Program. (This company really ticked me off when it convinced Yahoo! to automatically opt every store into its program without asking us first, but now you actually have to turn it on.)

✔ **Item Options Validation:** This security setting makes sure that all your Item Options (size, color, style, and so on) are in the correct format and match your database as customers place an order. If you have tons of orders (100-plus a day) and a high rate of fraud, you probably want to set this option to Yes. However, if you're like I am and know you have some improperly formatted item options, then select the Allow Items With Unrecognized Options To Be Placed In The Shopping Cart check box. This setting allows all orders with options to go through whether or not they're properly formatted. For a lot more information on options, see Chapter 12.

Fax/e-mail order notification

When you get an order, you want to know about it as soon as possible. The Order System Settings page is where you set up your e-mail addresses for order notifications, when they're sent, and how the e-mails are formatted. Credit-card information is not included in the e-mail. You can also set up fax notification, time sent, and format. (Merchant Starter accounts don't get faxes.) We use faxes as pick tickets in our warehouse.

For example, I found out how handy the Resend feature was the first time our ancient fax machine ran out of toner and kept printing (although you couldn't read anything). All you do is set the range of orders you want to have re-sent and the merchant e-mail and fax notifications are resent (but not the customer e-mails). This option is also helpful when your e-mail software or fax machine has been down or offline.

Configuring inventory

Set your inventory options to None (which does nothing); Real-Time inventory (for power users only), which queries a script on another server to check your inventory; or Database inventory, which checks a CSV file you upload to see whether an item is in stock.

If you ever want any repeat orders, you have to be honest with your customers about what you have in stock and how long it will take for items to be delivered. However, I recommend *not* using the inventory feature unless you have a huge inventory (thousands of items), your inventory isn't very deep (only one or two of a product, and reorders take forever), or your inventory fluctuates a lot (on a minute-by-minute basis). Even then, you must keep your computer files current and update the Yahoo! Store.

When you turn on Database Inventory, an Inventory link appears under the Process column. This link takes you to a page where you can upload or download inventory files.

Payment methods

With the addition of the new Checkout Manager, Yahoo! Stores are now completely integrated with PayPal. Adding PayPal as a payment method is relatively new, and it requires you to use the new Checkout Manager (which should be out of beta test mode — or pretty close — by the time you read this book; see Chapter 14). Please see the Yahoo! Help section at `http://help.yahoo.com/help/us/store/order/paypal` for lots more info than I can fit in here.

Here's what you need to know about using PayPal as a payment method:

✔ You must be a PayPal Premier or Business member to use PayPal as your merchant account. If you have a personal account, you can upgrade it. If you don't have an account, you can apply for a new one.

✔ After you have an account at PayPal, you have to log in to your PayPal account and turn on the APIs so that PayPal can talk with Yahoo!. See `http://help.yahoo.com/help/us/store/order/paypal/paypal-02.html`.

✔ Back at Yahoo!, you need to identify yourself as who you say you are by logging in to your PayPal account, testing your account, and saving any changes.

✔ Setting up a Yahoo! Store to accept PayPal as an alternate payment option is kinda complicated. In the Checkout Manager's Page Configuration module, you have to enable PayPal on each of the various pages, including the Shopping Cart, the Shipping/Billing page on a merged checkout, or the Billing page on a two-step checkout.

✔ Because you're bypassing the Yahoo! checkout, PayPal can't be in the drop-down list of Pay methods like Visa or MasterCard, but displays as a button below Payment methods. This button takes the customer from the retailer's site to the PayPal site and then back to the retailer's site to complete the transaction.

✔ If a retailer's PayPal account isn't set to automatic capture, the transaction acts much like a typical credit-card procedure, where authorization is requested at the time of purchase.

✔ Within 29 days of authorization, the retailer has to capture the authorized funds (when the order ships) by going into the Store Manager's Process Orders, finding the order, and clicking the Capture Funds button.

✔ After 29 days, retailers have only one more chance to reauthorize by browsing to the order in the Store Manager and clicking the Reauthorize button.

Again, read the documentation. The new Checkout Manager should be out of beta testing sometime in early 2006, probably by the time you read this.

Setting tax rates

Setting up taxes is pretty straightforward. Pick your state, and the tax rate appears in a field that you can edit. State legislatures seem to raise state sales tax rates faster than Yahoo! can keep up with the changes, so contact your local tax authority for current rates. For more information on tax settings, see `http://help.yahoo.com/help/us/store/manage/ordersettings/ordersettings-61.html`.

Setting Up Your Sites for Success

The Store Manager gives you all kinds of different controls over your store. Here's how to control who accesses your store, set up custom 404 "file not found" error pages, and password-protect your published site if you ever want to keep customers out of your site:

- ✔ **Use the Store Manager's Editor access page** to control who has access to the Store Manager and Store Editor by giving certain Yahoo! IDs limited permissions. Choose from three settings: All (which can do everything); Edit Content & See Stats; or see Orders Only. You can add or delete any Yahoo! IDs, but you can't delete the master Yahoo! ID that created the store account. You can't delete yourself, which is a good thing.

- ✔ **Email when site updates:** Under Notification Preferences, select the E-mail Me When My Site Is Updated check box and click the Change button to get an e-mail sent to the main contact address whenever the site is published. This option is very convenient for big stores with lots of products because it may take 15 to 20 minutes for large sites to publish. This e-mail lets you know that your site is published so that you can check out the changes on the published site or go back into the Store Editor.

- ✔ **404 Error Pages/Page Not Found Handling:** When someone types a URL for a page that doesn't exist or clicks an old link to a page you have deleted, Yahoo! automatically redirects him to a copy of your home page, such as `http://yourdomain.com/youraccountname`. This redirection may be confusing to users, but it's also bad for search engines because it may look like you have a duplicate copy of your home page. Search engines tend to penalize pages that they think are exact or close copies of other pages, so you need to create a custom 404 page.

  Go into the Store Editor and create a page with the ID 404 (or whatever you want the error page's ID to be). Make the Name field something like, "Whoops! Sorry! The page you are looking for no longer exists." Add some text like the following to the Caption field for users: "Try the site search to find what you were looking for, or try these links to our most popular pages." When you're happy with how your new error page looks, publish the site and then go back to the Store Manager's Preferences page and change Page Not Found Handling to "Use a custom Store Editor page Custom" and enter the ID in the field. Click the Change button. Publish your order settings and then, in about 5 minutes, look for a page that you *know* doesn't exist.

- ✔ **Domain Names:** Merchant Solutions stores (after 9/24/2003) control their domains under Manage My Services. See Chapter 24 for more on domains.

- ✔ **Customer Access:** The Customer Access link is sometimes mistaken for the Access link. This feature allows you to enable passwords for viewing the published site. You create the username and password. I have several wholesale clients who use this feature to hide wholesale pricing from their regular retail customers, but because the information isn't super, super secret, we just use customer e-mail addresses for both the username and password.

Customer ratings give you good feedback

Allow customers to give you feedback on shopping with your store by activating merchant ratings on the Order Form page (under Order Settings) in the Customer Ratings section. You can also specify a separate e-mail address for receiving customer ratings e-mails. See Chapter 3 for more info on ratings.

Customer ratings appear on the Store Manager page. You see how many responses you have, a graph of your ratings, and a comparable graph to all of Yahoo! Shopping. If someone gives you a bad rating and you fix her problem (and you know that she's a happy customer), or if someone screws up and rates you badly even when his comments were positive, or if someone doesn't respond to the first Ratings Request E-mail, you can always give it a second shot.

Click the Rating Request Email link on the right side of the individual order page to be sent to a form where you can add a message to your customer and resend the Ratings Request E-mail.

Customer ratings are visible on Yahoo! Shopping and, combined with a relevancy score, determine how well merchants who participate in Yahoo! Shopping rank in the search results. Y!Shopping merchants are required to enable ratings.

I wouldn't recommend surprising any (possibly) unhappy customers with a "second chance" customer ratings request. Also, folks who never rated you the first time may view a second request as spam, so be careful. See Chapter 22 for more e-mail dos and don'ts.

Setting Up Shipping Settings

A simpler shipping model is so much easier for you and your customers. Think about shipping as a marketing cost and not as a profit center. Free shipping sells stuff online, and if you make this offer, create a shipping method called something like: "FREE SHIPPING via UPS Ground (Orders over $99 US48)."

I use the Ship-weight field on individual products to add costs to super-bulky or heavy items, especially on express methods.

Shipment and order-status e-mails

The main reason I use Yahoo! Store is because it's so easy. A perfect example of this ease is setting up and sending customer Order Confirmation E-mails. To turn on this feature, all you do is click the Shipment & Order Status link, type your e-mail address in the Order Confirmation E-mail field, and click the

Publish Order Settings link on the Store Manager page. Order confirmation e-mails are then automatically sent to customers immediately after they place an order. Here are a couple of other things you need to know about:

- ✔ **Confirmation e-mail:** Please change the Confirmation E-mail because the default text is "This email is to confirm the receipt of your recent order from *Yhst-17192271484370*," which is pretty bland. I use the same information that's in my Order Confirmation page; see the section "Configuring Order Settings," earlier in this chapter.

- ✔ **Shipment tracking:** The Store Manager has some pretty impressive shipment-tracking features that notify customers via an e-mail alert and change shipping information on the Order Status page when you make a change in an order's shipping status. You can edit this information manually on the individual order page or (power users only) by e-mailing an XML file containing the order number, the status change, and a password. See `http://help.yahoo.com/help/us/store/order/retrieve/retrieve-12.html` for more information on automating shipment-tracking updates.

Shipping Manager

The Shipping Manager is a new addition to Merchant Solutions. Recently all the old Yahoo! Stores were automatically upgraded with the Shipping Manager, which allows you to calculate shipping, set free shipping, offer different shipping methods, accept foreign orders, create shipping tables, set up shipping rates and rules, and experiment with a shipping and tax test before publishing order changes. See Chapter 3 as well as Yahoo!'s Help page at `http://help.yahoo.com/help/us/store/shipping` for more on the Shipping Manager.

UPS shipping tools

UPS WorldShip is software that runs on your computer that's hooked up to a digital scale and thermal label printer you rent from UPS. Sometimes UPS loans you a PC at no charge when you ship enough stuff. WorldShip lets you import customer address information from your Yahoo! Store so that you don't have to retype labels.

After you pack and ship all your boxes, you can upload tracking numbers and update shipment statuses to your Yahoo! Store. WorldShip also shows you current UPS rates (without fuel surcharges), and you can track packages through `www.ups.com`, print labels for each package, view and print proof of delivery, create international documents, and batch-process end-of-day files so that your UPS driver doesn't have to scan every box you ship. I use it. It rocks!

See `http://help.yahoo.com/help/us/store/shipping/shipping-51.html` for more information on integrating UPS WorldShip with your Yahoo! Store or just download the files at `http://store.yahoo.com/lib/vw/Yahoo-UPSWorldShip-documentation.ZIP` for some cool stuff!

Merchant Starter accounts can't export to UPS WorldShip because they lack XML export ability.

Shipping foreign orders

It's a small world after all. And now they're telling me it's flat again. Shipping internationally is not as easy as some folks make it out to be, but if you have the profit margins and the ambition, maybe you can be the next Dutch East India Trading Company. Not me!

UPSOnline Tools: Is it the right tool for the job?

UPSOnline Tools is now integrated with Store Manager, so you can process orders and online shipments within the Store Manager. You can print UPS shipping labels from your information without having to retype info or even export data from Yahoo! to another platform. It also validates customer address information.

UPSOnline Tools is kind of like UPS WorldShip but it's an online application, so you need Internet access to print shipping labels and process orders. To get UPSOnline Tools to use real-time shipping methods, you have to use the official UPS Rates and Service Selection for shipping methods.

In theory, it sounds great! Personally, I get really nervous when several unrelated technical things I have no control over have to work at exactly the same time for orders to come through or for me to process orders. The original reason I didn't use real-time UPS shipping is because the UPS shipping server had to be functioning when someone was placing an order. I'm the guy who processes credit cards offline, too, so when someone's card gets declined, at least I have the chance to call him and try to save the order.

I also don't want UPS giving my customers error messages at the point of purchase when they don't type their addresses in just right. I prefer having a simpler shipping rate table, which is easy for customers to understand, than exact UPS rates. My shipping rates with free shipping offers are a marketing tool, not a profit center. I prefer to process my shipments offline, but I do export order information from Yahoo! Store.

You control which countries can place orders under the Foreign Orders link under Order Settings. You can choose from a default list of countries, opt for USA only, pick the countries you want from a list, or select all countries. Just because a country isn't listed doesn't mean that international customers not on your list won't try to place an online order. Also, not to be an isolationist, but we eliminated all foreign orders except Canada (home of Geddy Lee, Todd "Oilman" Friesen, and Andrew Goodman), and our sales dropped 2 percent, but our problem orders dropped 25 percent, which was a very, very, very big deal, eh. I recommend that beginning retailers avoid the complications of international e-commerce until they have totally mastered the domestic arena.

Part IV
Profiting from Internet Marketing

The 5th Wave   By Rich Tennant

Ted's getting real impatient and wants you to finish our FAQ page NOW!

Q: WHY IS TED SUCH A PSYCHOPATH CONTROL FREAK?
A: HIS MOTHER.
Q: DOES TED HAVE A BRAIN?
A: NO.
Q: HOW MUCH LONGER BEFORE YOU STRANGLE TED?
A: NOT MUCH LONGER.

In this part . . .

In this part of the book, I talk about my favorite subject:
profiting from Internet marketing no matter where you
live. I live out in the sticks, three miles out in the country
just outside a sleepy little college town in rural
Mississippi.

Living in Starkville (pop. 25,000) is great! All my family
is here (six nephews!), and with the university, you can
always find something to do, especially if you like college
sports. The cost of living is extremely cheap, the people
are nice and well-educated, crime is nonexistent, and the
town is almost recession-proof because the college is
here. But there's always been a downside.

As a brick-and-mortar retailer, my store's success has
always been limited by how many people could physically
get to my store and shop. That was a big problem. But not
anymore! With the Internet, I now have access to every
other retailers' customers! This makes a big difference in
what and how much I can sell. For example, one of my
stores just passed one million visitors for the past year.
Holy cow! I couldn't imagine that kind of foot traffic in a
retail store in these parts!

Finding your best keywords, optimizing your store pages
for search engines, and buying paid search ads are the
keys to successfully marketing your Yahoo! Store. In this
part, I cover how to get more Web traffic, how to maximize your use of keywords, and how to make sure that
your store is found when shoppers are looking to buy
what you're selling. I also introduce several other ways
to market your business online.

Chapter 16

Searching for the Right Words

· ·

In This Chapter

▶ Unlocking the secrets of how shoppers search

▶ Mining converting keyword gold from store orders and merchant e-mails

▶ Bucketing keywords into similar groups to save time and trouble

▶ Picking landing pages for both keyword buckets and products

▶ Seeing how shoppers search when they're almost ready to buy

· ·

Choosing the right keywords for your business is the foundation of a smart Internet marketing strategy. The key to driving more qualified visitors to your online store is to make sure that you rank well in the search engines when folks search for your best keywords.

After eight years of selling online, I've figured at least one thing out: You'll make more money when you focus on the exact search terms buyers use to find your store, and then optimize your site and buy pay-per-click ads for those converting keywords. By targeting more of these potential buyers at the exact moment they're in a buying mood, you get much more bang for your buck out of your advertising budget.

Whether you target online traffic by optimizing your site to appear higher and higher in the free search results or by buying your way to the top with paid-search ads, or both, you're much more likely to increase your Yahoo! Store's sales by focusing on the keywords that convert into cash than by chasing any other kind of traffic.

In this chapter, I show you the difference between good search terms and great ones. I also cover how to mine keyword gold hidden deep within your Yahoo! Store, how to discover new keyword phrases using online keyword research tools, and how to continuously collect, categorize, classify, and consequently cash in on your converting keywords.

Introducing Keywords

Keywords are the search words users type into search engines when they're looking for something on the Internet. *Keyword, keyword phrase, search word,* and *search term* all mean the same thing: The words folks are typing into that search engine's search box to find your Yahoo! Store.

The most important thing about search marketing is knowing the most popular and the highest converting search terms buyers use to find what you sell. These search terms are your converting *keyword phrases.* When you know what exact keyword phrases convert for you, you can do everything possible to make sure that your store ranks as high as possible in the search results for those specific words and phrases in both the free search results and pay-per-click results.

Some keywords are more popular than others. Some keywords generate more sales than others. But what you're interested in is the subset of search terms called *converting keywords.* These phrases are the words actual shoppers type into the search engines when they're ready to buy what you sell.

 Lots of Yahoo! Store owners get distracted chasing extremely popular keywords. These popular keywords have a lot of searches, drive a lot of traffic, and sometimes convert into sales. They're also very, very competitive. Popular keywords are extremely hard to rank for search engines, and premium positions with paid-search ads are often cost prohibitive. I've had much more success going after the less popular but higher converting keywords, but if I rank well for the popular words, too, that's great.

Often, my consulting clients aren't aware that they're sitting on buried keyword gold in their e-mail inboxes and Yahoo! Store References and Order data. You have valuable information hidden all over the place, and I'm about to tell you how to find it and dig it out!

Considering Where Keywords Come From

Because keywords are so important, it's very helpful to see where keywords come from. Consider what happens when a searcher types a specific keyword phrase and clicks the Search button. The search engine results page (or SERP) that appears is a combination of several different sources of information working together to find what the searcher is looking for, whether that's free information or product pages. This chapter is about making sure that your store is found in as many of those different places as possible when folks are looking to buy what you sell. Conquering keywords is the key to making the most of Internet marketing.

Figure 16-1 shows a search results page from a search on Yahoo! for the keyword phrase *dog beds*. Take a closer look at a search results page and notice all the different elements, especially paid-search ads and free search results.

When you surf to Yahoo!, type a keyword phrase into the search box and click the Search button, several things happen:

- ✓ **Yahoo! Search pulls free results from its search index and shows the Top 10 Web pages for that search phrase.** These Web pages are listed in descending order by relevancy sorted by a top-secret, always-changing algorithm. The free search results from Yahoo!'s search engine appear under the sponsored results.

  Pre-2003, Yahoo!'s free search results were limited to searches from the Yahoo! Directory supplemented by secondary results from another search engine. Yahoo! then used rebranded results from Google until last year, when Yahoo! started its own search engine.

- ✓ **Yahoo! Search Marketing displays paid-search ads, which are triggered by the keyword phrase searched for.** These Sponsored Results (pay-per-click text ads) are sorted in descending order by bid and appear above, to the right, and at the bottom of the free results. The top three to four ads (Premium Results) appear above the free listings and get most of the clicks, so advertisers are willing to pay top dollar for premium positioning.

Figure 16-1:
The Yahoo! Search Results Page shows both paid-search ads and free search results.

Paid-search advertising is one of the best ways you can get qualified shoppers to your online store. Because most businesses can't break into the Top 10 positions in the free search results to save their lives, they get their wallets out and buy their way to the top. For the lowdown on paid search, see Chapter 18.

Advertisers bid for position by keyword, and their rankings move up and down all day as advertising budgets get maxed out, or advertisers change bids.

✔ **Yahoo! Shopping links appear when Yahoo! recognizes a search term as a product search.** Yahoo's shopping portal was built on the Yahoo! Store database with thousands of merchants with millions of products. At one time, the only way into Y!Shopping was to open a Yahoo! Store or sign a $250,000.00 annual Featured Merchant contract. Now anyone who is willing to pay-per-click can participate in Yahoo! Product Submit. Yahoo! charges different rates for different industries. These pay-per-click (PPC) rates can range anywhere from 15 cents to $1 a click. For a current rate card, see `https://productsubmit.adcentral.yahoo.com/sspi/us/pricing`.

✔ **Yahoo! suggests several more specific keywords when search terms are pretty generic.** When you use pretty broad search terms, Yahoo! helps you out with a list of popular, related, more specific keywords. This "Also try . . ." list is good for surfers, but great for marketers looking for more keywords.

Most people search for general phrases and then become progressively more specific as they home in on what they want. For example, if you sell pet products, you might see more search traffic from the keyword phrase *dog beds,* but more specific searches like *big waterproof dog beds, large red cedar dog beds,* or *discount acme dog beds* will convert at a much higher rate than general phrases.

Oddly enough, search results pages for Yahoo!, Google, MSN, AOL, and Ask.com look very similar. These search engines also change their search results page design often and switch advertising network partners every time I turn around. Most of the SERP layouts are similar to the format initiated by Google, with free (organic, natural) search results on the left and paid-search ads on the right, with sometimes two or more ads in the premium real estate at the top above the free listings.

AOL Search has a slightly different feel than the other search engines. AOL now offers Smartbox Suggestions on the fly while you type. AOL also shows more keywords with Web Offers & More, which gives you more AdWords ads.

Conquering Converting Keywords

Converting keywords are as good as cash because they're the search terms that result in online sales. While the majority of online searches are queries for one- or two-word phrases, converting keywords are usually three-word, four-word, five-word, or even longer keyword phrases. These keyword phrases are often very specific, including the product name with the manufacturer's name, brand, model number, and/or a modifier or two. A good example of a very specific converting keyword phrase is *Eastover 05 Stealth Connexion -9 Senior Bat,* which weighs in at seven words!

When you know your top converting keywords, you can easily monitor your progress in attracting traffic from both free search-engine traffic and paid-search ads.

Converting keyword phrases can be very obscure. They don't tend to show up in the various keyword tools. You won't find most of these phrases in the top 100 traffic keywords. The last time I analyzed my own sites' converting keyword phrases for the last six months, more than 300 of the single-order converting keyword phrases were so obscure and specific that they had 100 percent conversion rates. That percentage means one search, one order.

If you follow the search-marketing industry at all, you hear industry folks talk about the "long tail of search." What they mean is that millions and millions of unique keyword phrases get only one or two searches a month, at best.

If you stop and think about it, the longer a keyword phrase is, the more specific it is, which really helps a search engine deliver only the most relevant pages in its search results. When your product pages are relevant enough to rank for extremely specific keyword phrases, the odds are visitors will find what they're looking for and convert into sales at a much higher rate than visitors who don't really know what they're looking for.

Also, if your paid-search ad or free listing in the organic results has the exact keyword phrase a customer typed into a search box, you're much more likely to get the click because your page speaks the customer's language. And if your product is named exactly what a shopper is looking to buy, you're going to get the sale. I call this phenomenon the "Hey! That's exactly what I'm looking for" effect.

Think about the language potential customers use when you name your products. Sell folks exactly what they're looking to buy. Consider making multiple versions of your products with different names to sell the same thing to different types of buyers.

It's so easy to optimize your store for these phrases because you have virtually no competition. The best way to rank well on Google, Yahoo!, and MSN searches for these very specific search terms is to beef up your store's product pages and write tons of unique content for your site. Write FAQs and articles about the products that you sell, answer customer questions, write product reviews, provide solutions to problems your customers may have, and generally inform the people who use the products you sell. (See Chapter 19 for more on optimizing your store for search engines.)

Lots of folks keep keyword lists. You're more interested in your list. My converting keywords are different than your converting keywords, even if we sell the exact same thing. Different stores have different styles, attract different kinds of customers, and sell differently.

Collecting converting keywords

Collecting converting keywords may be the most important concept in this book. Your Merchant Emails and the orders themselves from Yahoo! have keyword gold in them, and I'm not talking about the credit-card information, either. A little more than half of the orders in my Yahoo! Stores show which search engine the order came from and which keyword search was used to find the site and turned into a sale. Look at the Referrer for the referring search engine (and sometimes the keyword used). Look at the Rev-Share URL field for the full search-engine search string, which shows both keyword and engine. For example, a URL might look like `www.google.com/search?hl=en&q=keyword+phrase` where you can see the keyword phrase embedded in the URL.

You can pinpoint your converting keywords using many different methods, but my favorite is looking at referring search-engine data in your Merchant Order E-mails and in the orders themselves shown in the Store Manager.

Digging keywords out of your orders

One way you can find your converting keywords is to look at the orders themselves. In Store Manager, click the Orders link under the Process heading to see orders placed on your Yahoo! Store. The Retrieve Orders screen appears. Click the View button, and the last order placed appears.

If an order has referring search-engine and keyword data attached to it, you see the Entry Page (which is the first page someone went to on your site), the Referrer (which shows you the source of the traffic and sometimes the keyword), and/or the Yahoo! Rev-Share URL (which sometimes has the keyword embedded in the URL). If you use Yahoo! Store's Track Link feature, this information appears on the order, too.

Figure 16-2 shows you an example of an actual order containing converting keyword information. In this order, the customer purchased about $130 worth of stuff.

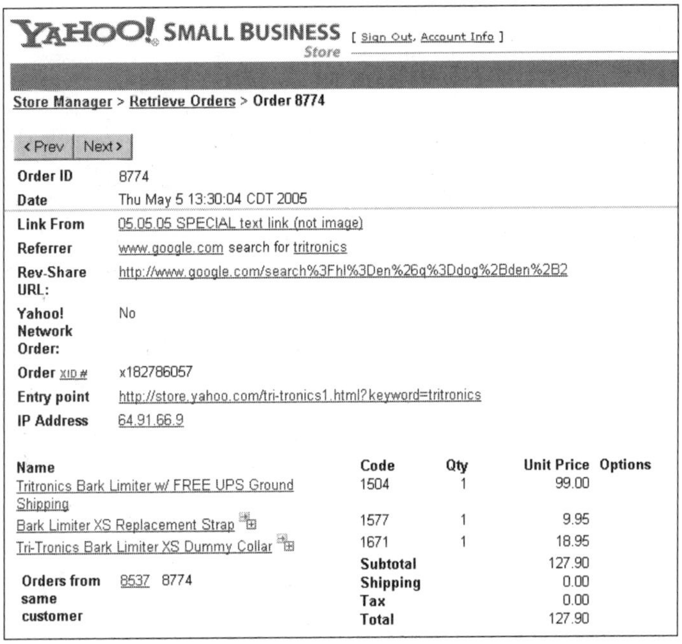

Figure 16-2: Sometimes an order shows you the Referrer with converting keyword, the Rev-Share URL, and the Entry Page.

The order shown in Figure 16-2 gives me a lot of valuable information:

- ✔ The order from this customer came from a repeat visit. I can tell because the click came from an e-mail newsletter, which means that the customer placed a previous order or signed up on the newsletter list. The Track Link appears as Link from 05.05.05-SPECIAL Text Link, which even tells me what link the customer clicked on in a specific e-mail. For more on track links, see Chapter 18.

- ✔ I know the customer originally came from a Google AdWords ad because the Referrer shows him coming from a www.google.com search for the word *tritronics,* and his Entry Point shows his entry page on the site to have a Google AdWords landing page embedded in the URL string: tri-tronics1.html? engine=adwords &keyword=tritronics.

- ✔ The customer bought two additional items from the related cross-sell items we display in the shopping cart, which you can see by the icons next to the items with little arrows and plus signs. For more on cross-selling and other merchandising techniques you can use to increase your sales, see Chapter 13.

✔ The Rev-Share URL shows another search on Google for Dog Den 2 — **www.google.com**/search%3Fhl%3Den%26q%3Ddog%2Bden%2B2. The %2B are encoded space characters. If you hold your nose just right, you can see the keywords *dog den 2* right there in the URL. I don't know how many times I've seen Dan Boberg of Yahoo! Search Marketing (formerly Overture) present at search conferences, but the last time I did, he said that the average customer makes more than a dozen different searches before buying something. Holy cow!

When I'm looking at orders in the Store Manager, I click the link shown in the Referrer or Rev-Share URL and visit the search engine to try to re-create the exact search results page that the customer saw, so I can see exactly what the customer saw. I discover more about how people search (and shop) by replicating these exact customer searches on an order-by-order basis. I see what ads and free listings prompt customers to click. I don't check every order, every day, but I try to do it as often as I can. The search engines seem to change results every few days, and paid-search ads change as budgets get spent, so the closer to the actual order time I check on the link, the more likely I am to see exactly what the customer saw.

Prying keywords out of product reports

You can extract your converting keywords product by product through a cool report that most Yahoo! Store owners don't really know about. The Sales report lists the products that are selling well. You can sort the various products by the number of items sold, order count, or revenue, but I always sort by revenue because that's where the money is!

Playing with orders

When you do a Sales report, when an item has 50 or fewer orders in a given date range, the Orders number becomes a link back to a summary report of all the original orders for that specific product. When you see 50 orders for the same product with all the search-engine and keyword data for one specific product all on one page, you can see some really cool things — converting keywords being the coolest! You can usually see where the customer came from (Referrer) and what he searched for (Rev-Share URL).

Only products with less than 50 orders in a given time frame have a link to the orders. Why exactly? My guess is that because it takes a while for the Store Manager to generate these pages of orders, more than 50 orders would take too long or overtax the server.

On your bestselling products, you'll have more than 50 orders in a year. How can you see all the orders? Simply shorten the time frame to get the number of orders down to less than 50 by selecting the radio button with the next shortest time frame. Try the last 180 days (6 months), but if you have a ton of orders, you can do it month by month for the last 6 months.

Converting keywords really are worth more!

The following table shows stats from a real Yahoo! Store with about eight weeks of really good sales data from early 2005. I exported the data from software called EngineReady (www. engineready.com) and totaled up the date in Excel. More than 10,000 unique keyword phrases generated almost 81,000 visitors from free search-engine traffic and paid-search ads. It's time to start separating the wheat from the chaff!

Nonconverting keyword phrases: The bad news is that almost 9,100 of the top 10,000 keyword phases sent more than 55,000 visitors to this Yahoo! Store, but those visitors didn't place a single order. Ouch. Still, it's good to know what keywords are popular, but didn't convert. I'm sure some of these folks may have placed a phone order, bookmarked the site for later use, or deleted their cookies so that I lost the ability to track them, but for now, I'm not losing sleep over these keyword phrases.

Converting keyword phrases: The good news is that more than 900 other keywords converted into sales and sent 34,000-plus visitors who spent over $142,000. That's more like it!

What's weird is that the top 150 converting keywords (ranked by revenue per phrase) didn't generate the majority of the sales. By dollar volume, 55 percent of all sales came from 758 unique keyword phrases with just one order per search term. These single-sale keyword phrases averaged almost a 9 percent conversion rate, too! These obscure phrases are literally worth their weight in gold. What phrases do you think I'm optimizing for and buying pay-per-click for now? Oh, yeah!

It's pretty sad, but thinking about what I can do with converting keyword data keeps me up at night! I think I need to get a life.

Bucket	# Orders	Revenue ($)	# Visitors	# Keywords	Conversion Rate (%)
Converting keywords	1,374	142,360	34,181	902	4.02
Keywords with 2+ orders	616	63,697	25,679	134	2.40
Keywords with 1 order	758	78,662	8,502	758	8.91
Keywords with no orders	0	0	55,251	9,098	0
All keywords	**1,374**	**142,360**	**80,930**	**10,000+**	**1.70**

Here's how to get your top 200 converting keywords out of your Sales reports:

1. **Go to your Yahoo! Store Manager.**

2. **In the Statistics column, click the Sales link.**

    Your top 50 product sales from the last 365 days appear sorted in descending order by the number of items sold. The first 50 items appear by default, but you can change that by clicking the See All link or the See More link (which doubles the number of items shown).

3. **Click the See More link to display 100 items.**

   The screen refreshes, and you see sales by product for the bestselling 100 products from the last 365 days.

4. **Click the By Revenue link to sort the products in descending order by dollars.**

   Revenue is really what you're really interested in. Configuring the Sales report by revenue shows you your Top 100 Best Sellers, which probably represent 70 to 80 percent of your gross sales if your store is like most stores I work on.

5. **Click the See More link again to bump up the number of products to 200 products.**

After you have six months or so of sales on your Yahoo! Store, you can really see what words buyers use to find what you sell. Until then, you just don't have a big enough sample. You can compile a list of converting keywords from simply looking at your orders. Having access to all this converting keyword info is kinda cool, but it sometimes takes years to develop these lists. If you have a new Yahoo! Store, you probably don't have years and years to wait to jump into PPC advertising.

Working with Your Top Converting Keywords

Now you're convinced that converting keywords are critically important and that you must collect them. I keep my converting keyword list of all the words that converted into sales on all my Web sites in Microsoft Excel, and I have thousands of these phrases. Here's what I do with this very valuable information after I collect all my converting keyword phrases:

- ✔ **Classify converting keywords.** I split the list into product-specific keywords and more generic searches that need to be sorted into groups.

- ✔ **Categorize nonproduct converting keywords by sorting them into different buckets so that you can save time and work on similar search terms at the same time.** A *bucket* is a just a funny name for a group of similar things (keywords, products, customers, landing pages, or anything else you want to organize). I like saying "bucket" and using it as a verb! You can group your keywords into buckets in a variety of ways.

You can bucket keyword phrases by manufacturer, by product type, or by the type of customer. Most keyword phrases are easily sorted into their corresponding bucket.

For example, say that someone bought a baseball bat and the converting keyword phrase was *Eastover Junior League baseball bat.* I have at least three different ways to bucket that phrase: by manufacturer (Eastover), by league (Junior League), and by product type (baseball bat). Usually a store has anywhere from 40 to 100 different buckets or groups of keywords, depending on the variety of merchandise sold and how detailed you want to get in your categories. I prefer to work with one bucket at a time when buying paid-search ads and optimizing pages for search engines, but especially when I'm slopping the hogs. Woooo, pig, sooey!

✔ **Pick a page for each converting keyword phrase so that you use that page as a landing page for paid-search ads (see Chapter 18) and so that you can optimize that page for free search-engine traffic (see Chapter 19).** The easiest way to select a specific page is to ask yourself what the most relevant page on your site would be if a new visitor could see just one page. Look over your most popular section pages and make sure that you have good landing pages for these converting keywords. Here's how I pick pages for several different types of converting keywords:

- **Product-specific keywords should use the actual product page as a landing page.** For example, someone searching for the phrase *Dental Kong DK1* needs to be directed to that specific product page, so I optimize the DK1 product page for that converting keyword phrase.

- **Buckets of similar keyword phrases usually match up nicely with a specific Yahoo! Store section page or two.** Make sure that these words are used in the Caption on their matching section pages. For example, with my softball site, if the keyword phrase is *Eastover Junior League baseball bat,* then the section is Eastover and the subsection would be Junior League bats.

- **Keyword phrases without a matching section page give you the opportunity to create new section pages to match those keywords.** For example, if you have a dog store and folks are searching for *Irish Setter chew toys* and *Irish Setter dog beds,* you probably need to make an Irish Setter section in your Shop By Breed category.

- **Brand-specific keyword searches do better matched to Shop By Brand pages.** Experience tells me that folks who search by brand are ready to buy, and they want that specific brand. For example, if someone searches for *Konga brand chew toys,* she needs to be directed to the Konga product page, not the more generic Chew Toys page, which has products from Kong as well as other brands.

Unfortunately, you don't control which pages come up for search queries in the search engines, but you can control exactly which page prospective customers land on when you buy paid-search ads. See Chapter 18 for what you need to know about buying paid-search advertising.

✔ **Check your rankings on the top three search engines to see how well you're positioned for each converting keyword phrase.** You want to be in the top ten results on Google, Yahoo!, and MSN, but I aim for the top three rankings. You'll definitely see a correlation between high rankings of specific keyword phrases and record-breaking sales. When the search engines are churning all around like they tend to do, I can tell how my sales are directly affected by how well I rank for certain critical converting keyphrases.

Here's how to keep up with your search rankings:

- Begin by checking your search engine position by hand on each engine for each keyword, one at a time. Just do a search for the phrase and pray. Your site should appear in the top ten results. If not, you have some work to do. I tell you how to optimize your Yahoo! Store for search engines in Chapter 19.

✔ **Eventually you can automate your ranking reports for your top converting keyword phrases.** I love using Bruce Clay's tools at SEOToolSet.com to check my ranks and analyze my pages. In the past, I've also used Web Position Gold (www.webposition.com). See Chapter 25 for more info on the tools you can use.

After you start ranking well for lots and lots of converting keywords, you don't have to worry about your search-engine position for every single word or phrase on every single engine so that you sleep a little better at night.

✔ **Buy paid-search ads on Google and Yahoo! Search Marketing (and soon MSN) for the exact same collection of converting keywords.** I buy anywhere from 5,000 to 10,000 keywords on a given project, so I never can remember what I've bought and what I haven't. To help keep track, I take my converting keyword phrase and do a quick PPC check.

I search on Overture.com to see whether I'm buying that word with Yahoo! Search Marketing, and I search on Google to see whether I'm buying it on Google AdWords. If not, I add it to my list of words to buy. Because I've already got a landing page for each keyword (or bucket of keywords), the only work I have to do is to write a compelling search ad. See Chapter 18 for more about buying your way to the top with paid search.

I record all this information in my Converting Keywords Excel file and do it again tomorrow when (hopefully) I'll have a whole new batch of converting keywords.

Seeing How Your Shoppers Search

You need to know how shoppers search. People don't just search for something, click an ad or free listing, and then go to an online store and buy something. Shoppers go through several different stages of searching.

They start with gathering information about what's available. Then they shop the features of different brands until they find what they want to buy. Finally, they compare retailers by looking at prices, shipping options and costs, taxes, and product availability.

Shoppers who are ready to buy use more brand-name queries right before they make their purchase. These customers know what they want to buy, including the make, model number, and style of the product. If you have a competitive price, they just want to see whether you have it in stock, when they can get it, and how much shipping is going to cost them.

You want these customers to find you when they're searching, because they're about to open up their wallets. Sometimes these folks haven't even been to your store. They may have been doing their information gathering on other competitors' Web sites. This search is your only shot at getting these folks to your store, so you want to rank well, so hopefully Joe Customer will click your store's listing.

The higher a product's price, the longer the *buying cycle* (the time it takes for someone to buy it). For more expensive purchases, shoppers have to think about their purchases, do their homework, and generally get more comfortable with a retailer before shelling out their dough. I cover increasing conversion by earning visitors' trust in your Web site in Chapter 21. If you sell lower priced items or impulse-buy items, then you'll have a much quicker selling cycle with customers spending less time on research, fewer searches to actually buying something, and generally higher conversion rates.

Researching Keywords

Several online tools are available to help you with your keyword research. The paid-search advertising networks (Google AdWords and Yahoo! Search Marketing) have some free tools, and several third-party software companies have tools like Wordtracker (`www.wordtracker.com`), Keyword Intelligence (`www.keywordintelligence.com`), and Trellian's Keyword Discovery (`www.keyworddiscovery.com`), where you pay a reasonable subscription fee to access their massive online databases.

Overture's free keyword selector tool

Overture, formerly Goto.com, is now Yahoo! Search Marketing. Its ad network has millions of keyword searches each month, which are incorporated into a big database, usually after the first of the month. Fortunately for you and me, the folks at Y!SM are nice enough to share their data.

To access Overture's free keyword suggestion tool, go to `http://inventory.overture.com`, type your keyword phrase into the search box, and click the arrow button. The search results page appears and tells you the number of times that phrase was searched for last month across Yahoo! Search Marketing's entire network. Every time a person does a search on Yahoo!, MSN (for now), Overture.com, and the rest of their network partners, those searches are added to the total number of searches. You also see a list of related searches that include your keyword phrase (with up to 100 subphrases).

When you know a few things about these numbers, you'll take these monthly search figures with a grain of salt:

 ✓ Overture Keyword Selector Tool combines singular, plural, misspellings, and even some broad matching terms in these search counts.

 ✓ More popular search terms have their monthly counts skewed by PPC rank-checking software, where PPC advertisers automatically check their Overture position by running search queries every few minutes.

 ✓ Lots of advertisers search on Overture.com to see their ads' position, and these searches inflate the monthly keyword counts. Some popular words seem to have a lot of rank-checking inflation, while some obscure terms have none.

For example, when you read that 64,639 searches occurred for *dog bed* in March 2005, that number includes *dog bed, dogbed, dog beds,* and every time an advertiser (or his software) checked his ad position for that keyword phrase on Overture, as shown in Figure 16-3.

When you play with the Overture keyword tool, start with your most general root keyword so that you can see all the related subphrases containing that word. For example, if you're selling dog beds, type the word *dog.* The tool shows you every related keyword phrase that contains the word *dog,* which may give you some ideas on other popular products you should carry.

Google AdWords free keyword tool

You can use the Google Keyword Sandbox at `https://adwords.google.com/select/main?cmd=KeywordSandbox` to generate additional keywords or to see which related keywords can trigger your ads.

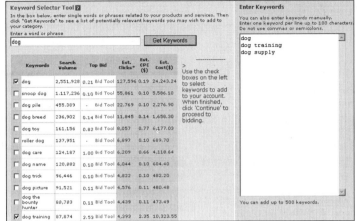

Figure 16-3:
Overture's
Search
Selector
Tool as seen
in the
Yahoo!
Search
Marketing
control
panel.

Google gives you three types of keyword suggestions: More Specific Keywords, Similar Keywords, and Additional Keywords:

- **More Specific Keywords** is a list of other keywords that includes your keyword phrase. Google advises you to buy these specific phrases instead of using broad matching to catch these keywords. If you're selling dog beds, then some examples include *best dog beds, big dog beds, bolster dog beds, bowser dog beds, cedar dog beds, cheap dog beds,* and so on.

- **Similar Keywords** are keywords that are related to your keyword phrase and that trigger your ad if you select broad matching. (For more on broad matching, see Chapter 18.) These keywords are synonyms and singular or plural variants. For example, if you're searching for dog beds, then some examples include *dog bed, pet beds,* and *pet bed.*

- **Additional Keywords** are mostly modifiers that you can use to expand your entire list or add to your negative match list for words you don't want to buy. For an ad campaign on dog beds, my negative match list starts with the word *cat.* (For more on negative matching, see Chapter 18.) Negative matches for dog bed ads include *cat, club, hammock, humane society, kennel club, photos, pics, picture, pictures, pictures of, rescue, shelters,* and *spca.*

  Additional keywords are usually modifiers and include other names for your products, synonyms, trademarks/brands, styles, retailer names, misspellings, geographic terms, and other related products.

  For example, good modifiers for a dog bed ad campaign include *heating, igloo, kuranda, large, luxury, orthopedic, outdoor, pads, pet bedding, puppy beds, therapeutic, thermal, warmer, waterproof,* and *wicker.*

(Meaning) elements of style

Search marketer Tor Crockatt created the concept of keyword *meaning elements* to break keywords into their smallest components that still have a meaning relevant to your site. After she has a keyword list broken down into the various meaning elements, she can mix and match all these modifiers with all these root keyphrases and build massive lists of keywords in a big ol' Excel spreadsheet.

Sometimes the smallest meaning element is a two-word phrase. A perfect example is the keyword phrase *Yahoo! Store,* a compound phrase with a singular meaning. I really don't care how I rank for *Yahoo!* or how I rank for the word *Store,* but I'm very concerned with ranking well for *Yahoo! Store.* Tor says there are seven types of meaning elements: comparison words, product/price adjectives, intended use, type of product, manufacturer, geographic modifiers, and action verbs. Here's an example using most of these element types: *hire best US Yahoo! Store designer for cheap online store facelift.*

Wordtracker keyword research tool

Wordtracker (`www.wordtracker.com`), shown in Figure 16-4, is a subscription-supported keyword tool based in the United Kingdom. The Wordtracker keyword tool pulls its data from various *meta-crawlers* and their search queries for the past 60 days with a database of keywords from 373 million search queries. Meta-search engines combine results from multiple search engines (Google, Yahoo!, MSN) so that their numbers aren't skewed by PPC bidding tools or SEO position-checking software like Overture. I log into Wordtracker the first thing every morning and run the tool all day long.

Wordtracker may be a little expensive, but it offers many benefits:

- Wordtracker gives you separate search counts for each search term for singular and plural, all misspellings, and even capitalization.

- You can import a list of keywords from another source to see how many searches a day your keywords receive.

- Wordtracker has a deal with Yahoo! Search Marketing (formerly Overture) so that you can automatically see what different Overture clients are bidding for each keyword phrase, which saves a lot of time when you have a big list of bids to check.

- Wordtracker allows you to drill down into each keyword, find related phrases, add the words you want to your keyword list, and expand the list to include all the related phrases you want. You can then get the Overture bids for each keyword phrase and export them in several formats.

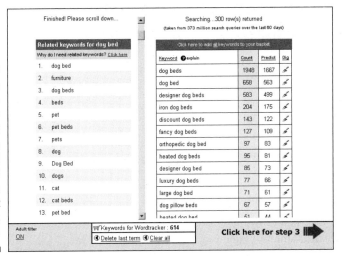

Figure 16-4: Wordtracker keyword tool is the best $200 I spend all year. You get what you pay for, folks!

- Wordtracker has a synonym generator, which simply pulls a list of synonyms from a thesaurus database.

- Wordtracker's *KEI (keyword effectiveness index) analysis* allows you to see how many competitors (and competing pages) you have on each search engine for each keyword. I don't really use this tool, but some keyword researchers swear by it.

- You can keep up to seven separate projects or lists of keywords.

- *Compressed search* (combining results from capitalized and noncapitalized search results) is wonderful for grabbing keyword data. I use it multiple times a day.

Okay. With less than 400 pages in this book, I can barely scratch the surface of what you can do with Wordtracker, much less all these other tools. Take a day when you have nothing to do (yeah, right!) and play on Wordtracker all afternoon or evening. For around $8, you can get full-day pass access to Wordtracker. I bet you'll sign up for the $200-a-year deal the next day.

Tracking Converting Keywords

Converting keywords from your paid-search ad campaigns are easier to track than the converting keywords from free search-engine traffic because you can use free conversion tracking tools offered by Google AdWords and Yahoo! Search Marketing (formerly Overture), in addition to watching Yahoo! Store referrer data.

Other keyword resources

Here are some additional resources for finding more keywords:

Google AdWords: *21 Pay-Per-Click Campaign Secrets Your Competition Doesn't Know (2004 Edition),* by Andrew Goodman (Page-Zero).

Webmasterworld's Keyword Research Forum: www.webmasterworld.com/forum8/.

SEO Research Labs: www.seoresearch labs.com offers information on keyword research and a free 90-page guide to SEO.

Open Directory Project: Online Keyword Tools: http://dmoz.org/Computers/ Internet/Web_Design_and_ Development/Authoring/Online_ Tools/Keywords.

When you put this tracking code on the Order Confirmation Page of your store's checkout, it tells Google or Overture that a visitor from a paid-search ad bought something, and this code ties this order to the keyword search that resulted in a sale. Google or Overture then pulls this data back into its database, and you can see which of your keywords and which of your ads are converting and driving the most sales to your Yahoo! Store. See Chapter 20 for more on the magic of metrics and consult Chapter 21 for conversion rate improvement ideas, but commence collecting converting keywords quickly or consider the consequences!

Chapter 17

Driving Traffic That Converts

In This Chapter

▶ Revving up the search engines with SEO and paid search

▶ E-mailing for fun and profit

▶ Discovering multiple marketing methods

You don't just want to attract more traffic to your Yahoo! Store; you want more folks to actually buy something. You need to fish for the right kind of fish, use the right kind of bait, and fish where the fish are biting, or you're going to go hungry tonight.

In this chapter, I tell you all you need to know and more about fishing for the right buyers, introduce you to search engine optimization and pay-per-click ads, and fill you in on lots of other ways to get more buyers to your Yahoo! Store.

Fishing the Right Way

When I tell you to "Fish for the right kind of fish," I mean that you should target the folks who spend the most money, buy the most profitable products you sell, and buy from you again and again. You don't want the little minnows who may place a small order and then never return. You probably also don't want the Great White sharks — international buyers who want to order a container-load of what you sell and pay you cost plus a dollar.

You also want to fish with the right kind of bait. You're an expert in what you sell, right? Your search-engine marketing must show that and speak your customer's language. Your search listings have to tell that guy to click your ad and buy from you. Shopping with you is better than shopping with the other guy, even though he probably sells the exact same things you do.

Lastly, you need to fish where the fish are biting. If your customers are soccer moms who have never changed their home page from MSN.com, you'd better show up under the MSN free search results and buy Yahoo! Search Marketing (formerly Overture) ads. If your customers are tech geeks who only search on Google, then you need to rank in the free search results and buy Google AdWords. If your customers are sports fans who live on Yahoo! Sports, then you need to be all over Yahoo!

"What one man can do, another can do."

The Edge (1997) is one of my favorite movies. I can watch it every time it shows up on my TiVo. A billionaire (Anthony Hopkins) and his super-model wife's favorite photographer (Alec Baldwin) survive a pretty horrific seaplane crash and are trapped in the Alaskan wilderness. Things get really hairy when a big ol' grizzly bear gets a hankering for a billionaire sandwich. In short, Mr. Billionaire (realizing that humans have survived bears and worse for centuries) motivates Mr. Baldwin's character to help him fight the bear with this mantra: "What one man can do, another can do."

He's absolutely right. Things are a lot easier to do after someone else has shown you that's it possible! Not only does this mindset work with man-eating grizzly bears, it also works with succeeding online. Thousands and thousands of other people are making a living selling online, and you can do it, too. Here's my grizzly-bear story:

My brother and I launched our first Yahoo! Store way back in April 1997, when Yahoo! Store was still called Viaweb. My mom and dad's dog-supply store was under siege from a new PetSmart store, which opened literally across the highway. Our store's sales had taken a tremendous hit, and we were looking for anything to generate revenue. Fortunately, we had an 18-month head start because we knew PetSmart was coming, and large companies make a lot of noise when they sneak into a market. My folks had started the business as a mail-order company way back in 1972, and we went back to our roots, ramping up the catalog side of the business. We spent hundreds of hours

creating a small black-and-white dog-supply catalog that we mailed to everyone on our mailing list, which got almost no response — maybe $5,000 in orders in six months, which was nowhere near enough to offset our lost sales.

One night, Mom saw an AT&T commercial on TV where two (fictional) female inventors/entrepreneurs opened an online store to sell their floppy sunglasses because they couldn't get snooty brick-and-mortar retailers to carry their products. The light bulb went off! Mom became obsessed with that commercial. All she ever said was, "Get me on the Internet. I know we need to be on the Internet!" She would not stop talking about getting online, so to appease her, I built a simple five-page site with a catalog request form. After I got listed in the Yahoo! Directory, we started getting hundreds of catalog requests. My dad freaked. He said we couldn't afford to mail all these catalogs without knowing that they would generate sales, so I had to either cut off the Web site or put our catalog online and sell products that way.

In 1997, I knew absolutely nothing about Web-store design, Web-site development, or online marketing. I was a graphic design major turned retailer selling comic books and baseball cards for a living. I was also in charge of all our print marketing campaigns. I had friends who were Webmasters, and were supportive, but I had no Web-development experience. To get an online store built seemed doable, but I didn't know where to start. Then Steve found Viaweb's online store builder and everything seemed to come together.

Fortunately, we already had the raw materials to build a site with 50 or 60 pages of catalog descriptions and graphics from our failed paper catalog attempt, and we started our store. While building the most basic online store, I did research at night for ways to get people to the Web store. I knew I needed traffic, but had no idea how to get it. How about buying some banners? Because the Yahoo! Directory seemed to do so well, I called Yahoo! advertising, and those folks wanted a one-year contract with a $10,000-a-month minimum for a banner campaign. Wow! There was no way we could afford that. What about finding some other small guys like me and partnering with them?

One of the first things I did was to poke around and try to find all the popular sites where, unbeknownst to them, our future customers were hanging out. I found a very active community of dog enthusiasts that had a hopping message board, tons of classifieds, a full calendar listing dog events all over the world, and many free articles. The site had a huge user base and did regular e-mail newsletters. I contacted the owner of the site and got his rates for banner ads, which were extremely reasonable.

I talked to my dad about running $750 worth of banners, and I thought his head was going to explode. "No way." Well, I thought it would work, so I did it any way. I told Mom what I was doing and put it on *my* credit card, so it was my gamble. Eventually, I signed a contract for three months for $250 a month.

That one site generated the majority of our revenue until we got picked up in the search engines and in the Yahoo! directory. The first month, we sold more than $5,000 worth of dog products, which is actually still a pretty good first month for an online store, but this was way back in May 1997. Ever the loveable curmudgeon, my dad, ponied up the $750, and I was in charge of online marketing from then on!

I think our initial success with sponsoring banners on a content site really spurred us on to take Internet marketing seriously and discover the ins and outs of selling on the Net. It bothers me to no end to think what may have happened had I not taken that calculated risk (besides being out $750). Some risks are worth taking, and you'll never know it if you don't try. "What one man can do, another can do."

Cranking Up Search-Engine Marketing

Search-engine marketing (SEM) is just a part of Internet marketing, but these days, search engines drive the most traffic. Search-engine marketing consists of two parts: free search and paid search. You use search engine optimization for getting listed and improving your rankings in the free search results (sometimes called organic, natural, or unpaid), and you buy paid-search advertising (called paid-search, pay-per-click, or sponsored results).

Every day, millions of folks search Google, Yahoo!, and MSN for stuff that they want to buy. Anywhere from 60 to 80 percent of search-engine traffic comes from free search results, and anywhere from 20 to 40 percent of users click on pay-per-click ads. You need to crank up your search engine marketing to drive this traffic to your Yahoo! Store.

Driving free traffic from search engines

Google, Yahoo!, and MSN can send you hundreds of thousands of visitors a year. I have seen free search-engine traffic generate millions of dollars in real sales to real Yahoo! Stores.

Nowadays, only three search engines matter: Google, Yahoo!, and MSN. AOL is powered by Google, and the fifth engine that almost matters is Ask Jeeves (which is powered by Teoma). The Big Three are so big that the smaller crawlers, directories, and portals just don't have enough traffic to move the needle. You'll get some traffic and sales from all these little sites, but if you want to sell something, you'd better be well-ranked in the Big Three.

Introducing search engine optimization

Search engine optimization (SEO) is the art and science of making changes to your Web site to rank better for relevant keywords in the search engine results pages (SERPs). Most effective SEO is done in two ways: by implementing the current best practices and by testing new methods, tracking your results, and then keeping what improves your rankings.

The two basic building blocks of search engine optimization are text and links. *Text* refers to the words on the page — visible text you can see and a search-engine spider can read. If you can see it on your screen and highlight text with your mouse and cut and paste it in a text editor like Notepad, then it's visible text. A *link* is a hyperlink pointing to the page from other pages on your site or from other sites. I go into a lot more detail about SEO in Chapter 19, but here's what you need to know:

✔ **Text:** You want to have keyword-rich text on each of your pages using your most relevant keywords in well-written product descriptions and other useful content such as product reviews, articles, FAQs, and more. These keywords also appear in various HTML elements in places like your title tag, meta keywords and description tags, inside header tags, body text, and links on your site.

These HTML elements are generated by the product information you type in your Yahoo! Store product database in the fields Name, Headline, Code, Caption, Abstract, Label, and the site-wide variable Final-Text, and you can see them on any Web page by choosing View➪Source and viewing the actual HTML source code of the page.

✔ **Links:** You also need links pointing to each page. The links can come from your site (internal links from your other pages or navigational text links), or the links can come from other people's Web sites linking to your Yahoo! Store. Good examples of other folks linking to you are directory listings, resource pages, reciprocal link exchanges with similar sites, suppliers and manufacturers linking to their retailers, product review sites, and even people linking to you from their blogs.

Buying search-engine traffic with PPC ads

The search engines finally figured out how to make money and still provide value to their users. In addition to the free-search results, search engines now display *paid-search ads* (also know as *sponsored links* or *pay-per-click ads*) above and to the right of the free results. Shoppers are searching — a lot. Here's how paid-search ads work:

1. **Select the search terms or keywords relevant to what you sell that you want to trigger your text ads as folks search for those words.**

   For more info on keywords than you ever probably want to know, see Chapter 16.

2. **Write search listings (text ads) for each keyword.**

   These text ads consist of a title, a short description, and your URL. Writing good ads is important to get qualified buyers to click your ads. Tell folks why they should shop with you, but ads with less hype do better. See Chapter 18 for more on creating effective paid-search advertising campaigns.

3. **Determine how much you can bid for each keyword.**

   Paid-search ads are sold by the keyword, and ad position is auctioned off to the highest bidder. Advertisers who bid more get better position on the page, which drives more traffic. You control your ad's position by how much you bid on each search term.

4. **Submit your keywords and ads.**

   Yahoo! Search Marketing ads get reviewed by a person, and a few days later, they appear across the Ad Network. Google AdWords spot check your ads with software and then get around to reviewing your ads. The folks at Google like to automate everything through software with an algorithm, which is pretty smart. I guess I would, too, if I could!

5. **When users search for your keyword phrases, your ads appear in the search results pages in order by bid amount.**

   You pay only when someone clicks on your ad.

If you want to guarantee that you're in the search engines, buy pay-per-click ads. If you want to guarantee top positions for your keywords, then bid high amounts for your keywords. He who bids the most gets positioned the highest. Fund your account and sell some stuff online!

Marketing with E-Mail Newsletters

E-mail marketing with newsletters is a great way to keep in touch with your customers and prospects, target offers to specific groups of customers, and boost your Yahoo! Store's sales and profits. The flip side is that when used incorrectly, e-mail marketing is the easiest way to tick off your customers. By spamming them with too-frequent or irrelevant e-mails, you can also run afoul of ISP bandwidth or spam filters, and nowadays, the legal implications of sending unwanted e-mail have huge penalties for the smallest mistakes. E-mail marketing can be extremely effective, but it does have many pitfalls. I cover e-mail marketing in detail in Chapter 22.

Before you start your e-mail marketing, stop and read Seth Godin's *Permission Marketing* to change your marketing mindset. *Permission Marketing* (Simon & Schuster) is an awesome book and a must-read for any online marketer. Mr. Godin was way ahead of his time in recognizing the value of someone saying, "Hey. I'm interested in what you sell. Please e-mail me when you have something I need to know about."

Directing Traffic from Directories

Directories are the Web's equivalent of the yellow pages, essentially huge lists of links, where Web sites are reviewed, cataloged, sorted, and categorized by type of site, usually by human editors. Directories are important for many reasons, but mostly because they offer you a source of qualified traffic, an easy way to get high-quality links, and a place where search-engine spiders begin crawling the Web to find your site.

Sometimes you have to pay to get a directory listing, and sometimes you get a free listing. There are big directories that try to cover everything on the entire Internet, little niche directories that focus on specific industries, and everything in between. These tips get you started in the right direction:

  ✔ **The Yahoo! directory (**`http://dir.yahoo.com`**) is probably the most popular example of an online directory.** Yahoo! started off in February 1994 as Stanford grad students David Filo and Jerry Yang's personal bookmarks and has since grown into a world-class media company.

In the good ol' days, a Yahoo! Directory listing was free. A good Yahoo! listing was the Holy Grail of the Internet because Yahoo was the #1 source of visitors and sales. It's ironic, but Yahoo! doesn't use the directory as the main source for search results on Yahoo.com because Yahoo! now has its own search engine.

A Yahoo! Directory listing is still a good thing to get if you can afford the $300 or so a year. Links from the Yahoo! directory are very helpful from an SEO standpoint with the other engines. Lots of search engines start spidering the Web following links from directories like Yahoo! and DMOZ, so being in the Yahoo! Directory gets you in some search engines right away.

✔ **DMOZ (a.k.a. the Open Directory Project) began as an alternative to the Yahoo! Directory, offering free listings for quality sites.** The directory is staffed by an all-volunteer army of editors who maintain their individual category pages in their particular areas of expertise.

There is no cost to submit a site to the DMOZ, but there's also no guarantee that your site will get a listing, even if your site rocks! Almost everything depends on your category editor. Before you submit your store to the directory, you need to make sure that your site meets several requirements:

- **Make your site unique.** The DMOZ isn't anti-commercial, but if your store looks like a hundred other stores in the same category with the same exact products and descriptions, you probably won't get a listing.

- **Make sure that you submit your site to the proper category, and only submit your site once.** Multiple submissions only get your site deleted because the DMOZ keeps up with how many times your domain has been submitted and in which categories.

- **Be patient after submitting.** Wait a couple of months before even starting to worry about it. You can always ask the powers-that-be to take a look at your site's submission by posting a help request at www.resource-zone.com.

- **Be polite and respectful.** Read the site's guidelines and lots of other posts before you ask senior editors to review your listing request because you may only get one shot.

If you get a link in the Yahoo! Directory and the DMOZ, you're ahead of 95 percent of the other stores out there, but take a look at other directories, too. Lots of these directories are free or cheap. I recommend taking a look at About.com, JoeAnt.com, GoGuides.com, BOTW.com, Gimpsy.com, and Zeal.com for folks really hungry for links!

Heeding the Call of the Mall

What better place to be than in a mall when you're a retailer? Shopping portals like Shopping.com, Yahoo! Shopping, and BizRate have lots of shoppers, but they also have high rent and tons of competitors. If you're buying paid-search ads, you're probably in the shopping engines already because many of them feed their supplemental results with ads from Google AdWords and Yahoo! Search Marketing.

Sometimes you get listed at no charge because the shopping sites (Froogle, Shopping.com, and BizRate) sometimes pull product data from your Yahoo! Store's XML feed. Every Yahoo! Store has an XML document containing product information that's updated every time you publish your product catalog data. For more information on the turning on the XML feed, see Chapter 15.

Getting listed in Yahoo! Shopping

With tens of thousands of stores, millions of products, and more than a billion dollars a year in sales, Yahoo! Shopping combines product search with comparison shopping. Yahoo! Shopping was originally built on a database of Yahoo! Store merchants and products, and now it's open to anyone who will pay, pulling product data from both Yahoo! and non-Yahoo! merchants, and additional results from crawling the Web to find stores and products.

Yahoo! Shopping is currently in third place after Shopping.com and BizRate, with a 14.4 percent market share in the shopping search business.

Users can compare prices and features among merchants as well as review products. Shoppers also get to rate merchants in multiple categories (customer service, fulfillment, pricing, and so on), which is why Merchant Solutions customers are required to enable customer ratings.

Yahoo! Merchant Solutions customers and Yahoo! Store (legacy) customers have their product data pulled directly from their stores. To flesh out the database, Y!Shopping also actively spiders the Web, looking for additional products, and includes nonpaying Yahoo! Stores data, but these stores rank poorly.

Get your wallet out because you're gonna have to pay. To sign up for Y!Shopping, go to your Store Manager and click the Yahoo! Shopping link. Create a new Product Submit and fund your account with a credit card. You pay a cost-per-click fee for each visitor (anywhere from $0.15 to $1, depending on how your products are categorized). You get a leg up on the competition because Yahoo! Stores get a 20 percent discount off the rate card, which you can see at the following Web site:

```
http://productsubmit.adcentral.yahoo.com/sspi/us/pricing
```

Your success in Yahoo! Shopping depends in a large part on whether your products appeal to the average consumer, how much competition is inside Yahoo! Shopping, and how well you optimize your product listings. Yahoo! Shopping is now an open platform, which means more competition for me and you. Shopping search results are sorted by several factors, including how relevant your product listings are, the quality of your customer ratings, and your relationship with Yahoo! Merchants who pay to get better listings in Yahoo! Shopping than results from the Web crawl. Merchants are ranked by a ratings system that favors merchants who have given good service and have been positively rated.

✔ **Froogle:** Froogle is Google's shopping search engine and Google's answer to Yahoo! Shopping. Getting your products in Froogle is pretty easy when you're a Yahoo! Store because Froogle uses the XML feed from all Yahoo! Stores. You can also submit your products in a datafeed via FTP, which allows you to optimize your product listings. See `https://www.google.com/froogle/merchants` for Froogle for merchants. (Google makes money from advertising off of the Google AdWords that run alongside the free product listings. See Chapter 18 for more on Google AdWords.)

✔ **Feed Services:** Some companies take your Yahoo! Store product data, chop it up, reformat it, and submit it to all the different shopping engines for a fee. My favorite would have to be Don Cole's feed service (`www.ystoretools.com`), which I talk about a bit more in Chapter 25.

Buying Text-Link Ads for Traffic and Link Popularity

By now, you probably know you need to get links to your Yahoo! Store to get traffic as well as the SEO benefits. One way to get links is to buy them. An easy way to buy links is to hook up with text-link brokers like Text-Link-Ads.com.

Make buying text links another part of a real *link-building campaign,* which is anything you do to get folks to link back to you. Request links from quality content sites, directories, your own suppliers' and manufacturers' Web sites, industry associations you belong to, and any other sites related to your industry that will link to you. See Chapter 19 for more on the power of links and link building.

Here are a few tips for buying text links:

✔ **Buy text links on sites with a similar theme to your Yahoo! Store.** You want to benefit from the additional traffic that you'd get from that site, regardless of any search engine optimization benefits. For example, if you have an online pet store, buy text links on sites that have articles about pets, not automotive shop sites.

  ✔ **Buy links not only to your home page, but also *deep links* (links to interior pages of your store) as well.** Make sure that you use different keywords in the *anchor text* (the text in the link).

  ✔ **Don't buy *run-of-site* links (links on every page) on huge 100,000-page sites.** After a few dozen pages, you quickly reach a point of diminishing returns. Including 100,000 links from a single site looks like spam to most search engines.

I've got a general rule that I use for budgeting funds for buying text links. I take 10 percent of what I'm spending on paid-search ads, and I use that number as my text-link budget.

Sponsoring Forums, Directories, Nonprofits, and Clubs

Odds are that most of the affinity sites, hobby sites, interest sites, or community sites similar to your Yahoo! Store niche sell advertising (links or banners) or have sponsorship opportunities. Some sites, especially nonprofits, don't want to look like they're out for the money, so you see the word *sponsorship* used, but it really means the same thing: advertising.

If these sites don't currently accept advertising, you can always suggest that they do. Contact the owner or Webmaster and ask about sponsoring the site, underwriting the site's hosting expenses, or donating prizes for events or contests in exchange for some marketing attention. All sponsoring a site means is that you give the site money, and it gives you exposure (with ads, links, mentions in their newsletters, and so on).

Many sites related to what you sell have *forums* or bulletin boards that are teeming with potential customers. By sharing your expertise, lending a helping hand, answering beginner questions, and participating in discussions in an online community, you can build your reputation in the industry as an expert, which lends credibility to your store. Make sure that you always abide by forum rules and posting guidelines and really participate. Forums can be fun!

Commissioning Sales through Affiliate Marketing

Affiliate programs are marketing relationships between retailers and Web sites. Affiliates send traffic to the retailer's Yahoo! Store in exchange for a percentage of sales. Retailers provide sales copy, product databases, advertising graphics, and banners for the affiliates to advertise their stores. These ads have links that use a tracking code and go through a third-party like Commission Junction (www.cj.com). Commission Junction's tracking software keeps up with which affiliate sent the retailer the traffic, and when someone buys something, the affiliate gets credit for the sale.

Affiliate marketing has its upsides:

- ✔ You can get a ton of traffic very quickly.
- ✔ Merchants pay only when someone buys something.
- ✔ Merchants don't pay for phone orders, newsletter signups who convert later, people who surf at work but buy at home, or users who delete their cookies. (Sometimes there are sales affiliates should get paid for, but they don't because their sales don't track.)

Commission Junction is the only Yahoo! Store–approved affiliate solution. CJ is a little expensive, but the interface is great, and CJ's people know affiliate marketing. Last time I talked with CJ, it had a one-year minimum commitment, which ran about $5,000.

CJ gives you an independent third party to connect you with the affiliates (it calls them *publishers*). You have an interface where you watch your stats, upload your ads, and promote your program. Once a month, you pay CJ. CJ pays your affiliates and charges you a fee of 30 percent of whatever you pay your affiliates. For example, if you have a $100 sale where you pay your affiliate 10 percent, you pay 13 percent to CJ and CJ pays 10 percent to your affiliate.

One of the most successful marketing methods I've seen has been *revenue share programs*. These deals are much like affiliate programs, but you usually have a single affiliate dealing with a single Yahoo! Store.

In this model, the marketer gets a percentage of sales for designing, developing, improving, and maintaining a store, in addition to driving search-engine traffic though search engine optimization and paid search. If the store doesn't sell anything, the marketer goes hungry, so you usually have an extremely motivated search-engine marketer. If the store does sell something, the marketer participates in the success of the store. This model allows the retailer to concentrate on retailing and the marketer to concentrate on driving qualified traffic to the online store.

Exploring eBay Auctions for Yahoo! Store Owners

Auctions are a great way to sell things when you're not selling products at full retail or when you have samples or other products you want to liquidate.

Factory seconds, returned products, overstocks, and scratch-and-dent products make good auctions. While other auctions sites exist, eBay is about it unless your industry has a niche auction site with a lot of activity.

If you think you may be interested in auctioning on eBay, check out the following titles, all by Marsha Collier and all published by Wiley Publishing: *eBay For Dummies; Starting an eBay Business For Dummies;* and *eBay Timesaving Techniques For Dummies.*

Blogging for Retailers

I have to admit that I got caught up in the blogging phenomenon in the last 18 months. A *blog* (short for *weblog*) is a loose-format online journal where you can write about almost anything. Blogs can address almost any subject, but industry-specific blogs do well as marketing tools. Blogs are a lot less formal than most corporate communications, so they allow you to present a more personal face to your customers and vendors.

My Yahoo! Store Blog (http://ystore.blogs.com) started out as an archive of some marketing columns I had written and turned into a soapbox where I could rant and rave about various Yahoo! Store issues, and list tips and tricks or marketing resources as I ran across them. I knew my clients, my fellow developers, and even my friends at Yahoo! corporate headquarters could read my posts.

Use blogs to feature new products and services, demonstrate your expert knowledge about what you sell, and leverage all the content you've written in e-mails and other places to a much larger audience.

Sometimes blogging really pays off:

- ✔ **Get access to opportunities in your industry.** My acquisitions editor, Steve Hayes, read my 100-plus blog posts (http://ystore.blogs. com), which ultimately led to me writing this book. Had he only read what was on my regular Web site trying to sell my marketing services, I may never have gotten the phone call that resulted in this book.

- ✔ **Network over the Internet.** I live in rural Mississippi, okay, which means I never run into my dot-com peers down at the tractor pull. (Okay, I've never *really* been to a tractor pull.) Frequent blog posts about my obsession with converting keywords got me in on the beta test of Swivel's (www.swivel.com) cool new online marketing tool that tracks and graphs your online advertising spending and conversion data with an intuitive, visual interface. Participating in the beta test gave me input on product development, which I never would have gotten otherwise.

✔ **Tap into unknown customer needs.** I wrote a blog post just the other day about a company called SLI Systems (`www.sli-systems.com`), which offers a Yahoo! Store–friendly customized search solution. While somewhat expensive, the search is light-years ahead of the free-search tool included in Yahoo!. Now I have multiple clients asking me to set up custom searches for them. I had no idea my clients would be interested in something like this, but one blog post, and wham!

Exploring Other Ways to Get Traffic

You can market your business and sell online in many ways. Realize that I hyperfocus on two or three (SEO, paid search, and blogging) because they work really well for me. Each client of mine has a unique approach to selling online. I guess you just have to keep looking until you find what works for you. Here are some other marketing avenues you should pursue:

✔ **Swap links with related sites.** Become a resource yourself with links and reviews to the best content so that your customers come back to your site even when they're not specifically looking to buy something.

✔ **Collect e-mail addresses and create weekly e-mail newsletters with specials.** Have contests to collect some e-mail addresses and get folks excited about your site. Run a survey or offer an online quiz to your readers.

✔ **Write interesting articles and offer them to other sites.** Give your visitors this free content in exchange for an e-mail address. For example, think about something like a "Buyer's Guide: Ten Things You Should Know Before Buying Anything."

✔ **Advertise offline.** Trade journals and industry publications have cheap classified ads. Consider radio, TV, billboards, direct mail, and catalogs. The list is practically endless.

For a great article on more ways to get Web traffic, read Brett Tabke's article "The Mostly Viral Top Traffic Alternatives to Search Engines List" at `www.webmasterworld.com/forum10/906.htm`.

Peeling One Potato at a Time . . .

You can easily get overwhelmed with all the things you have to do. My dad had a saying that probably has saved my sanity: "Peel one potato at a time. You can only do one thing." But how do you pick which thing to do? My Uncle Paul always tells me to make sure that whatever you're doing is the highest priority and best use of your time.

The secret weapon for prioritizing my work is to apply the 80/20 rule to everything I do. Also known as the Pareto Principle, the 80/20 rule is simply the observation that not all customers, products, or activities are created equal and that the results you get from similar activities may vary widely.

If you focus on what activities get the most results, instead of trying to work on everything, you'll go much farther, much faster.

For example, 20 percent of your customers may generate 80 percent of your revenues, 20 percent of your products can make up 80 percent of your sales, and 20 percent of your keywords may generate 80 percent of your traffic and conversions. After you know what the most effective 20 percent are, you can concentrate more of your time and effort on those items and get a huge boost in productivity.

For example, when you work on improving your product pages, start with your bestsellers and work your way down the list in order of descending sales. By the time you stop or run out of time, or something catches on fire, odds are you've done the most important work. If you have a site with thousands of products, odds are that most of your sales come from your top 100 items. If you work alphabetically, you could optimize hundreds of pages before getting to any of your bestsellers, which is probably not the best use of your time.

The 80/20 rule applies to many things, including marketing to your customers, schmoozing with your vendors/suppliers, managing your PPC accounts, working on your SEO campaigns, maximizing products sales, writing buyer's guides, managing your keywords, grooming your employees, and so on.

Chapter 18

Buying Your Way to the Top

● ●

In This Chapter

▶ Discovering paid-search advertising

▶ Starting your PPC campaign by picking keywords

▶ Writing clickable ads to get more customers

▶ Landing on pages designed to convert

▶ Managing paid-search campaigns to maximize results

▶ Tracking your ads to make sure that you get your money's worth

● ●

Search ads are a fast and effective way to drive extremely targeted, qualified Web traffic straight to your store. Your ads are shown only to potential customers because you get to choose the keyword phrases that trigger your ads. Open an advertising account, pick your search terms, write your ad copy, set your budget, and off you go. You decide how much you can afford to pay per visitor, and you budget your advertising up and down as needed.

Paid-search advertising works, too, and you can prove it with conversion-tracking software. You can track almost everything, so throw money at what's generating sales while culling the losers. You have total control over where you send the person who clicks your ad, too, so you can make sure that potential buyers land on the most relevant page on your site for their search query.

In this chapter, I give you a quick overview on how to cost-effectively use pay-per-click advertising to help push up your sales in your Yahoo! Store, and I tell you everything you need to know to improve your pay-per-click performance. You find out how to track your visitors, create a winning landing page, fine-tune your campaigns, and more.

Introducing Paid-Search Advertising

The search engines have finally figured out how to make a buck or two. Scratch that. More like ten billion. Analysts estimate global spending on paid search was close to $10,000,000,000.00 in 2005. The search-engine advertising business is on fire, growing at a whopping 40 percent-plus a year. Holy cow. And I'm supposed to cover all you need to know in less than 20 pages?

Paid search, sometimes called *pay-per-click (PPC) advertising,* is the advertising part of search-engine marketing. Paid-search ads usually appear at the top or right of a search engine's free results page, triggered by keyword searches. Only ads relevant to the specific keyword-phrase search display alongside the search engine's regular or free results. Here's how you buy into paid-search advertising:

1. **Open a search-marketing account.**

   Google AdWords and Yahoo! Search Marketing are the ones you want, and all you need is a credit card. Check out the promotional offers page at `http://sbs.smallbusiness.yahoo.com/marketing/promotional_offers.php` with a $50 promotional credit available for folks opening new accounts with Y!SM and Google AdWords. The paid-search companies are always giving away coupons at all the search conferences I attend, so hit me up for some freebies, too!

2. **Select keywords relevant to your business.**

   See Chapter 16 for more than you want to know about choosing keywords.

3. **Write search listings ads with titles and descriptions.**

   Describe the benefits of doing business with you — the less hype, the better. Read about writing effective search ads in the section "Creating clickable ads," later in this chapter.

4. **Determine how much you want to bid for each search term.**

   You control your ad's position by how much you bid compared to your competitors. Discover bidding strategies in the section "Bidding smart from the start," later in this chapter.

5. **Pick the most relevant landing page.**

   Each keyword phrase and search ad should point to the one page on your site that solves that specific customer's problem. Sometimes every keyword needs a separate page. Read about landing pages in the section "Coming in for a landing," later in this chapter.

6. **Submit your ads and cross your fingers.**

   Your ads must pass Google's or Yahoo!'s editorial review to make sure that the words you buy are relevant to your landing page. When approved, your ads start to appear across the ad network and, if you choose, on content sites as well. Read all about the network and different distribution options in the section "Choosing syndication and distribution options," later in this chapter.

7. **Track what works (and what doesn't) with free conversion-tracking software.**

   Monitor your ads. Test different keywords, ad copy, and landing pages. Start cramming on improving your search-ad campaigns in the section "Measuring Search-Advertising Results," later in this chapter.

Deciding between Paid and Free Searches

The instantaneous gratification of pay-per-click ads can be tempting. Here's where paying to get listed in the top results beats hoping to be listed in the free results:

- ✔ **With paid search, you're totally in control.** You choose the keywords, write the ads, and pick which pages get promoted. With SEO, the search engines (and sometimes the spammers) are in control of the rankings.

- ✔ **With paid search, your ads appear almost immediately.** You don't have to wait weeks or months for your site to appear in paid-search ads like you do in the free search results.

- ✔ **With paid search, you're not at the mercy of search-engine spiders and ranking algorithms to determine the most relevant page.** Just get out your wallet and buy your way to the top, because (like in the real world) the highest bidder gets the best real estate.

- ✔ **With paid search, you choose what keyword phrases you rank well for by how much you're willing to pay.** Free search-engine rankings for keywords sometimes seem almost random, even though you optimize for your best words. For example, my #1 referring keyword phrase from Google on my dog-supply site is *Dog Boots,* but we sell only two kinds of dog boots and have around 1,500 other kinds of products. Go figure.

- ✔ **With paid search, you can test keyword phrases that you don't rank well for in the free results.** That way, you can see whether you want to optimize for those words, too. Sometimes very competitive or expensive keywords don't convert like you think they should.

- ✔ **With paid search, you also write the ads so that you determine what users see.** You choose the link text (title) and the little snippet of text (description) that appear on the search results pages. With the free listings, you have little or no control over what the search engines display.

- ✔ **With paid search, you also choose what pages folks land on for each keyword.** Instead of hoping that your best landing pages rank for your best keywords, you get to pick where folks go on your Web store. You can also change your landing pages as often as you want to maximize their effectiveness. When your pages rank really well for your best keywords in the free search results, you're almost afraid to touch the pages.

Unfortunately, paid search has a dark side as well:

- ✔ **Paid-search advertising is expensive and consumes a lot of time.** Babysitting your ad campaigns takes a lot of time and mental energy. If you don't closely monitor your campaigns, a good campaign can go down the tubes fast.

- ✔ **Customers trust the free, natural, organic results.** Free results are seen as independent and more authoritative than ads. More sophisticated surfers seem to avoid clicking ads.

- ✔ **Competitors can be foolish and bid insane amounts, thus temporarily making your search-ad campaign ineffective or unprofitable.** Competitors can also click your ads. Click fraud can be costly and frustrating.

- ✔ **More retailers lose money than make money on pay-per-click ad campaigns (in my experience).** This loss is probably due more to ego-bidding, mismanagement, or neglect than from evil-doers.

- ✔ **Keywords just keep getting more and more expensive!** The average cost per click just keeps going up. Two or three years ago, most traffic was free. You can still get thousands of people per day to your Web site at no cost-per-click with good old-fashioned SEO. There's nothing like free traffic from search engines. Develop some good unique content, get a ton of links, and that's pretty much it.

Combining the one-two punch of SEO and PPC

Truth be told, 'round here we like both kinds of search marketing: paid *and* free. Search marketing is the one-two punch of search engine optimization (SEO) + paid search, which can be an effective match to your SEO campaigns.

Free search is not enough. According to an iProspect study in May 2004 (IProspect, Search Engine User Attitudes, 5/2004), almost 40 percent of the traffic from the Big Four portals comes from PPC ads.

I believe you should buy paid-search (PPC) ads when you already rank well for your keyword terms in the free results from your search engine optimization (SEO) strategy. When do you normally get *two* chances to make an advertising impression with a prospect who is ready to buy? It's like buying an ad in the newspaper that runs right next to your feature story. You can't control what they write about you, but the ad is all yours!

Planning Your PPC Ad Campaign

You need to start any advertising campaign with a good plan. Before you start shelling out greenbacks to Google and Yahoo!, ask yourself the following questions to determine the best way to spend your ad dollars:

✔ **What are my store's PPC goals?** Decide what you want prospects to do when they come to your store. Usually the primary goal is to get browsers to turn into buyers by placing an order. Secondary goals include signing up for a newsletter or downloading a buyer's guide.

✔ **How much is this campaign worth to my business?** Take time to figure out how much you're willing to pay for an order. I give you an equation to follow in the section "Knowing what to bid," later in this chapter, that can help you determine this amount. You also need to decide how much you're willing to pay per customer, as well as the lifetime value of a customer.

✔ **What are my store's numbers?** Determine your store's conversion rate. *Conversion rate* is the percentage of unique visitors that actually buys something. You can figure this rate by dividing the number of orders by the number of unique visitors. Next, figure your *gross profit margin* (your retail price minus the cost of the goods sold) and the amount of your average order.

✔ **What is my store's budget?** Determine your initial monthly budget for PPC advertising, how much time you can spend managing your PPC campaigns, and, for every dollar you spend, the amount of sales you have to generate to make a profit.

Buying Traffic with Paid-Search Ads

The paid-search advertising networks — for example, Yahoo! Search Marketing and Google AdWords — serve ads on hundreds of Web sites and give you access to millions of searchers each day, and they want to rent them to you for mere pennies a click. If you want to guarantee that your company shows up on the first page of search-engine results, get your wallet out because it's time to buy some ads. The good news is that you incur little or no upfront costs, make no commitment whatsoever, and you pay nothing if no one clicks your ads.

Picking keywords

The *keyword phrase* is the word or words that someone types into a search engine. When the user clicks the Search button, that search phrase triggers both free results and paid ads (sponsored links). Before investing in a PPC campaign, you need to know exactly what keyword phrases your customers use when they're looking to buy what you sell because these converting keywords are the words you'll bid on for your ads to appear on Yahoo! and Google.

You can determine the best keywords for your business in a number of ways. Did a keyword phrase convert into a sale? Did a keyword phrase generate traffic to your Web site? Are your competitors buying that keyword phrase or optimizing their Web site for that keyword phrase? For more information about keywords than you'll probably ever want to know, see Chapter 16.

Deciding on matching types

When you advertise on a keyword, you also choose how specific the keyword matching is. One major difference between Google and Y!SM is default matching type. With Google, you get broad match by default. Overture's standard match (default) displays your ads for exact matches to your search terms, as well as singular/plural variations, common misspellings, and "topics that are highly relevant to your keywords, titles and descriptions."

Here are your matching choices:

- *Broad match* (or standard match) shows your ad on every search containing your keywords in any order.

- *Phrase match* shows your ad only on searches containing your exact phrase.

- *Exact match* shows your ad only for searches that contain that exact keyword phrase.

Eliminate keywords you don't want with negative matching

Negative matching allows you to pick stop words that kill your ad for any searches containing that term, because sometimes you don't want to be found for certain keywords phrases. Usually, these negative keywords are either very popular searches that don't match your business model (*free, cheap, wholesale, downloads, samples,* and so on) or phrases where your keywords overlap with phrases in other unrelated industries.

Buying your company name and domain

One way to improve performance is to buy your company name and URL. This strategy may seem a bit obvious, but no one does it. You probably already rank very well for your domain name and your company name, but buy them anyway. When someone is searching for me, I want to make sure that I'm found.

Buy every possible variant of how someone could search for your company name. Buy misspellings of your name. Buy your name as all one word. Buy every variant of your domain name. Buy the singular and plurals of your name. Buy your e-mail addresses. Watch for other ways folks butcher your name and buy those variants, too.

Creating clickable ads

Keywords are only one part of a PPC campaign. You also need to write an actual advertisement to appear along with the keyword. After I assemble my list of keywords, I start out writing ads for each bucket of keywords.

- **Headline/Title:** The *headline* or *title* is the blue underlined link that folks click to go to your Web site. Google AdWords gives you up to 25 characters. Yahoo! Search Marketing limits you to 40 characters in titles.

    A headline is the most important marketing copy you'll ever write. I have better results when the title of the ad is exactly what folks are searching for. I try to include something to make the title/headline relevant.

- **Description:** The *description* is the ad text that appears after your link. Yahoo! Search Marketing gives you 190 characters in your caption, but some search partners show an abbreviated listing with only 70 characters. Make sure that your description makes sense with only 70 characters.

    With a Yahoo! Search Marketing ad, you can actually write a more descriptive sentence than with a Google ad because Google gives you only two lines with a maximum of 35 characters on each line, which can be a little frustrating. After you get the hang of writing concisely, creating Google ads can be fun, almost like writing a marketing haiku.

- **URL:** Your paid-search ad also has a *URL,* which is the address of a page on your site where you want to send visitors who clicked on that specific ad. Every ad could have a unique URL to a unique landing page designed especially for that ad. Both Yahoo! Search Marketing and Google AdWords give you 1,024 characters for your URL so that you have plenty of room for long page names and tracking codes. Y!SM displays only your domain name.

- **Display URL:** Google AdWords also gives you an additional field called *Display URL* with a maximum length of 35 characters. Name your landing page with your keywords or ad copy so that you can call additional attention to your AdWords ad. Make your Display URL something like `http://domain.com/keyword-phrase-sale.html`.

Coming in for a landing

Usually, when someone clicks one of my ads, I either send them to the front page (rarely), a section page (uncommon), a product page (more often), or a search results pages from my Yahoo! Store's internal search engine.

Lazy marketers land folks on the home page. Sometimes that's appropriate for the most generic words. People can discover what your company is about and poke around your site, but you can usually choose a more relevant page depending upon the search word.

If folks are looking for information about various product groups using more generic keyword phrases such as *Plasma HDTV* or *Automatic Swimming Pool Cleaners,* I like to send them to my Product Buyer's Guides. Section pages are also good places for these folks to land on your site, but I usually link to the sections from the Buyer's Guides. Product-related keywords definitely need to use product pages as landing pages.

Here are a few more tips about landing pages:

- ✔ If you have to think for more than two seconds about where you want a prospect to land on your site, then you know that you need to create a specific landing page for that keyword phrase.

- ✔ Check to make sure that your landing pages are up, especially if you have multiple people working on your Web site. There's nothing like paying for terms that have a 404 error page when folks click on a $5-a-click ad.

- ✔ If you're targeting very specific terms, consider making a landing page template without normal site navigation, but experiment with different types of landing pages to see which types of pages get you a better conversion rate.

- ✔ Use the search term in the headline of your landing page. I always try to get the "Hey! That's exactly what I was looking for!" response.

- ✔ Talk about the benefits of buying the product in the first screen shot of the landing page. Tell your reader what problem this product solves. Bullet points are great for pointing out features and benefits.

Determining bid amounts

The *bid amount* is how much money an advertiser is willing to pay for someone to click his ad and go to his Web site. They're called *pay-per-click ads* because an advertiser only has to pay when users click the ad. You don't have to pay for *impressions* (the number of times your ad is shown), only for clicks on your ad.

Looking at bids with the View Bids tool on Y!SM

Yahoo! Search Marketing will show you advertisers' maximum bids at any given time. To view them, follow these steps:

1. **Go to** www.overture.com **and do a search for the keyword you want to research.**

2. **In the upper-right corner, click the View Advertisers' Max Bids link.**

   A screen appears, asking you to type the search term again and a random code word.

3. **Type the term and random code word.**

   The maximum that all the current advertisers are willing to pay for clicks appears (see figure). At the top of the screen is a spot for you to type the search term you want to see the maximum bids for.

4. **Type your search term and click the Search button.**

Y!SM has a very straightforward auction where the highest bidder gets the highest number position. Google is a little different and rewards advertisers with ads that generate the most revenue with better positions. Let me explain.

For example, imagine if you will, one advertiser bidding $1.00 a click for a certain keyword phrase, and getting a 1% *click-through rate,* or CTR, on the ad. Google makes $1.00 for every 100 people seeing the ad. Imagine a second advertiser bidding a little more than half as much, say only 51 cents a click, but this second advertiser had a 2 percent CTR (perhaps because she had a better written ad). Google would make $1.02 per 100 visitors because of the higher CTR and reward the second advertiser with the #1 position.

Bidding smart from the start

When planning a PPC advertising campaign, an important early step is determining how much you can spend per click. When you set up an advertising account, you set the maximum amount you're willing to pay for a visitor for each search term. You can change these bids at any time, and you can pause your ad campaign with the click of a button. However, you need to have some general ideas of how much you can pay for an average sale to set a baseline for building a profitable campaign. When you have some real conversion data, it's easier to pay a lot more for the big fish and ignore the minnows and the snapping turtles.

There's a very delicate balance between bidding high enough to be well-ranked in the paid-search results and converting enough of those shoppers into buyers to make sure that your advertising makes money.

My good friend, David Karandish of FindStuff.com (who some folks will recognize as the SEO on *Martha Stewart's Apprentice*), gave me this advice about *bid throttling* — the process of bidding much higher in the short term than you're willing to pay in the long term — and how it's fundamental for establishing a click-through rate on new AdWords campaigns:

> *Google's advertising revenue is maximized by getting more and more clicks. It is in their best interest to show ads that get clicked on as often as possible. New advertisers must bid significantly higher to get activated in order to establish a click-through history. Once a track record is established, you can slowly throttle down (lower) your bids and maintain better positioning for a much cheaper cost per click.*

Knowing what to bid

You need a pretty good idea of the most you can spend per visitor before you get started. After a campaign gets going, you can then optimize different keywords with different bid amounts, but you need to know your numbers for an average visitor to your Yahoo! Store.

Are you advertising products that tend to generate repeat orders? Take this factor into account when deciding how much you can afford to pay for that first sale. Raise your maximum cost-per-order (CPO) for ads for products that create repeat buyers.

Remember that customers from PPC convert at somewhat different rates than free traffic, and all keywords convert at wildly different rates, so aim to beat your averages. Some ads and keyword phrases perform better, and some perform worse. You can adjust individual keywords and bids accordingly as you develop your campaigns.

Getting the best bids for your bucks

The top spots above the free search results on a search engine are called the *premium listings*. These listings are the same as the text ads that run down the right side of the page. If you want your ad to go to the top — or even appear at all — you have to pay premium dollars. Some of Google's and Y!SM's partners only use the top three or four bids.

If you're in the #1 spot, you can expect about a 10 percent click-through rate (CTR), which means you get 1 click per 10 impressions. A #2 position generates somewhere around a 5 percent CTR and a #3 position around 4 percent, and the amount of clicks you get drops almost exponentially as your position decreases.

To get premium positioning on Google, you also have to pass an editorial review where someone at Google performs a hand-check on your ad to make sure that your ads are relevant to the search term. After you get your ads to the top, if you have strong bids with high click-through rates, it's somewhat difficult to get knocked off by a competitor unless he's willing to bid two to five times what you're paying.

So is it worth it to be the #1 ad on a search engine? Actually, I've had better luck in the #2 or #3 position, and the industry thinking seems to be along the same lines. Sometimes the #1 position gets all the clickers who are just curious and don't really read the ad. The #1 position also is vulnerable to competitors who like to click other advertisers' ads.

Choosing syndication and distribution options

Right now, only two paid-search advertising networks really count: Yahoo! Search Marketing (a.k.a. the ad network formerly known as Overture) and Google AdWords. The Big Four Portals — Yahoo!, Google, MSN, and AOL — and their affiliates drive 94 percent of all traffic (millions upon millions of visitors) from search engines to Web sites.

Yahoo! and Google also syndicate their search ads across multiple search partner sites, which run ads on their much smaller search engines or other Web sites.

Content ads: PPC by any other name

Content partners are just like search partners, but instead of running search ads on search-engine search queries, content partners display ads on top of articles, using sophisticated spidering tools to read the content of a page and then display relevant ads on top of that content.

In my experience, content ads do not convert at anywhere near the level of search marketing ads because folks visiting those content sites aren't actively searching for information or looking to buy products, so you may be burning through your valuable advertising dollars on content match ads when you think all your dollars are being spent on paid search.

Setting different distribution options

Sometimes you want your ads to run in only certain cities, or states, or parts of the world, or you want your ads to run everywhere except a particular area. When you're setting up a campaign, you usually have to indicate whether you want your ads to run in the United States and/or across the entire world, but you have other options, too. Exploring the details of the various geographic ad distribution options may be for you if you only sell locally or have certain limitations on your sales territory.

Measuring Search-Advertising Results

Conversion-tracking software allows you to see what ads drive tire-kickers and what ads drive buyers. When you have this information, you can start improving the efficacy of your paid-search campaigns. You can cull the non-performing ads, tweak the underperforming ads, and study the overperforming ads to see whether you can take the magic and sprinkle some of it back on the rest of your campaign.

Here's a conversion-tracking tip: When you start using conversion tracking, *put the start date in the campaign name.* If you run conversion rate reports where the date range overlaps the time before you were tracking conversions, your data will be off because all the clicks you got before adding the code look like they had 0 percent conversions.

Using free conversion tracking

Google AdWords and Yahoo! Search Marketing now offer free conversion-tracking code, which shows you which campaigns, ads, and keywords are turning into sales and which are turning your stomach. If you advertise on both networks, you need both tracking codes.

Google conversion-rate tracking doesn't count all Google partners, and it's likely that Y!SM has similar problems. You get what you pay for, and 100 percent accuracy is impossible. I always use multiple tracking methods to be sure.

Getting your JavaScript tracking code from Google and Yahoo! Search Marketing consoles is pretty straightforward, but if you have any problems, just consult their Help pages. After you have one or both of the tracking scripts, all you do is paste them inside the message field on your Order Confirmation page. Here's how:

1. **Log in to your Yahoo! Store and click the Store Manager link.**

   The Store Manager page appears.

2. **In the Order Settings column, click the Order Form link.**

   The Customize Your Order Form page appears.

3. **Scroll down to the Order Confirmation section and paste your tracking code(s) inside the Message field.**

4. **Scroll to the top of the page and click the Done button.**

   You return to the Yahoo! Store Manager.

5. **Click the Publish Order Settings link to publish your Google and/or Y!SM tracking code.**

Buying third-party tracking tools

If you spend more than $500 a month on PPC, you need Yahoo! Store–friendly conversion-tracking software. You just put a little snippet of code in your Head-tags field and on your Order Confirmation page, and these programs track where visitors come from, what they search for, and what they do. You can use tools, such as Clicktracks, Keywordmax, or Indextools that have workarounds or hacks that actually do capture the amount of the sale. I like all three programs and have used them on various projects. I talk more about these products in Chapters 20 and 25.

Working with trackable links

The Store Manager's Track Links feature is an easy way for Standard and Pro accounts (sorry, Starter accounts!) to track sales from paid-search and other campaigns so you can see which campaigns or banners or keywords are working. Here's how Track Links works:

Create a link with a descriptive name. The Store Manager then generates a URL with a unique tracking code. You use that link as the URL in the ad you want to track. When someone visits your site using this URL, the Store Manager makes a note and redirects him to the normal URL for the landing page.

Go to the Store Manager's Track Links page to see stats of the number of visitors, number of orders, and sales per link within a day or so of user activity. Orders from customers who clicked on Track Links are also marked with the name of the link right on the order so you can see which campaigns are working as orders come in.

Here's how to create a trackable link:

1. **Log in to your Yahoo! Store and go to Store Manager.**

2. **Click the Create Links link.**

   The Manage Trackable Links page appears.

3. **In the blank field, type the name of the link.**

   Name your links with obvious names and as much information as possi-
   ble so that you know which campaigns convert when you look at your
   Track Link stats. I like names like "041305 Google AdWords, Campaign 2,
   AdGroup 3, Ad 2" or "050506 Cocker Spaniel Keywords."

4. **Click the Create New Trackable Link button.**

   The Link page appears with your track-link URL, which includes your
   account name, a random-looking unique alphanumeric code (uXEP5p),
   and the name of the page you link to. For example, here's a Track Link:

   ```
   http://store.yahoo.com/cgi-bin/clink?YourAccountName+uXEP5p+index.html
   ```

Track Links point to the home page (index.html) by default, but you can
change the page name to whatever page you want to send clickers to by
replacing index.html with any other page name. For example, if you want
to track links to a landing page called buy-this-product.html, you'd use
something like this code as your URL in your PPC:

```
http://store.yahoo.com/cgi-bin/clink?youraccountname+MAyg4J+buy-this-product.html
```

After creating my trackable links, I usually place a test order to make sure
that everything is working. Just allow 24 to 48 hours for the stats to update.

Improving Your Campaigns

Running an ad campaign is about more than just coming up with winning keywords and great landing pages. You have to maintain your campaign, just like
you would regularly do yard work to have a great yard. You need to get rid of
keywords that aren't paying off and replace them.

Just to be absolutely sure that all my ads are working, I dig in and cull the
losers. I'm looking to pause or fix ads where I'm spending a lot of money to
get traffic that either doesn't convert at all or where the cost-per-order is way
out of whack with what we make on an order.

Nonperforming keywords

Some keyword phrases do send me traffic but for some reason don't convert
into sales. Eventually, I set a dollar threshold with the maximum amount of
money I think I can spend on a keyword phrase over a given period of time
without getting a conversion (usually $10 a phrase), and I pause or delete any
keywords above this threshold.

Other paid-search resources

PPC is a multibillion dollar business which makes it kind of hard to cover in a couple of chapters. If you want to know more about PPC, check out these great books and Web sites:

Building Your Business with Google For Dummies, by Brad Hill (Wiley Publishing).

Google AdWords: 21 Pay-Per-Click Campaign Secrets Your Competition Doesn't Know (2004 Edition), by Andrew Goodman (Page-Zero).

Yahoo! Search Marketing's Resource Center at `http://searchmarketing.yahoo.com/rc/srch/?mkt=us`. You can find tools, information, and case studies to help you improve your search-marketing campaigns.

Google AdWords Learning Center at `www.google.com/adwords/learningcenter`. This site gives you an introduction to AdWords; helps you set up an account, track ad performance, and optimize ads; introduces the AdWords toolbox; and more.

SearchEngineWatch.com: Created by Danny Sullivan, Search Engine Watch is the premier source of info on search-engine marketing. Search Engine Watch also sponsors the very popular Search Engine Strategies conferences every year in New York (March), San Jose, CA (August), and Chicago (December). If you have the time and inclination, the conferences are money well spent. The contacts alone are worth the price of admission.

Webmasterworld PPC forums: Visit `www.webmasterworld.com/forum81` and `www.webmasterworld.com/forum33`. You can find interactive forums with official representatives from all major paid-search companies.

Underperforming keywords

Another group of keywords are relevant to my site, get a lot of traffic and clicks, and actually convert, but at an extremely low conversion rate. These underperforming keywords make my cost-per-order (CPO) higher than my profit per sale. Ouch. If my cost per order is, say, $20, based on what I'm getting paid as a revenue share partner, I can't afford to spend that. I can spend more like $12 CPO. So I go and I cut off any ads that are more than $15 CPO in a given time period, even though I know these words are relevant and convert.

I keep a list of words I removed from my PPC campaigns, and I check this list from time to time to see whether any words should be added back to my active campaigns. Sometimes I get inspired to see whether I can take an underperforming word and make the perfect ad and landing page to make it worth buying.

Chapter 19

Discovering Search Engine Optimization (SEO)

Search engine optimization (SEO) is sometimes looked upon as a mysterious, black art where you have to be a whacked-out mad scientist or an idiot savant or mathematical genius to crack the secret algorithms of the search engines to get free traffic. Nope! You've been watching too much TV. For e-commerce folks like you and me, the best search engine optimization strategy is a two-pronged strategy: make sure that the engines can tell exactly what your site is about and get more links than the other guy.

A couple of my SEO friends think I expose way, way too much of my personal search engine optimization methodology, but what the heck! Things change so fast, and I'm not telling you *everything* I know! I do think you'll get your $25 worth out of two specific pages in here. You find out the steps to successful Yahoo! Store search engine optimization, including how to know what HTML elements are missing from your store, assign keywords to pages, create compelling title tags, master meta-tags, write search-engine-friendly copy, and love links.

In this chapter, I really give you more strategy than specific tactics. The most important thing to do is to make sure that the search engines know that your site is really about what you say it's about. And keep your nose clean, because when you get busted, it *hurts!*

Discovering How Search Engines Work

When you do a search on a search engine like Google, Yahoo!, or MSN Search, the search-engine server checks its index for pages that contain the words matching your search query. This list of pages can literally be in the millions of pages, depending on your keyword phrase. The search engine then quickly sorts the pages to show you the most relevant listings at the top of the page. And it does this process almost instantly!

Order, please!

The order of search results is determined by these super, super secret *algorithms* (rules used to rank Web pages) and filters that are the secret behind the billion dollar search-engine companies' technology. If you knew exactly how a search engine ranked pages, in theory you could jump to the #1 position for almost any search keyword by building the perfect page. After playing with search engines for almost ten years, I now think of all the different algos and filters used to order search results kinda like a kaleidoscope where something's always changing. I guess it's harder to hit a moving target!

Back in 1997, search engines used what today would be considered extremely unsophisticated methods to rank Web pages, primarily using many different on-page factors (elements on the page) in their ranking algorithms. For example, *keyword density* (the percentage of the occurrence of a keyword compared to the total text) was extremely important, so SEOs spent a lot of time looking at pages that outranked them, measured their keyword density, and then tweaked their pages to match. *Keyword frequency,* the number of times a keyword appears in a given page, was somewhat important, too. Then everything changed.

Enter Google

A little startup no one had ever heard of, called Google, started using a radical new idea to dramatically improve the relevancy of its search results. With Google's search engine, it didn't really matter what *you* said about your site with meta-tags or even keyword density because Google relied more on what *other sites* said about you. Google performed *reputation analysis* on every page in its index by looking at the quantity and quality of links from other Web pages linking to a particular page. When more important pages linked to your page, the more important your page was. Google founder Larry Page called this ranking PageRank. Nowadays, all the big search engines do some sort of link popularity and reputation analysis and figure these rankings in their search algorithms.

Along came a spider

Search engines use special software called *spiders* (or *robots*) to crawl the Web looking for new pages to add to their index. The crawl starts from a database of pages already in their index so that the 'bot can make sure that old pages still exist, find and index changes to the old pages, and then follow any new links to discover new Web pages.

If you ever want to see what your site looks like to a search-engine spider, turn off images and JavaScript in your browser. All you see is text and links. It's pretty plain. Now you're probably starting to see why text and links are important to your search-engine rankings, because search engines can only index and rank what they can see!

When you have a new site, you want the search engines to find your site — and fast! The easiest way is to get links from sites already in the index. It's easy to find these indexed sites because they're the ones that come up when you do a keyword search. For example, the Yahoo! Directory is a great place to buy a link ($299 a year if approved) because spiders crawl all over Yahoo!'s directory. See Chapter 17 for more on the Yahoo! Directory and other places to get links.

After the 'bot finds your site, it crawls (visits) all your pages. The search-engine spider indexes the text on your pages and counts and follows links on your site. After your pages get indexed, you start to get a trickle of traffic to your site when folks search for phrases relevant to your site. The more links you get and the more relevant the text on your site, the more traffic you get.

Honestly, all that search-engine math makes my head hurt. I was an art major! I just find what works for ranking my sites, and I keep doing that until it doesn't work anymore. My best secret weapon is my really, really smart friends who I roll with at search-engine conferences all around the country.

Speaking of SEO buddies, SEOMike, whose real name is Mike Black, president of Internet Marketing Resources (www.im-resources.com), took a gander at the fourth or fifth version of this chapter and reminded me to plug something new. Google has a great way to allow you to help its spider find all your pages: Google Sitemaps.

Google offers free tools to help you create an XML file for Google's robot, which tells it what pages you want indexed, how frequently you want them indexed, and what new pages you have added. Google also provides you with spidering reports that you can view from your Google account. These reports tell you whether the Googlebot is having any problems with your pages, which makes me sleep better at night. Visit www.google.com/sitemaps/login for more information.

Uh, is this spam?

Don't do anything you *know* you're not supposed to do because search engines detect spam. Don't try to deceive the search engines. Don't link to spammy sites. Don't do anything you don't want your competitors reporting on a search-engine spam report.

I e-mail a couple of SEO friends of mine every week or so with examples of sites aggressively marketing their products online, and I always use the same subject line "Uh, is this spam?" Good friend Joe Morin of BoostRanking.com, SEO to the CEOs, always replies with some variation of "Cousin, if you have to ask, then you *know* it's spam!" I know, cousin. I know.

Matt Cutts, search quality engineer and spam fighter at Google, lists tons of examples of search-engine spam on his personal Web site, www.mattcutts. com/blog, as well as recipes for bacon polenta and how to pimp your ride on the cheap.

Appreciating Yahoo! Stores for Ease of SEO

Yahoo! Stores are search-engine friendly from the get-go with no custom programming required. I've sold millions of dollars over the years with Yahoo! Stores using the standard, built-in RTML templates, even though I make some pretty serious RTML tweaks these days. Here's why Yahoo! Stores work well for free search-engine traffic:

- ✔ **Store Editor–built pages are static HTML pages that are very search-engine friendly.** *Static* means that they sit in a folder on a Yahoo! server somewhere and are much better for search engines than *dynamic* (database-generated) pages. Dynamic pages are used by most other e-commerce packages because dynamic pages don't exist until someone asks for them by clicking a link or doing a product search.

- ✔ **Yahoo! Store pages are easy to edit, so making SEO improvements is very easy.** Anytime you're editing your store — for example, making price changes — you can also make tweaks to the various SEO elements.

- ✔ **Yahoo! servers have an extremely high uptime,** which is critical for searchbots. If your site isn't there when the search engine spider or 'bot shows up, the 'bot assumes that you most likely deleted the pages and removes them from the index. Ouch! "No, wait! Come back, Googlebot! I was in the shower. . . ."

Optimizing Yahoo! Stores without Programming

The secret to the Yahoo! Store standard template SEO is pretty simple:

- ✔ Put your keywords at least once in the Name field, and at least twice in the Caption field on all product and section pages using normal language to accurately describe your products.

- ✔ Link to up to 25 of your big-money section and product pages in the Variables Final-text field. Use the most important keywords for the anchor text (words in the links).

- ✔ Use the Abstract fields on section pages and the home page.

I also recommend that you go a little bit overboard in the link development category if you don't spring for custom RTML. A decently optimized page with tons of links to it beats a perfectly optimized page with fewer links every time.

Optimizing Your Store for Search Engines

Okay. Here's how I do SEO. If you're a competitor of any of my clients, this is really just a filler chapter, and none of this stuff works, anyway. Go check out Chapter 13. Serious, professional Yahoo! Store search engine optimization consists of five parts: custom RTML programming, keyword research, SEO copywriting, link development, and tracking results. This process is cyclical; as you add more content and expand what products you sell, your keywords grow and change over time.

Custom RTML programming

Custom SEO RTML templates are sexy! Make structural changes to your RTML templates to make your already SEO-friendly Yahoo! Store into a search engine's dream date. It's like building the perfect, uh, page. After this new RTML framework is built, most of the thinking work still has to be done, but now you have a place to put everything. It's like getting a new house with tons of storage space! Now pay your RTML guys, kick 'em out of the store, and get to work on the keywords.

Disclaimer: The "custom RTML" part is optional (see Chapter 26), because you really can optimize Yahoo! Stores right out of the box and do fine in the search engines. You may have to override several variables on every page, which is a major pain, but you can do it. RTML programming isn't for everyone, and not everyone has the couple of thousand dollars or so needed to hire the right programmers to make the right SEO templates for your store.

I'll let you in on a little secret: If you get only one extra order a day from super SEO RTML templates (and you should!), the extra orders you get within the first year will more than pay for the couple of thousand bucks you need to spend to get your templates done right. Plus, think of all the time you'll save by not having to override variables every time you make a new page! For more on RTML, see Chapter 26.

Here's what I do with my RTML tweaks. You can use this checklist when you complete your custom templates:

- ✓ **Replace or supplement the built-in image-based Nav-bar buttons.** Add text-link navigation, navigational text breadcrumbs, sidebars with text links, and text link footers to the pages. I think I see a trend here. . . .

- ✓ **Add certain missing SEO elements to the templates for custom title, meta descriptions, and meta keyword tags.** Create custom fields on each page to store this info or use existing fields, such as Label and Abstract, for other purposes.

- ✓ **Replace images with text wherever possible.** For example, replace the part of the template that generates Headlines as image files (pictures of pretty fonts) with more search-engine-friendly <H1> heading tags around the text in your Headline or Name field.

- ✓ **Create separate RTML templates for product pages.** I like products to have a more conversion-oriented focus. Section and content pages are more about navigation and education.

- ✓ **Separate products from sections.** Stores with more than seven or eight major sections, or sections with 100-plus products, need a separate RTML category template for each major section complete with section-specific navigation (to related subsections and products).

Keyword research

Keyword research is so important. You need a list of your top 200 keywords, which you then assign to about 40 or 50 pages. Every optimized page needs four or five keywords and phrases assigned to it. See Chapter 16 for more on keywords.

Different types of pages have different types of keywords assigned to them. For example, product pages are better for model numbers, specific brand names, and singular versions of words. Section pages are better for somewhat more generic keywords and plurals. Home pages are better for really broad phrases.

One of the best ways to figure out which keywords match up with a page is to ask yourself what the searcher is trying to find and see which page is most relevant. You can see how well your site is optimized by doing the same query on Google or Yahoo! with a *site:* filter. For example, if the keyword phrase for Big Ed's WidgetWorld.com is "Widget 2000 replacement parts," I do a search (without quotes) for:

```
site:WidgetWorld.com widget 2000 replacement parts
```

The search engine then returns only results from WidgetWorld.com containing the words widget *and* 2000 *and* replacement *and* parts. From this example alone, you can see the words you need to add to your section and product pages.

Honestly, you could do nothing else for SEO besides adding the words buyers use to find your site to the pages relevant to those keywords, and your site would rank better and better. It's virtually impossible to rank for words not on your site (unless someone links to your pages with those words, or the search engines start using synonym matching in their algorithms).

Someone needs to figure out your most valuable keywords. I prefer to use my converting keywords for my top 200 keywords, rather than the more generic words that drive traffic but don't convert into sales. See Chapter 16 for the secrets to unlocking keywords.

SEO copywriting

SEO copywriting starts after you've assigned the four or five page keywords to each page. Write a page title and a two- to three-sentence description. Then expand the page keywords list to 15 to 20 keyword phrases. Make sure your product description uses your keywords in a compelling Caption that sells your product.

Here are the different elements you need to write:

- ✔ **Title:** Every page needs a compelling title tag (anywhere from 6 to 12 words) that describes the page with the most valuable keywords used in it.

✔ **Description:** You need to write a 15- to 25-word abstract that sums up the page using all the page keywords in a couple or three sentences for the meta description.

✔ **Keywords:** Expand your page keywords to a total of anywhere from 12 to 18 keyword phrases (including singulars and plurals, misspellings, alternate spellings, related words, and so on) for the meta keyword list.

✔ **Caption:** Make sure that the four or five page keywords are used on the page itself within the Caption field. Sometimes you can use the copy you wrote for the Abstract for the first paragraph of the Caption.

✔ **Internal links:** Make sure that you link to this page from other pages on your site using these keywords in the link text (anchor text). For example, link to your replacement parts page with the anchor text *Widget 2000 replacement parts* from as many different pages as make sense.

Writing descriptive product names for title tags

Page titles (or titles or title tags) should describe the content of a Web page in a compelling and informative sentence filled with relevant keywords. For example, consider a real product page at `http://gundogsupply.com/ adremtrainsy.html`.

By default, the page title is the name of the product: *Innotek ADV-300.* A better page title would beef up the name with these keywords: *Innotek ADV-300 Remote Training Collar.* My dream page title would be *Innotek ADV-300 Remote Training Collar $129.99, You Save $39.96 + FREE Shipping UPS Ground* 1-800-624-6378.

A bad page title would be just using your domain name in the title. A worse page title would be stuffed with keywords like *Innotek ADV-300, ADV300, Innotech adv-300, INNOTEK Collars,* and *Cheap!* The worst page title would be no page title or using the same page title on multiple pages.

The page title displays in the upper left corner of your browser window when you view a page. Search engine results pages (SERPs) show the page title as the link to your site, so you need a well-written title to get searchers to click your site's listing to visit your Yahoo! Store.

Ultimately, page titles should be as long as they need to be, but I get better rankings using 6 to 12 important keywords in a headline-like sentence that offers solutions to my customers' problems. Every page on your site needs a unique title. Make sure that you use keywords in your titles, but don't be like some folks and just throw a list of keywords in the title.

Store Editor standard templates take the page title from the text inside the Name field unless a Page-title field is on the page, as in, for example, the home page. You can create a better title tag on Yahoo! Stores in three ways:

- ✔ Just add keywords to the Name field.

- ✔ Create a new property on a page called Page-title and totally customize your title tag however you want.

- ✔ Go all out with RTML and make super-smart title tags. I write RTML templates that look at each product page and add several details to the title tag. The template looks to see whether there is a Price and a Sale-price. If so, the template adds the retail price and the cost savings to the page title like this: *Name of Product,* Only $76, Save $24.95.

    If the Sale-price is higher than the minimum order needed to get free shipping, the template throws in "- FREE Shipping US48 UPS Ground" at the end of the title tag. RTML is cool!

You can make your titles better than the competition's by adding text that shows the benefits of doing business with you rather than with those other guys. For example, add phrases like "free shipping, money-back guarantee, your savings $10, special offer, free gift with $50 order," or whatever promotions you like to do to your title tags to get more folks to click your search-engine listings.

Creating keyword-rich content in captions

Well-written Caption fields with your keywords used at least twice are the key to search engine optimization. Don't just paste a list of keywords in the Caption field. Your customers will probably be more confused than the search engines! You need well-written product descriptions if you want to sell something, so make sure that you use your page keywords inside the content of your Caption field. Find out more about keywords in Chapter 16.

One of the hardest things I have to do is convince clients to create their own content for their Web pages. We all hear "Content is king," but what does that mean? From an SEO perspective, content is well-written copy, words, and unique text that you or employees write for your Web store, which includes everything from product captions, articles related to what you sell, buyers' guides, product reviews, forum posts, answers to FAQs (frequently asked questions), extended product descriptions, answers to people's questions, or even a glossary of industry terms. Content is really just text that the search engine can see, but it needs to be well-written content for your visitors!

You can even hire professional copywriters to write your content, but get your wallet out. Good copywriters are expensive. Writing is hard work, the mental equivalent of ditch digging. I understand that *so* much better than I did a year ago after writing almost 500 pages of content for the first draft of this book.

Duplicate content is a problem. These days, the search engines are really good about weeding out pages with *duplicate content,* or pages with exactly the same or very similar paragraphs of text that appear elsewhere on the Web. For example, if you sell the same products as a thousand other Web stores and you use the same product Names and Captions as all the other retailers, Google is going to push you to the bottom of the list. You don't really get banned, but a filter kicks your listings two or three pages down in the SERPs, which has almost the same effect as being banned.

The meta description isn't as important as it once was, but I still use it. I write a good description — a short paragraph that summarizes the products in each section page — and place it in the Caption field and inside the Abstract field on each section. I also show Abstracts on the section pages and the home page.

Google shows the meta description on the SERPs page when the keyword is found in the description. You really need a unique meta-description tag for each page, and the only way to do unique meta descriptions with the standard templates is to override the Head-tags Variable on each page, write a custom Meta Description tag, and paste it inside the Head-tags field.

Also, in a standard template store, you have to override the *Keywords* Variable on each page and paste in a list of 15 to 20 keywords phrases to have unique meta keywords for each page.

Standard templates also generate the Headline on section and products as an image using the pretty, but search-engine-unfriendly, vw-img tags. You can turn these headlines off by deselecting Display-text from the Head-elements setting under Variables, but then you have to hand-code <H1> tags and place them inside the Caption field. Without formatting, <H1> tags look big and clunky, but you can easily control the look using CSS (cascading style sheets). Take a look at *CSS Web Design For Dummies,* by Richard Mansfield (Wiley Publishing), for more information about CSS.

Even if you don't use the Headline field, put the text from the Name inside the field anyway because standard templates display the text inside the Name in bold right above the order functionality.

Linked development

Links are more than half of the SEO battle. There are three kinds of links: links to your site from other sites, links from your site to other sites, and internal links on your site to other pages within your site. Search engines use the *anchor text* (the words in the links) from all these kinds of links to figure out what your site is about. Link development on Yahoo! Stores includes getting links, giving links, and optimizing your internal links.

Manipulating your own links with no guilt

Internal links help search engines see how you structure your site, how you organize your site, and how you prioritize your pages. You have two kinds of links in your site: navigational links that run across the site on almost every page and spot links that occur only on one or two pages:

- ✔ **Site-wide text-link navigation helps because when each page on a site has a link to the top 20 pages in your navigation, you get a bump in the search engines.** When you're designing your site's navigation, concentrate first on helping visitors find what they're looking for, but include your best keywords in text links to your major section and product pages. Tightening up your internal text navigation links can really help your SEO efforts. If you're using the standard templates, stick these links in the Final-text field on the Variables page.

- ✔ **Internal links from the text in your Caption fields work great, especially when you use** `<strong>` **tags around anchors.** I like four or five internal links for each of my major keywords sprinkled around the site. Place these links on logical, related pages, but don't overdo it. For example, make your site more friendly by pasting links to related products inside the Caption fields on pages where they make the most sense. For example, if you sell duck calls and you also sell duck call lanyards, you can link to the lanyards page with the following code in the Duck Calls Caption:

```
Also check out our <a href=duck-call-lanyards.html>duck call lanyards</a>.
```

You also want to make sure that your site uses similar keywords elsewhere in links to the `duck-call-lanyards.html` page on other relevant pages. For example, you can put lanyard links on these pages: Gifts for Duck Hunters, Presents under $20, Retriever Training Supplies, LanyardCorp Products, and so on. Be helpful. If you mention a related product in a Caption field, link to it with keywords within the anchor text. If it's a high-priority keyword, put `<strong>` tags around the keyword, too.

Linking to other cool sites actually helps your site

Outbound links (links from your site to other Web sites) tell search engines what you think your site is about by the type of sites you link to. Momma always said you're known by the company you keep — birds of a feather and all that. Your outbound links are counted as personal recommendations, so link only to sites and pages your users would find useful and wouldn't embarrass you.

For example, on the Duck Calls section page, you can link to Tom Wiley's secrets of duck calling Web site. On product pages, you can link to the manufacturer's warranty page, other product information, industry news, forums, enthusiast sites, and even to indirect competitors' pages if they sell what you don't have and your customers would appreciate it.

Look. It's okay for people to leave your site! You're not going to lose all your traffic when you link to other pages. On average, you have five page views before the average surfer is off your site to visit another site. One thing you can do is make sure that your users can easily get back to your site after looking at a site you link to by simply making all external links open new browsers windows. Just add the target attribute `target=_new` to your anchor tags like so:

```
<a href=http://www.externaldomain.com/ target=_new>anchor text</a>
```

Getting links to your site

Inbound links (links from other Web sites) send you Web traffic, but they also help search engines understand your site by the content of the page linking to your site. You get links by buying directory listings, asking more established sites for links, buying text-link ads, doing reciprocal link exchanges with related sites, and more. You also get links (almost by accident) by creating a Web site with useful content (articles, reviews, buyers' guides) that folks consider enough of a resource to link to it from their Web site.

When you ask for links, you want all links pointing to your site to use the exact same *URL* (Web address) so that one domain gets credit for all those links. I prefer the URL www.*yourdomain*.com with the www in the URL. It's important to use a consistent URL so that all your link popularity will pass to one page for maximum bang for your buck.

I talk about buying text links, getting into directories (Yahoo! Directory, DMOZ, JoeAnt), and acquiring links in other ways in Chapter 17, but here are more links you need to know about:

✔ *Deep links* are links to a page deep within your site, not just your home page. For example, a deep link is a link to a URL like www.*yourdomain*. com/helpful-product-review.html or any other page other than your home page. Search engines really like deep links! The more good content you have, the more likely other Webmasters will link to pages deep inside your site. I asked a manufacturer we buy from for permission to put a copy of a great article on dog training up on my site. The article is really helpful, and I actually got a coveted DMOZ directory link to that page.

✔ *Reciprocal links* are an example of the "You scratch my back, I'll scratch yours" principle. Lots of folks know that they need links, so swapping links with other sites that swap links is a great way to get easy, if somewhat off-target, links. The search engines, especially Google, are devaluing the benefit of reciprocal links because most of those links are swapped to manipulate the search engines.

Without the SEO benefit, Webmasters probably wouldn't link to most of those sites. Make sure that any reciprocal links you swap are to related sites and that you have plenty of good links from places you don't link to, like directories, your wholesalers and suppliers, and customer pages.

How many links do you need? My friend Troy Matthews (www.1twc.com) says link building is a lot like fishing in a bass tournament. You don't have to be Bill Dance or catch a record-breaking fish to win the trophy; your fish just has to be a little bit bigger than anyone else's that day!

Look at your competitors' back links to get an idea of how big *your* fish has to be!

You know you need links, and sometimes it's just easier to get someone else to worry with the hassle! I'm hesitant to give away one of my secret sources, but I do have one person I completely trust and recommend for high-value link development. Debra O'Neil-Mastaler (www.alliance-link.com) is one of my search-engine conference buddies. She runs with Jill Whalen and the HighRankings.com crew, and I can't say enough nice things about her! She's like my mom away from mom.

Measured results

Measuring results is mission critical. You'll never know how well (or poorly) you're ranking on Google, Yahoo!, or MSN Search if you don't measure your results. The best measurement to track with your analytics software is how many orders (conversions) you get from each engine and what keyword searches converted into a sale. Who cares about traffic? I want orders! I'm in the e-*commerce* business, not the e-*visitor* business! See Chapter 20 for more information about seeing the details of search-engine traffic through the Store Manager's References reports.

You can also track how many pages you have indexed in the engines, how many back links (pages linking back to you) you have, and what position your site is ranked for each keyword phrase.

Use position checkers to see how well you rank for specific keywords. Get the Maalox first, though. I hope you don't get motion sickness because you're going to move up and down in the SERPs. Bruce Clay's SEOToolset.com offers a suite of SEO Tools that I love. It's an online tool, so you can check how you're doing from any online connection. See Chapter 25 for more on this and other tools I use for SEO improvement and reporting.

Before I start making any changes to a new site, I gather my top 200 keywords and take a baseline ranking. See where you rank today and check it pretty regularly. Hopefully, I can watch my position in the engines improve as I add more content and get more links. Engines don't like anything automated that queries their engines too much, so be careful. Every week or so should be fine for your top 200 keywords.

Create some SEO pet projects. Take more competitive keywords where you don't rank as well as you would like and work on them in particular. Develop more content and actively target links for those pages. Track a "favorite" competitor who is beating you on certain engines. Try to figure out how the company is beating you and then use its SEO techniques against it. Have fun and try not to stress out about your search-engine rankings.

Doing Your SEO Homework

"Free" search-engine traffic comes with a price to be paid. The opportunity cost of SEO can be very high. Staying on top of the search-engine game means that you're always working to keep up with changes the search engines make. You also have to stay ahead of folks in your industry who are trying to get your biscuit.

Search engine optimization is a zero-sum game. That means that it has winners and losers. A given keyword has only ten positions on page one. If someone moves up into the top ten for a keyword, that means someone else is moving out.

It's a jungle out there! Some of your competitors will do almost anything to get ahead of you in the search results. It can be incredibly frustrating when spammers try to cheat the engines by using short-sighted tactics to deceive the engines. Sometimes the engines don't catch the most blatant spammers because they have bigger fish to fry, such as the porn, pills, and casino guys.

Also, much of the information that is publicly available on SEO is either outdated, misinformation, or simply just wrong. There is also a lot of information on techniques that may work for a short while but result in getting you banned from various engines.

You can do basic SEO yourself, or you can outsource it to any number of SEO consultants or agencies. Most SEO is done by figuring out which factors the search engines use to determine which pages are most relevant for a given search and then making sure that your pages are as relevant as they can be for the topics they're about. My recommendation, like everything else, is to do a little bit yourself and see whether you have a knack for it; if so, keep on keeping on. If you find an SEO you trust and can afford, then give him the keys and let him drive.

One of my old clients was paying a major SEO firm $2,100 a month for "advanced" SEO. All the SEO company did was come in and write custom meta keyword and description tags for 100 section pages and then send him ranking reports every month. That's pretty cold! My client slept better at night knowing that he was doing something about SEO, but he was really getting, uh, underserviced for what he was paying.

If you're hiring someone for search engine optimization work, look at examples in her portfolio. View the source on the home page of one of her projects and make a list of all the keywords in the title tag. Do some rank checking to see how well this site ranks on Google, Yahoo!, and MSN for all the keywords listed in the keywords tag on her home page. If the site doesn't rank in the top ten results, you may want to consider hiring another firm.

Also, lots of snake-oil SEOs are aggressive telemarketers and cold-call folks with new domains with promises of top ten rankings. Buyer beware! These folks are sometimes so rude that you can't get a word in edgewise, so I often end up hanging up on them.

If you get anywhere near the amount of spam in your Inbox that I do, you're painfully aware that many folks describe themselves as "Search Engine Experts." Some of these folks use dangerous or deceptive practices, and in the end, you, the site owner, are the one who pays the price.

Need a good firm? You have friends. Ask around. Find someone else who is happy with his SEO firm and has been for years. Go with a solid referral and do your homework. Be careful!

I do my own SEO and most of my own link development, but because I go to all these search-engine conferences five or six times a year, I have a Rolodex full of world-class SEOs. Drop me an e-mail for a list of folks I recommend because Yahoo! Stores are a little funky. The RTML part makes some SEOs' heads explode.

Exploring more with SEO resources

Here are a few more resources for you — just in case you were mesmerized by this topic!

✔ Brett Tabke's WebmasterWorld.com has millions of pages on every subject from search engine optimization to e-commerce to basic Webmaster questions. The site is free, but all the really, really good stuff is posted in the supporters' forum, which you can access for $149 a year. Brett also hosts PubCon several times a year all over the world, and I attend every chance I get.

✔ Danny Sullivan's SearchEngineWatch.com is a tremendous resource on search engines and Internet marketing. SEW has forums, articles, and a valuable newsletter, and hosts the Search Engine Strategies conferences in New York, Chicago, and San Jose every year. SES is expensive, but worth it. I also go to every SES conference I can.

✔ Jill Whelan is a top white-hat SEO, author, and speaker, as well as owner of HighRankings.com, where you can sign up for Jill's newsletter, read articles, and participate in the forums.

✔ The name Bruce Clay has been synonymous with search engine optimization since 1997 or so. BruceClay.com has tons of free information. His other site, SEOToolset.com, has a suite of valuable search engine optimization tools, which I use. Bruce also offers a search engine optimization training course, which I took and highly recommend for retailers.

✔ Matt Cutts is a senior engineer at Google in charge of search quality, which is really just a polite way of saying he hunts down and kills spammy Web sites. Read his unofficial, but extremely relevant, search blog at `www.mattcutts.com/blog` for firsthand information on what Google wants and doesn't want in a Web site.

Part V
Making More Money with Your Yahoo! Store

The 5th Wave   By Rich Tennant

©RICHTENNANT

Serch Injin
Optamazashun

Kee Werd
Stratageez

1. Top

"How long has he been programming our meta-tags?"

In this part . . .

When I talk to most Yahoo! Store owners, I find that
every question they ask me pretty much fits into
one of two buckets: either *how to save time* or *how to
make more money.* I don't know about you, but I'm in this
business for the money. Don't get me wrong! I love what
I do, and people are way more important to me than profits, but when I'm at work, I'm here to make a buck. I'm
either working on things to take better care of my clients
(and sell more stuff) or automating repetitive tasks and
minimizing, or completely eliminating, mindless tasks
and busywork to save my ever-dwindling supply of time.

In this part, I show you how to do a little bit of both: save
time and make more money. You discover how to increase
traffic and sales by seeing where customers come from
and improving your store (reading store statistics), convert
more of the existing traffic you have into sales (conversion
rate), spend less time getting new products up on your
Web store (product uploads), get more sales from existing
customers (e-mail newsletters), and make sure that your
domain name is configured in a search-engine-friendly way.
I also introduce Yahoo! Small Business Web hosting and
the other ways to build Yahoo! Stores, Store Tags + Catalog
Manager, just so you know what you're (not) missing.

Look: Some of this part isn't for the squeamish or newbies.
Here, I talk about very powerful and effective ways to save
time building and managing your Yahoo! Store, but it's not
unlike working with a nail gun! There's a pretty big downside if things get out of control. Please be careful! Don't play
with database uploads if you don't feel extremely comfortable because you could blow up your store. And don't mess
with your domain name and where it points unless you
have a new store or understand the implications with
search engines.

Chapter 20

Running Your Business by the Numbers

In This Chapter

▶ Getting familiar with traffic, revenue, conversion rate, and more

▶ Keeping your eye on the most important metrics

▶ Crunching numbers to product profits

*W*hen I talk about running your business by the numbers, I'm more concerned with the "running your business" part than the "numbers" part. Minding the numbers is extremely important for the success of your business, but you don't want to get lost in a jungle of data. You have to see both the forest and the trees. Your Yahoo! Store Manager comes with all these cool tools, graphs, reports, and statistics, but you need to watch the right indicators to measure how you're doing and to see what you need to work on.

In this chapter, I show you what information you can get out of your Yahoo! Store Manager and which part of it is worth looking at. I explore the full range of Store Manager reports and introduce some third-party tools. I also explain why I track the things I do. Pretty much every evening, I take a quick daily pulse to make sure that my Yahoo! Stores are healthy. I track other numbers, too, so when a site has a hiccup and sales drop suddenly, I can quickly discover what's wrong and fix it.

Discovering What You Need to Know

This chapter is not about accounting! When it comes to the numbers in this chapter, I'm really looking at traffic and sales on your Yahoo! Store. As a business owner, you'd better be watching all the other numbers, too, especially your overhead and profit margin. Payroll seems to be the biggest expense for growing retailers, but pay-per-click advertising can eat you alive, as I discuss in Chapter 18. Your accountant (and you better have a good one!) can give you better benchmarks to make sure that your overhead doesn't pull you under. Fortunately, we have accountants in the family. Uncle Paul crunches the numbers and keeps us on track, but more importantly, he shares his Mississippi State tickets (and I mean the good seats)!

I really got into the Yahoo! Store stats back in 1997 when I opened my first Viaweb store. It blew my mind that you could see exactly how your customers found you and watch their actions in your store. Remember, I've always been a retailer, and prior to 1997, all my experience was in owning brick-and-mortar stores. I used to pour over my sales statistics from my point-of-sale system, but I never really geeked out on statistics until I opened a Yahoo! Store.

Every day I look at daily sales, visitors to the site, and number of orders. I also track conversion rate (percentage of visitors who order), number of Shopping Carts started compared to actual orders, how much I spent on Google AdWords and Yahoo! Search Marketing (formerly Overture) clicks, how much free traffic I got from the search engines, and even more. When something's on fire, I've got to know what the deal is.

Figure 20-1 shows the Store Manager of a real Yahoo! Store (and, no, I'm not telling what it's selling), which displays the sales and Page Views from the last 120 days. I wish the fine folks in Sunnyvale would let us pick which graphs to show on the front page, but having those two isn't all bad. You have to have traffic (visitors) to your site before you can sell anything, but for me, conversion rate is the most important number for a Web retailer.

Conversion rate (%) is the percentage of visitors to your Web site that buy something. You can find this number for your Yahoo! Store by looking at the Orders/Customer graph in the Store Manager. If you can increase your conversion rate even just a little bit, you can exponentially increase your store's success.

Tracking and improving your conversion rate is the secret to the e-commerce universe.

The longer the date range you're looking at, the larger the sample of data. Larger samples mean longer periods of time, which seem to even out the daily ups and downs of business. Larger samples give you more reliable information on trends. Any trend less than 90 days can be a fluke. Ask your favorite economics professor for his opinion, but my dad wouldn't listen to me when I got excited about a change in the site if the time period was anything less than three months.

You can choose from several date ranges in Store Manager's Sales report (under Statistics): Last 10 days, Last 30 Days, Last 60 Days, Last 90 Days, Last 120 Days, Last 180 Days, and Last 365 Days. You can also view stats by the calendar month (for the last five months). Graphs have custom date ranges so that you can see patterns over months or even years.

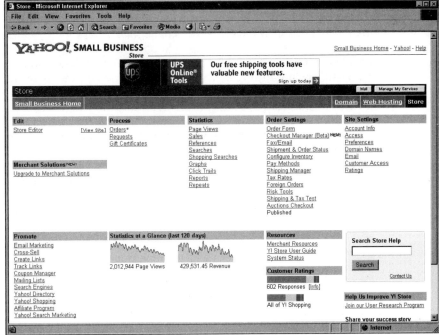

Figure 20-1:
Page Views
and
Revenue
graphs for
the last 120
days appear
on the Store
Manager.

Introducing Yahoo! Store Statistics

The smart folks who designed the Store Manager back in the mid-1990s understood that certain numbers are important to retailers, so the first thing you see when you log in to the Store Manager are graphs for Page Views and Revenue for the last 120 days. I love my Yahoo! Store stats, especially Store References. You can see where folks are coming from, what words they searched for, and whether that keyword resulted in a sale.

Yahoo! Store stats are good, but they're far from perfect. Sometimes the stats don't track certain types of sales. Sometimes they're way off, listing a referrer that was for another Yahoo! Store. Sometimes the cookie data gets garbled. It can be a little frustrating to have missing or plain wrong information. Even if Your Yahoo! Store stats aren't perfect, they're consistent, which means that you can use them to see how you're doing.

I overcompensate for the holes in Yahoo! Store tracking by running two or three additional Web analytics programs and return on investment (ROI) tracking tools. Multiple programs give me overlapping results.

If you use a third-party tracking tool, make sure that it's compatible with Yahoo! Store and can import the revenue number. More tracking packages will work with the new Checkout Manager (see Chapter 14), which should be online full-time in early 2006, but I highly recommend taking a look at ClickTracks (`www.clicktracks.com`), Keywordmax (`www.keywordmax.com`), and EngineReady (`www.engineready.com`) for more and better information about who's visiting your store and what's selling. I discuss it a little more in Chapters 18 and 25.

It's probably overkill, but I want to grab every converting keyword I can. I'm not ashamed to admit that I'm obsessed with conversion rate, and the secret to conversions is converting keywords, which you can read more about in Chapter 16 and at `http://ystore.blogs.com` in my Yahoo! Store marketing blog.

Most of the numbers I'm interested in are found under the Store Manager's Statistics tab, which links to separate reports for Page Views (shows most popular pages by hits), Sales (shows bestselling products), References (shows referral information on sources of traffic and sales), Graphs (creates graphs of page views, sales, customers, and so on), Click Trails (looks at individual customer click trails over time), Reports (provides downloadable reports of traffic and sales), and a few others. I cover all these reports in the upcoming sections.

Page Views

Page Views is the first link under the Statistics tab and shows you the top 50 section or item pages in descending order by hits (or page views) for the past 365 days. You can sort By Hits, By Count Of Items Sold, By Count Of Orders, or By Revenue.

Keep in mind that even though the Page Views report shows revenue (sales) info, the Sales report (see the next section in this chapter) is a much better report for looking at what's selling.

I use the Page Views report to see which section pages are the most popular pages. First, I make sure that my site-navigation features link to these pages. I also make sure that these pages feature links to my best deals and promotions. Finally, I want these pages to load fast, so I minimize slow-loading graphics. See Chapter 21 for more information.

Sales

Figure 20-2 displays the Sales report from a third real-live Yahoo! Store (and, no, I'm still not telling), which is the second link under the Store Manager's Statistics Column. Click the Sales link to see your top 50 products in descending order By Count Of Items Sold for the past 365 days. You can also sort the Sales report By Count Of Orders or By Revenue (sales).

Click the See More, See All, or See Fewer link to change the number of results in your report, but if you want to get all the data, click the Spreadsheet link to download a CSV spreadsheet file with the following fields: Name, Items Sold, Revenue, Page Views, ID, Code, and Price.

I use the CSV file to get all kinds of info. Having the IDs makes all the difference in the world!

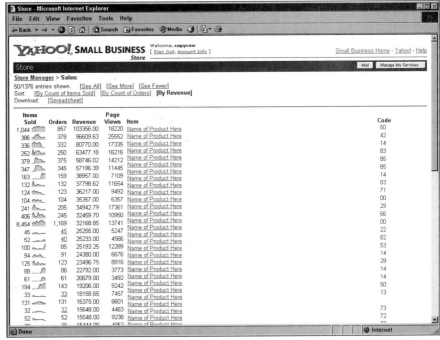

Figure 20-2:
The sales report shows you your most items by items sold, hits, or revenue.

For more established stores, the bestselling products tend to generate 50 or more sales per month, not per year, so this feature is best accessed on reports with smaller date ranges. For specific product information, set a really short date range, such as Past 30 Or 60 Days, to dig out those golden nuggets.

Also look at the products that sell the most dollar volume. If you sell a thousand products, the majority of your sales probably come from the top 200 items. I want to find out more about those top-sellers, and I'm not really interested in the conversion rate of whatever is ranked #878.

Don't forget to look at your bestselling products that have the highest conversion rates. You have to figure out this number yourself by dividing the number of orders by the number of page views, which is much easier to do in Excel. Popular product pages that don't convert as well as other product pages have a flaw somewhere. The product may be flawed or overpriced, or the page design may be the problem. The product page may be too heavy or lack compelling sales copy.

References

Figure 20-3 shows a References report from another real-live Yahoo! Store (where yet again I've erased all identifiable store data), with visits, orders, revenue, revenue per visit, and referring URL. Most of your traffic will be from Google, Yahoo!, MSN, and high-traffic sites that link to you. Roughly 60 percent of your sales will have referrer data, and the rest winds up in the Bermuda Triangle.

Some sales don't have referrer data because shoppers come from bookmarks or they type your domain name in their browser, which is a really good thing because it means that people like you well enough to remember your URL. Some third-party tracking tools (such as ClickTracks and Engine Ready) can track up to half of this "missing" referrer data, which is why I pay extra each month for my third-party analytic tools. I discuss these tools in Chapter 25.

Google bought an analytics company called Urchin last year and now gives away its analytics software to gather more information about how people use the Web, as well as in the hope that you'll use it to improve your site and spend more on Google AdWords. For more information on this free program, visit www.google.com/analytics. For more about Google AdWords and paid search, see Chapter 18.

Figure 20-4 shows that the dollars are in the details. All the really good data in Referrals is on the Details page. Click the Details link to the right of any referring URL for an eye-opening look at exactly what pages or keyword searches are sending you sales and traffic.

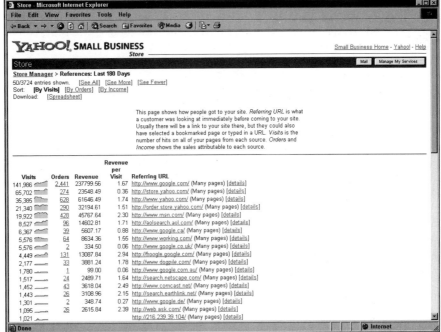

Figure 20-3:
References
shows you
where
visitors
come from
by referring
Web site
sorted by
Orders,
Revenue, or
Referring
URL.

You can find out a lot by reviewing the information in the Details link:

- ✓ **Scroll to the bottom to change the report's Period (date range) or the Sort method (Visits, Orders, or Income).** The report defaults to the last 180 days and sorts in descending order by visits.

- ✓ **Click the Referring URL link, and you see the current search results on the search engine for that particular keyword phrase.** Each of the Details links next to the Referring URL is a link to the search results for the keywords that sent you the traffic. Clicking is much easier than typing!

- ✓ **Click the By Income link to sort the Details page in descending order by revenue.** This is a great way to see your *converting keywords,* which are the search phrases that result in a sale. (For more on keywords, see Chapter 16.)

- ✓ **Look in the upper left corner of Referrer Details to see how many unique keyword phrases folks sent you traffic for that particular engine.** You can also see the total number of visitors sent on the References page or on the bottom of the Referrer details page. For example, the Google Details report says *50/8414 entries shown,* which means that 8,414 different keyword searches on Google drove those 140,383 people from Google to this client's site. See Chapter 19 for more on search engine optimization for free traffic.

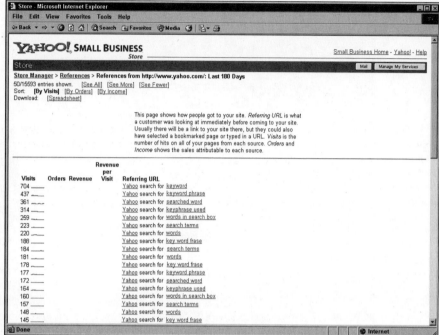

Figure 20-4:
The Details link in References displays the keywords used by visitors to find your store.

✔ **Click the Download: Spreadsheet link to download a CSV report from the date range set at the bottom of the report page.** Sometimes it's easier to view all the data offline than online.

✔ **The CSV export is limited to 10,000 lines, so if you have more keywords than that, the stragglers get cut off.** Kinda reminds me of dinner at the Snell house! Set a smaller date range to catch more keywords across multiple reports.

✔ **Set the date range to the earliest calendar month by selecting the applicable radio button, click the Show button, and then click the Download: Spreadsheet link.** Do this every month for each engine that sends you a lot of traffic. Your Yahoo! Store only saves this Referring URL info for the last six months. Every month, you lose a month's worth of keyword data. The converting keyword data is still attached to each individual order, but it's worth the trouble of grabbing this data every month to see which words you rank well for, which words get traffic but don't convert, and so on.

Store Searches

See what search words are popular on your internal store site search by clicking the Store Searches link under Statistics. Scroll to the bottom of the report and change the report from Search Strings (phrases) to Individual Words to see the most popular words used. Store Searches aren't available in the Merchant Starter package.

Results from Store Searches tell you a lot about what folks can't find on your store. Popular keywords give you ideas to improve your site navigation by seeing what folks couldn't find by simply navigating your store. See what people really call the things that you sell by the names they type into search. Collect popular misspellings to beef up your meta-tags and misspellings pages. Get new product ideas from popular searches for items you don't currently sell.

Shopping Searches

See last week's top 100 searches on Yahoo! Shopping. This report shows you how seasonal Yahoo! Shopping can be. In May, it's all about the prom dresses, and then the next month, wedding dresses are shooting up the charts. Around Halloween, Star Wars costumes are hot. For more information on Yahoo! Shopping, see Chapter 17. Shopping Searches aren't available in the Merchant Starter package.

Graphs

Graphs is the sixth link under the Statistics tab and gives you 20 different graphs over any date range you want. Although there may be 20 graphs, only four of them matter to me: Customers, Revenue, Number Of Orders, and Orders/Customer.

Because the information in graphs is pretty broad, it doesn't take up that much room, so Yahoo! doesn't delete any of it. There's also a custom date range, so I can set the date range to the month of June back in 1997 and remember the good ol' days. . . .

Figure 20-5 displays a store's Revenue. Orders/Customer is really your conversion rate, or the percentage of visitors who buy something. Everything else is what my dad would call "neat to know (but what can you do with it?)." Again, see Chapter 21 for more information on increasing usability and (more importantly) conversion rate.

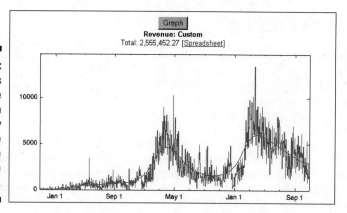

Figure 20-5:
This
Revenue
graph
shows daily
revenue
over the
past three
years.

Figure 20-6 shows Customers from another honest-to-goodness Yahoo! Store over the past 365 days. The label Customers is somewhat of a misnomer because to me, a customer is someone who buys something; these folks are visitors. Of course, 1.3 million "customers" is nothing to sneeze at!

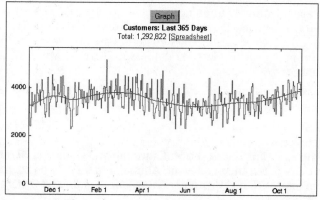

Figure 20-6:
This
Customers
graph
shows daily
unique
visitors over
the past
year.

Reports

Reports is the eighth link under the Statistics tab and lets you see Page Views, Customers, Page Views/Customer, (Number Of) Orders, Income, Items Sold, and Average Order. You can see this data Monthly, Weekly, or Daily, but Yahoo! only keeps the daily data for about six months.

Click the Export To Excel link to get this data in a handy CSV text file, which is cool for looking at trends over weeks or months. Sometimes the data in Reports doesn't update as fast as the rest of the site, and sometimes deleted orders still show up. This information is very good for broad decision making, but I don't use it for accounting or anything that needs to be 100 percent right.

Click Trails

Click Trails is the seventh link under the Statistics tab and gives you another (kind of wacky) way to measure customer traffic and see where folks went on the site. You can see the number of users as well as each individual Click Trail for each day's traffic with these three links: Click Trails, Trails Where The Order Button Was Pressed, and Trails That Resulted In An Order. Click Trails aren't available in the Merchant Starter package.

Unfortunately, you have to look at click trails day by day. You can't download them, and Yahoo! deletes them after 60 days or so. My assistant logs in every week and grabs those three numbers by hand for every store we track. It's that important! I call these trails, carts, and orders. On an average Yahoo! Store, for every 100 trails, I see 3 or 4 carts and 1 or 2 orders.

Here are a few things you should think about:

✔ Look at Trails That Resulted In An Order to retrace the steps used by an actual customer to place an order. I find out more about how customers use a site by looking at this level. Notice that almost all new customers look at your `info.html` page.

✔ Also look at Trails Where The Order Button Was Pressed (but didn't result in an order) to see whether you can figure out what happened from when the fish was on the line to why it didn't make it into the boat.

✔ When your traffic shoots up, sometimes your conversion rate suffers because you get a lot of junk traffic.

✔ If you ever want to see what time of the day people do things, select Graph Daily Cycle when you're playing with Graphs. Even in 1997, I see the same thing I see today: The majority of traffic and sales are in a 9 a.m. to 5 p.m. hump followed by a second, slightly smaller hump from 5 to 9 p.m. If you take phone orders, consider being open later for the folks shopping after work.

Chapter 21

Converting Browsers into Buyers

*F*irst impressions are critical for converting shoppers into buying customers. When new visitors first land on your store pages, your store must look as though you have what they are looking for long enough to keep them from clicking the Back button. Next, your online store must be easy enough to navigate and search so that customers can quickly find what they want.

Your customers might not know exactly what they want, so you must be prepared to help them out with informative articles, product reviews, and buyers' guides that tell them what kinds of products solve their problems. Product pages must sell using words and pictures to create enough interest and direct customers to buy through calls to action in the copy and on the Order buttons. Your store must look credible to instill enough confidence for customers to click the Add To Cart button. Finally, your checkout process must appear safe and secure, be easy enough to use, and focus on the task of completing an order.

In this chapter, I discuss the keys to improving your store's conversion rate and Web usability, show you how to make your store easier to use, and explore some things I've discovered over the past nine years to convert more browsers into buyers!

Getting Shoppers to Buy

Conversion rate is so important, but jumping through all those hoops sounds pretty hairy! Fortunately, it's not that hard. You can make a few simple (but extremely important) changes to your site that will increase your *conversion rate*. Conversion rate is the percentage of shoppers that visits your Web store and actually places an order. I believe that this is the most important number for most e-commerce businesses to be aware of.

Unfortunately, many merchants don't even track their store's conversion rate, much less attempt to improve it. You have several ways to increase conversion rate, but the easiest is to improve your Web site's *usability*. Web usability is the study of making Web sites easier to use by using established design conventions, making your site load faster, using positive language, communicating clearly, and testing your site with real users.

Increasing your site's traffic is not enough

Getting traffic to your Web site can be a full-time job in itself. After all this traffic gets to your site, you still have to jump over several more hurdles before you get the first order!

First, you have to make sure that your site grabs and holds the attention of your shoppers. Second, you have to do everything in your power to improve your customer conversion machine (your store) before you start spending big bucks to attract more visitors to it. Fixing the "machine" gets you more traffic. So, make your site easier to use by implementing Web usability best practices (which I discuss a little later in this chapter).

Make sure that you're selling something that folks want to buy, and at a competitive price. Check out Chapter 2 for some ideas on business models and how to figure out what else to sell.

Increasing sales by creating quality content

When you make a point of improving the quality of your content, something very cool happens: More and more shoppers are converted to buyers. Adding articles, buyers' guides, product FAQs, additional product pictures, reviews, and so on is like pouring chum into the water when you're going fishing. Customers just eat that stuff up, and the search engines do, too!

Explain which products are good for what, and take an editorial position on them; that is, describe what you like and dislike about certain models. Provide more information about products than what anyone can cut and paste from the manufacturers' sites: a stock product photo and a lame product description. Take additional photos of the product, explain its features, *and* describe how those features solve people's problems. This information is what makes folks want to buy what you sell.

For example, after our dad died, my brother, Steve, became the president of our family business, and Steve was much more willing than my dad ever was to share his expertise and opinions on dog-training gear in public. My brother is, uh, rather opinionated sometimes with online editorials and product reviews, but this works to his advantage because people want to know what real people think about products they are thinking about buying. After Steve began sharing his opinions on the site, sales immediately went up, especially for items with expanded product information or product reviews.

When you add content to your site, you also increase the *stickiness* of your site, or the length of time folks stay on your site. My friend, Internet marketing guru Craig Paddock, says that he sees a direct correlation between the amount of time someone spends on your site and that person's likelihood to convert into a paying customer. This fact alone is an argument in favor of bulking up the product information on your site.

Some folks don't buy on the first visit. It's completely understandable when a brand-new visitor says, "Uh, I just don't think we're ready to Place Order at this point in our relationship. I mean, I just found you on Google two minutes ago. I don't even know you. How about I just Add To My Cart for now?"

Craig Paddock believes in micro-conversions, or steps to conversions. He says that because it often takes many visits to your site before some people buy, your job is to get them one step closer to the Shopping Cart or checkout than they would have taken otherwise. This is the secret to increasing your online sales.

Some folks who visit your site will never buy. Period. This includes those conducting shopping research for purchases to be made offline, tire-kickers, competitors, and irrelevant traffic from weird search-engine queries that are the Internet equivalent of a wrong telephone number. You probably have a lot of unqualified traffic, too, or folks who might be interested in what you sell, but aren't very likely to buy something. These folks will click your paid-search ad just to see what your site sells.

Building Customer Confidence

Instill confidence in shoppers by looking like a professional organization, but at the same time, give your site a human face. It's like what Momma always said: "Just be yourself."

- ✔ **Have a professional-looking site.** Make sure that your information is always current (keep copyrights up to date, eliminate seasonal promotions and special offers that are past due, and so on). Spell-check your site. The only typos you want are for search engines on your "commonly misspelled words page," with links to the real pages. Watch out for any anti-customer language such as "We reserve the right to refuse service to anyone" or anything that sounds as though it were written by a bureaucrat.

✔ **Tell me how to reach you.** Provide full contact information. Divulge your physical address, phone numbers, fax number, e-mail address, business hours, and any other pertinent contact data I need to get in touch with you. Look like a real company, not someone hiding behind the anonymity of the Web.

✔ **Give me your number.** You need an 800 number displayed prominently on your site. Feature that number on every page, in the Shopping Cart, and all over the checkout pages. Put your phone hours under your 800 number. You might prefer that folks order online, but give them the option to order by phone. Offering customers the option of ordering via your 800 number significantly increases Web conversions because customers feel more secure when they have another way to reach you — even if they never use it.

Also, an 800 number is much better than the other free prefixes (such as 866, 877, or 888) because everyone knows what an 800 number is. Having an 800 number makes your business look more established, too. There aren't any "fresh" 800 numbers left these days, but if you insist, your telephone service provider will find you someone's old, discarded number, which will work just great!

✔ **Tell me your story.** Write bios of the company's principals. Write a compelling (but truthful) About Us or company background page.

✔ **Show me some pictures.** Provide real photos of you, your employees, your location (your building or shipping warehouse), and even some of your customers if they'll give you permission (by e-mail is fine). Don't use clip art or stock photography. Look, you don't have to be a supermodel to have your photo on the Web. The less slick the photos look, the more real they look.

✔ **Be your own company spokesmodel.** If you're in retail, you're probably the public face of your company, whether or not you want to admit it. Put your name (and reputation) on your Web site; doing so gives a significant boost to the credibility of your content.

✔ **Be small if you're small.** On the Internet, it's hard to tell the size of a company by the size or quality of its Web site. Take advantage of the fact that you're a tiny operation and that customers therefore receive personalized service and support from the owner of the company. It's okay to admit that you're a small, one-woman operation because you'll give a level of attention that someone won't get shopping at an Amazon.com.

Personally, I don't want to buy from BigBoxCo, Inc. with 24-hour phone support. I want to buy from someone real who knows what they're talking about. Someone who will be there *when* I have questions and *if* I have a problem. Someone who cares about me as a customer. I prefer to deal with the owner so that if I have a problem, I know I'm talking with some-one whose house payment depends on keeping me a happy customer.

✔ **Prove that you are a legitimate business.** Tell me your history. In the Internet age, the length of time you've been in business says a lot. No one will toot your own horn for you. Tell me about your certifications; that you're licensed, bonded, and insured; and that you've won industry awards for exceptional customer service. List your bibliography of credibility-building articles, books, or speaking engagements.

✔ **Collect and publish customer testimonials.** It's pretty cool for you to tell folks how great you are, but when folks who gave you money want to brag on you, let 'em brag. Get permission before using folks' names, but don't be shy about asking. When you get e-mails of praise, reply and simply ask permission to add their name and comments (but not their e-mail address) to your testimonials page. After I get permission, I put their comments online and then e-mail them the URL to make sure that they're happy with how it looks; if they're not, I fix it to their satisfaction like a duck on a June bug. Link to these customer comments pages from your Shopping Cart and checkout where appropriate.

Employ trust symbols

Trust symbols are visual icons or logos representing known institutions that are somehow affiliated with a retailer to verify an online merchant's credibility. Trust symbols work even better when they are linked to independent Web sites and offer independent reviews or complaint resolution. Examples of trust symbols that you pay for one way or another (through dues, fees, percentage of sales, and so on) are industry trade associations (shop.org), shopping sites (Yahoo! Shopping), consumer protection groups (TrustE, BBBonline), and Internet security companies (ScanAlerts's Hackersafe logo, www.scanalert.com).

Some trust symbols that don't cost a thing are credit-card logos such as Visa, MasterCard, Discover, American Express, and PayPal, and you can use these to show accepted payment methods. Show the Y! hosting logo and, as noted previously, Yahoo! Shopping logo. Shipping carrier logos (UPS or FedEx) linked to your shipping info pages work well. Show manufacturer and brand logos on product pages. Display a graphic emphasizing that your checkout is safe and secure through *SSL* (Secure Socket Layer) with 128-bit encryption.

Offer better customer service

Reduce or eliminate risk with a 100% Satisfaction Guarantee. Make returns, exchanges, and canceled orders easy. Have a well-organized Info page with FAQ-style links. Answer e-mails quickly — within one business day, tops. Take the time to write answers to FAQs and put them on the site. Consider an *autoresponder,* which is an automated e-mail tool that instantly replies to e-mail questions with links to FAQs when you'll be away from your e-mail for a while. I use www.aweber.com for all my autoresponders. Ask for questions and feedback on the Web site. Offer help everywhere with links to info and privacy pages. Have a simple, understandable privacy policy.

Improve product pages to increase sales

The product page is where the decision to buy occurs. Improvements on the product level give you the best chance to sell more to folks on your site. Get the biggest bang for your buck by spending your time grooming your best-selling products' product pages. Don't distract folks from focusing on the task at hand because of hyperactive navigation. In fact, I like to isolate product pages from site-wide navigation to minimize distractions.

These tips can help you improve your product pages:

- ✔ **Write a compelling headline that gives a benefit.** Turn features into benefits. For example, "This car goes 180 mph, which means that you'll never be late to work again. . . ."

- ✔ **Call it what it is.** Make sure that the Name field contains the exact product name, brand, and model number as well as what everyone else calls it.

- ✔ **Tell me all about it.** Write a unique product description in your Caption field with more information than the manufacturer's product page provides. Link to warranty information and show all accessories and related products.

- ✔ **Make the price bigger.** No, even bigger than that. And red. Have a Sale-price and List price (if you discount) because you'll sell more when people know they're saving money.

- ✔ **Show product availability.** Display estimated ship date and delivery time on the product page before customers add a product to their Shopping Cart. Add a quantity field if you sell items commonly bought in bulk. You'll need RTML to do this (see Chapter 26). When something sells out and you can't get it anymore, either delete these extinct items or link to alternative or replacement products, but either way, remove these links from normal section or category pages. Nothing is worse than having a customer wanting to buy something that you can't sell her!

- ✔ **Show more photos, bigger photos, better photos.** Show a picture of the box. Show product details that you couldn't see even if you were in a real store. Make sure that you watermark your name or domain all over these photos, because competitors will steal them. See Chapter 8 for more info on images.

- ✔ **Nothing succeeds like success.** Put the word *Bestseller* in your best-selling products Name field (top 40) for another boost in sales. Shoppers feel more comfortable buying what other folks buy.

- ✔ **Write a Buyer's Guide for each product category.** Write a product *FAQ* (frequently asked questions) list if you get asked many questions about specific products.

- ✔ **Change text on your Buy buttons from Order to Add To Cart.** This is the Order-text setting under Variables in the Store Editor. Add To Cart is much less of a commitment than Order or Buy.

- ✔ **Change the name of the button that links to your Shopping Cart.** The default Show-order-text setting under Variables is Show Order, which I change to Show Shopping Cart or My Shopping Cart.

- ✔ **Make the Add To Cart button really, really, really big.** And red. And place it high on page, preferably on the right side, and above the fold so that folks can see it when they first see the product page without scrolling. You'll need RTML for this, so see Chapter 26 for more info.

This point is so important that it's worth repeating: The product page is where the decision to buy occurs. Make sure that your bestselling product pages put their best face forward with fantastic photography. Craft compelling headlines with a call to action (Order now!) and the benefits of buying. Produce personal, sales-driven copy with well-written product captions that turn features into benefits and motivate browsers to become buyers.

Convert more Shopping Carts

Here's a real-world example using a Yahoo! Store that's been around for at least three years. For every 100 people who visit Merchant X's online store, 5.2 percent of all shoppers click the Add To Cart button and place a product into the Shopping Cart; 4.5 percent of all shoppers start the checkout process; 3.6 percent of all shoppers make it to the second page of checkout (billing page); and 3.1 percent of all shoppers place an order online. Another 1 percent of all shoppers call in to place an order over the phone.

Almost 95 percent of visitors (what Yahoo! calls *customers,* or unique visitors) never even use the Shopping Cart. Ouch! Only around 5 percent of all visitors start a Shopping Cart, with 61 percent of those folks actually placing orders (completed carts). Around 70 percent of folks who start the checkout process actually finish and place an order, which I call a completed cart.

Ultimately, you want to make checking out fast, easy, and stress-free. Make sure that customers can focus on completing the checkout process by eliminating distractions such as external site navigation. Also, the only links to have here are ones that go back to the cart and that continue the checkout process. Make sure that your checkout *branding* (logos) and *look and feel* (colors and fonts) match the look of your store so that no disconnect occurs when customers move from store pages into the checkout process.

Improve your Shopping Carts

Call your cart a Shopping Cart, not a shopping basket or a shopping bag or a shopping bucket. The online Shopping Cart is a well-known Web convention at this point. Virtually everyone knows that e-commerce sites use Shopping Carts, so don't be cute. Here are some tips to get more folks to the Checkout pages:

- **Place a View Cart button or link prominently on every page.** I prefer to place a Shopping Cart/Checkout icon or link (or both) in the right-uppermost corner of every page.

- **Make the Proceed To Checkout button big and place it high on the Shopping Cart page.** See Chapter 14 for more on the new Checkout Manager. I like to minimize the branding and navigation that appears above the cart's contents to pull up that Proceed To Checkout button.

- **Make the Keep Shopping button or link go back to the previous product page.** By default, the Yahoo! Store's Keep Shopping link takes customers back to the previous product page unless you change the variable Continue-url. Don't change this unless you have a very good reason.

- **In the Shopping Cart, tell customers how to do three things: keep shopping, edit the contents of their cart, or check out.** Show your 800 number and phone hours. Push your 100% Satisfaction Guarantee. Link to your info.html page for contact information. Push the free shipping offer.

Talk about shipping and delivery on the Shipping Info Checkout page

Tell customers that you have their stuff (Availability), what company you'll ship it through (Shipping Options), and how fast they'll get their stuff (Delivery Time). Push free shipping or other shipping promotions. Here's more on what to show on the Shipping Info Checkout page:

- **Display all shipping charges before checkout to reduce the number of abandoned carts.** Show shipping prices on the product page if you can. Estimate ship date and delivery time.

- **Make your shipping rates easy to understand.** I like having a free shipping promotion on all domestic (US48) orders above a certain dollar amount (usually my average sale), and flat-rate shipping for all other domestic orders, which covers 95 percent of your orders. I have separate shipping rates for bulky items, express delivery, Alaska/Hawaii/Puerto Rico, APO, and Canada.

- **Free shipping works great if you can afford it.** Make free shipping an incentive to increase order size. Push FREE SHIPPING on every page and in title tags and abstracts for items that qualify.

- **Remove unnecessary data fields on the checkout forms.** Don't collect any info you don't need. See Chapter 14 on how to remove unnecessary fields and clean up your store's checkout.

✔ **Use a Progress Indicator graphic.** This graphic says, "You are here. Here's what's left to do to place an order," and it is now provided in the new Checkout Manager (Chapter 14). Back in the good ol' days (2005 and earlier), we had to make our checkout progress indicators by hand and we liked it that way.

✔ **Link to shipping information pages.** Links to helpful info pages, policy pages, express shipping options, and international info should open in pop-ups or new windows to avoid taking the customer out of the checkout path.

✔ **If you must use coupon codes in your checkout (please don't), rename the coupon code field something else (such as Source-code).** This way, the 95 percent of customers who don't have coupons won't feel like they're getting screwed because they *don't* have a coupon. Trust me. Your conversion rate will thank you.

✔ **Provide links to contact information.** Show your 800 number with phone hours and other contact info. Link to Cart Help pages.

Talk about safety, security, and privacy on the Billing Info Checkout page

Tell shoppers that they are on a secure server and that their personal information is safe and secure. Assure customers that their satisfaction is completely guaranteed (if you do that). Display or link to pages with testimonials from satisfied customers. Here are more ways to make your customer feel comfortable buying from you:

✔ **Link to other ways to order or pay.** Link to a fax or mail-order PDF order form if you can accept those types of orders.

✔ **Emphasize privacy when you ask for customers' e-mail.** Tell them you'll safeguard their personal information, and that you don't spam.

✔ **Accept a variety of payment methods.** Accept four major credit cards (Visa, MasterCard, Discover, and American Express) plus PayPal, and show their logos on-site. Consider taking online checks, too. I like to put a GIF file with these trust symbols in the Variable Final-text field.

Improving Your Store's Usability to Increase Conversions

Improving the usability of your Yahoo! Store is one of the most effective things you can do to increase your conversion rate, and thus your sales. Achieving this usability includes perhaps boring but definitely important stuff such as increasing the load speed of your store; optimizing and reducing image files to make them load faster; designing your store to display correctly on the browsers and monitors that the majority of folks visiting your site are using; writing copy in a Web-friendly style; using established Web-design conventions; and more.

Web usability isn't a magic bullet! Just because you make your site easier to use doesn't mean that you will sell anything. Shoppers will jump through hoops of fire and shop in the world's worst online store if it's the only place that sells what they want to buy. The opposite is true, too! If your prices are too high, your site looks amateurish or shady, your shipping rates and policies are hard to find or nonexistent, your returns and exchanges policies are draconian, or you're selling something that no one wants to buy in the first place, *no matter how much you improve the usability of your site, no one is ever going to buy from you!*

Here are some ways to improve your Yahoo! Store's usability and (I hope!) your conversion rate:

- **Follow well-established Web-design conventions.** Blue underlined links look like links. Buttons look clickable when they look three-dimensional and raised off the page. Pages less than 800 pixels wide mean no horizontal scrolling. Intrusive pop-ups get blocked by browsers or run folks off your site.

- **Use better error pages.** Make a custom 404 error page that pops up when a page cannot be found with a site search box, links to popular pages, and uses a friendly "Whoops! Page not found but it's not your fault" tone. (See Chapter 15.)

- **Watch others use your site.** Find a newbie. Get "civilians" to surf the site and have a specific tasks such as finding a type of product with a specific feature, or finding a product that will solve a particular problem and is priced below a certain point. Watch what users do, not just what they say — but do get them to verbalize their thought process as they click around.

- **Ask customers for feedback about your site design on your Web site.** Put a Feedback link in the Final-text field.

Understanding how little time you have

Jakob Nielsen (www.useit.com) is best known as the father of *Web usability,* which is the study of how people use the Internet and how to make Web sites easier to use. Nielsen's research says that you have about 10 seconds before the average user starts to give up on a slow-loading page and clicks the Back button. Other research shows that the average dialup user waits an average of 30 seconds for each new Web page he or she views.

There's a big difference between 10 seconds on a super-fast DSL or cable modem and 10 seconds on a bad dialup connection. Ten seconds on a modem gets you anywhere from 34K to 50K worth of files, depending on everything from modem speed to where the files actually are on the Internet. Ten seconds on a broadband connection gets you anything from 250K on up.

Fortunately, you are probably a typical e-commerce retailer and your target customer base mirrors most of America, with about half the users on high-speed Internet connections with DSL or cable modems and the other half on telephone dialup. This means that some of your users need faster-loading Web pages than others because the faster your page loads, the more pages the average visitor will view. The more pages visitors view, the more they will buy.

A fast-loading Web page is never a bad thing, even if someone is on a high-speed Internet connection. There is a direct relationship between fast-loading Web pages and higher conversion rates.

Revving up your site's load speed

Load speed is the first critical function of your Web site. Remember that if a page doesn't load within 10 seconds, it doesn't matter how cool your site is; you will lose some customers. One client's sales jumped up tens of thousands of dollars the first month after I put his site on a "diet." I decreased his thumbnails to make the section pages load faster, and I actually increased the size of his product images. The slow load was causing customers to bail before having a chance to order.

Think 50K file as a maximum file size for a Web page and all its elements. This maximum gives you about 10KB for your HTML file (compressed) and 40K for images. With a section page, this gives you ten 4KB thumbnails or twenty 2K thumbnails.

Use HTML or text over graphics. HTML text downloads faster because HTML code files weigh much, much less than image files, and search engines can read the text. For example, the headlines created on the Yahoo! Store product pages are actually images, or pictures of words, not words themselves. These image files are small but at least ten times the file size of the same text in HTML.

Your biggest problem: Images

Images are the main culprit when it comes to load speed. Here are some solutions to common problems with images:

- ✓ **Compressing individual image files works wonders.** For example, an uncompressed photograph for a product image can result in an 80K JPEG file, which is way too big! Compressed, that photo is a 20K file.

The slightest amount of compression can vastly reduce file sizes, so make sure that you adjust your compression settings in your graphics software. I set my JPEG compression to 15 percent, and I reduce my GIF files to 16 colors with no dithering. Adobe Photoshop and Corel's Paint Shop Pro both have compression wizards. You can always use an online tool such as those found at www.jpegwizard.com or www.321webmaster.com/optigif.php if you prefer.

✔ **Reduce the number of images on a page to increase load speed.** Usually, the problem with images is that the file size of all the images put together is too large. The easiest way to speed up image load speed on a Yahoo! Store is to have fewer items in section pages (up to 20 products per section, maximum). For example, 40 thumbnails of product shots on a section page load very slowly! My average thumbnail icon is usually about 3.5K.

✔ **Use smaller thumbnail images (closer to 45 x 45 pixels than 125 x 125 pixels).** In the Store Editor under the Variables settings, change Thumb-height to 55 and Thumb-width to 55 and click the Update button. Now see how your thumbnails look by browsing your most popular section pages.

Multiply the number of thumbnails you have by the Variables Thumb-height and Thumb-width to get a rough guess at the weight of those graphic images based upon pixels. For example, if you have 45-x-45-pixel thumbnails, you can have up to 20 products in a section. Twenty thumbnails x 45 pixels x 45 pixels = 40,500 pixels.

✔ **Optimize your Icons for faster-loading thumbnail images.** The best way to reduce the load time of section or category page is to crunch the stuffing out of a 45-x-45-pixel GIF file. Don't get stuck with a big, fat 5KB autogenerated thumbnail. Take that image, compress it to 2 or 3KB, and upload that to the Icon image property. If you want to get the biggest bang for your buck, maximize your top 20 section pages.

✔ **Save images in a Web-friendly format and file size.** When you create or edit your images in a graphics program, save photographs as JPEGs and save graphics such as logos as GIF files. I aim to make any custom icons (thumbnails) no larger than 2K. Product photos should be less than 30K, and preferably 20K.

✔ **Formatting images helps.** Crop product photos on a white background to remove white space around the image.

✔ **Recycling images works, too.** I've been guilty of this: using one logo on the home page, a slightly different one in the footer of every page, and yet another version of my logo on my info pages. What a waste of bandwidth! Now I use the same logo across the site. When users visit a second page that contains that logo, the image is already on their hard drive and it doesn't have to be downloaded again.

When you have an image-heavy navigation scheme, remember that these images have to be downloaded only once. Reuse persistent navigation and other elements (Search button, Add To Cart button, Info graphic, and so on) on other pages.

Don't use big images below the fold. Almost half of Web users won't scroll down even on Web pages that are longer than their browsers are tall. If an image doesn't show in the first screen shot (above the fold), then don't have an image there.

Everything depends on access speed

Speed is everything. Fifteen years ago, I accessed Usenet newsgroups with a 1200/2400-baud modem that let me read the words a letter at a time on the screen as files downloaded. Ten years ago, 28.8K modems were the standard. Five years ago, everyone had upgraded to 56K modems, and DSL and cable were first coming online. Now, half the country is using broadband at home with speeds anywhere from 256KB to 3 megabits, with folks living in the boonies (like me) stuck on dialup or satellite. Today, people access the Web at many, many different speeds.

A user's Internet access speed determines how long it takes for an HTML page and all the images and other elements on that page to download and display in a browser. The faster a user's Internet access speed, the less time it takes for a page to load. The faster the load speed of a page, the better the experience will be for your average shopper. Better shopping experiences turn into sales. Slow-loading pages are extremely frustrating, and after 10 seconds, most folks give up.

You may have no control over the speed of your visitors' Internet access, but you have total control over the size of your Web pages, how many images you display on a page, and the file size of each image. If you want to sell to only 50 percent of the population, don't worry about the file sizes of your images and HTML pages. For my part, I'd rather have a shot at every dollar.

Looking at Who's Looking at You

Read on as I share some demographic information from one of my higher-traffic Yahoo! Stores. Besides telling you what pages were the most popular, what keywords converted into sales, and where all this traffic is coming from, most third-party analytics software also collects demographic information. This includes the browser, browser version, and monitor resolution settings of all your visitors.

Operating system and browser software

Depending on your customer mix, most users (95.5 percent) will be using some version of Windows. Less than 5 percent will be using a Macintosh or the Linux operating system. If you sell to early adopters, designers, musicians, or anyone else who fits the Macintosh profile, you need to make sure that your site looks good on a Mac, too.

You need to know the types of browsers that visitors use to look at your Web store. Web sites display somewhat differently (and sometimes very differently) in different browsers.

Most people surfing the Internet today use Microsoft's Internet Explorer (IE). I prefer Firefox for surfing the Internet, but when I'm building a Yahoo! Store, I like to see what the vast majority of my customers will see, so I use Internet Explorer.

Screen resolution in pixels

A Web page of an online catalog is very different from the printed page of the mail-order catalog. With print, you have absolute control over how the shopper sees your catalog page. You make the images and text fill up the page with a pleasing design. On the Web, you have some control, but visitors will see different-looking catalogs depending on their browser settings and monitor's *screen resolution* (how many pixels tall and pixels wide a monitor displays).

Most monitors can display multiple settings. The higher the settings, the smaller everything appears. You've probably seen the super-geek's computer with a 23-inch monitor whose screen resolution setting is so high that you can't read the text, and Web pages appear the size of postage stamps.

In July 2005, the most popular screen resolution on one of my sites was 1,024 x 768 (favored by 54 percent of users). In a very distant second place was 800 x 600 (22 percent). This means that if you design a store that's around 800 pixels wide (or just a little smaller), it will look good on more than 99 percent of the users looking at your Web site, which is good enough for me!

By default, Yahoo! Stores have an absolute width, meaning that if you're looking at a 790-pixel-wide store on a 50-inch plasma monitor, it might look a little small. Most folks don't surf the Web on a 50-inch plasma monitor but rather on a regular old CRT monitor set to 1,024 x 768. Make sure that you design your store to look good on the average shopper's monitor!

Free speed test

Use this free speed test on your pages to see the total load time of any Web page. The Results page tells you the file size (weight) of all the elements on the page including scripts and images, gives you links to them in descending order by file size, and then gives you some helpful tips based upon your results. You can find it here:

```
www.websiteoptimization.com/
    services/analyze
```

It's fun! Run your competitor's pages through the tool either for laughs or a wake-up call, depending on how fast they are. My top five competitors' home pages weighed in at 265K, 252K, 182K, 165K, and 73K. I weighed in at 51K. Zoom, zoom!

So, how big can your pages be?

There's a very delicate balancing act between using pretty pictures and determining how patient visitors can be to wait for images to download. There are three types of files: the HTML page itself, site-wide navigation/branding images, and page-specific product images.

You don't have much control over the file size of your HTML pages. The file really has to be as big as it needs to be. You can cut down a little on file size by doing a couple of things: moving some code off the page by externalizing some files such as JavaScripts, and moving some formatting off the page by using cascading style sheets (CSS).

Yahoo! seems to be compressing HTML files on its servers. This is a fancy way to increase the load speed of a page by compressing the HTML file into a Zip file that the browsers can read. My home page on one site weighed in at 79K, but after I looked at the file with the download speed analysis tool, I found that it weighed in at just over 55K.

Focus on what makes money

While most of my ad agency–based Web-development friends were mastering all the ins and outs of the latest version of Flash and Photoshop to make sexy Web pages, I made the very conscious decision not to. Instead, I focused on discovering how to make my sites convert better and how to drive more and more traffic through search-engine marketing to my very profitable, but not quite as flashy, Web stores.

I'll admit that sometimes I feel as though I'm searching for the magic bullet for improving my conversion rate. If I could only find that one magical phrase (100% Satisfaction Guaranteed) that keeps folks from dropping their Shopping Carts and bailing out of the checkout process, I'd be rich! If it were only that simple!

The truth is that all these little things add up to increasing your conversion rate. It's not just one thing. As you make changes to your store, document what you do, and make changes slowly to see what the impact is over time. Every site is different, so techniques that work on one site may not work for another site. Some changes may decrease sales and conversions, so watch out!

Conversion and usability resources

Check out these resources for more information on increasing your sales:

- ✔ **GrokDotcom** (www.grokdot.com)**:** This conversion-rate marketing newsletter is from Future Now, written by the Eisenberg Brothers.

- ✔ **Jakob Nielsen's Web site** (www.useit.com)**:** This site features Jakob Nielsen's weekly Alertbox column, "Web usability, usability engineering, and Jakob's minimalist approach to Web design."

- ✔ *Designing Web Usability,* by Jakob Nielsen (New Riders Publishing, 1999): This book is the Bible of Web Usability and is worth every penny of the $45.00 list price, but you can get it on Amazon for $30.98. Buy his other books, too!

Chapter 22

E-Mailing Your Customers for Fun and Profit

E-mail is the #1 killer app of the Internet. More people use e-mail than use the Internet for e-commerce, online dating, and reading the news combined.

Marketing through e-mail is a great way to keep in touch with your customers, educate them about things they're interested in, "shake the tree" to get traffic to your Yahoo! Store, and sell lots of cool stuff.

E-mail marketing is also the easiest way to tick off your customers, get your domain banned from major service providers, get booted off Yahoo! Merchant Solutions, and even do some hard time in the big house. You want to be careful before you e-mail thousands of people on your customer list.

In this chapter, I outline the various ways you can use e-mail to communicate with your customers, talk about dealing with spam, explore managing your e-mail lists, and touch on creating newsletters to connect with and sell to your customers and prospects.

Discovering E-Mail Marketing Tools

E-mail is the most popular online activity and one of the most powerful ways to communicate with your customers. You can use e-mail in several ways to tap into the power of e-mail marketing:

- ✔ **E-mails to customers who placed an order, such as:**

  - Order Confirmation e-mail or Thanks For Your Order message.

  - Shipping notification with tracking number and delivery info. You can send it by hand or use UPS (or another carrier) to automatically notify customers that their orders have shipped.

  - Rate This Merchant e-mail sent two weeks after the order was placed.

  - Order Status message (if you use this feature). For example, if an item is delayed, back-ordered, or being sent in separate boxes, you can change the status setting on the order and notify the customer by e-mail.

- ✔ **Personal replies to questions:** You can also shine when folks e-mail you with questions about products or your shipping policies.

- ✔ **Viral marketing:** Customers can use their e-mail to spread your marketing for you (like a virus). You can encourage them to "e-mail this page (or newsletter) to a friend."

Thanking customers with e-mails

The main reason I use Yahoo! Store is because it's so easy. A perfect example is customer Order Confirmation E-mails. To turn on this feature, just click the Store Manager's Shipment & Order Status link, type your e-mail address in the Order Confirmation E-mail field, click the Update button, and then click the Publish Order Settings link on the Store Manager page. Order confirmation e-mails are then automatically sent to customers immediately after they place their orders. This confirmation also contains additional shipping information, answers to other frequently asked questions (FAQs), and full customer service contact information with names, phone numbers, e-mail addresses, and hours of operation.

One of the best ways you can reduce your workload is by including very detailed shipping and customer service information in your Order Confirmation e-mail. Edit this e-mail on the Store Manager's Shipment & Order Status page. Scroll to the Confirmation Email message field, type or paste your message text, and click the Update button. When the Store Manager appears, click the Publish Order Settings link to make your change permanent.

Include all the information that folks are most likely to call you about, such as business hours, shipping schedules, and links to your shipping information pages and FAQs.

Here's a pretty good "Thanks for your order!" message:

> *Thanks for your order! Most orders ship out via UPS the same business day received. International orders and orders with personalized products may take a little longer. We will contact you by e-mail if we have any questions regarding your order, or if there will be a significant delay in processing your order.*
>
> *Some quantity discounts, free shipping on certain Internet specials, and shipping costs on international orders may NOT be shown on this copy, but WILL be reflected on your final invoice. If you have any questions about your order, comments about our site, or anything else you think we need to know, please e-mail me at sales@yourdomain.com.*
>
> *We appreciate your business! Thanks,* Owner's Name
>
> Company Name *Customer Service, 1-800-555-1212*

I would also recommend including a link to your information page (info.html page) as well as your FAQ page if you have one. If some products take a certain amount of time to ship, I try to include that in the availability field, which also reduces the amount of customer service e-mails and phone calls. About one-third of the calls we get are "where is my order" (WISMO) calls, but we would get a lot more if we did not include this information.

One last thing! One of the most important things I believe you can do in your Order Confirmation e-mail message is to really thank the customer for his order. Be a bit more personal about it. Set the tone of your relationship with your customer. Say something like "We appreciate your business. We are a small business and without customers we wouldn't be here, so thanks for your order," or "Our job is to take care of you. Customer satisfaction is extremely important to us, and if you have any questions, here is what you can do. . . . "

Sending Order e-mails

Consider the following tips when sending Order e-mails:

- ✔ When the orders have shipped, I send a "Your Order Just Shipped" e-mail to thank customers again for their orders and to notify them that the orders are on the way.

- ✔ UPS WorldShip software also sends each customer a generic e-mail that contains her UPS tracking number with links to the UPS Web site for real-time tracking info and the package's expected date of delivery.

✔ When merchants enable the ratings feature in the Store Manager under Customer Ratings, customers receive an automated Yahoo! Shopping "Rate This Merchant" e-mail two weeks after placing their order.

Taking advantage of personalized replies

When customers e-mail you directly to ask product questions or query about the status of their order, you have the opportunity to shine. Here are some ways you can maximize the personal contact you have with customers via e-mail:

✔ **Stay on top of your e-mail.** Customer service and order inquiries are extremely time sensitive and usually need an immediate response. These days, folks expect a reply within hours, if not minutes. The faster you can jump on a problem, the greater the chance of fixing something before it spirals out of control.

✔ **Writing and speaking are totally different ways of communicating information.** When people read your e-mail, they can't hear the inflections or the pitch in your voice. To avoid coming across as too blunt, I always turn on my "polite" filter when replying to customer e-mails.

My dad always started his replies with "Thank you for e-mailing Gun Dog Supply" and then responded to a customer's e-mail. Whatever your personal style, remember that while the customer isn't always right, he is always the customer. Spelling and punctuation are important, too. If you can't spell, run a spell checker before you send your e-mail.

✔ **Be a real person, not a nameless, faceless automaton.** Sign your e-mails with your name, not "*yourdomain.com* customer service." I think that being a small company, where customers can get personalized customer service from a real person (sometimes even the owner), is an extremely important advantage when competing with big, impersonal corporations.

✔ **Dress up your signature file.** At the bottom of every e-mail that I send is my *signature file* (or sig file), which is a text file that lists all my contact information: my name, phone numbers, mailing address, e-mail addresses, Web-site URL, and a link to my blog. If I'm promoting anything specifically, I can promote it in my sig file. You send lots of e-mails on a daily basis, and most of these folks will eventually need your contact information.

Get the benefit of branding your URL in their brain. Customers can see "Click here to read my blog" or "Click here to buy my book."

✔ **Pimp up your *reply name*.** I usually stick my 800 number and URL in my reply name. Instead of an e-mail saying it's `From: Rob` it says `From: Rob Snell, 1-800-332-7601, http://ystore.com`, which is usually a clickable link in most e-mail software. When folks preview my e-mail in their Inbox, they actually see some, if not all, of my 1-800 number in the From line, which makes it really easy for folks to call me.

Responding to e-mail addresses on your Web site

You may notice that all the e-mail addresses you have published on your site seem to get a lot of spam. If you get much e-mail, you probably have a hard time picking the wheat from the chaff. Certain e-mails I receive need my immediate attention, so I use different addresses for different things.

To make sure that the important messages get to the top of your Inbox, use a different reply address for customers than your generic "contact us" e-mail address on your Web site. For example, you can make orders@yourdomain. com the reply address to your Order Confirmation e-mail. That way, you know that e-mails to that address can be only folks who ordered something who are asking questions. *Note:* Make sure that e-mail address appears nowhere else on your site to reduce the amount of spam you get by 80 or 90 percent.

Referral e-mail marketing

Another way to market yourself via e-mail is to ask your customers to pass along your info. Tell them to tell their friends! Unfortunately, Yahoo! Store doesn't come with a service that allows you to add an E-Mail This Page To A Friend button. However, many third-party services, such as Constant Contact, offer this feature. Usually, your bulk e-mail or newsletter service gives you the code to add this capacity to your Web site. The Constant Contact service is easy to use, offers a free trial, and has tons of other cool tools you can use to market to your customers. Take a look at www.constantcontact.com.

Advertising in e-mail newsletters

Buying ads in other folks' e-mail newsletters is a very cost-effective form of e-mail marketing. It's a great way to use e-mail to get access to folks who are not on your customer list. No matter what your industry, people create newsletters somewhat related to what you sell, and they'll let you sponsor their newsletter. You can actually buy a text ad with a link for $50 on up. Most ads are sold on a CPM (cost per thousand people) basis.

Create an ad, put a tracking link in the URL, and see whether it converts into sales. If you get any sales or new customers from it, keep doing it. If not, try some different ads or offers. If newsletter publishers archive their content on their Web site, sometimes you get the added bonus of a link to your Yahoo! Store.

Marketing products and services with autoresponders

Another way to collect e-mail addresses of potential customers is to offer free reports via e-mail using autoresponders. An *autoresponder* is an e-mail program that automatically sends a response when someone e-mails that specific address. Sometimes a series of messages are sent over several days, and then the prospect is added to your regular newsletter.

I like using autoresponders because they're a quick way for folks to get instant information in exchange for their e-mail address. For more information on using autoresponders, visit www.aweber.com, which is my favorite e-mail vendor.

Marketing in a Spam-Filled World

About a year ago, it looked like the spammers had destroyed e-mail marketing, but now it looks like things are actually getting better. The software people have created better spam filters, Internet Service Providers (ISPs) have done a better job blocking spammy domains, and now the Feds have stepped in to try to take down the spammers. Industry initiatives are also under way to help address the problem of e-mail spoofing and phishing by verifying the domain name from which the e-mail is sent. Right now, spammers can hide behind fake e-mail addresses.

I am not a lawyer. You need to have your attorney look over how you run your business and address any of your concerns. Best practices, acceptable use, terms of service, and laws change every day. By the time you read this book, everything in this chapter may have changed, but this section is meant to give you a general idea of what's considered spamming and what's not. In other words, don't e-mail people who haven't done business with you or who ask you not to e-mail them.

The CAN-SPAM Act and you

The CAN-SPAM (Controlling the Assault of Non-Solicited Pornography and Marketing) Act of 2003 was effective January 2004. The CAN-SPAM Act applies to American businesses that use e-mail for commercial purposes, spammers, and those who hire spammers. The CAN-SPAM Act is the federal government's first step dealing with e-mail spam.

Now businesses can send unsolicited commercial e-mail to an e-mail address, but they have to stop sending e-mails to folks who don't want it. The law also created guidelines for marketers, and created consequences for those who violate the law. The punishments aren't just a slap on the wrist, either. They have some teeth, with serious fines and even jail time for violating CAN-SPAM. Spammers are also liable for civil damages.

The CAN-SPAM Act classifies commercial e-mail into three kinds of messages: transactional or relationship messages, messages to an opt-in list, and other types of commercial e-mails:

- **Transactional or relationship e-mails** include order confirmations, order status e-mails, and messages to existing customers. Yahoo! Store Order Confirmations and Order Status messages are not spam because the customer placed an order and gave you an e-mail address. This relationship allows you to e-mail him. You can also send newsletters to the folks that have ordered from your Yahoo! Store before because you have a prior relationship with them, but an Opt-In approach is preferred.

- **Opt-In List e-mails** are messages to folks who gave you permission to e-mail them. For example, when folks signed up for your newsletter, they gave you permission to e-mail them. (For more on opting in, see the nearby sidebar "Opting In, double opting in, and opting out.")

- **Other types of commercial messages** include ads, newsletters, or commercial solicitation being sent that don't qualify as the relationship messages or opt-in messages. These messages must state that the e-mail is an ad or a commercial message somewhere in the e-mail.

Here's what you need to do to comply with CAN-SPAM:

- **State somewhere in your commercial e-mails that the e-mail is a commercial message or ad.** Just in case someone doesn't have a prior relationship with you or doesn't opt-in, I recommend saying this somewhere in the footer of the message:

  "You are receiving this message with our special offers because you are on our list of friends and customers. If you don't want to receive promotional messages from us, simply give us a holler, and we'll take you off the list."

- **Include your postal mailing address with all e-mails.** It is a good idea to put this and other contact information, such as links to your Web site, at the bottom of all your e-mails anyway, but the U.S. government requires it now.

- ✔ **List clear removal or unsubscribe options in every e-mail.** Most bulk or newsletter e-mail vendors do this for you by attaching an unsubscribe option at the bottom of all the newsletters. Honor the remove request within ten business days.

- ✔ **Live by your privacy policy.** If you tell people that you're not going to sell, rent, or give away e-mail addresses and personal information that you collect on the site, then you shouldn't do it.

- ✔ **Don't use misleading From addresses or misleading subject lines in your e-mails.** In other words, your e-mail needs to say that it is from you, and the subject lines need to be about what the e-mail is about.

Having permission to send commercial e-mail to someone is a privilege. Don't abuse it by mailing your list too often. Weekly e-mails are about as often as I want to get promotional e-mails. Live by your privacy policy or die. If you say you won't rent, sell, or even reveal personal information, then don't.

Opting in, double opting in, and opting out

E-mail marketing is confusing enough as it is, so I opted to include some information explaining the ins and outs of opting in and out of e-mail lists.

Opt-in means that a person took action to add her e-mail address to your list and gave her permission for you to e-mail her. *Subscribers* (folks on e-mail lists) can opt-in several ways:

- ✔ When they buy something, by checking a box that says "Yes, I want to receive your weekly e-mail newsletter with money-saving coupons" on a form

- ✔ When they type their name into an e-mail newsletter signup form on your Web site

- ✔ When they tell someone on the phone that it's okay to add them to your e-mail newsletter list

Double opt-in is opt-in with an added hurdle: After subscribers give you their e-mail address, they receive a confirmation e-mail to double-check that they really want to be on your list. If they don't reply to that confirmation e-mail, they don't get added to your list. Double opt-in actually radically reduces the number of folks who make it to your mailing list for several reasons. Some folks change their mind. Some folks get the e-mail and never respond to it. Some e-mail confirmations get caught in spam filters. However, double opt-in e-mail newsletters virtually guarantee you that your new subscriber actually owns that e-mail address, verify that they wanted to receive e-mail from you, and are a pretty good indicator that someone is a very qualified prospect.

Opt-out is when you have a customer's e-mail address and assume that you have permission to e-mail him until he tells you otherwise — and we all know what happens when you assume. A customer can opt-out by replying to your mailings with a remove request or by using the automatic removal link usually included at the bottom of automated, bulk e-mail newsletters. From a permission marketing standpoint, opt-in and double opt-in are the way to go because you have the express permission of the customer or prospect asking for more e-mails from you. Opt-out is a little bit spammier.

Yahoo's take on spam

Yahoo's Terms of Service require you to follow the Yahoo! Store guidelines, which are pretty specific about spam. Yahoo! says that you can't send mass e-mail to folks who don't request it; send e-mail with a fake e-mail address; promote a store with multiple submissions in public forums; use inappropriate links, titles, or descriptions; or use content that doesn't belong to you. For more details, see `http://store.yahoo.com/guide.html`.

If someone is spamming you from a Yahoo! Store, report it here:

`http://add.yahoo.com/fast/help/us/sbiz/cgi_abuse.`

Managing Your E-Mail Lists

When someone places an order, her name and e-mail address is added to your Yahoo! Store's Mailing List database. This database is located under the Mailing Lists link under Promote on the Store Manager page. From this database, you can add the new names to different lists (customers, prospects, and so on), create new mailing lists, add names and e-mail addresses, delete names and addresses, and export your entire list. Also, you can export these names in a *CSV* (comma separated value) text file, which you can use to export the names to a third-party mailing list, such as Constant Contact or Aweber.

Managing your e-mail list can be complicated. I like to use my Yahoo! Store as my master list.

Sign 'em up!

How do you get people to sign up for your newsletter? The first thing you can do is use the Catalog Request form. Yahoo! Store has a catalog request form that you can use to collect names and e-mails. I personally don't like this form because it has many other fields that your customer has to complete, which makes it a little more difficult to collect the information.

Usually, when you have a third-party bulk e-mail vendor, the vendor gives you a very simple signup form. We use Bcentral. I've had clients who have used Constant Contact, Relevant Tools, Got Marketing (Yahoo!'s designated partner), Aweber, and Topica. Signup forms are a great way to collect e-mail addresses from folks who are actually interested in receiving marketing materials and product information from you. Your bulk e-mail vendor gives you a snippet of code that allows you to put a signup box or form on any HTML page. It's really easy to add that to your Final Text field (under Variables) or elsewhere on your site.

Offer free downloads

One way to collect e-mails is to have a free download in exchange for an e-mail address via newsletter signup. If I can give away a free report, free e-book, marketing piece, software sample, or PDF report, then I'm more likely to acquire subscribers. This worked really well for one of my clients, an attorney who specializes in real estate investing. He has all these free legal forms you can download. I suggested that he "charge" an e-mail address as the price for downloading all these free boilerplate legal documents. He said that one idea (not really invented by me) was perhaps the best piece of marketing advice he ever got because that ten minutes of conversation exponentially increased the size of his mailing list. See his site at www.legalwiz.com.

Keep signup forms as simple as possible. I ask for name and e-mail address only. Make sure that you tell people why they should sign up for your newsletter (free coupons, product information, reviews, contests, and so on). I usually emphasize the fact that I never give away, rent, or sell my customer's personal data.

Every week, I take all the new customers and newsletter signups, add them to the Yahoo! Store list, and then copy the addresses to my Bcentral account. A mailing list is born!

Weeding your list

When someone asks to be removed from future e-mails, I actually delete his name twice. I go into the Yahoo! Store and delete his name from the Yahoo! Store mailing list. I then go into Bcentral and delete his name from that software, too, to make sure that we don't have his e-mail address anywhere inside our marketing system. The system automatically removes e-mail addresses that bounce multiple times.

Some folks get e-mails and never read them, never reply, never ask to be removed, and never order anything again. E-mailing customers is so cheap, that I just keep on e-mailing these folks, hoping that one day they may order again. The profit from an average order pays for the cost of sending around 10,000 e-mails, so I'll e-mail a customer forever on the chance that he might just order again!

Crafting Effective E-Commerce Newsletters

The appearance of e-mail messages is much like Web pages because the presentation to your subscribers totally depends on what software they're using to read their e-mail. Messages read on AOL or Gmail are going to look different than e-mail read with Outlook Express, and messages on a PDA are going to look totally different. You don't have absolute control over how messages appear to your customers, but you can do a lot of things to help.

Nowadays, most subscribers' e-mail software is sophisticated enough to receive complete Web pages with full HTML, rich with multimedia content. In the good old days, you didn't have to worry about how your message was going to look because we had only text available. Now you have to choose among sending plain text, HTML-enabled e-mail, or both.

I try to send the simplest e-mails possible. I usually include an image at the top of the e-mail to look sexy, but I try to make my e-mails as simple as possible. When you use simple text, you know folks are going to be able to read it. The more complicated the HTML, the more likely you are to set off spam filters, and your e-mail will never get opened, much less read or responded to.

With HTML e-mails, most third-party bulk e-mail vendors allow you to have an alternate message, which usually just consists of a paragraph of simple text and a link to a page on your Web site, and it appears whenever the full HTML e-mail doesn't display.

Did you get my e-mail?

You need to make sure that the e-mail you send actually arrives. The only way I've ever been able to tell for sure is to set up test accounts at Gmail, Hotmail, Yahoo! Mail, and AOL. If your e-mails don't arrive, it may be because your domain is a blocked domain because you appear on a *blacklist*. Blacklists are lists of spammers and their domains compiled by independent third parties.

To be safe, I have several AOL accounts. I want to see whether AOL subscribers are actually getting my e-mails and how the e-mail looks in the different versions of AOL's e-mail software. Lots of times, HTML-rich e-mails don't appear on AOL. AOL's e-mail software is a little strange, and you have to do some things when you send your e-mail to make sure that it shows up. AOL is important! Ten percent of the people on any given mailing list these days seem to be AOL users. AOL users like to shop online, so you don't want to miss out on selling them stuff.

Connecting with your customers through a weekly newsletter

Chuck Rosanski's weekly e-mail newsletter from Mile High Comics (www.milehighcomics.com) is the best retailer's newsletter I've run across in eight years of selling online. Mile High Comics is the world's largest comic book retailer and sells millions of dollars in comics every year. Here's why I like it:

✔ The format is simple HTML, mostly text with a photo or two. His copywriting isn't commercial at all, which doesn't trip off spam filters.

✔ Chuck's newsletter is personal and makes customers feel like they're part of his family. Chuck's writing style is real, down home, and conversational. I don't really have the time, but I want to read it when it comes out. Every week, you get to find out what Chuck has been up to this week, and what kind of crazy deals and specials he'll have next.

✔ Chuck has a great "hook." He travels all over the world to buy all these huge comic book collections, so he has to sell his existing stock at ridiculous prices to be able to afford to buy the next collection. Every week, some other group of comics is 20 to 80 percent off retail.

✔ When he's not running his comics empire, he works in his garden and grows organic produce that he sells at the local farmer's market.

Why do I know this? I read his newsletter. I don't even really collect comics anymore, but Chuck still gets my money, usually because I see something that would make a great present. You need a cool e-mail newsletter? Subscribe to the Mile High Comics newsletter to see how it's done right!

Chapter 23

Getting Down with Product Uploads

*O*ne of the most powerful tools in your Store Editor toolbox is database uploads. Both the Store Editor and the Catalog Manager allow you to upload product databases to build, rebuild, or update your online store. You can edit your product data offline and then quickly upload the updated information for extremely fast and easy Web-store maintenance.

This chapter is about the Store Editor Database Upload feature. Stores using the Catalog Manager should stay out of the Store Editor and refer to the Yahoo! Store Help files for more information. If you use the Store Editor, you should never really use the Catalog Manager to create, edit, and manage your products. I prefer the Store Editor hands down for store building.

You can use database uploads to manage your store in two ways: You can update existing products and add new items with load files, or you can completely rebuild your store from the ground up with a master database file you build offline. If you're comfortable with Excel and CSV files, database uploads are extremely easy. It's almost like trimming your nose hairs with a Bowie knife.

In this chapter, I show you how to create a product database, upload it to the Store Editor's server, preview the uploaded file to make sure that the data is correct, update the store with the uploaded file, and publish your changes.

I'll be very upfront about this. I'm trying to scare you. Newbies do *not* need to mess with database uploads. This is my disclaimer: Don't think about touching a functioning, money-making Yahoo! Store with database uploads unless you're prepared to completely rebuild your store from scratch. If you're not comfortable with Microsoft Excel and CSV files, you have some work to do before you can play with database uploads. Open a second account and play with a test store.

On the other hand, if you have a new account with no product pages, creating and uploading a CSV via the database upload functionality is really a no-lose proposition. There's no better time to explore the power of database uploads than on a brand-spanking new store, especially if you have Microsoft Excel and have your product info in a CSV file.

A Word of Warning

If you think you're up to the challenge of database uploads, you need to be aware of the potential consequences. You can do the following:

- Nuke your entire site and overwrite old products with new data. You can make enough changes that you cannot undo without calling Yahoo! engineers to restore your account from backups.

- Change or corrupt the prebuilt Yahoo! function pages (index, norder, nsearch, info, and privacypolicy).

- Totally mess up your site's hierarchy and navigation if you screw up the Path and Contents fields. You can accidentally create multiple versions of the same section page, resulting in some products being in the first section and some in the second section.

- Drop hundreds or thousands of new products on your home page if you forget to include where the new products are supposed to go.

- Dump the contents of your Clipboard and never know it. Usually things on your Clipboard are new products not yet available or out-of-stock products, so you discover that you made this mistake after someone orders something you can't sell her. Frustrating!

Think about setting up a test store to practice doing database uploads. It's worth the $40 a month when you consider the real cost of accidentally deleting your real store. I mean, how much is your ulcer worth? Master doing database uploads, practice your RTML skills, and try other design tricks behind closed doors. Train new employees in a safe environment instead of learning on a live store without a net. I found out more by building new stores from scratch and blowing things up before the client ever got to see the first demo.

When you're playing with your demo account (or a brand new store), you can totally destroy all the products and sections in a store and use the magic of the Rebuild button to wipe the slate clean.

This stuff changes from time to time. Read the Help files and be careful!

Introducing Database Uploads

Database uploads make dull, repetitive work easy! Instead of using the Store Editor to add products, you build a simple database of products in a spreadsheet and upload store data in a matter of minutes. You can create hundreds or thousands of products and sections in a single text file. You can also update existing products and move products around on your store with load files. Database uploads can only create or update product data (text and numbers) and don't allow you to upload graphics like Images, Icons, or Insets. (See Chapter 8 for info on uploading product images. See Chapter 25 for unofficial, third-party tools for uploading and downloading other image files.)

You have to be in the Advanced mode of Store Editor to do database uploads. If you don't work in Advanced mode, you can't even see the Database Upload button, and you have no business playing with database uploads. This feature is for power users only.

Store Editor database uploads are really pretty straightforward. You create a product database file that contains product information, such as name, price, code, and maybe some other fields, too. You save the file as a CSV text file. You log in to the Store Editor and navigate to the Database Upload page.

The upload is really a two-step process: You upload your CSV, and then, after you've previewed the file, you commit to updating the store. If you make a mistake, you have a chance to undo your snafu with the Revert function. If the file looks fine, click the Publish button, which updates the public version of your store with your changes.

Creating Products with Uploads

You really have to know what you're doing when you're working with database uploads, or you can overwrite your entire store with the click of a button. You don't have to have custom programming skills. I teach "civilian" retailers how to do database uploads all the time. All you really need are basic chops in Excel.

The only software you need is a text editor and spreadsheet software like Microsoft Excel. If I'm not using Excel because the files are really small or simple, I use Notepad (which comes free with Windows) or UltraEdit-32. You can download a 30-day free trial of the latter from www.ultraedit.com or just go ahead and pay the $40 and get the world's best text editor.

You have to be able to open a file, sort and filter records, use find and replace to correct data, add and remove text, and export files (or "Save As") in the CSV (comma separated variable) format. Knowing how to do triple back flips with text such as concatenating multiple fields into a single field helps, too!

If you want to tweak your geek chops, check out *Microsoft Excel For Dummies,* by Greg Harvey (Wiley Publishing).

Formatting Your Upload Files

The Store Editor accepts database upload files in two formats: CSV text files and Bar-Delimited files (fields separated by pipes: |). Bar-Delimited files are much harder to use, so just don't!

CSV files are simple text files where the fields are separated by commas and have no font or color formatting. CSV files are really easy to make in widely available programs like Notepad or Microsoft Excel. Here's an example of a simple CSV database upload file:

```
Name,Code,Price
iPod,1234,$200
iPod Case,2345,$18
```

This file creates two orderable products on the home page. All the other fields are blank or the default. Because there is no ID field, the code generates the ID.

Here are some basic things you need to know about CSV files for Store Editor uploads:

- ✔ The first row of any database upload file is for the field names.
- ✔ At a minimum, you need an ID or Code field, and one other field.
- ✔ Fields can be in any order.
- ✔ Prices can have dollar signs or not.
- ✔ Empty database fields are not a problem, but empty lines are a problem.
- ✔ The ID and Code fields for each item must be unique.

✔ The ID field determines the object-ID. If you don't have an ID field in an upload, then the Code field also becomes the ID. Naming products with the same Codes and IDs is good product management. If your upload file doesn't have a Code field or an ID field, the Store Editor randomly generates an ID, such as gensym-1234.

✔ You don't have to upload something to every field, but empty YES/NO fields (such as Taxable, Orderable, and Leafed) default to Yes unless you upload something different.

I like to build my files in Microsoft Excel, save them as CSV text files, and close Excel. I open the CSV file in Notepad to make sure that my file is properly formatted. I name my CSV file with the time it was created somewhere in the filename so that I can tell which is the latest version. It seems I always have to tweak my upload files for some reason or another, because I always forget a field or something or have an error message usually caused by me mistyping a field name.

Uploading Data in the Right Fields

Here are the various product fields you can upload to a Yahoo! Store using the database upload functionality:

✔ Yahoo! Help files say that you can upload the following fields: Abstract, Availability, Caption, Code, Headline, Label, Name, Options, Orderable, Path, Price, Sale-price, Ship-weight, and Ypath.

✔ I upload the ID as a separate column instead of letting the code determine the ID. I also like to upload Contents fields with a list of object-IDs.

✔ Yahoo! Help files say that you can't upload content on section pages, but I do it all the time. Here's a two-item load file:

```
Name,ID,Caption
Section,sample-section,Looking for what's in this section?
Section,sample-subsection,It might be in this subsection!
```

Doing Uploads

Doing your first database upload can be very exciting. Instead of uploading thousands of products with every field imaginable, start small.

Here's an example of an upload file:

```
Name,Code,Price,Path
Gadget,1234,$199,Widgets:Gismos
```

This file creates a Widgets section page with a Gismos subsection. It also creates a Gadget product page, which shows up at www.*yourdomain.com*/ 1234.html because the order-ID determines the document name.

The following file adds the Sale-Price to the same product:

```
Name,Code,Price,Sale-Price,Path
Gadget,1234,$199,$165,Widgets:Gismos
```

The following file adds a drop-down option menu named Color, where you can choose Black or Red for the same product:

```
Name,Code,Price,Sale-Price,Path,Options
Gadget,1234,$199,$165,Widgets:Gismos,Color Black Red
```

Uploading Data with the New Upload button

After you click the New Upload button on the Database Upload page, the New Upload page appears (see Figure 23-1). Four drop-down menus let you select a data format (CSV or Bar-Delimited), the item type and template, and the section type and template. An Upload field with a Browse button lets you choose the file from your disk and upload your product database file to the server.

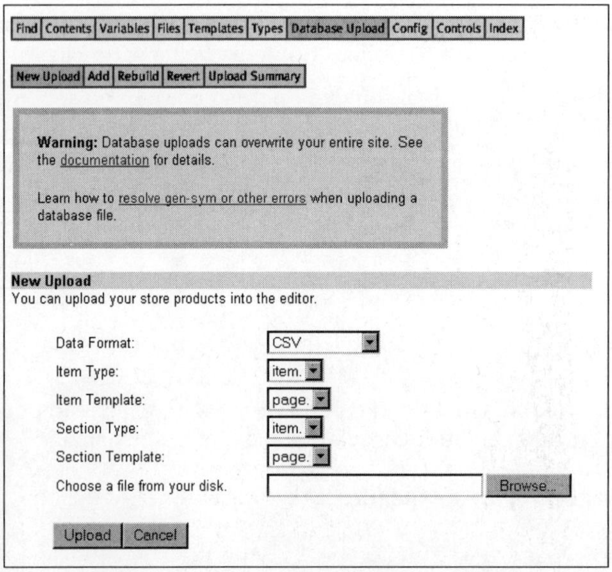

Figure 23-1:
The New Upload page lets you choose your upload file format, specify templates and types for items and sections, and upload your product database file.

If you're not using custom types and templates, just leave everything set to the defaults (CSV, item., page., item., page.), click the Browse button to select a file from your computer, and then click the Upload button to upload the file.

For the data format, you can choose either CSV or Bar-Delimited:

- **Bar-Delimited** is old-school. Think: 1997. Bar-Delimited files have pipes (|) delimiting or separating the various fields in your database. Type a pipe. Look in the upper-right corner of your keyboard. Press Shift+\. I can't believe they still allow bar-delimited database uploads, because in 1998, the Viaweb folks started saying they were going to discontinue it any day now, so I figured out how to do CSV files in Excel.

- **CSV** (comma separated variable) files are much easier to make using Microsoft Excel. I talk a lot more about CSV files earlier in this chapter.

If you're using custom types and templates, select the type and template you want for this upload, click the Browse button to select a file from your computer, and then click the Upload button to upload the file.

Reviewing your data

No matter whether you're using the standard or custom types and templates, the Upload Summary page appears with a Summary, Warnings And Errors, and View Individual Records fields:

- **Summary** displays the upload file's time and date, a list of all the fields in the file, and a count of how many records are in the upload file. If you misspelled a field name, it appears here as well.

  Check the number of records. If this number is way off, then something's wrong with your formatting.

- **Warnings And Errors** shows you all the records with problems, links to those individual records, and the corresponding error messages for each record. Each record that has a problem, such as a blank line or missing field, appears here.

- **View Individual Records** starts with the first record of upload. Here you can jump to any record in the file or use the Next button to page through individual records. At a minimum, I like to check the first record, a middle record, and the last record to make sure that I didn't screw something up.

You need to check your data before you add it to your store or completely rebuild your store. Start by making sure that your upload file is the right file type (CSV), is not corrupted (has no garbage characters), has the correct number of records, has correctly spelled field names, and has the data in the right fields. After you're pretty happy with your file, you have to decide how you want the data added to your Yahoo! Store.

Updating product data

Store Editor database uploads have two options for updating product data:
Add or Rebuild.

- ✔ The Add button creates new products and updates the fields for existing
  products.
- ✔ The Rebuild button totally deletes all products and sections and literally
  rebuilds your store from the ground up (except your prebuilt Yahoo!
  function pages, such as index, info, privacypolicy, and so on), which
  allows you to wipe the slate clean and upload a brand new store. Be
  careful! You can delete your entire store by clicking one button.
  Fortunately, Yahoo! gives you an extra chance to cancel before completely rebuilding your store (see Figure 23-2).

Figure 23-2:
Rebuild
gives you
one last
chance to
cancel
before
deleting all
sections and
products
and
rebuilding
your store
from your
database
upload file.

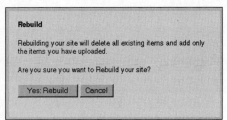

Rebuild

Rebuilding your site will delete all existing items and add only
the items you have uploaded.

Are you sure you want to Rebuild your site?

[Yes: Rebuild] [Cancel]

My experience is that Add is better than Rebuild unless you have a completely new database every time you need to do an upload. I like to be able to
make tons of adjustments and edits in my Store Editor when I want to and not
have to worry about overwriting them with a database upload. Add is good
for this task!

BobtheJanitor.com is a revenue-share store I manage. Almost once a month, the product database experiences major changes, such as added or dropped products, price adjustments, and product availability changes. Instead of updating each of these products by hand, I use the Rebuild function to delete all sections and products and rebuild the store with the most current information.

Rebuild is perfect for sites that receive complete product databases from third-party vendors. Rebuild also works great for retailers who generate their Yahoo! Store data from an internal master database file — for example, from customer service and inventory-tracking software like OrderMotion or Stone Edge.

Any changes you make to the Store Editor on any page other than the home page, info page, or Variables is deleted when you click the Rebuild button. This is extremely dangerous because it is too easy for new users to completely overwrite their store.

The reason the home page doesn't get deleted with Rebuild is because the home page is a Main. type. A cool trick that Luke at Yahoo! Tech Support taught me a few years back was that you can create pages with Main. as the type on the Contents page. These new Main. pages survive a Rebuild because the Store Editor thinks that they're the home page.

Revert button

If you accidentally delete something important while updating your store, you can try the Revert button. The Revert button reverts all your products and sections to the way they were before you did the last upload and add/rebuild. Revert also has a great warning message: "Revert will restore your items to the state before your last upload Add or Rebuild. Are you sure you want to Revert?"

You only have one chance to use Revert to undo your last upload. If you upload a database (for example, `rebuild205am.csv`), rebuild your store (which deletes everything and rebuilds your store using the file `rebuild205am.csv`), decide that's not right and upload another database (for example, `rebuild217am.csv`), and press the Rebuild button again, pressing the Revert button reverts your data back only to your first mistake (`rebuild205am.csv`); the Revert button doesn't work after that.

The Revert button reverts only your product data or objects (products/sections) back to how they were before you clicked the Add or Rebuild button. It doesn't restore changes to Variables, templates, types, or anything else.

The worst thing that could happen is that you do two uploads, realize that you've made a tragic mistake, and now you can't go back two steps.

When you really screw up . . .

If Revert doesn't fix your problem, the only thing you can do is contact Yahoo! Store Technical Support and beg the folks to restore your data. They really don't like to do this task, because it involves pulling the data tapes from the last 36 hours of backup files and choosing the most current version — and even then, you still lose hours and hours of work. Unfortunately, Yahoo! can't press a magic button and have your Store Editor magically transformed to match the published version of your store.

I've only had to go to the backup one time, and that was in 1999 when Mom deleted a redundant site map page, which deleted every single category and product on the site. Man, she freaked! Getting the site restored almost instantly involved much groveling and bribery including a huge overnight shipment of Mom's famous homemade chocolate chip cookies for the Yahoo! Sales and Tech Support folks, but mostly for Dave Greten, the engineer who saved the day!

Troubleshooting Database Uploads

Performing Yahoo! Store database uploads is like shaving with a chain saw! It's very effective and powerful, but the slightest wrong move and you have a real problem on your hands! You can totally gum up your site hierarchy with database uploads, dump tons of items on the home page with no path information, fragment your site, and create multiple versions of section pages where some products are on the original section page and the rest are on the alternate section pages, and even worse.

Here's a cool trick: I like to make the first column and the last column in an upload file the ID field. As long as the data in both columns is exactly the same, the file is fine, and it's a good way to make sure that every record in your file has the correct number of fields.

Here are a few more things you need to know about database uploads:

- ✓ **"Unknown field will not be used" means you have a typo in your field names.** Don't Add or Rebuild; just fix the field name, save the file, and re-upload the file.

✔ **When you upload a CSV file, you also dump the contents of the Clipboard to the site.** They may be orphaned items, but you can find them with site search. Before doing an upload, I make a temporary section on the home page called *storeroom*. I paste all the objects on the Clipboard into the storeroom section. I upload my product database and then cut the storeroom section to the Clipboard.

✔ **If you accidentally use the same ID for a new product that you were using on an old product, you create a Frankenstein's monster of a product.** Your upload adds the new information to the old product, thus screwing up two items. The old product has some data from the new product, but will probably have the old product's picture and be in the old product section. Make sure that you use unique IDs. If you have a big site, with tens of thousands of items, sometimes weeks or months can pass before you figure out what happened.

✔ **You can accidentally change the templates on Yahoo! function pages: index, info, norder, privacypolicy, ind, and so on.** Be careful when creating a product upload database. Make sure that you don't have any objects in the file that you don't want to create or update. Several third-party sites take the XML feed of all your sections and products and turn this information into a CSV file.

These files sometimes include the object IDs of the Yahoo! Store Editor prebuilt function pages: your home page (index), your info page (info), your alphabetical index (ind), your search page (nsearch), your privacy policy page (privacypolicy), and your Shopping Cart (norder).

When you do a database upload, you specify the type and template of each object-ID in your file. The defaults are "item." for type and "page." for template. Remember, you can't change the type of an object, only the template. Each of these prebuilt function pages uses separate templates and is made of separate types. If you do a database upload for these object-IDs, you change the template to whatever you specify, before you upload your file, which can really mess up your info and index pages. It's easy enough to change these back to the correct template by editing each function page, but you shouldn't upload these object IDs in the first place!

Chapter 24

Mastering Domains

In This Chapter

▶ Discovering domain basics

▶ Registering the perfect domain name for your business

▶ Pointing domains at the right place

▶ Managing and protecting your domains

*C*hoosing your domain name or dot-com address is one of the most important Internet marketing decisions you'll make. When you open your Yahoo! Store/Merchant Solutions account, you start by either registering a brand new domain or pointing another domain you already own to your new Yahoo! Merchant Solutions account.

Domains are serious business, too. Anytime you make changes to your domain setup, a bone-headed mistake, a technical glitch, or even a bureaucratic snafu can take your Yahoo! Store offline. Horrors! It's not as scary as it sounds, though. You just need to pay very close attention when messing with your domains. Think of managing your domain like you're changing a fuse in a fuse box.

In this chapter, I talk about what you need to know about domains, how to choose a good domain name, how to decide whether to point a domain name to your store or to your hosting account, and other stuff. If you're already master of your domain, use this chapter as reference when you need it and skip ahead. It's a *Dummies* book!

Exploring Your Domain

Your domain name is the foundation of your Yahoo! Merchant Solutions account, as well as the center of your Internet marketing universe. You must have a domain name or register a new domain to open a new account with Yahoo! Merchant Solutions.

A *domain name* is simply your dot-com, the unique address on the Web that points to your Yahoo! Store or Web site. Your domain is your *URL* (Uniform Resource Locator or address of something on the Internet). When someone types your domain into his Web browser, that address can only point to one place: your Yahoo! Store. A domain name is a lot like a phone number, and having a great one is a very good thing.

Registering Your Domain Name

When you want to get a domain name, you just go to a *registrar,* a company licensed by ICANN (the official licensing body of the Internet) to register and manage domain names, to see whether the domain you want is available, select a domain, agree to lots of terms and conditions, fill out a form, and then pay the registrar around ten bucks to reserve that domain name for the next year.

Do us both a favor and use one company to register all your domain names. There are too many passwords and logins these days as it is!

Here are a few tips to remember when registering your domain:

- ✔ **When registering your main domain, go ahead and pay to reserve your domain for as long as you can (think five to ten years).** That way, you don't have to think about reregistering it for a long period of time.

- ✔ **Make sure that your contact information has an e-mail address that you'll be using for a long time.** Use a permanent mailing address, perhaps your parents' address or a permanent P.O. box. See the nearby sidebar "Don't panic: Changing your domain info" for good reasons why.

- ✔ **Have separate e-mail and mailing addresses for your administrative, technical, and billing contacts.** That way, when you have trouble, someone from the registrar will be able to reach you or someone working with you.

- ✔ **Make sure that you keep your contact information current when you change e-mail addresses, mailing addresses, or phone numbers.** ICANN requires that your data be correct. Domains with false information can be taken away.

- ✔ **If you're buying multiple domains, do yourself a favor and use the same registrar.** It makes keeping up with your domains a little easier.

Don't panic: Changing your domain info

In 1997, I registered a domain for the next eight years. The contact information was my CompuServe e-mail address and parents' mailing address. Fast-forward to 2004, and it was the first time I needed to make a change to my domain. By then, my parents had moved, their area code had changed, and that e-mail address hadn't been good for five or six years.

It is a major pain to get your domain information changed, but it's doable. Depending on your registrar, you fax in a statement on company letterhead with a photocopy of your driver's license and a legal statement saying that you're the rightful owner of that domain. Unless someone contests it, the registrar will give you access to your domain, usually the same day you fax in your information. Remember that you're signing a legal affidavit, so no monkey business!

Registering domains with Yahoo!

When you create your Merchant Solutions account and you sign up for a brand new unregistered domain name, Yahoo! registers your domain with one of its partner registrars, but you manage all the details through your Yahoo! account. Very convenient! Yahoo! says the domain registration is free, but you're paying enough in your monthly hosting bill (which runs anywhere from $11.95 to $300 a month, depending on the package you buy) to more than cover the annual cost (around $10) of your domain registration fee.

The only downside to registering through Yahoo! is that after you've opened your account, the domain is welded to your Merchant Solutions account so that you can't register the same domain multiple years in advance. Yahoo! automatically renews your domain every year unless you close your account, which makes you responsible for reregistering your domain with its registrar.

Registering domains with other companies

A few years back before domain names became a commodity item, Yahoo! was charging full retail (around $35 a year) for registering domain names, so I used GoDaddy.com as my registrar of choice. Now I keep using GoDaddy.com for its great technical support. The folks at GoDaddy.com don't outsource their tech support phone calls to an offshore phone bank, and the friendly, knowledgeable folks understand that you probably don't have a computer science degree from MIT. They don't even make fun of me when I can't figure out which button to click to make the simplest changes or when I forget my customer ID, login, and password. GoDaddy.com also has great TV commercials.

When you use a different registrar than Yahoo!, there's a little more work involved in creating and maintaining your account. You have to log in to your account at that registrar's Web site to point your domain to Yahoo!'s nameservers (yns1.yahoo.com and yns2.yahoo.com), which causes your Web site or Yahoo! Store to appear when people type your domain name. You also have to use the registrar's Web site to make changes to your contact information and to renew your domain. It's not as convenient as using http://smallbusiness.yahoo.com/domains, but for me, it's too late!

GoDaddy.com charges only $8.95 a year to register a domain, but watch out for all the add-on stuff in the checkout process. GoDaddy is very good at upselling in its shopping cart and checkout (so take notes!) and tries to sell you services that you really don't need, such as e-mail, Web hosting, marketing software, clip art, and so on.

Non-Yahoo! registered domains and DNSs

When you already have your domain registered with a different registrar, Yahoo! makes it easy to sign up. Just click the link next to Already Have A Domain Name? Use It With A Yahoo! Plan. After signing up for your Yahoo! account, you have to go to your registrar and point your domain name servers (DNSs) to the Yahoo! Store Name Servers. The Yahoo! Store Name Servers are the following: yns1.yahoo.com and yns2.yahoo.com.

It's pretty easy to log in to your account at the registrar, change your DNS settings, and save your changes. Usually within 24 to 48 hours, your domain name will be working. Every registrar is slightly different, so check with technical support if you have any questions.

Mastering Your Domains

Yahoo! makes setting up and making changes to your domain settings easy. When you log in to Yahoo at http://smallbusiness.yahoo.com/services, you're one click away from your Domain Control Panel, shown in Figure 24-1. In the Domain Control Panel, you can manage your domain and subdomains, edit your Domain Registration Information (WHOIS), and work with your Advanced DNS settings, which you'll probably never touch.

Figure 24-1:
The Yahoo!
Domain
Control
Panel
allows easy
access to all
the things
you ever
want to
change on
your
domain.

Figure 24-1:
The Yahoo!
Domain
Control
Panel
allows easy
access to all
the things
you ever
want to
change on
your
domain.

Determining your site entry point

Yahoo! Merchant Solutions is two, two, two stores in one! You have pages you build in the Store Editor and pages you build offline and upload and host in your Web-hosting account. By default, www.*yourdomain*.com points to your Web-hosting account, and http://store.*yourdomain*.com points to the Store Editor–built pages. Having two different ways to build stores is very confusing to folks. It's even confusing for developers! If you're old school like I am, the Store Editor is fine. (See Chapter 5 for more information, where I talk a lot more about the Editor versus Web hosting and Store Tags.)

Figure 24-2 shows where you change your *site entry point* (where the www.*yourdomain*.com URL points). You have to decide whether you want your site entry point to be your Store Editor–built pages or pages hosted in your Web-hosting account.

Figure 24-2:
Your Domain
Name
Destination
is also
called your
site entry
point.

What this decision really means is "Do you want the front door to be the main entryway to your store, or do you want to go ahead and make that side door that everyone is really going to use the main entrance?"

If you use Editor, make it the site entry point. If not, leave well enough alone. (If you don't use Editor, you probably bought the wrong book, but hopefully you'll get your $24.95's worth in marketing and other advice!)

To fix (okay, change) your site entry point, you need to log in to your store and follow these steps:

1. **Click the Domain Control Panel link on your Manage My Services page.**

   Your Domain Control Panel appears (refer to Figure 24-1).

2. **Click the Manage Domain & Subdomains link.**

   You see a table that lists your domain and address and shows the destination My Web Hosting Site. This destination is what you want to change.

3. **Click the Edit link.**

   The Edit Your Domain Name Destination page appears.

4. **Read all the notes and warnings.**

   If you disagree with anything, defer to Yahoo!'s expertise and call tech support at 1-866-800-8092.

   You see two radio buttons. Right now, it says Keep The Current Destination As My Web Hosting Home Page.

5. **Select the Change The Destination To My Store Editor Homepage radio button, scroll to the bottom, and click the Submit button.**

   You return to the Manage Domain & Subdomains page, where the Destination should show My Store Pages.

   For those of you who are familiar with traditional Web hosting, all the pages, images, and other files you upload to your Yahoo! Web-Hosting account will be located in the subdomain site http://site. *yourdomain*.com. All the pages built in the Store Editor will be inside www.*yourdomain*.com. It takes a little while for Yahoo! to figure out where to point your Web store.

6. **Type your domain name in your browser.**

   If it's a new domain hosted by Yahoo!, you see a page that says "This site is under construction" until it points to your Store Editor home page.

Redirecting store URLs to your domain

Search engines don't like *mirror sites* (when the same content or the same Web site exists in multiple places on the Web) because duplicate content fills up their index with redundant Web pages. If spammers thought they'd profit from it and could get away with it, they'd crank out thousands of copies of their Web sites.

Google is very good at picking out dupes and has a pretty harsh duplicate content filter, which figures out which is the main site and then nukes all the duplicate pages.

One of the problems that Yahoo! Stores have traditionally had is that multiple URLs point to the exact same page. Search engines see this one page with multiple addresses as completely separate Web sites. You see how this can be a problem: There's really one page on a Yahoo! Store, but all these URLs point to it: `http://store.yahoo.com/youraccountname`, `www.yourdomain.com`, `http://stores.yahoo.com/youraccountname`, `http://youraccountname.store.yahoo.com`, `http://youraccountname.stores.yahoo.com`, `http://youraccountname.shopping.store.yahoo.com`, and several other URLs. It looks like you're spamming their index with multiple copies of the same site. Google's pretty good about figuring out which site is the real site, but Yahoo!'s search engine and MSN Search both index and list all the URLs.

To fix most of this problem, Yahoo! added a feature to automatically redirect store URLs to domain URLs using a permanent 301 redirect. SEO guru Greg Boser (of Webguerrilla.com) says that a 301 redirect is just like a change-of-address form to a search engine, which says that the page at this old Web address moved to this new Web address. Don't worry about what a 301 redirect does in technical terms; just consider using 301's good manners for search engines. Your store pages show up in the search engines, and all the *back links* (links back from other pages to your store) still count for link popularity. (I discuss back links, link popularity, and other lucrative geeky topics in Chapter 19.)

Always have links to your store point to one consistent URL so that your site's link popularity ("votes" from other pages) counts for the same "candidate" page. For example, any links to your home page should point to the URL `http://www.yourdomain.com/` (with the `www`). Also, links to any interior pages should point to `http://www.yourdomain.com/pagename.html` to maximize link popularity. Search engines see `www.yourdomain.com` and `http://yourdomain.com` (without the `www`) as two separate pages, so any link popularity is split between the two.

Here's how to turn on the 301 Change Of Address Form inside your Store Manager:

1. **Click the Domain Names link under Site Settings on your Store Manager.**

   Yahoo! Store most likely asks you for your *security key*, which is your second-level password for scary things such as changing your credit billing information or seeing customer orders. If you haven't created your security key, you're going to have to create one. I detail all the information about the security key in Chapter 3. Yahoo! is very good about not allowing authorized people to make changes to your store.

2. **Type your security key and click the Continue button.**

   The Domain Name Management page appears. You can add host names, as well as adjust your Yahoo Domain Redirect Settings on this page. When you first open a Merchant Solutions Account, all your published editor pages are on the Yahoo! Domain URLs `http://store.yahoo.com/yhst-youraccountnamehere`, as well as the subdomain `http://store.yourdomain.com`. That's what you *don't* want.

3. **Select `www.yourdomain.com` from the pull-down menu and click the Set Redirect button.**

   After you select this setting, you should never need to change it again.

   Your Domain Name Management Confirmation page is where Yahoo! helpfully explains "You have selected to redirect all Yahoo! Store generated URLs to `www.yourdomain.com`" and shows you a list of all the duplicate URLs now redirected to your domain. The redirect takes effect usually within a day or so. For example, after it is activated, when someone goes to my `http://store.yahoo.com/yhst-17192271484370` page, Yahoo! instantly 301s (or redirects) her to `www.ystorebooks.com`, which is my Store Editor–built home page. Pretty cool, Yahoo!

Part VI
The Part of Tens

The 5th Wave   By Rich Tennant

"Somebody got through our dead-end Web links,
past the firewalls, and around the phone-prompt
loops. Before you know it, the kid here picks up
the phone, and he's talking one on one to a customer."

In this part . . .

This part of the book is The Part of Tens, a *Dummies* book tradition where every chapter is a list of ten things. In The Part of Tens, I cover the ten types of tools I use on a daily basis and tell you ten times why you should turn to RTML.

When you're building and managing your Yahoo! Store, you have to have the right tool for the right job. In this part, I list ten types of tools I can't live without (with examples!), including keyword-research programs, search-marketing tools, store-backup software, additional Web analytics, helpful utilities, and graphics software.

I also introduce you to RTML, the proprietary template scripting language you can use to customize stores built in the Store Editor. You discover the basic concepts of RTML and all the cool things that you can do (or pay someone to do) with RTML.

Chapter 25

Ten or So Tools of the Trade

In this chapter, I give you ten or so types of tools you need to run your Yahoo! Store and list the specific tools I use and recommend. Enjoy!

Searching for All the Right Words

(See Chapter 16 for a whole chapter on keywords and their importance to your Yahoo! Store's success.) Your Yahoo! Store References can tell you what keywords are currently driving your traffic and sales, but you need to know all the popular keywords in your market so that you can optimize your site for search engines (see Chapter 19) and buy the words in paid-search ad campaigns (see Chapter 18). Enter keyword research tools!

Wordtracker is my favorite commercial keyword tool. Type a general keyword, and Wordtracker shows you how many people searched for that query in the last 60 days and gives you a list of all the other phrases containing your keyword query. Check out the free trial at www.wordtracker.com, where you can sign up for a year's subscription for around $250.

Keyword Discovery from Trellian is my new keyword tool of choice, generating even more keywords per search than Wordtracker. The Trellian folks live in Australia and, besides making some cool SEO and keyword-research tools, are also very successful sheep farmers. They'll happily share SEO secrets or how to deal with your wombat problem, but whatever you do, don't ask them to share their sheep. Visit www.trellian.com, where you can get Keyword Discovery from only $32.50 a month.

Searching Engine Queries/Filters

Search engines are pretty good at finding what you're looking for, but search results can only be as good as the searcher's query. Power users can use these queries and filters to see how many pages they have in the engines and who links to them and then use these tools to do a little recon on the competition. (Find more about what you're searching for in Chapter 19.) You can use many advanced search filters and advanced operators to do super-focused surgical strike–style searches on the various search engines and their indices, but here are my favorites:

- Search for **site:*YourDomain*.com** on Google, Yahoo!, or MSN to see whether a site is indexed in a particular engine and to see how many pages are in the index.

- Search for **link:http://www.*YourDomain*.com** on Google, Yahoo!, or MSN for a list of pages that link back to a specific URL or domain. I like to do the *link:* query for specific pages, not just home pages, to see which interior pages have external links.

- Search for **intitle:** *keyword phrase* on Google or Yahoo! to see only the pages that contain that keyword phrase inside the Title tag. This is a great way to see how many pages are really optimized for a given keyword phrase.

- Search for **inurl:** *keyword phrase* on Google or Yahoo! to see only the pages with that specific keyword phrase in the URL.

- See Google's page listing all their advanced operators at `http://www.google.com/help/operators.html`

- See Yahoo!'s page listing search filters at `http://help.yahoo.com/help/us/ysearch/tips/tips-03.html`

- See MSN's page for Search Builder and advanced options at `http://search.msn.com/docs/help.aspx?t=SEARCH_REF_AdvSrchOperators.htm`

Using the Right YstoreTool for the Job

YstoreTools.com, an independent, third-party software site, offers tools that make creating and managing your online store easier. Get the right tool for the right job. Programmer/developer Don Cole has created a whole suite of software tools and services available for the Yahoo! Store owner, including Graphic Downloader, Graphic Uploader, Order Checker, Order Processor, and the famous RTML Transfer Utility. Yahoo! Store Backup & Feed is Don's relatively new monthly service where he converts your Yahoo! Store product data into files you can upload to almost any other shopping site or engine, including eBay, Amazon, Yahoo! Shopping, Froogle, and about 20 other major online shopping portals. See www.ystoreservices.com for more info.

Exporting Your Yahoo! Store

Yahoo! Store Export Tool, from David Burke's VisualFuture.com, is one tool I cannot live without! Export your entire store with the click of a button. Visit www.visualfuture.com for access to this free service. Chapter 15 has more information about enabling the XML export of your store's items and sections.

Checking Your Web Position

SEOToolSet is SEO guru Bruce Clay's suite of online search-engine tools for tracking, analyzing, improving, and optimizing your Web pages for the best search-engine ranking results. Track your position on the top engines for up to 200 keywords. Reverse-engineer SEO secrets of pages that outrank you for any given keyword phrase. Keep up with who links to you and figure out who links to your competition. It's available at www.seotoolset.com and www.bruceclay.com for $99 a quarter.

Webposition is a similar Web position tracking application, except it runs from your desktop. I use it for larger lists of keywords. Available at www.webposition.com with a free demo, the standard edition is $149 and the Pro Edition is $389.

Tracking Trends with Analytics Software

As I discuss in Chapter 20, Yahoo! Statistics are pretty good, but if you want to really know your visitors' every move on your Web site, you need some additional software. ClickTracks Pro Hosted rocks! John Marshall and the ClickTracks crew have always had user-friendly Web analytics software, but they went the extra mile to make their software Yahoo! Store compatible. See which keywords on which engines generate traffic and sales with custom ROI analysis. I love ClickTracks' visual interface that maps visitor behavior over a copy of your Web store so that you can see what navigational elements work to drive traffic and sales. Now the new version (ClickTracks Pro 6.0) has built-in A/B testing. I can't wait to try out the new version, which is available at www.clicktracks.com starting at $179 per month.

EngineReady is another Web analytics software package I use to track which keywords are driving traffic and sales. My favorite feature is a daily e-mail containing an Excel file of my converting keywords from the previous day. Available at `www.engineready.com`, it starts at $49.95 per month for up to 50,000 page views. Tell Justin I said howdy!

Checking Out Other Cool Tools

Wow! I almost ran out of room. Domain tools I like using are DNSStuff.com, Whois.sc, and Godaddy.com's DomainsbyProxy. For customer service and inventory management, take a look at StoneEdge.com or OrderMotion.com.

Not only am I a slow typist, but I also edit while I type, so I'm extremely slow at typing, but get me running my mouth, and I can talk a bookload! This *For Dummies* manuscript is brought to you by Dragon Naturally Speaking. You talk, and it types.

Google Tools I use almost every day: Gmail gives me access to my e-mail from anywhere I have Internet access. Searching your e-mail instead of sorting is great if you don't mind the ads. Google Alerts is great for news and searches to alert you of new pages in the search engine. The Google Toolbar lets you search from your browser as well as see information about sites you visit. Google Desktop Search organizes files on your personal computer and makes finding files almost as easy as searching on Google.

Finally, don't forget `http://my.yahoo.com` for your Yahoo! calendar, organizing RSS feeds for keeping up with blogs, and news, too.

Chapter 26

Ten or So RTML Resources and Recommendations

In This Chapter

▶ Dipping your toe into RTML

▶ Navigating the possibilities of RTML

*R*TML is the proprietary template scripting language that the Store Editor uses to generate HTML pages for products, sections, and other pages. RTML is extremely powerful and is able to do things that regular old HTML just can't do. For example, RTML pages can know where a product is inside the store's hierarchy or display information on a Web page that's stored inside another page.

Don't be scared of RTML! Some folks are extremely intimidated by RTML and avoid it, but the reality is that your store already uses RTML. Every time you click the Publish button, the prebuilt templates create static HTML pages based upon settings you control on the Store Editor's Variables page (and a few other places). Yahoo! provides no tech support for RTML, and the official documentation just whets your appetite for modifying templates, but isn't enough to get you started. Also, be aware that when some tech support folks see custom or modified RTML templates, they use that to punt on the easiest support questions.

Most retailers don't need to know how to program RTML. Unless you're going to develop Yahoo! Stores for a living, it's probably not worth learning the RTML operators and syntax, but any retailer can benefit from knowing what RTML can do. It's much easier to hire a developer and know that you're paying a fair price for custom templates or RTML modifications when you know just a little about RTML. That's why I'm giving you ten or so RTML recommendations and RTML resources you should check out.

Know HTML before Playing with RTML

Much of RTML is based upon regular HTML, so before you dive in to modifying or customizing templates, you must be familiar with basic HTML, especially table tags. I recommend *HTML 4 For Dummies,* 5th Edition (Wiley Publishing), by Ed Tittel and Mary Burmeister.

Experiment with RTML

There's a big difference between modifying copies of RTML templates (pretty easy), customizing copies of RTML templates (more complicated), and creating new RTML templates from scratch (you'd better know exactly what you're doing). The best way to understand RTML is to dive in and start playing with copies of the prebuilt templates. Also, make new templates from scratch to discover how operators work with simple examples. Finally, beg, borrow, or buy someone else's RTML templates so that you can reverse-engineer how she did something. If you're going to experiment with RTML, invest $40 a month to get a second Yahoo! Store for testing so that you can play with RTML and not worry about blowing up your real store.

Read Mike's Books on RTML

This section is going to sound like an ad for my good friend (and this book's technical reviewer) Michael Whitaker, but I'm not getting paid for it, and it's a great resource, so take a look at it. Mike's first book, *RTML for Yahoo! Store — A visual quick-start tutorial to modifying templates* (Monitus), is a perfect entry-level how-to guide for playing around with RTML, as well as a great brushup for more advanced users. He shows you exactly how to do many RTML modifications that folks want to do on their stores, including adding a search box to every page on your store, modifying your site's navigation, and using a custom image button for your Add To Cart button. See www.monitus.com/ebook.htm and www.ystore101.com for more information.

Mike's new book, *Yahoo! Store Tips & Tricks* (Ytimes Publications), just came out and is cowritten with Istvan Siposs. Read that one, too. It's got tons of really specific tips for Yahoo! Store owners, with some useful advice even if you never touch RTML, so take a look at it. He and Istvan have a series of very educational Yahoo! Store training seminars where I've been a guest lecturer on marketing. See http://ytimes.info/yahoo-store-tips-and-tricks.html for more on this book.

Read Istvan's Books on RTML

RTML guru Istvan Siposs knows more about RTML than anyone I've ever met. I was blown away when he told me he reverse-engineered everything he knows about RTML simply by experimenting with the prebuilt templates in the Store Editor. Holy cow!

Unfortunately, I doubt there will ever be an *RTML For Dummies* book because there might be 500 people who would buy it. Fortunately for you and me, Istvan has written and published multiple books on RTML, including *RTML 101: The Unofficial Guide To Yahoo! Store Templates, Custom Templates NOW!* (e-book), *Deconstructing Y-Times* (e-book), and *Yahoo! Store Template Reference* (e-book), all published by Ytimes Publications. Visit his Yahoo! Store at `http://Ytimes.info` and check out his stuff!

Use Don Cole's Template Transfer Utility

Don Cole is one of my heroes. He's a programmer, store developer, and all-around nice guy. Not only does he develop these incredibly cool Y!Store tools (`www.ystoretools.com`), but he also makes them available to other developers and the general public at extremely reasonable prices. Don even has a free RTML Transfer Utility template upload tool that you can use to download, archive, modify, and upload your custom RTML templates. You can download templates at no charge, and he only charges you $1 (or less when you buy upload credits in bulk) for every RTML template you upload. If you have ever hand-built templates using the RTML Stack Editor, you'd probably pay $20 per template to never do that again.

Don's template upload tool saves your custom RTML in text files that you can edit with any text editor (like Notepad) or even Microsoft Excel. Even if you don't code your own RTML, you can download and back up your templates and sleep better at night knowing that you have the blueprints to your store design safely tucked away.

Read the YstoreForums.com RTML forum

Lots of developers and power users hang out at Don Cole's Yahoo! Store forum (`www.ystoreforums.com`), and you can gain a lot of knowledge by reading it. Ask seasoned development pros your RTML questions in the RTML General Questions & Information forum at `www.ystoretools.com/forums/forum.asp?FORUM_ID=17`.

Look at Lots of Custom RTML Stores

One of the best things you can do is look at as many custom-built RTML stores and make a list of the features you like and want on your store. Most stores have similar needs (text link navigation, breadcrumbs, SEO modifications, related items, and so on), so lots of "custom" stores look very, very similar. Look, the last thing you want to do is pay $2,500 and get a cookie-cutter template that took an hour for some guy to tweak and upload.

Search on Google or Yahoo for *RTML Yahoo -telescope*, and you get a list of around 400 sites that mention both Yahoo! and RTML. RTML also stands for *remote telescope markup language,* so the *-telescope* removes those pages. I found around 389 sites mentioning RTML and Yahoo! (and not telescopes!) on Google. Look at the portfolio pages of developers listed in the top 30 sites, and you'll have a very good idea of what you can do with RTML.

Add Missing SEO Elements

RTML is perfect for adding a few missing search-engine-friendly elements to a copy of the (Page.) template. I customize my copies of RTML templates to beef up my title tag, add a unique meta keywords tag (for each page), create a unique meta description, change the headline from an image to <H1> tags, add the name at the bottom of the page in a page summary, link to the next item within a section (with the name of the next item) to get the benefit of the anchor text, link up to the previous section, create an SEO-friendly site map, and lots of other things — but I've been sworn to secrecy and cannot reveal them in print! If you can do it with text, you can do it with RTML.

Add RTML Navigational Elements

RTML is a great way to add more navigational elements to your Yahoo! Store. The easiest elements to add are *breadcrumbs,* those navigational You Are Here links, because Yahoo! Store has a hidden breadcrumbs RTML template (Walk-up.) already built. I also like to add Previous/Up/Next links, a Browse Next Item: Name of Item link at the bottom of every product page, and sometimes related products links to all the other items in the same section.

Index

• C •

CAN-SPAM Act of 2003, 352–354
Caption field, 65, 67, 185
Cart. *See also* Checkout Manager
  Add To Cart button, 65–67
  conversion rate, 337–339
  customizing, 175–176
  design, 67–68
  editing, 175–176
  functionality, 67
  Keep Shopping button, 67
  navigation, 99
  new features, 215
  ordering process, 67–68
  Secure-basket variable, 141
  Update Quantity button, 67
cascading style sheets (CSS), 224
Catalog Manager, 229–230
catalog requests, 236
changing
  colors, 94
  domain information, 373–375
Checkout buttons, 225
Checkout Manager
  activating, 218
  Advanced Settings module, 217, 224–226
  Beta test, 216
  bugs, 226
  Checkout buttons, 225
  cookies, 224
  CSS (cascading style sheets), 224
  custom fields, 223
  customer messages, 222
  Customer Ratings, 221
  design, 224–225
  disabling, 226
  documentation, 216
  enabling, 226
  fields, 222–223
  flow settings, 218–220
  "Getting Started Guide for Checkout
    Manager," 216
  Gift Options, 221
  Global Settings module, 216, 219–221
  Help files, 216
  Item Option Validation, 226
  multiple-page checkout, 219
  new features, 215–216

  opening, 216
  Page Configuration module, 216, 221–223
  previewing, 217
  progress indicator, 225
  publishing Order Settings, 218
  Revert panel, 226
  single-page checkout, 219
  test orders, 218
  Visual Customization module, 216–217
Checkout Manager Guide, 228
Checkout Wrapper, 220–221
child pages, 171
choosing a domain name, 371
Clay, Bruce, SEO expert, 316, 383
click trails, 98, 329
clickable ads, 291
ClickTracks, 322, 383
Clipboard, 193–194
Code field, 182
Cole, Dan
  Graphic Downloader tool, 382
  Graphic Uploader tool, 382
  Order Checker tool, 382
  Order Processor tool, 382
  RTML Template Transfer Utility, 382, 387
  Yahoo! Store Backup & Feed tool, 382–383
  Yahoo! Store forum, 387
Collier, Marsha
  eBay For Dummies, 282
  *eBay Timesaving Techniques For
    Dummies*, 282
  *Starting an eBay Business For
    Dummies*, 282
color blindness, 94
colors
  background colors, 137
  changing, 94
  color schemes, 131
  design, 93–94
  progress indicator, 225
  RGB (red green blue), 94
  variables, 137
  Variables button, 94
Columns variable, 138
Column-width variable, 138
Commission Junction affiliate
    programs, 281
community of Yahoo! Store owners, 11

• *Q* •

• T •

• *U* •

• W •

• Y •

BUSINESS, CAREERS & PERSONAL FINANCE

0-7645-5307-0   0-7645-5331-3 *†

Also available:

- Accounting For Dummies †
  0-7645-5314-3
- Business Plans Kit For Dummies †
  0-7645-5365-8
- Cover Letters For Dummies
  0-7645-5224-4
- Frugal Living For Dummies
  0-7645-5403-4
- Leadership For Dummies
  0-7645-5176-0
- Managing For Dummies
  0-7645-1771-6

- Marketing For Dummies
  0-7645-5600-2
- Personal Finance For Dummies *
  0-7645-2590-5
- Project Management For Dummies
  0-7645-5283-X
- Resumes For Dummies †
  0-7645-5471-9
- Selling For Dummies
  0-7645-5363-1
- Small Business Kit For Dummies *†
  0-7645-5093-4

HOME & BUSINESS COMPUTER BASICS

0-7645-4074-2   0-7645-3758-X

Also available:

- ACT! 6 For Dummies
  0-7645-2645-6
- iLife '04 All-in-One Desk Reference
  For Dummies
  0-7645-7347-0
- iPAQ For Dummies
  0-7645-6769-1
- Mac OS X Panther Timesaving
  Techniques For Dummies
  0-7645-5812-9
- Macs For Dummies
  0-7645-5656-8

- Microsoft Money 2004 For Dummies
  0-7645-4195-1
- Office 2003 All-in-One Desk Reference
  For Dummies
  0-7645-3883-7
- Outlook 2003 For Dummies
  0-7645-3759-8
- PCs For Dummies
  0-7645-4074-2
- TiVo For Dummies
  0-7645-6923-6
- Upgrading and Fixing PCs For Dummies
  0-7645-1665-5
- Windows XP Timesaving Techniques
  For Dummies
  0-7645-3748-2

FOOD, HOME, GARDEN, HOBBIES, MUSIC & PETS

0-7645-5295-3   0-7645-5232-5

Also available:

- Bass Guitar For Dummies
  0-7645-2487-9
- Diabetes Cookbook For Dummies
  0-7645-5230-9
- Gardening For Dummies *
  0-7645-5130-2
- Guitar For Dummies
  0-7645-5106-X
- Holiday Decorating For Dummies
  0-7645-2570-0
- Home Improvement All-in-One
  For Dummies
  0-7645-5680-0

- Knitting For Dummies
  0-7645-5395-X
- Piano For Dummies
  0-7645-5105-1
- Puppies For Dummies
  0-7645-5255-4
- Scrapbooking For Dummies
  0-7645-7208-3
- Senior Dogs For Dummies
  0-7645-5818-8
- Singing For Dummies
  0-7645-2475-5
- 30-Minute Meals For Dummies
  0-7645-2589-1

INTERNET & DIGITAL MEDIA

 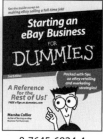

0-7645-1664-7   0-7645-6924-4

Also available:

- 2005 Online Shopping Directory
  For Dummies
  0-7645-7495-7
- CD & DVD Recording For Dummies
  0-7645-5956-7
- eBay For Dummies
  0-7645-5654-1
- Fighting Spam For Dummies
  0-7645-5965-6
- Genealogy Online For Dummies
  0-7645-5964-8
- Google For Dummies
  0-7645-4420-9

- Home Recording For Musicians
  For Dummies
  0-7645-1634-5
- The Internet For Dummies
  0-7645-4173-0
- iPod & iTunes For Dummies
  0-7645-7772-7
- Preventing Identity Theft For Dummies
  0-7645-7336-5
- Pro Tools All-in-One Desk Reference
  For Dummies
  0-7645-5714-9
- Roxio Easy Media Creator For Dummies
  0-7645-7131-1

* Separate Canadian edition also available
† Separate U.K. edition also available

Available wherever books are sold. For more information or to order direct: U.S. customers visit www.dummies.com or call 1-877-762-2974.
U.K. customers visit www.wileyeurope.com or call 0800 243407. Canadian customers visit www.wiley.ca or call 1-800-567-4797.

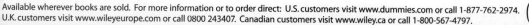

WILEY

SPORTS, FITNESS, PARENTING, RELIGION & SPIRITUALITY

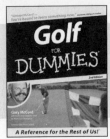

0-7645-5146-9

0-7645-5418-2

Also available:
- Adoption For Dummies
  0-7645-5488-3
- Basketball For Dummies
  0-7645-5248-1
- The Bible For Dummies
  0-7645-5296-1
- Buddhism For Dummies
  0-7645-5359-3
- Catholicism For Dummies
  0-7645-5391-7
- Hockey For Dummies
  0-7645-5228-7

- Judaism For Dummies
  0-7645-5299-6
- Martial Arts For Dummies
  0-7645-5358-5
- Pilates For Dummies
  0-7645-5397-6
- Religion For Dummies
  0-7645-5264-3
- Teaching Kids to Read For Dummies
  0-7645-4043-2
- Weight Training For Dummies
  0-7645-5168-X
- Yoga For Dummies
  0-7645-5117-5

TRAVEL

0-7645 5438-7

0-7645-5453-0

Also available:
- Alaska For Dummies
  0-7645-1761-9
- Arizona For Dummies
  0-7645-6938-4
- Cancún and the Yucatán For Dummies
  0-7645-2437-2
- Cruise Vacations For Dummies
  0-7645-6941-4
- Europe For Dummies
  0-7645-5456-5
- Ireland For Dummies
  0-7645-5455-7

- Las Vegas For Dummies
  0-7645-5448-4
- London For Dummies
  0-7645-4277-X
- New York City For Dummies
  0-7645-6945-7
- Paris For Dummies
  0-7645-5494-8
- RV Vacations For Dummies
  0-7645-5443-3
- Walt Disney World & Orlando For Dummies
  0-7645-6943-0

GRAPHICS, DESIGN & WEB DEVELOPMENT

0-7645-4345-8

0-7645-5589-8

Also available:
- Adobe Acrobat 6 PDF For Dummies
  0-7645-3760-1
- Building a Web Site For Dummies
  0-7645-7144-3
- Dreamweaver MX 2004 For Dummies
  0-7645-4342-3
- FrontPage 2003 For Dummies
  0-7645-3882-9
- HTML 4 For Dummies
  0-7645-1995-6
- Illustrator CS For Dummies
  0-7645-4084-X

- Macromedia Flash MX 2004 For Dummies
  0-7645-4358-X
- Photoshop 7 All-in-One Desk Reference For Dummies
  0-7645-1667-1
- Photoshop CS Timesaving Techniques For Dummies
  0-7645-6782-9
- PHP 5 For Dummies
  0-7645-4166-8
- PowerPoint 2003 For Dummies
  0-7645-3908-6
- QuarkXPress 6 For Dummies
  0-7645-2593-X

NETWORKING, SECURITY, PROGRAMMING & DATABASES

0-7645-6852-3

0-7645-5784-X

Also available:
- A+ Certification For Dummies
  0-7645-4187-0
- Access 2003 All-in-One Desk Reference For Dummies
  0-7645-3988-4
- Beginning Programming For Dummies
  0-7645-4997-9
- C For Dummies
  0-7645-7068-4
- Firewalls For Dummies
  0-7645-4048-3
- Home Networking For Dummies
  0-7645-42796

- Network Security For Dummies
  0-7645-1679-5
- Networking For Dummies
  0-7645-1677-9
- TCP/IP For Dummies
  0-7645-1760-0
- VBA For Dummies
  0-7645-3989-2
- Wireless All In-One Desk Reference For Dummies
  0-7645-7496-5
- Wireless Home Networking For Dummies
  0-7645-3910-8